THE END OF THE WORLD AS WE KNOW IT?

CRISIS, RESISTANCE, AND THE AGE OF AUSTERITY

ADVANCE PRAISE

"*The End of the World As We Know It?* contains snapshots from around the world of capitalism's most recent crisis and the attempts of affected populations to create real alternatives through struggle, study, and contestation. Highly recommended reading for the contemporary dissident." —Ruth Kinna, author of *A Beginner's Guide to Anarchism*

"*The End of the World As We Know It?* will be an invaluable resource for students of political economy in our momentous times.... [it] offers an indispensable array of perspectives on the crisis in contemporary global capitalism, with an eye toward dismantling it." —Alessandro De Giorgi, author of *Re-thinking the Political Economy of Punishment*

"*The End of the World As We Know It?* is a must-read for those interested in navigating the turbulent waters of economic uncertainty, political instability, and global resistance. The contributors—including political economists, organizers, workers, and students—not only provide clear and accessible analyses but also, and more importantly, a range of thought-provoking proposals for change which challenge an increasingly unequal and unsustainable status quo." —Nathan Jun, Author of *Anarchism and Political Modernity*

"There is nothing more important for anticapitalists than providing sharp analysis and relevant answers to the problems of our time, rather than merely propagating noble ideals. Here is a book that lives up to the task." —Gabriel Kuhn, Editor of *All Power to the Councils!*

"The contributions in *The End of the World As We Know It?* provide us with important lessons concerning the economic crisis and the attempts of working people to create a world worth living in." —Andrej Grubacic, Co-author of *Wobblies and Zapatistas: Conversations on Anarchism, Marxism, and Radical History* and author of *Don't Mourn, Balkanize! Essays After Yugoslavia*

THE END OF THE WORLD AS WE KNOW IT?

CRISIS, RESISTANCE, AND THE AGE OF AUSTERITY

Edited by Deric Shannon

AK Press
674-A 23rd Street
Oakland, CA 94612
USA
www.akpress.org
akpress@akpress.org

AK Press
PO Box 12766
Edinburgh EH8 9YE
Scotland
www.akuk.com
ak@akedin.demon.co.uk

The above addresses would be delighted to provide you with the latest AK Press distribution catalog, which features the several thousand books, pamphlets, zines, audio and video products, and stylish apparel published and/or distributed by AK Press. Alternatively, visit our websites for the complete catalog, latest news, and secure ordering.

Cover design by Kate Khatib.
Interior design by Magpie Killjoy.

Printed in the USA on acid-free paper.

ACKNOWLEDGMENTS

I FINISHED THIS BOOK UP MOVING AMONG FOUR DIFFERENT CITIES ON two coasts, often broke. But I'm a millionaire in friends, many of whom welcomed me into their homes and lives in this process. I'd like to first acknowledge all of them who I can think of: Abbey Volcano—for giving me her extra room as a crash pad and storage space multiple times; Maggie Spallina, Richard Rex, Colin O' Malley, Jake Allen, Crescenzo Scipione, Shane Burley—all for putting me up (and putting up with me) in upstate NY; Mark Bray and Yesenia Barragán for giving me the couch in their balcony room in their New Jersey apartment during nights when I desperately needed space away from my life; Maria Yates, Naitha Bellesis, Melany Pinick, Nestor Guillen, Jesse-James Bentley, Cindy Smith, Tom Wetzel, the entire Juliana/Sasha/Charles/Bill household—for making the Bay lovely; my brother and sister Bill Armaline and Nicole Steward and my friend, Adam Weaver—for helping me navigate San Jose; my new friends, Mike McQuaide and Stacy Bell McQuaide—for helping me settle into a small Georgia town and acclimate to life in the South and a new job; and my mom and pops and brothers, as always for varied reasons.

Special thanks are also due to Abbey Volcano for a careful and iron editorial hand, Charles Weigl and Zach Blue for critical guidance, Kate Khatib for continually amazing cover art, and all of the folks at AK Press for their generous support of the project.

My gratitude to all of you.

To the dispossessed.

CONTENTS

PART 4: THE RULING CLASS RESPONSE

PART 5: EDUCATION AND THE STUDENT RESPONSE

CONCLUSION

SNAPSHOTS OF THE CRISIS, AUSTERITY, AND THE MOVEMENTS AGAINST

DERIC SHANNON

The law doth punish man or woman
That steals the goose from off the common,
But lets the greater felon loose
That steals the common from the goose[1]

BY NOW, DOZENS—IF NOT HUNDREDS—OF COMPETING NARRATIVES
that outline how we arrived at this particular global moment are circulating, typified by multiple crises (economic, social, ecological, political, etc.), multiple contestations over the means of life, and multiple possibilities for the future, some certainly more pleasant than others. Much of this work on crisis is (justifiably, I think) rooted in the
market collapse of 2008, and the rise of austerity politics and various
new social movements. While neither capitalist crises, nor economic
policies focused on cutting social spending and upwardly distributing
wealth, nor movements of affected populations are particularly *new,*
we do seem to live in a time of multiple possibilities—perhaps an acceleration and amplification of these things.

It *is* important to pose the sense of possibility such a historical
moment provides as an open question: *Is it the end of the world as
we know it?* I can save any readers waiting for the answer to that

particular question some time by stating categorically, here in the book's second paragraph, that this collection never answers that question. However, plenty of examples exist all over the world of what look like instances of society coming apart at the seams. Sometimes social explosions are global in scope and we are living in what could be a huge conflagration.

It makes sense, then, to begin this collection with the market collapse. Capitalism, after all, is assembled in such a way to invisibilize its attendant social relations, to make them seem natural, and, perhaps most importantly, to make them seem inevitable—as if there can be no alternative.[2] When historical moments of crisis hit—when peoples' expectations are undercut by austere social realities—they shake the faith in capitalism that allows it to be continually reproduced in our daily lives. People begin to see that the way that we've organized our lives is one option, but that other possibilities may also be on the table. While global movements have also arisen in times when capitalism has not been in crisis, in the current historical moment, crisis was a primary spark.

SNAPSHOTS

"A good [short story] would take me out of myself and then stuff me back in, outsized, now, and uneasy with the fit."
—David Sedaris

I want to begin by explaining the purpose of this collection and the way it is organized. This book begins with a few assumptions, the first of which is that we can only ever have a partial understanding of the world we live in and possibilities for the future. However, our understanding can be more or less partial, more or less informed, and bringing together analyses and stories from around the world, particularly during a historical moment such as ours, can be valuable in deepening our understanding of the present and possibilities for the future.

What I have assembled here, with the help of contributing authors, are *snapshots*. This isn't an attempt to tell the whole story of the crisis or various responses to it, but rather a way of sharing stories and analyses in one place, so we might learn from each other. As such, the book is missing a lot—there is an entire globe to cover; a wide array of social relations; a near-infinite number of possibilities for looking at how power is arranged in our lives and how it might be re-arranged. No collection could possibly hope to cover all or perhaps even the most important aspects of existing human social relations.

Secondly, I want to make a case for what should be a rather uncontroversial point. Our understandings of the economy cannot coherently be separated from analyses of social movements and the struggles between those who largely own and operate our society and the rest of us.[3] That is, economics cannot be abstracted from politics (or vice versa)—some people refer to this understanding, or type of analysis, as *political economy*—and for those of us who want to make a break with capitalism, a critical political economic understanding of the present is important.

Finally, given this understanding, we need a complex look at challenges to capital-as-it-is-composed as well as capitalism as such; the reaction to crisis by both the ruling class and the dispossessed; and the ways that these challenges and conflicts make up our social world and shape possibilities for the future.[4] Again, this is not a particularly original argument and should not be controversial for radicals (it is basic political economics), but I want to position the contents of this book and argue that a collection like this—one that includes analyses of economics, movements, and the state, from the broad to the narrow, the global to the local, the general to the specific—can be particularly useful for those of us opposed to capitalism and the state. Indeed, collections with this kind of range can provide us with tools to work together, to struggle more effectively.

I have been gathering valuable analyses, interviews, and stories since at least 2010. By the time this collection sees the light of day, some content will be old, while newer, important pieces will be missing.[5] In some ways, it's just a truism that the world moves, history marches on, and no collection could hope to cover everything. However, I think we are living in a special historical moment: there has been a general acceleration of events of huge importance, the implications of which we are still grappling with and trying to understand. Worth mentioning is that other valuable books and collections looking at specific pieces of our social puzzle exist, which might address questions missing here.[6] This book focuses specifically on the crisis, its effects, and the contestations over power that have taken place over the last few years. And it begins with the origins of the crisis and its rippling effects.

THE CRISIS AND ITS EFFECTS

"But lo! Men have become the tools of their tools."
—Henry David Thoreau

CRISIS IS CERTAINLY nothing new to capitalism—rather it is integral to how capitalism is arranged.[7] But crises in capitalism call into question deeply held myths about its necessity, its supposed naturalness, and, perhaps most famously stated by Margaret Thatcher, what is one of our most deeply entrenched beliefs: *there is no alternative.* In moments of crisis, the misery produced by rising wealth inequality, and the gap between material expectations and material reality, can bring about an acceleration of conflict over resources that, in turn, provides space for imagining different futures.

Many economists suggest the current crisis is a direct result of the inflation and burst of the housing bubble in the US. Greedy bankers gave bad loans to eager families under false pretenses, so the story goes. Increasingly bizarre and mystical financial instruments were created to sell and resell those loans, in their entirety and in bits and pieces, in an inexplicable process of speculation, then speculation upon that speculation, then speculation on that speculation of speculation, and so on. This process created a form of financial protection to the original lenders—for a while. But these were *bad loans* given to people by predatory lenders. The returns could not last forever and eventually the bubble burst, having a domino effect globally. Huge hedge funds and financial firms began declaring bankruptcy, consumer confidence plummeted, and financial markets reacted nervously, and eventually collapsed.[8] Thus was created the Great Recession in which we are now living.[9]

There's some truth to this narrative, although, as with most explanations of current events provided by our thirty-second, newsbite-driven media, there's also an awful lot missing. Like all large-scale institutional arrangements involving millions or, rather, billions of human beings, very specific historical, material, and ideological circumstances laid the foundations for the economic crisis. Though origin stories can go back as far as one likes, even thousands of years,[10] and although crises seem endemic to capitalism, it does make sense to root analysis of this particular crisis in the rise of a few different trends in contemporary capitalism, namely deregulation, neoliberalism, and financialization—developments tied to struggles between labor and capital.[11]

Neoliberalism arose as a response to the regulatory mechanisms that were in place until the early 1970s, the result of large-scale battles between labor and capital that led to high rates of unionization and other forms of worker organization.[12] Some historians suggest that the "New Deal" policies in the US and social democracy in Europe resulted from strategic alliances between labor and capital, awarding unions with a greater share of the social wealth in key industries, creating social provisions to provide for the poor, and increasing safety standards (and living standards more generally). As a remedy to this, neoliberalism was advanced by a number of well-financed think tanks, perhaps most notably the Mont Pelerin Society, whose membership included well-known economists such as Milton Friedman and Friedrich Hayek. The hallmark of neoliberalism is often referred to as *deregulation*, although I think that might be a bit of a misnomer. While neoliberal capitalism certainly saw attacks on existing regulations that benefited workers, it also saw increasing state regulation *on behalf of the wealthy*.[13] Neoliberalism was a sign of the defeat of labor, an end to the "alliance," and a part of the ruling class offensive against workers all over the world. The privatization endemic to neoliberalism also opened up crucial new spaces into which capital could expand, part of a broader move, inherent in capitalism, toward the expansion of commodification and marketization.

Since the ideology of neoliberalism was founded on the idea of removing state intervention from markets, in practice, it meant lowering the tax rates of the wealthy, decimating social programs and safety nets for workers, and allowing capital to move across borders with as little hindrance as possible. But it's important to understand that these practices were in conjunction with the rise of international lending institutions like the International Monetary Fund (IMF), the World Bank, and the World Trade Organization (WTO). Attached to loans for "development" to "underdeveloped" countries (i.e. often former colonies, now neocolonies, typically in the global South), these institutions demanded "structural adjustment programs." These "structural adjustments" meant removing barriers to trade from developed nations, privatizing industries and social services, and removing "troubling" regulations (economic, social, environmental) that would get in the way of doing business.

With trade barriers eliminated, manufacturing companies in developed countries like the US could move production facilities to more business-congenial environments. This led to the process of what many American economists refer to as *deindustrialization,* the systematic transfer of manufacturing jobs from the overdeveloped world to developing economies reliant on IMF loans, and thus beholden to structural adjustment programs. Those manufacturing jobs, before they were moved from the overdeveloped world, were often union jobs that allowed workers to eke out a decent living. Replacing those jobs were unemployment and a rise in low-paying service-sector jobs, leading to *downward* mobility for many workers in the overdeveloped world.

In order for capitalism to continue functioning, workers in the overdeveloped world needed money to spend on commodities (now often produced abroad for cheaper labor costs), and unemployment and low-paying service jobs didn't provide enough capital for such spending. While in the past, credit and loans were a risk undertaken by lenders and creditors directly, the credit extensions and loans given to workers, particularly in the US, were increasingly rolled into complex financial instruments and speculative capital, with lenders and creditors protected by the padding of speculation, institutions like the IMF, and (as seen with global bailouts of financial institutions) the state. As David Graeber explains, "This leads to insane speculative bubbles, a situation in which 90–95 percent of all money is actually speculative with no connection to production or trade, and people becoming effectively enserfed."[14] Due to neoliberal ideology, these heavily protected and financialized loans were made even more readily available through federal programs that saw the deregulation of banks, home loans, and the subsequent rise in subprime home loans offered through predatory lending practices. The housing bubble expanded and eventually burst, causing global effects that we are still living with today, due in large part to historical events tied to social struggles.

This overly simplified account is fleshed out in some detail by contributions to Part 1 of this collection. Paul Bowman historicizes accounts of the economic crisis, providing a materialist analysis that "attempt[s] to avoid falling into the pitfalls of geopolitics or economic determinism and keep[s] sight of the human agency of real processes of struggle and production, and productive struggle." In my interview with Noam Chomsky, he roots the crisis in the post-World War II changes to the economy, while offering suggestions for political practice based on current conditions. Davita Silfen Glasberg, Angie Beeman, and Colleen Casey focus specifically on predatory lending practices in the housing market, and their racist roots, as factors leading to the financial crisis. They build upon years of research compiled in Chicago, Indianapolis, St. Louis, Cleveland, and Hartford.

Since financial institutions all over the world owned parts of these loans and mortgages through financialization and speculation, the effects of the housing market bubble bursting have also been globally felt. Evidence of this is easily found: in the ruins of the global economy; the aggravation of racist and gendered oppressions, as the working class is divided by racist, anti-immigrant, and sexist ideas and, importantly, movements; and the rise of forms of contestation and struggle that were unimaginable just a few years ago, such as the Arab Spring and the movements within public squares (e.g. Tahrir Square, Zucotti Park, Puerta Del Sol, Syntagma Square). More poignantly, evidence of this can be found in the suffering of working people all over the world.

As the EU struggled to cope with widespread unemployment and people were being evicted from their homes as a result of being unable to pay their mortgages, four people committed suicide in Spain in one week in February of 2013 because of eviction proceedings.[15] South of Spain, in North Africa, suicide in the form of self-immolation became a common reaction to "poverty, frustration, [and a] lack of opportunities." One news report noted "five men have set themselves on fire in Egypt, four in Algeria, and one in Mauritania."[16] Like Spain, Algeria saw four suicides in a single week, demonstrating what reporters described as "signs of social misery" throughout the region.[17] Similarly, in Israel, two flower-growers, immersed in debt and reeling from the confiscation of their vehicles, took their own lives. These stories "of desperation" have become "increasingly common in Israel, where living standards have plummeted in the past three years as the economic boom generated by the post-Oslo-Accords optimism unraveled into the worst economic crisis in the country's history."[18]

Meanwhile, in Ireland, management of the supermarket giant Tesco was accused of affixing armbands to warehouse workers, in order to track their movements and "reprimand them for breaks."[19] Far from Ireland, in Southeast Asia, after a factory collapsed in

Bangladesh, killing over a thousand people, workers poured into the streets, smashing cars and barricading roads in "anger at the faceless system that grinds their daily lives into hours making garments and minutes for rest."[20] Moving north and east, in China and Taiwan, at the Foxconn factories, where cheap electronics parts for computer giants like Apple, HP, Sony, and Nokia are produced, workers also experienced a spate of suicides, likely a result of the "labor camp" conditions, in which workers were sometimes "forced to work 80 to 100 hours of overtime per month."[21] In one particular cynical attempt at public relations, the company claimed that "success" was "the root of the morale problems it's trying to excise from its workforce," as it held rallies to raise morale, and hung suicide-prevention nets from its factory walls to catch any workers who might decide to jump from the misery of their conditions.[22]

And precisely under these conditions of immiseration, the right wing all over the world has undertaken a dizzying series of attacks on women, queer folks, immigrants, people of color—any scapegoats it can find. In the US, Republican Party politicians have recently made a number of embarrassingly reckless comments about rape, most often in transparent ploys to attack abortion rights and the bodily autonomy of women.[23] Religious fundamentalists in Uganda, "whose lobbying is generously funded by conservative U.S. Christian organizations representing every denomination from evangelicals to Catholics to Mormons," are some of the "most influential supporters" of proposed legislation that "would impose draconian new punishments" for same-sex sexual practices. "Among them: a seven-year prison sentence for consenting adults who have gay sex, life sentences for people in same-sex marriages and even jail for those who don't report gays and lesbians in their midst."[24] Southern Europe generally, and Greece in particular, has seen a rise in far-right, anti-immigrant panic, resulting in an increasing interest in fascism and the emergence of new right-wing, populist parties, whose members have terrorized migrant workers in public.[25]

Amidst this crisis-ridden landscape, contributors to this volume have cataloged various effects of the market collapse in Part 2. Antonis Vradis writes of a sense of self-defeat in Greece, where the crisis has taken on such proportions that even *meaning* itself is a casualty of conditions. Harpreet K. Paul traces the global effects of the crisis on human rights, rooting her analysis in neoliberalism's triumph.

Ernesto Aguilar and Ayn Morgan discuss some of the ways people of color, particularly in the US, are touched by an economy in decline. Gayge Maggio takes a critical look at gender and reproductive labor in capitalism's most recent catastrophe. Dustin Shannon interviews Miguel Ángel Fernández about the CNT, and crisis and response in Spain. Jasmin Mujanović outlines the ways that crisis has become *institutionalized* in Bosnia-Herzegovina, while Jorell Meléndez Badillo takes a look at Puerto Rico, asserting that "capitalism is not in crisis, capitalism is the crisis."[26]

By the way, in case any readers were wondering, while most of this was taking place throughout the world, the richest seven percent in the US actually got richer.[27]

AUSTERITY AND THE RULING CLASS RESPONSE

"The State is the altar of political freedom and, like the religious altar, it is maintained for the purpose of human sacrifice."
—Emma Goldman

IN THE FACE of this global catastrophe, while the majority of the world's population has seen a decline in living standards, people have lost their homes, companies have increased pressure on workers to generate greater productivity, and the wealthiest few continue to profit and grow richer, the response of the ruling class has been centered on *austerity*. Austerity can be seen, along with neoliberalism, as part of the ruling class'sdecades long offensive against the working class. In one recent example, prior to austerity policies, the financial institutions largely responsible for the housing market crash were rewarded for their predatory practices with hundreds of billions of tax dollars in the form of a bailout.

Austerity does bear some resemblance to neoliberalism, consisting of deregulation when it comes to social spending, but otherwise, as the bailout makes plain, regulation in direct favor of the wealthy. Austerity also applies pressure on states similar to the structural adjustment policies of neoliberalism, but does so to *overdeveloped* nations, where debt crises (particularly throughout the EU) have caused nations whose economies are intimately connected through common currencies, trade agreements, and shared fiscal governance to plummet dangerously close to collapse and require "bailout" funds from their neighbors. This leaves vulnerable, collapsing nations dependent on their lenders in an eerily similar paternalistic pattern as the relationship between overdeveloped and "underdeveloped" nations under neoliberalism. Perhaps nowhere is this more obvious than in Greece, where politicians have been continually forced to accede to demands by international lenders such as the IMF for, as per usual, privatization and an evisceration of social spending, effectively giving up control of fiscal policy in exchange for loans to keep an ailing economy afloat.

These economic "fixes" have been applied across the globe, in attempts to recover from the economic crisis. The results have been staggering for workers—particularly younger workers. Globally, the "youth unemployment rate is projected to reach almost 13 percent in 2013—the equivalent of 73 million young people" without jobs and that "is not expected to decline before 2018."[28] In Spain and Greece, youth unemployment is particularly high, with an astonishing 56 percent in the former and 62.5 percent in the latter.[29]

Naturally, this has led many youth to question the presumed truths conveyed by their elders—namely, that education and hard work would lead to jobs and prosperity. In turn, this has led to the formation of large youth and student movements. And the ruling class's response to those movements has been, almost uniformly across the globe, repression. Some of this I witnessed firsthand, when police charged Spanish "15-M" protesters in the center of Madrid in December, 2011, and pulled occupiers from the sidewalks in New York City, beating and arresting them, at the end of a massive general assembly held after the May Day march in 2012.

Stories of militarized police violently attacking protesters are almost commonplace at the time of writing this introduction. And those attacks have been coupled with other forms of police/state repression, such as the grand jury summonses used to intimidate organizers in the US. From New York City to Seattle to Santa Cruz, grand jury resisters have emerged from youth movements and the state has jailed them, in fairly obvious attempts to silence dissidence and create an atmosphere of distrust and paranoia among movement participants. Further, police brutality continues to be a common feature in Egypt, where protesters who toppled one regime are now dealing with a military coup of the ruling class that followed. In Greece, where, according to one senior officer, police have been infiltrated by the fascist Golden Dawn,[30] the police captured, abused, and tortured antifascist protesters in one particularly widely covered attack.[31] In reaction to the student movement in Chile, "police attacked passersby, beat up journalists and staged a…brutal attack on student leaders immediately after they had held a press conference" during a march in 2011, where "(h)undreds of protesters were injured, and 250 were arrested."[32] And in South Africa, police shot and killed striking miners in what has now been dubbed the "Marikana Massacre."

These directly repressive forms of policing have been utilized in conjunction with an increase in state/police spying and surveillance. The recent revelations by ex-contractor Edward Snowden of the monstrous Orwellian surveillance apparatus in the US are a case in point. As the US collects data on its citizens, foreign nationals, and foreign governments—and those data collection efforts are made public—the state's distrust of its own people and supposed allies is made clear. This, of course, is not a new phenomenon nor, for that matter, is heavy-handed police violence. As far back as 1851, one well-known French antagonist noted:

> To be governed is to be watched over, inspected, spied on, directed, legislated, regimented, closed in, indoctrinated, preached at, controlled, assessed, evaluated, censored, commanded, all by creatures that have neither the right nor wisdom nor virtue… To be governed means that at every move, operation, or transaction, one is noted, registered, entered in a census, taxed, stamped, authorized, recommended, admonished, prevented, reformed, set right, corrected. Government means to be subject to tribute, trained, ransomed, exploited, monopolized, extorted, pressured, mystified, robbed; all in the name of public utility and the general good. Then at first sign of resistance or word of complaint, one is repressed, fined, despised, vexed, pursued, hustled, beaten up, garroted, imprisoned, shot, machine gunned, judged, sentenced, deported, sacrificed, sold, betrayed, and to cap it all, ridiculed, mocked, outraged, and dishonored. That is Government. That is its justice and morality![33]

What *is* new in this age of austerity and large-scale antagonism toward the state is the sheer amount of data being collected (particularly digital communications and networks), as well as the increase in police militarization. Yesterday's riot police are today's street cops and today's riot police are yesterday's National Guard. The state seems to be waging a counterinsurgency against its own citizens.[34]

And this certainly is not limited to the United States. In Europe, entire cities are under surveillance through the use of CCTV cameras, and some people have made a sport of destroying them.[35] Additionally, in Greece, since around 2008, one report indicates "wiretaps have increased...by a staggering 1,050 percent."[36] In Italy, in "2010 alone, over 100,000 people were wiretapped, with the total cost reaching €284 million."[37] In Spain, online surveillance recently took on ridiculous proportions, when five people were arrested for posting comments on anticapitalist Facebook pages. While announcing an inquiry into US spying programs in July of 2013, the European Union Parliament expressed "grave concern about allegations that similar surveillance programs are run by several EU member states, such as the UK, Sweden, the Netherlands and Germany," and urged "them to examine whether those programs are compatible with EU law."[38] These systems of surveillance and data-collection have gotten so bad that even state organizations are expressing concerns about their own members!

Austerity, surveillance, and police violence are not the only options for ruling class responses to the crisis. Capitalists and their states could respond in softer ways. Perhaps we will see a return to Keynesian fiscal policy or some other set of reforms attempting to create a new labor-capital alliance, although many radicals argue that such a proposition is unlikely or impossible.[39] The turn toward sustainable technologies, localism, and what has been dubbed "green capitalism" could form a new asset bubble in a "Green New Deal." We are already starting to see such attempts, as various states around the world subsidize so-called "green energy" efforts.

In Part 4 of this collection, contributors deal with various aspects of the ruling class response. Drawing on work he published in 2011 and 2012, Nate Hawthorne deals with the question of whether deep and meaningful reform is possible, while arguing that we should be prepared to deal with what he calls "militant reformism"—an admonition to anticapitalists not to mistake *form* for *content*.[40] Yesenia Barragán looks at so-called "green capitalism," noting possibilities of a "Green New Deal," while charting transnational resistance to this particular elite response. Adam Quinn argues that the militarization of police since the economic downturn can be seen as a crucial form of austerity. Rooting his analysis in representations of the crisis, particularly in Greece, Chris Spannos suggests that major media gives us a one-dimensional view of capitalism in crisis, rather than a multidimensional view that questions the logic of the rule of capital. Sean Parson and Luis Fernandez contend that police have developed *insurgency control*, a combination of tactics of repression, surveillance, and suppression to deal with "the movements against." Uri Gordon analyzes how Israeli politicians use nationalist fervor to pacify and recuperate movements, using Israel's "tent protests" as a case study. Finally, Benjamin Fogel examines the case of the Marikana Massacre, developing an analysis that first appeared in *Insurgent Notes* in October 2012.[41]

THE MOVEMENTS AGAINST

"As happens sometimes, a moment settled and hovered and remained for much more than a moment. And sound stopped and movement stopped for much, much more than a moment."
—John Steinbeck

THERE ARE MOMENTS in history when social antagonisms become so great that global tidal waves of contestation, insurrection, and revolt roll over the planet. I believe we are living in one such moment. As Paul Mason, economics editor of BBC2's *Newsnight* argues, it seems things are "kicking off everywhere."[42] The economic crisis is only one crisis, which could serve as a catalyst for the continued mobilization of people, amidst mobilizations that have already began. Living in an age of multiple crises creates multiple possibilities for the widening of antagonisms between privilege and power, on the one hand, and the dispossessed, on the other. In many ways, the economic crisis is interconnected with the environmental crisis in which we are living.[43] And both the economic and environmental crises have contributed to a crisis of legitimacy for our ruling institutions. According to one commentator, "protests from Istanbul to São Paulo have one thing in common—growing dissent among the young, educated and better-off protesting against the very system that once enriched them. And therein lies the danger for governments."[44]

I have termed the movements that have arisen in this recent global wave "the movements against" to indicate two things. First, what these movements are *against* is a question up for debate, debate that is often vigorously undertaken from within movements themselves. Are these movements against authoritarian regimes, austerity, rising inequality, lowering standards of living, unaccountable governments, etc.? Or are they movements about something more fundamental? Are they movements against capitalism, the state, and domination in all of its various forms? The answers to these questions, it seems, are simultaneously "yes" and "no." It's part of what fascinates, impresses, irritates, and exasperates various participants and observers about the movements.

Secondly, I use the term to point out that these are *antagonist* movements, by and large. Part of why they escape easy categorization is because most of these groupings have avoided affiliation with political parties, unions, NGO-ization. They have often quite consciously attempted to remain autonomous from and antagonistic to institutionalization. In societies where the relevance of any social grouping is judged by their representation among major institutions, this can make for an amorphous and near-unintelligible social body, bewildering to onlookers and participants alike. Defining them as movements *against* aims to describe antagonist movements in relation to institutionalization.[45]

Finally, while most of the pieces in this collection refer to *movements* in a general sense, just as the ruling class response is complex, the response of the dispossessed is also plural. Some of the responses to the crisis could not be described as movements in the traditional sense. They include riots, looting, and a wide range of attacks on property relations, the state, and domination. But I'm not sure there is always a clear separation between the latter and what I'm calling "the movements against," where some of these attacks have either emerged from movements or catalyzed them.

Most people narrate the existing wave of social movements by beginning with the Arab Spring. Far from a unified phenomenon, the Arab Spring refers to a grouping of events in the Middle East and North Africa still taking place (an awful long "Spring"). The causes are multiple, as are the methods and the outcomes. Multiple governments have been overthrown (in Tunisia, Yemen, Libya, and twice now in Egypt, the latest as a result of a military coup); in Syria, there is civil war; and elsewhere, there have been sustained protests, sacking of cabinets and parliaments, or deep changes in governmental policies.[46]

In Egypt, much of the public attention was focused on Tahrir Square. While the square has a history as a space of protest, it was occupied during the 2011 revolution, at one point attracting over a quarter million people and shooting off into side streets. This set the stage for occupations of public squares across the globe: Puerto Del Sol in Spain; Parliament Square in the UK; Syntagma Square in Greece; in the US, the two most dynamic occupations were in Oakland, in the renamed "Oscar Grant Plaza," and in New York City, in Zuccotti Park, where the "Occupy Wall Street" movement first emerged. Protesters in Egypt set the stage for a global wave—a "movement of squares," so to speak.

Of course, the response of the dispossessed took on many other forms as well. In Wisconsin, as a response to Governor Scott Walker's legislation limiting the public bargaining rights of public sector unions, people descended on and occupied the State Capitol in Madison. This struggle ended in a failed recall strategy and the victory of Governor Walker's union-busting bill. In Argentina, over 130 people were arrested in poverty-stricken cities, following outbreaks of looting at supermarkets.[47] In Mexico, self-organized defense squads were formed to combat violence.[48] In Port Said, in Egypt, attempts were made at taking and self-organizing the city.[49] In Spain, house-less families are setting up housing networks in vacant buildings, forming the *corrala* movement.[50]

Also included in these various forms of movement have been student attempts at organizing, occupying, and combating the powers-that-be. In the US, before the Occupy Wall Street movement emerged, students had occupied buildings in New York and California, perhaps popularizing the language of "occupation" in key movement texts. In the fall of 2010, approximately 50,000 students and academics took to the streets in London, UK, destroying property and eventually occupying Tory Party headquarters for a short period. And in Chile and Quebec, the student movements have become known throughout the world for their recent militancy.

Part Three of this collection deals with the response of the dispossessed, while Part Five deals specifically with the student response. By organizing these responses into distinct sections, I do not mean to suggest that students are a group apart from the world's dispossessed. Nor do I intend to suggest that students have some special role in contemporary struggles or that educational institutions are a special locus of struggle.[51] Rather, I included a section specifically about students and higher education workers because of the dynamism of recent movements on campuses, and because, as Paul Mason suggests, the "graduate without a future" does seem to figure significantly among the people who have populated the movements against. This means that higher education, at least, might warrant its own discussion, although we might debate prioritizing these sorts of fights.

Part Three begins with Mark Bray, an organizer with Occupy Wall Street's Press Working Group, who writes about how Occupy Wall Street provided strategic narratives of the economic decline of the US, a subject bound up in all sorts of elite ideological assumptions, and what it means for struggle in the present. Abbey Volcano provides examples of direct intervention around gender and sexuality in the movements against. Marie Trigona writes on Argentina's antagonist movements, rooting her analysis in the rise of neoliberalism, and notes how space is organized and contested. Nick Driedger provides a brief analysis of the struggle of the Canadian Union of Postal Workers, of which he was a part. Shane Burley looks at the development of the housing movement and its response to crisis. Christian Garland examines the 2011 Tottenham Riots, suggesting that we might find insurrectionary potential in the precariat. Matthew Adams gives us history and case studies of solidarity networks as a means of resisting austerity.

Part Five—the section on education and the student response—begins with a contribution from William T. Armaline and Abraham DeLeon on the role of education in larger social struggles, providing suggestions for how educators might intervene in institutions of higher learning. Abbey Volcano interviews student organizer Jamie Burnett about the Québécois student movement. Marianne LeNabat surveys student organizing in New York City in the wake of Occupy. Yesenia Barragán and Mark Bray interview Rudy Amanda Hurtado Garcés, a student organizer in Colombia and a longtime militant in Colombia's antineoliberal movements. Finally, Mónica Kostas and Scott Nikolas Nappalos provide an analysis of the student movement in Chile, along with an interview with Felipe Ramírez, a Chilean student organizer.

The pieces—the snapshots—in this collection, I think, speak for themselves. Undoubtedly, readers will draw widely differing conclusions from what they encounter in this book. But the intention is not to provide a single, coherent line on social struggle (I'm beginning to believe those can't exist anyway), but to provide stories by movement participants and analysts for those of us who want to widen social antagonisms and create a new future. I conclude the collection with my own short analysis on developing a critical understanding of possibilities for the future, relying on the contents of the book, personal experiences as a participant in the movements against, and what I think are important lessons recently advanced by radicals.

I end this introduction with a quote by Immanuel Wallerstein, taken from a longer piece in which he argues that one can see the spirit of '68 in existing movements. He provides a cautionary warning for those who think the existing movements are on the wane and suggests what might happen when the next asset bubble bursts (student loans, anyone?): "Those who believe that Arab unrest, that world unrest, is a passing moment will discover in the next major bubble burst (which we can anticipate quite soon) that the '1968 current' will no longer be so easily contained."[52] I hope he's right, for my own sake and for all of us.

ENDNOTES

1   Anonymously attributed, as quoted in Raj Patel, *Stuffed and Starved: The Hidden Battle for the World Food System* (Brooklyn: Melville House Publishing, 2007), 76.

2   For one of my personal favorites on this, see Mark Fisher, *Capitalist Realism: Is There No Alternative?* (Winchester, UK: Zero Books, 2009).

3   I want to be clear here: these conflicts, between the rulers and ruled, the owners and the dispossessed, only *sometimes* manifest as social movements.

4   There is a difference between opposition to "globalization," "austerity," or "neoliberalism" and opposition to "capitalism."

5   As I pen this introduction, the world has seen an open rebellion develop in Turkey; a former US contractor revealed major domestic and foreign surveillance operations by the National Security Agency and is

currently seeking asylum while stranded in a Russian airport; protests and riots have broken out in parts of the US, in reaction to a Florida judge finding George Zimmerman "not guilty" in the shooting death of an African-American teenager, Trayvon Martin—all developments worthy of their own analysis.

6   A few such collections that I've found particularly valuable are:

Paul Craig Roberts, *How the Economy was Lost: The War of the Worlds* (Oakland: AK Press, 2010).

Greg Albo, Sam Gindin, and Leo Panitch, *In and Out of Crisis: The Global Financial Meltdown and Left Alternatives* (Oakland: PM Press, 2010).

Aragorn! (ed.), *Occupy Everything: Anarchists in the Occupy Movement, 2009–2011* (Berkeley: LBC Books 2012).

Kate Khatib, Margaret Killjoy, and Mike McGuire (eds.), *We Are Many: Reflections on Movement Strategy From Occupation to Liberation* (Oakland: AK Press, 2012).

John Bellamy Foster and Fred Magdoff, *The Great Financial Crisis: Causes and Consequences* (New York City: Monthly Review Press, 2009).

Sasha Lilley, *Capital and its Discontents: Conversations with Radical Thinkers in a Time of Tumult* (Oakland: PM Press, 2011).

Geoff Mann, *Disassembly Required: A Field Guide to Actually Existing Capitalism* (Oakland: AK Press, 2013).

7   For one explanation, see John Asimakopoulos, "Globalized Contradictions of Capitalism and the Imperative for Epochal Change," in *The Accumulation of Freedom: Writings on Anarchist Economics*, Deric Shannon et al., eds. (Oakland: AK Press, 2012).

8   As an aside, it's interesting to note how economists personify markets. This observation allows one to make all sorts of interesting inferences about our society.

9   For an interesting look at how racism played a central part in these predatory lending practices—typically ignored in mainstream economic analyses of the lead-up to the crisis—in addition to the chapter by Davita Silfen Glasberg, et al. in this collection, see Davita Silfen Glasberg, Angie Beeman, and Colleen Casey, "Preying on the American

Dream: Predatory Lending, Institutionalized Racism, and Resistance to Economic Injustice," in *Human Rights in Our Own Backyard: Injustice and Resistance in the United States* (Philadelphia: University of Pennsylvania Press, 2011), 34–45.

10   Although not intended as an explanation of the crisis, for one notable example, see David Graeber, *Debt: The First 5000 Years* (Brooklyn: Melville House Publishing, 2011).

11   Although the roots of this particular crisis of capitalism lie in neoliberal deregulation, financialization, globalization, or some combination of those things, it's *not* the position of the editor that the solution is a return to regulated "New Deal" capitalism. Such a return may not even be possible at this point, an argument that Nate Hawthorne deals with in this collection at some length. Rather, capitalism itself is a crisis and even if it could be stable, it would still be misery-inducing, alienating, and exploitative for the vast majority of the planet's inhabitants, human and nonhuman.

12   Typified by the state intervening in the economy to provide social programs and protections for the working classes.

13   This introduction is, perhaps, not the place to develop this particular argument, but consider, as one example, the regulation of borders under "free trade" agreements such as the North American Free Trade Agreement (NAFTA). NAFTA allowed a tremendous amount of capital mobility and an easier time for companies and their wealthy owners to move themselves and their assets into so-called "underdeveloped" countries (and back). Also consider the sorts of obstacles workers from those same "underdeveloped" countries face when they decide to migrate to the overdeveloped world in search of work. What looks like *deregulation* for capital and the wealthy looks an awful lot like *heavy regulation* for workers.

14   David Graeber and Jamie Stern-Weiner, "Debt, Slavery and our Idea of Freedom (Part 2)," *ZNet*, http://www.zcommunications.org/debt-slavery-and-our-idea-of-freedom-part-2-by-david-graeber (accessed July 15, 2013).

15   Meredith Bennett-Smith, "4th Eviction-Motivated Suicide Rocks Indebted Spain; Protesters Shout Eviction Is 'Murder'," *Huffington Post*, http://www.huffingtonpost.

com/2013/02/15/4th-eviction-suicide-spain_n_2697192.html (accessed July 15, 2013).

16 Al Jazeera, "Tunisia Triggers Copycat Suicides," *Al Jazeera*, http://www.aljazeera.com/news/africa/2011/01/20111179413130528.html (accessed July 18, 2013).

17 Ibid.

18 Iason Athanasiadis, "In Crisis: Where Now for Israel's Economy," Al Jazeera, http://www.aljazeera.com/archive/2003/04/20084915620503371.html (accessed July 18, 2003).

19 Kevin Rawlinson, "Tesco Accused of Using Electronic Armbands to Monitor its Staff," *The Independent*, http://www.independent.co.uk/news/business/news/tesco-accused-of-using-electronic-armbands-to-monitor-its-staff-8493952.html (accessed July 18, 2013).

20 Vijay Prashad, "Bangladeshi Workers Need More than Boycotts," *The Guardian*, http://www.guardian.co.uk/commentisfree/2013/apr/30/bangladesh-workers-need-more-than-boycotts (accessed July 18, 2013).

21 Fiona Tam, "Foxconn Factories are Labour Camps: Report," *South China Morning Post*, http://www.scmp.com/article/727143/foxconn-factories-are-labour-camps-report (accessed July 18, 2013).

22 Eliot Van Buskirk, "Foxconn Rallies Workers, Leaves Suicide Nets in Place (Updated)," *Wired*, http://www.wired.com/business/2010/08/foxconn-rallies-workers-installs-suicide-nets/ (accessed July 18, 2013).

23 Stephen D. Foster, Jr., "The Party of Rape Culture: 40 Republican Rape Quotes Everyone Should Remember," *Addicting Info*, http://www.addictinginfo.org/2013/07/16/the-party-of-rape-culture-40-republican-rape-quotes-everyone-should-remember/ (accessed July 18, 2013).

24 Tim Padgett, "Viewpoint: Uganda's Anti-Gay Bill a Christmas Alarm for Christians," *Time*, http://world.time.com/2012/12/04/viewpoint-ugandas-anti-gay-bill-a-christmas-alarm-for-christians/ (accessed July 18, 2013).

25 For one interesting discussion, see Marianne Maeckelbergh, "The Real Struggle Begins: Europe Descends into Fascism," *Dorset Eye,* http://www.dorseteye.com/north/articles/the-real-struggle-begins-europe-descends-into-fascism (accessed July 18, 2013).

26   Borrowing from Michael Truscello's documentary, *Capitalism is the Crisis: Radical Politics in the Age of Crisis,* 2011.

27   Associated Press, "Richest 7% Got Richer During Recovery," *The Star Democrat,* http://m.stardem.com/news/national/article_8b97d88e-acf8-11e2-9cef-001a4bcf887a.html (accessed July 18, 2013).

28   José Manuel Salazar-Xirinachs and Reeta Roy, "Young People Deserve a Better Start," *Huffington Post,* http://www.huffingtonpost.com/jose-manuel-salazarxirinachs/young-people-deserve-a-better-start_b_3246840.html (accessed July 19, 2013).

29   Derek Thompson, "Europe's Record Youth Unemployment: The Scariest Graph in the World Just Got Scarier," *The Atlantic,* http://www.theatlantic.com/business/archive/2013/05/europes-record-youth-unemployment-the-scariest-graph-in-the-world-just-got-scarier/276423/ (accessed July 19, 2013).

30   Aris Chatzistefanou, "Golden Dawn Has Infiltrated Greek Police, Claims Officer," *The Guardian,* http://www.guardian.co.uk/world/2012/oct/26/golden-dawn-infiltrated-greek-police-claims (accessed July 19, 2013).

31   Maria Margaronis, "Greek Anti-Fascist Protesters 'Tortured by Police' After Clash with Golden Dawn," *The Guardian,* http://www.guardian.co.uk/world/2012/oct/09/greek-antifascist-protesters-torture-police (accessed July 19, 2013).

32   Luis Arce, "President Piñera Unleashes Repression Against Chile's Student Movement," *World Socialist Website,* http://www.wsws.org/en/articles/2011/10/chil-o11.html (accessed July 20, 2013).

33   Pierre-Josef Proudhon, *General Idea of the Revolution* (London: Pluto Press, 1989), 294. Available online at http://fair-use.org/p-j-proudhon/general-idea-of-the-revolution/ (accessed December 20, 2013).

34   See Kristian Williams, Lara Messersmith-Glavin, and William Munger, *Life During Wartime: Resisting Counterinsurgency* (Oakland: AK Press, 2013) for a collection of discussions on this topic.

35   Oliver Stallwood, "Game to Destroy CCTV Cameras: Vandalism or Valid Protest?" *The Guardian,* http://www.guardian.co.uk/theguardian/shortcuts/2013/jan/25/game-destroy-cctv-cameras-berlin (accessed July 20, 2013).

36   Yiannis Baboulias, "Southern Europe is Becoming One Big Sur-
     veillance State," *Vice*, http://www.vice.com/en_uk/read/southern-
     europe-is-becoming-one-big-surveillance-state (accessed July 20,
     2013).

37   Ibid.

38   European Parliament Press Service, "Parliament to Launch In-Depth
     Inquiry into U.S. Surveillance Programmes," http://www.europarl.
     europa.eu/news/en/pressroom/content/20130701IPR14770/html/Par-
     liament-to-launch-in-depth-inquiry-into-US-surveillance-programmes
     (accessed July 20, 2013).

39   For a look at some of these arguments, see Juan Conatz, "Is Reform
     Possible?," *Libcom.org*, libcom.org/blog/reform-possible-22122011 (ac-
     cessed July 20, 2013).

40   One can find some of those earlier analyses at http://libcom.org/blog/
     nate (accessed July 20, 2013).

41   http://insurgentnotes.com/2012/10/marikana-a-point-of-rupture/ (ac-
     cessed July 20, 2013).

42   Paul Mason, *Why It's Still Kicking Off Everywhere: The New Global
     Revolutions* (Brooklyn: Verso Press, 2013).

43   For two interesting pieces on these interactions, see Michael T. Klare,
     "The Economic Crisis and the Environment," *Huffington Post*, http://
     www.huffingtonpost.com/michael-t-klare/the-economic-crisis-and-
     t_b_135631.html (accessed July 20, 2013) and Wayne Price, "The
     Ecological Crisis is an Economic Crisis; the Economic Crisis is an
     Ecological Crisis," *Anarkismo*, http://www.anarkismo.net/article/17024
     (accessed July 20, 2013).

44   Peter Beaumont, "Global Protest Grows as Citizens Lose Faith in
     Politics and the State," *The Guardian*, http://www.guardian.co.uk/
     world/2013/jun/22/urban-protest-changing-global-social-network (ac-
     cessed July 20, 2013). I might take issue with his characterization of
     these movements as consisting of the "better off."

45   When I refer to these movements, I do not mean to include every
     movement that has arisen in response to the crisis. The world has also
     seen a rise in reactionary movements, neo-fascist outfits and the like. I
     exclude them from the designation "the movements against" because

those groups represent another face of control through and through, and quite directly.

46 It is certainly a failing of this book that there is no account from antagonists in the various "Arab Spring" movements. This is not due to a lack of trying—indeed, I had interviews lined up with one scholar who has studied the region and written extensively on the situation in Libya in particular, as well as with two organizers in the Egyptian movement. The first didn't work out due to time constraints, the latter due to a desire to be in the streets instead of writing (can't say I blame them). Nevertheless, with westerners' history of orientalism and exclusion, I feel it necessary to acknowledge this lack, given that the book is going to press and I don't have time to find another contributor.

47 Working Class Self Organisation, "Supermarket Sweep Across Argentina," *Libcom.org*, http://libcom.org/blog/supermarket-sweep-across-argentina-21122012 (accessed July 20, 2013).

48 Mark Stevenson, "In Mexico, Self-Defense Squads Battle Violence," *Yahoo News*, http://news.yahoo.com/mexico-self-defense-squads-battle-violence-082925460.html (accessed July 20, 2013).

49 Infoaut, "Egypt: The Self-Management of Port Said and the Workers' Struggles," *Anarkismo*, http://www.anarkismo.net/article/25022 (accessed July 20, 2013).

50 Dave Stelfox, "How the Corrala Movement is Occupying Spain," *The Guardian*, http://www.guardian.co.uk/world/2013/mar/04/corrala-movement-occupying-spain (accessed July 20, 2013).

51 This is an analysis that I'm particularly uncomfortable with, given that academics do a lot of writing on existing social struggles and it is easy for them to center the experience of the institutions that they inhabit, often at the expense of analyzing other struggles.

52 Immanuel Wallerstein, "The Contradictions of the Arab Spring," *Al Jazeera*, http://www.aljazeera.com/indepth/opinion/2011/11/20111111101711539134.html (accessed July 21, 2013).

PART 1

THE CRISIS

"I have found a flaw."
—*Alan Greenspan, October 23, 2008*

FROM THE FALL OF SAIGON TO THE FALL OF LEHMAN

PAUL BOWMAN

IN A BLURRY, BLACK-AND-WHITE PHOTOGRAPH TAKEN IN ITALY IN THE 1960s, a worker rides a Vespa past a factory wall on which is scrawled operaist graffiti: "Il Vietnam è in fabbrica." Vietnam is in the factory. Today, one would be more likely to find "the factory is in Vietnam" written on the walls of the long-closed factory. How did we get from the fall of Saigon to the fall of Lehman brothers, from Nixon to Obama? The answer from much of the Left seems to be "financialization," understood not as a materialist process, but as fulfillment of the *Communist Manifesto*'s apocalyptic vision that "all that is solid melts into air."

Financialization, credit, and debt become immaterial, intangible factors, things of air and fiction, and, in the process, become explanations that explain nothing. Trying to step back from such ultimately unsatisfying interpretations, this chapter attempts to outline a materialist history of how the global capitalist system has evolved since the demise of the post-WW2 Bretton Woods system, in the ruins of Saigon, to the present day rise of China as the world's foremost industrial power, and the onset of stagnation and decline of the West. In the process, I attempt to avoid the pitfalls of geopolitics or economic determinism and to keep sight of the human agency of real processes of struggle and production, and productive struggle.

REGIMES OF ACCUMULATION, CARE, AND SETTLEMENT

IN ORDER TO frame this narrative, it is useful to introduce some loosely structural concepts. We will use the ideas of regimes of accumulation, regimes of care, and regimes of settlement to tell the story of the rise of Keynesianism from the ashes of the gold Standard era, its breakdown and replacement by neoliberal globalism, and the crisis of the latter, which is where we find ourselves today.

A "regime of accumulation" is a phrase originally introduced by the French Regulation School of Marxist historians, although we use it here much more loosely, to refer to an ensemble of strategies and institutions that together define the dominant mode of making profit in a given state territory. As such, it must, by implication, also deal with the biopolitical needs of the population of that territory, both in a disciplinary and policing sense, but also as the living basis of the labor power that is the source of profit. To that extent, it has been argued recently, in "Careless Talk," a paper by Gareth Brown, Emma Dowling, David Harvie, and Keir Milburn, that each regime of accumulation necessarily implies a shadow "regime of care."[1]

A regime of care, in this formulation, is the totality of strategies and institutions that manage the reproduction of living labor and labor power. This includes health and education systems, but also prisons, madhouses, police, and questions of cultural reproduction, such as whether the leisure activities of workers are self-organized, state-controlled, or commodified by the market. The relationship between regimes of accumulation and regimes of care parallels and reflects the one between capital's cycle of accumulation and labor's cycle of social reproduction.

If we were to pick one vignette to illustrate the development of regimes of care, the Black Panther Party school breakfast program would be it. Set up through the agency of autonomous and politically conscious self-organization, it would be taken over by the state under the Keynesian policies of the Nixon/Ford era and ultimately fall victim to the cuts of the Reagan years. This trajectory, in a nutshell, is emblematic of the passage from classical to Keynesian to neoliberal regimes of care characteristic of the twentieth century.

Above and beyond the regimes of accumulation and care that shape the dynamics of struggle and development within a particular state territory, states use an international system to manage their economic interactions, trade, and the balances and imbalances of payment they lead to. The conventional framework used to understand the gold standard and Bretton Woods is to consider them international monetary systems. We choose instead to call them "settlement systems." In part, this is in homage to the Bank of International Settlements, the oldest, established, dedicated institution of the system, still at the heart of setting the agreed rules for international banking today. But mainly we use this term to step back from the fetishism that substitutes money, one of the tools of settlement, for the real processes and problems of international balances of payment. Whatever the merits of Marshall McLuhan's famous epigram, "the medium is the message," may be to communications theory, nothing could be more misleading or mystifying than applying the same principle to the role of money in economics. In any case, there is no such thing today as a truly international money, and has not been since the days of the Spanish *peso de ocho* of the mercantile era. On that note, let us remark in passing that the gold standard does not refer to the time when people used gold as money directly, thereby avoiding settlement problems, but rather to the system of setting the exchange rate of national token currencies in relation and convertibility to gold.

Without wanting to write an economic textbook, we want to point out that certain problems arise when payment of debt between countries is settled. Loosely speaking, an imbalance of payments between two countries occurs if one persistently buys more imports from the other than they sell in return. Additionally, the relationship between balance of trade and balance of payments does also involve other factors (export of capital, repatriation of profits, intangibles, distinction between a country's current account and capital account, etc.). But, to cut a long story short, one of the resulting problems is that the deficit country ends up with a shortage of the other currency, while the surplus party has more than they want of the deficit trader's money. When the surplus country decides they won't accept payment in the deficit currency any more, the problem of needing a third means of payment arises, as the deficit country has a shortage of the net exporter's currency. Ideally, this third means of payment would be widely accepted by other countries, to repay imbalances the surplus party might, in turn, need to settle with them. Who chooses this third means of payment, exactly what it is, and how its relation with national currencies is managed, are some of the key problems within a regime of international settlements.

Of course these three interrelated regimes do not exhaust all the aspects of political, social, and economic development in the modern era. We could also talk about the problems with an international analogue to national regimes of care. Of course, no such regime properly exists, as the problems of migrant and refugee struggles for even the most basic rights, including life itself, illustrate very well. Yet the system of international organizations and institutions does include some that address biopolitical concerns at a global level, such as the World Health Organization, the Office of the United Nations High Commissioner for Refugees (UNHCR), various development bodies, or the whole swarming host of those "mendicant orders of Empire" (to use Toni Negri's delightfully puckish phrase), the international relief and development NGOs.

But above and beyond that, the net effects of interactions between these three regimes produces definite and distinctive eras in the framework of global governance. From the colonial imperialism of the gold standard era, to the neocolonialism of the Keynesian, to a putative postcolonial era inaugurated by neoliberal globalism, the appearance of a correlation between regimes of material relations and the politics of global governance raises the question of the direction of causality between the two. It is one of the contentions of this chapter that the actual direction of causation is the opposite of the common assumption that the politics of global governance shapes the path of capitalist development according to its own conscious design. "The best laid plans of mice and men, gang aft agley," as Robbie Burns put it.

THE RISE AND FALL OF KEYNESIANISM

THE ENSEMBLE OF national regimes of accumulation, care, and international regimes of settlement that came to be known, somewhat misleadingly, under the single title of Keynesianism, grew out of the crisis of the gold standard era. It was a crisis that encompassed two inter-European imperialist wars; the Great Depression of the interwar period; and the loss of great swathes of the globe's territory and population by the imperialist powers, through the establishment of state socialist regimes, first in Russia, and in China and most of Eastern and Central Europe after World War II.

These losses, even more than the destruction of the wars, were existentially alarming to the newly dominant US and its surviving European capitalist allies. If the practices, traditions, and dogmas of the gold standard era had mostly evolved "organically" through precedent, improvisation, and imitation, those of its replacement would, of necessity, be carefully designed to ward off the looming catastrophe of the overrunning of the entire Eurasian landmass by the barbarian "Communist" hordes. To that end, in July, 1944, delegates from allied countries, including John Maynard Keynes for the UK and Harry Dexter White for the US, met at the Mount Washington Hotel in Bretton Woods, New Hampshire for most of the month. The system of international settlements and currency management agreed upon there has born the resort town's name ever since.

The Bretton Woods system aimed to restore the stability of fixed interest rates that the gold standard had provided until its breakdown. However, rather than pegging each state's currency directly to gold convertibility, they would be pegged to the US dollar. Only the dollar would be convertible. Keynes argued that currencies should be pegged to a synthetic, non-national currency, the Bancor, which would in turn be convertible, not simply to gold, but to a basket of basic industrial, raw material commodities. However, in its hour of triumph, either in possession of or owed virtually all the gold reserves of the remaining western capitalist powers, the US was having none of it. The US dollar would be the reference point and international reserve currency, convertible directly to gold.

As well as defining the mechanics of a fixed currency system, the principle of capital controls, allowing member countries to defend their exchange rate without sacrificing all control over their national economies, was accepted for the first time in mainstream economics. In addition, international institutions were established to defend the system against national currency crises and the dangers of the "beggar thy neighbor" protectionist wars that had caused chaos during the 1930s. Those institutions, the International Monetary Fund, the International Bank of Reconstruction and Development (now the World Bank), and the General Agreement on Trade and Tariffs (now the World Trade Organization) are with us still.

There was a controversy at the Bretton Woods conference over the Bank on International Settlements (BIS). The BIS was originally set up to manage the punitive war reparations payments imposed on Germany by the Versailles treaty after World War I. As such, it had a number of German treasury figures on the board that became Nazi placemen after 1933. The Norwegian delegation to the Bretton Woods conference charged the BIS with having aided the financing of the Nazis during the war, facilitating the looting of occupied Europe, and being complicit in the Holocaust. With the backing of Harry Dexter White and Henry Morgenthau of the US, the Norwegians called for the liquidation of the BIS. This move was opposed by Keynes, not because the BIS wasn't guilty as charged (they certainly were), but because he recognized the need for an independent international "*capi di tutti capi*" (boss of all bosses) bank regulator to make the system work. Had the Swiss-based BIS been liquidated, the chances of a replacement either being blocked entirely, or relocated to New York and subsumed under US banking, were overwhelming. Like all Keynes'sother battles against White at the conference, the decision went with the Americans. However, despite being passed, the order to liquidate the BIS was not implemented before Roosevelt's death, and the British were able to convince Truman to rescind the order. The motives for choosing the BIS as the emblematic institutional figure of contemporary regimes of settlement are not limited to its purely economic history or functions alone. Three things need to be said about the Keynesian regime of accumulation. First, this was a party to which not everyone was invited. Keynes was a loyal British Empire man and the battles he fought with Harry Dexter White were mainly aimed at trying to defend some British independence within the trans-Atlantic alliance, despite the reality that an economically ruined UK was totally in hock to the US by the end of the war. However, both Keynes and White were on the same side when it came to maintaining the old world order, a white supremacist Euro-American dominance of the globe, and the division of the world into a developed "inside" versus a colonial, or soon-to-be nominally independent neocolonial "outside." The new "Keynesian" world order was a fundamentally divided world, bolstered by capital controls, in which the Cold War forced Western capitalist powers to cease fighting militarily over exclusive access to colonial territories, and agree to share them—under US hegemony, naturally.

The fundamentally colonial character of the Keynesian world order is particularly worth recalling today, when so many veteran left-wing commentators, with honorable records for criticizing US and Western imperialism, show a contradictory nostalgia for the Keynesian world order that was built on those very same imperialist foundations.

The second point of note is that the critique of the causes of the Great Depression, out of which Keynesianism was born, explicitly made the connection between the breakdown of the gold standard's international regime of settlement and the failure of the national regimes of accumulation to provide employment or break out of the downward spiral of debt-deflation. This is also worth remembering now, as many of today's wannabe "retro-Keynesians" present their alternative to the neoliberal order as a purely national project of accumulation, under the slogan of "jobs and growth," divorced from any associated need for change to the international settlement system itself.

The third consideration, related to the second, is that, as a project for national regeneration and return to full employment, so-called Keynesianism is in fact much more a product of the policies of the New Deal and fascist corporatism, as re-articulated in Abba Lerner's "functional finance," the perceived need for government intervention and use of active monetary and fiscal policy to achieve goals such as full employment, economic growth, etc. Now derided by the Right as "tax and spend" policies, the kind of dirigiste government economic policies that many people now associate with "Keynesianism" are really functional finance or "Lernerism." Just as the systematization of Keynes's work into conventional economics, via John Hicks's IS/LM curve (as preached today by the likes of Paul Krugman or Brad De-Long), should more properly be known as Hicksianism.

If the Keynesian regime of care could be summed up in one phrase, it would be: state colonization of the space of social reproduction. This is a process that began in the 1930s under the New Deal and the various Fascist governments in Europe. Impelled by the pressure of the Great Depression, worker unrest, and the threatening example of the Russian Revolution, areas of worker's life outside of the shop floor that had previously been beyond the horizon of bourgeois concern became targets for intervention and co-option. Most famously this included the organizations of workers' economic defense themselves—the unions.

Here we find the famous Keynesian "productivity deal," which provided power of conjuncture while simultaneously containing the seeds of its eventual destruction. The inclusion of the organs of labor's social reproduction into a Faustian compact with a national regime of accumulation violated the core ontological foundation of capitalist society—capital's need for autonomy from any limits posed by labor's reproductive needs. Worse, the effects of a regime founded on an even partial subsumption of capital's expansion to human needs undermined the very ideological foundation of the productivity deal to start with, and ultimately contributed to the great revolt of workers against work, which began in the late 1960s and lasted throughout the 1970s.

Ultimately the Keynesian divided world order fell to a double pincer movement of anticolonial struggles on the "outside," and the smashing of the productivity deal by workers on the "inside." The struggle of the workers against the work discipline implied in the Keynesian productivity deal we have just talked about was the "inside" struggle. In terms of the "outside" struggle, the Cold War meant that the US found itself somewhat trapped on the horns of a political dilemma. Despite its initial willingness to see decolonization struggles succeed in freeing former colonies from their exclusive possession by one or other European power—all the better to open them up to American commercial interests—the US was moved by a contrary motivation—namely, the fear that support for decolonization struggles from the "Communist" world of Russia or China would gain enough support amongst national liberation movements to bring the ex-colonies into their orbit, and thus be lost entirely to the capitalist sphere of influence.

Thus, the "domino theory" came to mean that the US, rather than playing the role, however hypocritical, of liberator to European colonies, ended up taking over the European powers' counterinsurgency struggles, as "colonizer of last resort." Lest we forget, Ho Chi Minh, not a Communist at the time, wrote to the US president for support for the freeing of Vietnam from Japanese and French colonial domination at the end of World War II. Vietnam was not originally a "domino," rather it was US support for French imperialism that forced the Viet Minh into the Communist camp.

The US decision to opt for the military suppression of decolonization struggles for fear of losing territory to their Cold War opponents committed them to a struggle against the needs of the peoples of the colonial "outside"—a struggle that became unsustainable, both financially and politico-militarily.

The spiraling costs of the Vietnam War increased the flow of US dollars outside US jurisdiction from a river to a flood. By 1971, this brought the maintenance of dollar convertibility at $35 per ounce of gold, the Bretton Woods founding price, to impossible levels. But if the costs of the war accelerated the process to breaking point, this was in many ways a death foretold. In 1960, the economist Robert Triffin warned that the US dollar-based Bretton Woods settlement regime was doomed. If the American purgatory in Vietnam was the result of the political dilemma over decolonization, it was what came to be known as the Triffin dilemma that ultimately sank dollar convertibility.

Again, a full exposition of the Triffin dilemma is best left to economics textbooks, but for our purposes the rough outline is as follows: Triffin pointed out that, as the global reserve currency, the dollar, was trying to do two jobs at the same time. The first was to serve the domestic needs of US economic growth and global trade competitiveness. The second was to serve the needs of the global community of capitalist nations that needed dollars for their own reserves and international settlement needs. The dilemma was that the two roles were in contradiction with each other. For the same reasons we looked at in the sketch model of balance of payments problems above, for the US to supply external countries with enough dollars to support their own growth—thus keeping them from the clutches of the Cold War enemy—required running a massive current account deficit. As well as driving up inflation at home, the popularity of the dollar as reserve currency meant high demand and high value for the dollar, thus making US exports more uncompetitive relative to those of other countries. The compensatory factor of external demand for US treasuries making the rest of the world subsidize cheap deficit credit for the US, a kind of "seigniorage" tribute remarked upon by some left commentators, including David Graeber, for example, actually only aggravates the net secular effect of exporting productive capacity to the rest of the world.

The basic dynamic of the Triffin dilemma of the US dollar as global reserve currency has been, to a greater or lesser degree, the secular trend, from the establishment of the Bretton Woods system until the present day. Keynes's arguments for the Bancor turned out to be farsighted, a point recently made by the governor of the Central Bank of China and a good number of other commentators on the current woes of the global monetary system. To give some idea of the scale of what we are talking about, current estimates are that three out of four US dollars in global circulation are outside US jurisdiction.

GLOBALIZATION AND NEOLIBERALISM

IN 1971, NIXON's administration was forced to end the direct convertibility of the dollar to gold. A revaluation of currencies followed later that year and, by 1973, countries abandoned any form of exchange rate control over the dollar and other currencies. The resulting volatility in international exchange rates, combined with the chaos occasioned by the loss of the Vietnam War, rampant class struggle in the West, oil price shocks, inflation, spiraling public spending, and the general lack of any coherent alternative capitalist strategy to the broken Keynesian model, dragged on throughout the 1970s. It wasn't until Margaret Thatcher gained power in 1979 and became the first to unilaterally drop capital controls that the Keynesian system was finally put out of its misery.

But if the form in which the Reagan/Thatcher neoliberal "revolution" appeared was that of a political initiative, we need to understand that its material and financial precursors had gestated during the previous period. I have discussed the growth of the repurchase or repo market, currency swaps, and other elements of the derivatives revolution, as means of evading capital and interest rate controls during the breakdown period of Keynesianism elsewhere and will not rehearse it here, for reasons of space.[2] Suffice it to say that the cozy social-democratic myth that, had it not been for the deregulation of the neoliberal era, financialization could not have escaped state control the way it did is a fallacy based on ignorance of the real history. Deregulation was in many ways simply the legalization of evasive financial practices that the state was powerless to prevent (not for want of trying).

Leaving aside the question of financialization until later, we must recognize the logistical revolution in global freight transport affected by containerization. If the Vietnam War had bankrupted the dollar's gold convertibility, holding Bretton Woods below the waterline, its flip side was the cementing of a logistical revolution that opened the era of globalization. The combination of dropping any capital controls on foreign direct investment, the growth of a derivatives-based system of hedging cross-border risks, and the opening of a virtual trans-Pacific container conveyer belt provided the basis for David Harvey's famous "spatial fix."[3] Globalizing production chains allowed capitalists to outflank worker's revolt against productivity in the West by relocating production to the East. The income gap opened by the drop in real wages caused by deindustrialization and replacement ser-vice-sector "McJobs" was bridged by the importation of disinflation, in the shape of ever-cheaper wage goods from the East. So was born a new "post-Fordist" neoliberal regime of accumulation.

Initially, the container ships returning empty from Vietnam were filled by Japanese transistor radios, motorcycles, and other exports. But by 1979, Deng Xiao Ping's struggle to succeed Mao was com-plete, and he saw the opportunity to hitch Chinese industrial devel-opment onto the trans-Pacific container conveyer belt. So began the process of turning China into the world's leading exporter—a process that eventually saw China overtake Japan, plunging the latter into what is now nearly two decades of stagnation.

From the perspective of the birth of a new regime of international settlement, the contrast with Bretton Woods could not be greater. Whereas the earlier system had been consciously designed, built on the basis of nearly two decades of reflection on the failures of the gold standard, the "floating world" of the post-Bretton Woods order came about almost entirely as an improvisation in the face of a sudden rupture. When Thatcher made the decision to drop capital controls, much to the horror of all of Whitehall and the City's financial elite, she was impelled by dogmatic radicalism, rather than any understand-ing of what the likely outcome would be.

But the other aspect of the post-Bretton Woods settlement sys-tem is that it was not a wholly new replacement for the previous sys-tem, but rather its continuation, in a partially collapsed form. Fixed exchange rates and capital controls may be gone, but the US dollar remains the global reserve currency. This also means that the basic dynamics of the Triffin dilemma continue to operate.

In addition to the relocation overseas of production in "trouble-some" industries already discussed, the other strategy of the neoliberal regime of accumulation was privatization. Specifically, the privatiza-tion of those sectors of the Keynesian "mixed economy" model that had been in state hands both provided windfalls to cut taxes on the middle and upper classes, while increasing the terrain for finance capi-tal to valorize itself.

If the Keynesian regime of care was characterized by the colonization of previously autonomous workers' culture and institutions
around reproduction, then the neoliberal regime was based on, what
else, privatization. In other words, the retreat of the state from supporting the biopolitical needs of the working class meant the space
was ceded, not to a return to self-organized self-provision, but into
the clutches of the market, for the commodification of leisure, health,
education, culture, and life itself.

But it was not simply the commodification of the sphere of social
reproduction that interested the forces of neoliberalism, but also its
actual financialization. The demutualization of the mortgage industry
and the promotion of home ownership for the masses was once again
founded on the enormous expansion of the finance and credit sector—anchored particularly in the property sector, the one consumer
durable that could not be shipped across the ocean in containers from
China. Just as the importation of disinflation kept prices of other
wage goods down, despite the inflationary monetary policies of the
era of "the Greenspan Put," so the nontransportability of property
meant inflation appeared in this sector as "asset" inflation. Of course,
housing is actually a cost to labor, not an asset. In reality, rising housing costs make workers poorer, but it was the triumph of bourgeois
ideology to convince workers that, as members of the "property-own-
ing democracy," the legal possession (albeit mortgaged) of their own
homes made them into small capitalists. Such that house price inflation created a "wealth effect" of people believing that they were being enriched by the process that was objectively impoverishing them,
beyond the short-term perspective of the "home equity loan." But
then neoliberalism has always been about the short-term being the
only visible horizon.

This hiving off of the role of "deficit spender of the last resort"
from the state to private households, especially of ordinary workers,
was termed by some "privatized Keynesianism." The difference is that
when the crunch comes, the state can print money to pay the bills,
while working-class households cannot.

In addition to the financialization of everyday life and social reproduction, the other form of deficit spending engaged in massively by
neoliberalism was "military Keynesianism." Throughout the Reagan
years, the US state ran enormous deficits; not to fund health, education, or social programs, which were all being savagely slashed (in

the name of "balancing the books" —as if!), but on military spending. In part, this was simple pork barreling of the military-industrial complex, but it was also a Cold War strategy to engage the USSR in a financial arms race on military spending, in the hopes of bankrupting it—a strategy that ultimately proved successful in bringing about the downfall of the USSR and the end of the Cold War.

In terms of global governance, the turn of the US toward the repression of the former European colonies through the sponsoring of countless repressive "anticommunist" regimes continued unabated into the Reagan/Thatcher years. Outside the G7 nations of North America, Western Europe, and Japan, the so-called "free world" looked overwhelmingly like a dystopian-nightmare, prison-camp world of fascistic military dictatorships. The Bretton Woods institutions of the international settlement system were repurposed, to leverage the volatility of floating exchange rates and free-flowing capital, to make good use of "crisis opportunities," such as the default crises of Mexico and many other countries of the global South, to impose a "Washington Consensus" medicine of austerity and cuts to social and development programs.

Had the determining factor in global development been the political program of governance of the Washington Consensus, we could have expected this pattern of military and/or IMF dictatorship over the global South to continue indefinitely. Indeed, for much of the 1980s and early 1990s, this appeared to be what was happening. But beneath the surface, the contradiction between the neoliberal globalized regime of accumulation and its strategy of global governance was undermining the very foundation of the post-Cold War Washington Consensus itself. Beneath the "shock doctrine" tactics of neoliberal governance, the secular tendency to export industrial productive capacity, occasioned by the underlying international relations of production and exchange, continued unabated.

The apogee, and turning point, of the post-Berlin Wall unipolar world of unchallenged Washington hegemony came with the so-called Asian crisis of 1998. In Asia, it was and is pointedly called "the IMF crisis" and regional countries resented bitterly the way collapsed property bubbles, and resulting sovereign and currency crises, were used by US and Western finance as an opportunity for a smash and grab raid. This process has been documented, in different ways, by Naomi Klein and Paul Krugman, amongst others. It represented the high point of the "Washington Consensus." By the summer of 2008, the IMF was virtually out of business, having only two remaining clients, and serious plans were being made to close up the institution, before the fallout saved it from Lehman Brothers and the October 10, 2008 global financial heart attack.

One of the unintended consequences of the crisis was the Russian default, which led to the collapse of the infamous Long Term Capital Management hedge fund (LTCM). The fall of LTCM ten years before the fall of Bear Stearns and Lehman Brothers, set up by the math geeks who won the bogus Nobel economics prize for the Black-Scholes equation used to price options (and many other derivatives, by analogy), in many way foreshadowed the 2007–2008 financial crash. Of course, retrospect is a fine thing, and that aspect was obscured by subsequent events: the Internet tech bubble, its collapse, 9/11, the neocon military offensive, etc.

Another unintended consequence of the 1998 IMF crisis (let's go with the Asian perspective on this one) was the institution of a strong dollar peg by the pillaged Asian economies, imitating what had been China's policy since it opened to the trans-Pacific export market in 1979. This so-called "Bretton Woods II" policy, whereby the dollar peg was reintroduced, not by the US in the service of its own interests, but by its opponents in the service of theirs, massively accelerated the trans-Pacific exportation of industrial capacity from the US to China, in particular, and Asia more generally. In order to maintain low peg rates, the participants in this policy had to soak up (or "sterilize," to use the conventional term) the surplus dollars being imported and reinvest them in a safe store of value—either US treasury bonds or similar US dollar-denominated financial assets with a triple-AAA rating.

It was this element of massive demand for finance assets with a triple-AAA rating that drove the mania for invention of evermore obscure financial instruments, including the infamous securitization industry that turned semi-fictional (in risk terms) mortgages into mortgage-backed securities (MBS), collateralized debt obligations (CDO), and their ilk. The credit boom was the result not of the fictional conjuring up of money out of thin air, but rather the enormous, pent-up demand of very real money looking for financial assets in which to invest, to get some return for idle cash. In other words, the credit boom was supply-side driven, contrary to some interpretations.

THE CRISIS OF NEOLIBERAL GLOBALIZATION

SINCE THE 2007–2008 global financial crash—the story of which I tell in greater detail in the article "10-10 Event," named after the aforementioned date of the Lehman Brother's CDS auction—we have found ourselves in a no-man's land of stagnation and multiple crises.[4]

On the one hand, we have the continuing euro zone crisis. Accepting Marx's dictum that history repeats itself, first as tragedy, then as farce, then the euro zone is the gold standard as farce. The structural similarities of a fixed exchange rate area with free flow of capital, with a lack of fiscal or political union or democracy, are leading to similar governance outcomes. A pseudo-colonial dynamic exists, in which the core exports its financial and economic contradictions to the periphery. Naturally, the Eurotops are in total denial about this reality.

Similarly, the US power elite is in denial about the ongoing results of the dollar reserve currency status, and the Japanese, likewise, are trying to restore competitiveness through devaluation of the yen, leading to an undeclared, global, "beggar thy neighbor" currency war. Meanwhile, the Chinese ruling class have just completed their reshuffle of every ten years by tilting the balance of power between technocrats and party aristocracy in favor of the latter, thus demonstrating that they too are in denial, lip-service notwithstanding, of the systemic threat that corruption poses to an absolutist state where political and economic power, rather than being separated, are combined and concentrated in the hands of an unaccountable elite. The road to avoiding the revolutionary overthrow of Communist Party power in China is the road less traveled at this stage.

What's more, in this period of interregnum between the decline and fall of US global hegemony and the rise of its Chinese replacement, the structural problems of global finance that triggered the last financial crash have not been fixed in any way, leaving the system open to a recurrence of the same, perhaps on a bigger scale. The problem is a lack of agency. Although the global capitalist class has forums like the G20 to talk out their differences and make plans, so far the only element capable of uniting them over and above their differing interests is lacking. Only the threat of working class power can unite the differing national capitalist classes and, so far, this is missing. The destruction wrought upon Western workers by globalization has yet to be overcome by a recomposition of a postindustrial class power. Similarly, the rising industrial muscle of the East and emerging economies, while resulting in a proliferation of vigorous local battles and struggles, has yet to reach the level of providing an existential threat to the established order. The words of Gramsci, at the time of the last great epochal crisis, resonate once more: "The crisis consists precisely in the fact that the old is dying and the new cannot be born; in this interregnum a great variety of morbid symptoms appear."[5]

From the point of view of global governance, if neoliberalism was a project to not only restore capitalist profit rates, but to conserve the West's global dominance, then we would have to say that neoliberalism will go down as one of the biggest self-inflicted defeats in history. Its end result has been the decline of Western dominance, and the seemingly unstoppable rise of China and other emergent powers to not simply equal status but, in the case of China, to overtake the US as the world's largest economic power in the next decade or so. The white supremacist world order of the nineteenth and twentieth centuries is finally coming to an end. And good riddance to it! But, of course, it is the contention of this text that the dynamics of capitalist development have never been dominated by the conscious political projects of global governance.

If one thing about the recent history of the modern era is clear, it is that Marx was not wrong when he called capitalism a revolutionary force, capable of sweeping away the remnants of the *ancient regime*. However, the extension of capitalism across the world's surface and its human population does not reduce the problems of its contradictions but magnifies them a thousand fold. The ever-accelerating destruction of the global climate and human-friendly environment is only one sign of the existential crisis that global capitalism poses. Before we get too tied up in the minutiae of subprime mortgages and Gaussian copulas, let us remember the big picture: we have a world to win, and we need to win it to ensure the survival of the next generations.

ENDNOTES

1   The full paper can be found here: http://www.academia.edu/2453956/ Careless_talk_social_reproduction_and_fault-lines_of_the_crisis_in_ the_UK (accessed July 14, 2013).

2   The full text catalogued is here: http://www.anarkismo.net/article/9850 (accessed July 14, 2013).

3   See David Harvey, "Globalization and the 'Spatial Fix'," *Geographische Revue*, vol. 2, 2001, http://opus.kobv.de/ubp/volltexte/2008/2436/pdf/ gr2_01_Ess02.pdf (accessed July 14, 2013).

4   "The 10/10 Event: Origins of an Economic Meltdown," Workers Solidarity Movement, http://www.wsm.ie/c/1010-event-origins-economic-meltdown (accessed July 14, 2013).

5   Antonio Gramsci, *Selections from Prison Notebooks* (New York: International Publishers, 2003/Orig. 1971)

INTERVIEW WITH NOAM CHOMSKY
ON THE ORIGINS OF THE CRISIS AND METHODS OF RESISTANCE

INTERVIEW BY DERIC SHANNON,
JANUARY 19, 2011

Deric Shannon: *Thank you very much for your time. I appreciate it. I have a few questions—mostly concentrated on the crisis and how we can respond to it. First, something that is missing in popular discourse is just a really simple explanation of how we have gotten to where we are right now, post-crisis. And it's something that I think that there's a ton of writing on by economists, but there are not a lot of analyses in plain, simple language. I was wondering if you could describe how we got to this point.*

Noam Chomsky: Well, just going back to the Second World War or the New Deal period—after the Second World War, there was a period of about twenty-five years of very high growth and egalitarian growth. So, the lowest quintile did about as well as the upper quintile. Now, that still meant plenty of inequality, but the inequality essentially didn't grow. People across the board were able to have opportunities that they hadn't had before. That's particularly striking for the African American community, who lived under virtual slavery up until then, in one form or another, but during those years were able to more or less enter the society. So, a black worker could get a job in an auto plant and have a fairly decent salary and reasonable healthcare, buy a house, and send his kids to school. That went on until the seventies. In the 1970s...and it went on right through the Nixon years.

Nixon was essentially the last liberal president—the last New Deal president. So, during the Nixon years, there was an increase in government regulation for the benefit of the population—things like the earned income tax credit (it actually passed) after basically his initiative, it passed after he resigned; EPA, environmental concerns; protection of workers' rights. Now, the business world was pretty upset about this. They are used to running everything and the idea that there should be a partially democratic government is anathema to them. So, there was a huge mobilization of the business community—and it's a very class-conscious business community—it's working all the time, but there was a big increase in the seventies, new think tanks, like the Heritage Foundation, to try to take over discourse and discussion, a vast increase in lobbyists, a big increase in campaign spending, very well-organized in the Republican Party primarily. And, of course, television was becoming more significant, so that if you want to delude the public about elections the way you delude them about commodities, which is what television advertising is about, it takes a lot of money. And, of course, the money is coming from mostly the corporate sector. That's partly the result of the fact that the one counter to it, labor organization, had been under bitter attack since the Second World War. But by that time it is becoming pretty weakened, and it's not a true counter to concentrated private capital.

There were also big changes in the economy related to this. The main change was a shift toward financialization—huge growth of the financial institutions. Theoretically financial institutions can be of some help to the economy. Like, if they are working, they can take unused assets, like bank accounts, and transfer them to productive activities, like lending money for a start-up or something. And if it's done under regulation, it can be done so that it doesn't break down into a crisis. In fact, there were no financial crises, until the seventies, when the regulatory system was operating. Well, part of this huge offensive was the attack on any regulatory systems, so that the financial institutions not only grew, but they grew more and more unregulated.

Related to this was a decision to hollow out domestic production and produce abroad, where it's cheaper and wages are lower, with no environmental constraints. OK for profits, but not so good for the population, of course. And all of this was happening at once. It was beginning in the late Carter years, you could see the effects. One effect was that the Democratic Party was also becoming more right wing. They had to move in the same direction for the funding for elections and party building, and so on. And it ends up with…we have…you know, we've always had one political party, the business party, but at least it had different factions. Well, we now have two parties. One of them, from the standpoint of, say, the sixties and seventies, is extreme right-wing Republicans (that's called the Republican Party), who are so deep in the pockets of big business that you need a telescope to find them. And the other party is moderate Republicans (they're called Democrats), those who have some concern for the popular constituency, but not much. They're basically what are called New Democrats, mostly, essentially what used to be moderate Republicans. So, the political system has shifted very far to the right.

At the same time, as a result of all these developments, for the majority of the population, say for the last thirty years, life has pretty much stagnated. Real incomes have pretty much stagnated. Work hours have very sharply increased. American workers work way beyond European workers. There's very misleading accounts of how American growth rates compare with European ones. If you really do serious calculation, you ask, "What is the GDP, gross domestic product, per work hour?" Not even per population, but we have population growth too. If you do that, it turns out, it doesn't look very good. Benefits, which were never very great, declined. The US does not have much in the way of support systems, so if a husband and wife are both working, there's little support for taking care of their children, so you've got all kinds of family problems and social problems. And people were getting by through debt, by extra work, and by asset inflation. In a deregulated financial system, you're going to have regular crises. There will be big bubbles developing and then they will burst. That happened several times during the Reagan years. Reagan left office with the biggest financial crisis since the Great Depression, called the savings and loan crisis. Clinton sort of carried it off for a while, but a lot of that was a tech bubble, which crashed in another recession. And then came the housing bubble, which is the latest one. The government, the federal reserve, and almost all of the economists couldn't see that there was an eight trillion dollar housing bubble of fake wealth…paper wealth…not real…which of course was going to burst, and it did. And it's the immediate cause of the current recession. It was accelerated by the development of exotic financial instruments, which made it possible for the people who sell mortgages to give them away in cases when they knew that people would never be able to pay back. But they didn't care because banks immediately bought up the mortgages. And the banks didn't care because they immediately securitized them, broke them up, and sold them in bits and pieces to other investors. By this point, the investors had no idea what they were buying. They didn't know that they were buying a piece of a mortgage that will never be paid back. There were new instruments, which allowed people, investors, to bet in favor of its failure. So, you insure yourself against failure—a whole complex system developed, which nobody understood.

In the Clinton years, the economists insisted on leaving it all deregulated and breaking down regulation. And yes, you get crises. This one's the biggest one. We are going to get a worse one because the outcome of every one of these crises is that the taxpayer is called on to bail out the perpetrators. Just what's happened now. So, you get literally trillions of dollars given to the people who have created the crises, who are now getting bigger bonuses than ever. That's trillions of dollars we are not giving to states and local governments, or to the workforce, or even for developing productive capacity. For instance, Obama virtually owned a large part of the auto industry. There were options. One option was to reconstruct it so that you can give it back to the owners and they will be making a profit. The other option would be to…instead of closing down factories or sending them to Mexico, they keep them here and put them in the hands of the workforce, which would be a good idea, and let them produce things that are badly needed in the country. Seiously needed. People complain that you go to Shanghai and it makes the United States look like a Third World country, but the same is true if you go to Europe. You come back here, you know, and you can't take a train because they don't work. Electric wires fall down in every storm because we do not have them underground. Potholes, and infrastructures are in horrible shape. It's also a deregulated healthcare system. Privatized deregulated healthcare system is a total disaster. If we had a healthcare system like comparable countries, we would not have a deficit. We would have a surplus.

And it's going to get worse. Nothing is being done by the two right-wing political parties, and they differ slightly on how to deal with it. Maybe one is a little better than the other, but the basic core of it is untouched, because they're in the pocket of the insurance companies and financial institutions. That is a very fundamental reason why a deregulated financial system is going to lead to crises. And that is just based on the essential nature of markets, and it's well understood. You get a footnote about it in standard economic texts. In fact, back in the nineties, there were books by serious economists pointing this out. In a market transaction, say you sell me a car. If we know what we are doing, we'll each try to work it out, so that we benefit. You get enough money. I get the car I want. We don't pay attention to what is called *externalities*—what the effect is on him if you sell me a car. Well, one of the effects on him is there's more air pollution, there's more traffic jams, and so on. For each individual, that may be small. But that's multiplied over a lot of individuals. In the case of, say, Goldman Sachs, an investment firm, now when they make a transaction, if they are doing it right, they take account of the costs to them and the risks to them. They do not take into account the externality that is called *systemic risk*—the risk that if their investments tank, the whole system is going to collapse. Now once you have a complex system like the kind I described, that risk is very high, which means you're virtually guaranteed to have repeated crises. And not for profound reasons—it's in the nature of unregulated markets.

Shannon: *It sounds like, in your current analysis, you're advocating for forms of social democracy or greater regulations on capital, but I know in terms of visionary arguments that you actually argue for a postcapitalist world.*

Chomsky: I think it's *all* wrong, but we are talking about what can be done within the framework of the existing institutions. And the answer is, quite a lot. So, for example, the fifties and the sixties were not particularly radical, but these things didn't happen. It is part of a dedicated class war, which has led to extremes that are very dangerous. But yes, there are totally different ways of doing things. Like, take the auto companies. When Obama took them over, took over General Motors, he continued GM's policies—closing plants—to try to make a leaner, more effective, more profitable company. Or permitting plants to go to Mexico. There were alternatives to that. One alternative is to turn the plants over to the workforce. There's plenty of interest in that on the part of working people. In fact, there are things happening right near here where workers are trying to take over plants that are being left destroyed by multinationals. It's happening all over. That would be one possibility. It could require some government support—meaning taxpayer support. But that would mean plants could be run by the people concerned, by the workforce and the community, and they could be converted to produce for human needs. Or let's take high-speed rail, where the US is extremely backward. That's not only important for life and the economy, but also for future survival. The wasteful use of fossil fuel is endangering the possibilities of decent survival.

Well, those are all perfectly good policies. They are just inconsistent with having a state capitalist society run with the concentration of extreme wealth and privilege. But they are perfectly feasible. And things like that could happen all over and it could lead to a completely different kind of society.

Shannon: *I think one of the main questions people have is, "How do we get there from here?" You know, and there's a ton of arguments over strategy on how to get beyond capitalism and institutions like the state.*

Chomsky: Getting rid of the state—this is not on the agenda. I mean, as long as you have anything like a kind of a state capitalist system where the state and concentrations of private capital are very tightly linked. Now the state, to some extent, is responsive to public opinion, to a limited extent, but somewhat. On the other hand, private capital is not responsive at all. They are unaccountable. Their goal is to maximize profit and market share for the CEO, the managers, and shareholders. Period. So, they are unaccountable tyrannies. Well, the state offers some protection. In fact, right through the Nixon years, there was protection. In fact, it increased under Nixon. But often safety and protections…in fact, that is part of the reason why the business classes were so upset and carried out this enormous mobilization. They didn't want to have any more liberals like Nixon around. They wanted straight representatives of the concentrated power. Period. So, in a society like this, to say, "Let's get rid of the state," is just saying, "Let's hand over everything to private power—private tyrannies," and that's no answer.

But what you can do within this society is build the components of a free and just society like, for example, self-managed net production units, for bakeries, or laundries, or colleges, or whatever it may be. You can work on that very straightforwardly. In fact, yeah, there are things you could do tomorrow. Like, say, right here, near where we're speaking there's a town, Taunton, Massachusetts, where a multinational is closing down a factory—a pretty efficient factory, but for them not enough profit for the banks, and so on. So, they are closing it down, destroying it. And the workforce and the community have offered to buy the equipment to reconstitute the factory and run it themselves. They might need a little support. Or maybe they wouldn't. But even if they did need some support, it's OK. The multinational is refusing. They would rather lose money by destroying the plant completely. They would rather lose money to prevent a self-managed, worker-owned factory from running. And that's because they are very class-conscious. They know the danger in eroding authority and obedience by making it clear to people that you can run your own affairs. So, they're class conscious. They are essentially vulgar Marxists. They understand it.

And that's a conflict that could be won with participation. If the workforce and the community are not helped, they're never going to win. But if they are, they could win. And it's something extremely concrete—talking about strategy.

Now, that kind of thing is not happening. There's a lot like it all over. And part of the reason is that the developments that sort of came out of the New Left did do a lot to civilize the country. They created plenty of groups, advocacy groups. If you look at them, the advocacy groups are what are sometimes called post-materialist. So they are concerned with important issues. Gay rights, pro-choice, environmental protection, and all those things are real, but they have nothing to do with the actual problems that people are facing. They are facing material problems. How do we live? You know. And the rising left has been relatively educated, relatively affluent.

I mean take, say, women's rights. A lot has been achieved there and that's important. There is an advocacy group, Emily's List, which is one of the biggest PACs [Political Action Committee] around. It puts a lot of money into elections. And, as far as I know, they have primarily one plank, pro-choice, which is important. But that PAC is not devoted to helping working people.

There were organizations that advocated for economic rights. They were called labor unions. And that's one of the reasons there has been such a massive effort to destroy them. In the private sector, they have been very seriously weakened. They have been able to survive in the public sector because the usually illegal actions that were taken with the government to destroy the private sector did not work in the public sector. There was more protection. But right now we are in the midst of a dangerous and very interesting propaganda campaign to wipe out public unions—the last bastion of labor support. So there's all kinds of hysteria being manufactured about how the real problem in the crisis is the teachers, and police, and firemen, you know: "They're overpaid. And they get these big pensions. And we've got to do something about that. We've got to prevent them…and the unions are demanding all sorts of things for the workers, so let's go after them." This is pretty impressive propaganda.

And the people who are doing it, who are being caught up in the propaganda, you know, piece by piece, they know that this is created. They want to have decent schools for their kids. They want the police to have reasonable lives. They want people to be secure. But they are caught up in the propaganda. It's kind of like in the Nazi period, blaming the Jews. You go after vulnerable people—immigrants, overpaid teachers, allegedly, you know, and so on. There is a general effort to try break down the public education system, which is one of the achievements of democracy, and privatize it—or the more or less equivalent charter schools—so you'll have an educational system for the rich and privileged and the rest can disappear.

In fact, some of the things that are happening are kind of mind-boggling. Take, say, the state of California, one of the richest places in the world. They had a really fine higher education system—public—one of the best in the world. They are destroying it, consciously destroying it. Next year, in fact, they just announced that funding for the higher education system from tuition is going to be greater than the state funding. That's saying, "We are going to privatize this system for the rich." So, the big colleges, you know, Berkeley, UCLA, those will be private colleges like the Ivy League, and if you are rich enough, you can get into them. And the rest of the system will just decline. Who cares about the public? That's happening in the richest place in the world.

By accident, I happened to go there a year ago after talking in Mexico, one of the poorer countries, you know, not super poor, but fairly poor. I was talking at the university, public university, national university. Pretty high quality. Very low salaries by our standards, but high quality, good teaching, active students, reasonable facilities, but not like you get at a private university here. *It's free.* Hundreds of thousands of students were there in a poor country. But in the richest country in the world, we're purposefully destroying it. And that's happening all over. Well, these things don't have to happen. In fact, in Mexico, there was an attempt some years ago to raise tuition and there was a massive strike all over the country—a student strike. Others participated. And the government had to back down and keep the colleges free. Well, unfortunately that's not happening here. There's a little protest, but nothing like that. But these are all apparently sound strategies, short-term. They are not creating utopia. But they are steps toward creating a different kind of society, in which people all manage their own affairs. The multinational in Taunton knows what they are doing: if you let these sparks kindle a flame, it will be understood. Others will do the same thing. So, you want to stamp it out right away. By the same token, we want to support them.

Shannon: *You mentioned the advocacy for pro-choice and the New Left's turn away from class struggle politics. And feminists of color and working-class feminists were always very critical of that. What good is legal choice if you can't afford an abortion anyway? How do we redirect energy back into class struggle and recognizing the working classes as agents for social transformation?*

Chomsky: The first thing we have to do is work really hard to reconstitute unions. First of all, protect those that are being attacked. There is a major attack underway right now, at bringing in a lot of the population, including the poorer population, to destroy the last remaining unions. It's happening right in front of our eyes. OK, it's something concrete that you can get involved in. In fact, the way it's working is…I mean you've got to admire this propaganda achievement. Like, the lame duck Congress. A great achievement, great praise for Obama, is the tax bill. So, the primary issue was should there be tax cuts for the very rich. Now the Republicans, of course, the extreme business communities, they say, "Sure, have tax cuts for the rich." At the same time, they are screaming about the deficit. Of course, that will be increased by the tax cuts for the rich, but they somehow carried this off over the objections of about two-thirds of the population. If Obama had stood up for something minimal like keeping the tax cut for the middle class but not for the super rich, not for the top few percent, he'd have had overwhelming public support. But, his interest is financial institutions, not the public. So, he gave that one away without even a struggle. Well, that's a pretty good achievement in itself, especially with all the screaming about the deficit.

But something else happened, which I don't think was even reported. That was, at the same time, Obama instituted a tax increase, exactly what he was not supposed to do, for federal workers. Now of course, it was not called a tax increase because if it had been, you'd get a lot of protest. And the press and others cooperated by not calling it a tax increase, but that's exactly what it was. It was called a pay freeze. Why could you sell a pay freeze? You know. They're taking things away from us. But, what is a pay freeze for federal workers? It's identical to a tax increase. It takes money away from the workers—just like a tax increase. It adds it to the treasury—just like a tax increase. So, in fact, it's a tax increase, but repackaged as a freeze for "these overpaid workers, who are the real problem of society." And they got away with it. It's impressive. Well, if we're trying to turn toward class politics, you know, you broadcast this all over the place. You organize people about it, and so on. And in case after case, there's a lot of things you can do, but you have to want to do them.

PREDATORY LENDING AND THE TWENTY-FIRST CENTURY RECESSION

PREYING ON THE AMERICAN DREAM AND REASSERTING RACIALIZED INEQUALITY

DAVITA SILFEN GLASBERG, ANGIE BEEMAN, AND COLLEEN CASEY

INTRODUCTION

POLITICAL PUNDITS ARGUE THAT, WITH THE RE-ELECTION OF BARACK Obama, we are now living in a post-racial society. This ideology helps to reinforce prevailing notions of subprime lending in the United States, which deny that the new economic reality is one of deepening racialized wealth inequality. We see neighborhood front lawns festooned with "foreclosure sale" signs, thick newspaper sections filled with real estate listings of foreclosure auctions and "short sales" on homes, and read heart-wrenching stories of lives disrupted and destroyed by the loss of homes and futures. Congress and state legislatures have held hearings to examine and define strategies for managing the crisis, but have come no closer to offering real relief or even fully appreciating the broader problem. But a clear grasp of the roots of the problem are essential, because this mortgage and foreclosure crisis is at the heart of the economic collapse of the twenty-first century, and a major part of why the economy is struggling to climb out of it. It is key to understanding why poverty, hunger, and homelessness continue to deepen, even while Wall Street indicators suggest a more robust economic recovery. And it is a vital factor in explaining why the racialized gap between wealth and poverty in the US is growing, not shrinking.

The term *subprime lending* results in a social construction of the problem as an unfortunate symptom of an economy in crisis, affecting people exclusively on the basis of their class position, and at least some of the press accounts (as well as former President George W. Bush) suggest that it may be the result of individuals making very poor financial decisions and thus making themselves vulnerable to a recessionary economy. Policy and program responses tried to address such decision-making, by providing greater transparency and financial services education to consumers through the establishment of the Consumer's Financial Bureau. While these efforts seek to address important issues, such social constructions treat subprime lending as a symptom of the recession, and ignore the role that the lending practices actually played in contributing to the recession, as well as the underlying racial and class biases that continue to characterize mortgage markets. These constructions also mask the important distinction between *subprime* and *predatory* lending.

Predatory lending is a more explicit, widespread, institutional practice that perpetuates inequality. In particular, predatory lending has deepened racialized inequality, ironically, at precisely that historic point in time when many believed we had overcome racism. The reality is that racism plays a central role in the foreclosure crisis and, therefore, played a central role in the market collapse. The reason why the crisis did not get widespread attention until 2007 was because, until that point, it was largely affecting people of color. As David Harvey argues, "The ultimate human and financial cost to society of not heeding clear warning signs because of collective lack of concern for, and prejudice against, those first in the firing line was to be incalculable."[1]

The questions then remain: what happened to the economy and the American Dream in the twenty-first century, and why is Wall Street bouncing back from the deep economic recession, while the working classes on Main Street in general, and working class people of color in particular, are still mired in an unchecked downward spiral? If the key to this picture is the mortgage and housing industry, how did the housing crisis happen and why hasn't it changed?

THE ROOTS OF THE MORTGAGE CRISIS: BANK DEREGULATION

After the Great Depression of the 1930s, Congress sought to impose restrictions on the financial industry, in order to prevent a repeat of that economic disaster. The result was the enactment of the Glass-Steagall Act, which established serious restrictions defining the legal behaviors in which banks occupying varying niches of the market could engage. Those restrictions in effect reduced or eliminated competition between huge commercial banks and smaller savings and loan banks. Each had their own market niche, and each operated in accordance with laws governing how they could do business. For example, no single bank could legally lend more than 10 percent of its available investment capital to a single borrower, in an effort to reduce exposure and risk for individual banks and to protect the savings of individual customers. For large commercial banks, this meant that none of them could single-handedly open their coffers exclusively to any corporation or government; since the borrowing needs of these customers were generally much greater than the capacity of any one bank, many banks had to "chip in" together, and that spread the risk.

By contrast, Glass-Steagall also established a niche for a mortgage industry by creating smaller savings and loan institutions. Their mission was to provide affordable standard mortgages to the working classes, thereby making the American Dream accessible to those for whom the goal of home ownership might otherwise be out of reach. These banks were not allowed to engage in speculative, high risk ventures like junk bonds. Thus, huge commercial banks and smaller savings and loan banks operated in very different markets, the working classes were given a far greater shot at a piece of the American Dream of home ownership, and the economy was relatively protected from the fundamental meltdown of the Great Depression, even if the inequalities inherent in capitalism remained intact.

This arrangement of federal regulation governing the financial industry worked pretty well for decades. Until, that is, the 1980s and 1990s, when we began to see vastly different behavior by financial institutions, not just by individual rogue banks, but as standard operating procedures. The 1980s saw the rise of junk bonds and eventually the meltdown of the savings and loan industry. By the 1990s, we began to see a dramatic increase in subprime lending, fueled perhaps by a host of mortgage innovations and a fragmented mortgage industry characterized by lenders, intermediaries, and brokers. Subprime lending, both for refinancing of existing mortgages and of initial origination loans, increased dramatically over the last quarter-century. For example, refinancing mortgage loans rose from 80,000 in 1973 to 790,000 in 1999; the number of financial institutions specializing in such lending rose during this time period from 104,000 to 997,000.[2] Furthermore, between 1994 and 2003, the total dollar value of subprime loans rose from $35 billion to $332 billion, an increase of 948 percent.[3]

This rise in subprime lending was followed very quickly by massive foreclosures on homes whose owners had defaulted on mortgages. Mortgage refinancing has been the leading use of subprime lending, constituting 80 percent of the massive increase since the 1970s.[4] Of greatest concern is that this increase in subprime mortgage refinancing occurred when refinancing loans were aggressively marketed to consumers as a way to bundle accumulated credit card debts, home improvements, and other outstanding liabilities into the mortgage, increasing the possibility that the homeowners could lose their homes.[5] As Harvey suggests, one of the ways that capitalism solves its many problems is through credit. To solve the demand problem, Harvey argues, credit had to be extended to low income people:

> Financial institutions, awash with credit, began to
> debt-finance people who had no steady income. If that
> had not happened, then who would have bought all
> the new houses and condominiums the debt-financed
> property developers were building? The demand prob-
> lem was temporarily bridged with respect to housing
> by debt-financing the developers as well as the buyers.
> The financial institutions collectively controlled both
> the supply of and demand for housing.[6]

By the end of 2008, foreclosures rose by more than 129 percent in a single year; subprime adjustable rate mortgages were at the root of more than one-third of all new foreclosures.[7]

Observers were increasingly complaining about "predatory lending," and research was mounting documenting that there was indeed institutional preying upon the American Dream. The rise in predatory lending and mortgage foreclosures just as quickly ignited the Great Recession of the twenty-first century (which in some towns and cities is a Depression). How could this have happened? Wasn't the industry supposed to be regulated to curb these excesses and prevent the very economic crisis we're now in? Didn't we learn anything from the Great Depression? What unleashed this seemingly swift sea change in the economy?

THE ROAD TO THE TWENTY-FIRST CENTURY IS PAVED WITH GREED

Let's begin, first, by unpacking the housing foreclosure crisis. To do so, we interviewed people whose homes were threatened with foreclosure or who had already lost their homes, as well as activists trying to help them. We first discovered that not all subprime lending is predatory. Subprime lending extends credit to borrowers who have risk factors such as poor credit ratings and, as such, has higher interest rates to offset the higher risk such loans pose. Its purpose is to "reward consumers trying to get out of debt and improve their credit by allowing them to build equity in their homes and to transition into prime loans as their credit improves."[8] By contrast, predatory lending is a subcategory of subprime lending, in that it harms rather than helps the borrower with interest rates well beyond the risk posed, carries terms far more punitive than those applied to prime lending, and in general attacks and erodes the equity position of the borrower rather than helping to build it. In general, predatory lending involves practices of extending credit that injure the borrower, usually by depleting equity the borrower has previously amassed in home ownership.[9] Let's look at exactly what sort of practices we're talking about here, which are associated with prime, subprime, and predatory lending.

SUBPRIME LENDING VS. PREDATORY LENDING PRACTICES

Predatory lending practices may involve one or more of several subprime lending techniques. Prime rate lending is credit extended only to the lowest-risk borrowers. Prime markets typically serve individuals with excellent credit, some asset accumulation, and a number of other factors that influence a high credit score. According to the Department of Housing and Urban Development (HUD), the prime market typically serves "A" borrowers whose credit scores are above 650.[10] Subprime lending is credit extended at rates higher than the prime rate. The subprime market provides credit to borrowers with an A to D rating, which includes credit scores below 650. Typically, these products have higher interest rates and less favorable terms than products serving the larger mainstream market. Almost everyone who borrows money accesses credit at interest rates above the prime rate or subprime loans.

Not all predatory lending is illegal. Lenders may aggressively pursue borrowers to engage in transactions that threaten their financial position or equity by encouraging them to shift unsecured consumer debt (such as credit card debt) into mortgages, refinancing when it's not in their best interests to do so, and adding additional hidden costs in the form of higher interest rates, points, fees, and closing costs. These practices were repeatedly reported and identified in our study of homeowners in danger of foreclosure. One respondent in this study indicated that the bank called her and said, "You know you can make your payments right at the bank…. They [the bank] were selling… credit cards and they dumped everything in [the mortgage]." Sometimes lenders vigorously encourage repeated refinancing. This occurred in at least one of our respondent's cases, where the lender came to his house to talk him into rolling his credit cards into a refinanced mortgage: "He [the banker] said, 'See, it's gonna be this much less because you won't be paying this for your credit cards…'cause that's all being paid off [with the mortgage] and you'll have the monies….' He made it look like I'd be stupid if I didn't get the loan."

Lenders may also apply extraordinarily high annual interest rates, points, and closing costs, well beyond those justified by the risk. One interview subject indicated that he paid 15 percent for a loan at a time when the going mortgage rates were close to 7 percent. Or banks will push the use of adjustable rate mortgages, or balloon loans, which are significant elements in foreclosures. The respondent who was convinced to roll his credit card debt into a refinanced mortgage also noted that he asked repeatedly for assurances that the loan he was getting was a fixed rate loan. He received reassurances that it was. It was not until he faced foreclosure that he found out he had, in fact, received an adjustable rate mortgage, and the rate had ballooned to a height he could not afford. The adjustable rate mortgage is a legal instrument; the dishonest sales tactic used to get this borrower to sign for one is not.

Other predatory practices are not legal, but are still common. For example, predatory lenders often fail to disclose loan terms, provide a Good Faith Estimate, inform the borrower that they have a specific number of days to change their mind, or itemize all charges on the loan before or during the closing. One interview subject was asked if he was shown any of these documents before or during the closing. He said, "No, I don't know. I know that there was a ton of stuff sent *after* the closing." [emphasis added]

One of our respondents said that the bank kept coming to his house pressuring him to refinance his home. The lender initially briefly reviewed some of the documents, but then demurred, telling the borrower, "Well, just sign it, don't worry about a thing, just sign it." The subject said the lender "kept talking to me about anything…and kept my mind totally off the loan…. I didn't even know I was signing loan papers. I mean he was really good…. I kept asking him, well what's this paper for. And he …shrugged everything off." Worse yet is the practice of falsifying loan applications, including forging signatures on loan documents; There was evidence of this in one of our cases, where a respondent stated, "He [the banker] kept saying, 'Well, just in case, why don't you fill out a couple of those [documents] in case I mix up this one, I can at least fill them out, you know without me having to come back to you.'"

These are just a few examples of the legal and illegal practices that are rampant in predatory lending, which dramatically increase the likelihood that borrowers will default on a mortgage and lose their homes.

RACIAL AND WEALTH PATTERNS AS IMPLICATIONS OF THE TWENTY-FIRST CENTURY RECESSION

WHILE BANKS AND brokers have routinely engaged in predatory practices, both legal and illegal, which have had such a disastrous effect on the overall economy, there is also the disturbing pattern of targets of such practices. Subprime lending appears to be related at least in part to social characteristics.[11] This relationship is important because, in addition to the large number of subprime refinancings, first-time home ownership gains for many borrowers historically excluded from mortgage markets have been fueled by higher-priced, subprime innovations.

In Connecticut, subprime lending increased by over 42 percent in the 1990s and into the new century; notably, the increase was more than 85 percent in neighborhoods where more than half the population were people of color.[12] Case studies in major metropolitan areas around the country indicate similar patterns in their findings.[13] One study found compelling evidence of broader correlation between subprime lending and race (beyond individual metropolitan areas in case studies).[14] More recently, our own research using data for low-income communities in Chicago, Indianapolis, St. Louis, Cleveland, and Hartford echoes these results. We found a strong association between the racial categorization of the borrower or the borrower's neighborhood and the likelihood of becoming a target of predatory lending: in essence, as the borrower becomes "less white," the odds of an equitable loan origination decreases, and that is the case not only for low-income but for moderate-income African American borrowers, suggesting a relative independence of racism operating in these practices. In stark terms, for example, African American borrowers in Hartford are almost three times more likely than white borrowers to receive high-cost mortgages, *regardless of their income*. Similarly, the higher the proportion of people of color in a community as a whole, the lower the odds of an equitable loan origination. As the National Community Reinvestment Coalition noted, "Income is no shield against racial differences in lending."[15] One activist we interviewed who worked to help victims of predatory lending keep their homes estimated that "90 percent of our clients are minorities." In particular, subprime lending has been found to be concentrated among borrowers of color, and in neighborhoods with high proportions of people of color, borrowers who decades earlier had been redlined and denied mortgages.

A number of studies point to the association between higher levels of subprime credit and specific racial and social characteristics of the borrowers and their neighborhoods. For example, the assessment of subprime lending in five cities (Atlanta, Baltimore, Chicago, Los Angeles, and New York) found that subprime loans were over three times more likely to be issued in low-income neighborhoods than in high-income neighborhoods, and five times more likely in black neighborhoods than in white neighborhoods.[16] Another study found that, as the percentage of African American population increased, the amount of subprime lending increased in Cleveland, Milwaukee, and Detroit, cities with extensive histories of racial residential segregation.[17] In another study, Williams et al. found that, between 1993 and 2000, at least half of the gains in home ownership in underserved markets, minority or low-income, were the result of subprime loans rather than prime loans.[18] These disparities are not limited to the neighborhood level, but exist at the individual borrower level as well. Based on the racial characteristics of individual borrowers, black and Hispanic mortgage holders pay more for mortgages. For example, one study found that both groups have home loans with higher interest rates when compared to whites, and are 1.5 to 2.5 times more likely to pay interest of 9 percent or more.[19]

Other research shows an applicant's race has a significant relationship to what type of lender they receive loans from. Applicants reporting African American, Hispanic, American Indian or Alaskan Native, or American and Pacific Islander racial identity were found to have a significant, positive effect on the likelihood they applied to a nonregulated lender—lenders who are far more likely to offer subprime, high-risk, creative mortgage instruments, such as adjustable-rate mortgages (ARMs).[20] That means that borrowers of color are especially exposed to the vulnerability of losing their homes, particularly in an economy caught in the grip of an economic tailspin such as that of 2008–2009. This, in turn, fuels and exacerbates racialized economic inequality. Access to finance capital then becomes a key element in the de facto continuation of racialized segregation and inequality that was once upon a time overt, blatant, and a clear violation of the Universal Declaration of Human Rights, as well as the US Constitution and civil rights legislation (though, of course, business-as-usual under US capitalism). This is important and we want to stress this fact: *while one can pinpoint the role that bank and mortgage deregulation played in the twenty-first century recession—the market collapse that is affecting people all over the world—because of the racialized nature of the predatory lending practices that developed in the United States, white supremacy and institutionalized racism were also primary factors in causing the economic crisis.*

POLITICAL ECONOMY, BANK DEREGULATION, AND PREDATORY LENDING

WHY WAS IT possible for banks to so aggressively pursue these non-standard instruments with customers who would have been defined as poor risks just ten years ago? We find the answer lies in both the logic of capitalism and the simultaneous deregulation of lending markets that created financial powerhouses. Congress deregulated banks as part of a quid pro quo of the agreement to bail out the near-bankrupt Chrysler Corporation in 1978, allowing banks to engage in practices not allowed under the old regulations. Banks were now free to pursue junk bonds and "exotic" instruments, which they did aggressively. The savings and loan and junk bond crises of the 1980s and 1990s were the early warning signs that deregulation had opened an institutional Pandora's Box.[21] Predatory lending and the consequent tsunami of foreclosures is the latest incarnation of that structural reorganization; it is not a result of rogue outliers in the financial industry or of individuals making very poor financial decisions—rather, the problem is structural.

The massive increase in the number of predatory home loans and the intense pace of that increase became the match that sparked the economic free fall of the twenty-first century. This is because housing is an industry central to the economy. Every time a house is built, it contributes to business for a wide range of support industries: lumber, steel, aluminum, glass, bricks, roofing, electrical products, plumbing products, home siding, durable goods (such as refrigerators, stoves, dishwashers, washers, and dryers), textiles, furniture, the trucking industry, the rail industry, and corrugated boxes (to transport many of these products and to move new homeowners into their homes), to name just a few. Home ownership infuses neighborhoods with stability, which encourages the rise of support services and commercial development. And all of these industries mean jobs, many of them paying living wages and more. It is easy to see how a healthy housing market can significantly stimulate the wider economy.

The tragic corollary is that the collapse of the housing market means all of these industries suffer contractions along with foreclosures because new home construction slows to a crawl, which means significantly fewer jobs in those industries. Whole communities may be pushed into recession or economic depression when that happens (and have been). And when substantial proportions of the population lose their jobs, they not only cannot feed and house themselves and their families, they also have no disposable income to spend and help fuel the economy's rebound. So, when banks engage in predatory lending, they are not just preying on individuals' grip on the American Dream of home ownership; they are attacking the working classes' share of the American economy, for the benefit of the most affluent, whose wealth mainly derives not from producing products and wealth, but from moving money and manipulating markets, to accumulate and concentrate more wealth in their own hands. For example, massive layoffs, which once signaled a firm in trouble and thus made investors nervous, now is interpreted as an indicator that a firm that is becoming "more competitive," as it gets lean and mean, and is therefore an attractive investment for hedge funds and the like. Is it any wonder that the gap between wealth and poverty in the US is at levels unseen since the 1930s? Is it any surprise that hunger and homelessness are on the rise, even as the stock market has rebounded to levels at or near those reached before the recession of 2008? Additionally, the logic of capitalism dictates that financial institutions must turn quarterly and annual profits in order to remain robust in the eyes of hungry shareholders. Placing mortgages, even high-risk ones, can provide at least the short-term appearance of profit-making, particularly if the originating institutions immediately sell the mortgage to a secondary bank. That quick sell to the secondary market gets the mortgage off the books of the originating banks, who collect a profit in the sale. Moreover, these mortgages, while certainly high risk, help the originating bank establish the appearance of compliance with the Community Reinvestment Act (CRA) directive to provide mortgages to underserved or redlined communities (hence, the reason why so many ARMs and consequent foreclosures appeared first and most forcefully in communities of color). Since these practices target those most in need of help getting into the mortgage market (people of color and the poor), we define these aggressively-placed mortgages as predatory lending.[22] Predatory lending reproduces and institutionalizes racialized economic inequality as an aggressive strategy for banking institutions to survive the pressures of capitalism. This is because one important element of wealth is access to mortgage lending and the acquisition of property.[23] And while these predatory practices may help financial institutions navigate the vagaries of capitalism, they do so on the backs of the poor, the working classes, and people of color.

Taken together, this body of research suggests that banking practices are promoting and reinforcing racialized economic inequality, robbing people of color of an equal opportunity to build equity and wealth. Furthermore, we argue, this is significant because it is a contemporary element of a history of practices and policies that together *institutionalize* racialized inequality, insofar as individual prejudice is no longer necessary for the continuation of racialized inequality.

CONCLUSION

Some observers would prefer to emphasize the "feel good" conclusion that the United States has entered a "post-racial" period of history, and that the ravages of the twenty-first century recession are color-blind, hitting people purely on the basis of their prior economic standing. However, the problem of predatory lending suggests a very different new reality: predatory lending strikes people of color disproportionately, robbing them of the economic advantage and equity many had only just begun to accrue. Even if one were to argue that subprime lending is extended simply on the basis of economic risk calculations, what is clear is that prior historical disadvantage and exclusion from equity acquisition has institutionally positioned people of color to be most vulnerable. What's more, predatory lending practices have helped to sustain the legacy of undeserved enrichment and impoverishment. The weakening economy in the twenty-first century caused adjustable rate mortgages to balloon out of the reach of many people, and the consequent escalating foreclosure rate contributed to one of the worst economic meltdowns in US history since the Great Depression. Although many whites clearly lost their homes and their equity due to foreclosure, people of color suffered a disproportionate setback in wealth accumulation.

Far from a post-racial society, the US is actually experiencing a new phase of racism, one that does not require individuals to harbor racist attitudes, but where racism is instead institutionalized and embedded in the very way our economy is organized. The deep recession of the twenty-first century is much more than a new economic reality driven by a casino-mentality stock market and individual overextension of debt; it is a racialized economic reality of heightened inequality fueled by institutionalized historical arrangements. Moreover, it is critical to keep in mind that that the 2008 economic crisis and the subsequent austerity measures served as the framework for deepening that racialized divide, much in the same way as previous recessions had done. That is, it should come as no surprise that, because racism and racialized inequality were already embedded in economic institutions, any "race blind" policies to address economic crises with austerity measures were bound to reproduce and intensify preexisting racialized divides, rather than improve them. To interrupt the latest incarnation of racism in the new economic reality of the twenty-first century will require the courage of affirmative institutional change and a recognition that past policies and practices really do matter—and in the context of organizing against austerity and capital in the US, this means foregrounding the experiences of people of color.

ENDNOTES

1 David Harvey, *The Enigma of Capital and the Crises of Capitalism* (New York: Oxford University Press, 2010), 1.

2 US Department of Housing and Urban Development-US Treasury National Predatory Lending Task Force, *Curbing Predatory Lending* (Washington, DC, 2000).

3 Richard Lord, *American Nightmare: Predatory Lending and the American Dream* (Monroe, ME: Common Courage Press, 2005).

4 US Department of Housing and Urban Development, "Unequal Burden: Income and racial disparities in subprime lending in America" (Washington, DC, 2000), http://www.huduser.org/publications/fairhsg/unequal.html (accessed July 13, 2013).

5 Cathy Lesser Mansfield, "The Road to Subprime 'HEL' Was Paved with Good Congressional Intentions: Usury Deregulation and the Subprime Home Equity Market," *South Carolina Law Review* 51, no. 3 (2000): 473.

6 Harvey, *The Enigma*, 17.

7 Mortgage Bankers' Association (MBA), "Delinquencies and Foreclosures Increase in Latest MBA National Delinquency Survey," www.mbaa.org/NewsandMedia/PressCenter/64769.htm (accessed July 11, 2013).

8   Jeanette Bradley, *The Community Guide to Predatory Lending Research* (North Carolina: Community Reinvestment Association of North Carolina, 2000), 160.

9   Deborah Goldstein, "Understanding Predatory Lending: Moving Toward a Common Definition and Workable Solutions" (Cambridge, MA: Joint Center for Housing Studies of Harvard University, 1999). See also Bradley, *The Community Guide*, 2000.

10   Elizabeth Renaurt, "An Overview of the Predatory Lending Process," *Housing Policy Debate* 15, no.3 (2004): 467–502.

11   Debbie Gruenstein and Christopher E. Herbert, "Analyzing Trends in Subprime Originations and Foreclosures: A Case Study of the Atlanta Metro Area" (Washington, DC: Neighborhood Reinvestment Corporation, 2000), www.nw.org/network/strategies/campaign/predatory/abt.pdf ; National Community Reinvestment Coalition (NCRC), *Income is No Shield: Against Racial Differences in Lending: A Comparison of High-Cost Lending in America's Metropolitan Areas*, www.ncrc.org (accessed July 13, 2013); Richard Williams, Reynold Nesiba, and Eileen Diaz McConnell, "The Changing Face of Inequality in Home Mortgage Lending" *Social Problems* 52, no. 2 (2005): 181–208; Bradley, *The Community Guide*, 2000.

12   J. Michael Collins, "Analyzing trends in subprime originations: A case study of Connecticut" (Washington, DC: Neighborhood Reinvestment Corporation, 2000).

13   ACORN, Pennsylvania, "Equity strippers: The Impact of Subprime Lending in Philadelphia," www.acorn.org/pressrelease/equity.htm#_ftn1 (accessed July 13, 2013); Harold L. Bunce, Debbie Bruenstein, Christopher E. Herbert, and Randall M. Scheessele, "Subprime Foreclosures: The Smoking Gun of Predatory Lending?" in *Housing Policy in the New Millennium Conference Proceedings,* (ed.) Susan M. Wachter and R. Leo Peene (Washington, DC: US Department of Housing and Urban Development, 2001): 257–272, Available at http://www.huduser.org/publications/pdf/brd/12Bunce.pdf; Gail Cincotta, Testimony before the US House of Representatives Committee on Banking and Financial Services, http://www.financialservices.house.gov/banking/52400wit.htm (accessed July 13, 2013).

14   Stephen L. Ross and John Yinger, *The Color of Credit: Mortgage Dis-crimination, Research Methodology, and Fair-Lending Enforcement* (Cambridge, MA: MIT Press, 2002).

15   NCRC, *Income is No Shield.*

16   US Department of Housing and Urban Development-US Treasury National Predatory Lending Task Force, *Curbing Predatory Lending* (Washington, DC, 2000).

17   John Taylor, Josh Silver, and David Berenbaum, "The Targets of Preda-tory and Discriminatory Lending: Who Are They and Where Do They Live?" in (ed.) Gregory Squires, *Why the Poor Pay More: How to Stop Predatory Lending,* (Westport, CT: Praeger Publications, 2004).

18   Williams, Nesiba, and McConnell, "The Changing Face," 2005.

19   L. Krivo and R. Kaufman, "Housing and Wealth Inequality: Racial-Ethnic Differences in Home Equity in the United States," *Demography* 41, no. 3 (2004): 585–605.

20   Colleen Casey, Davita Silfen Glasberg, and Angie Beeman, "Racial Disparities in Access to Mortgage Credit: Does Governance Matter?" *Social Science Quarterly* 92, no. 3 (2011): 782–806.

21   Davita Silfen Glasberg and Dan Skidmore, *Corporate Welfare Policy and the Welfare State: Bank Deregulation and the Savings and Loan Bailout* (Hawthorne, NY: Aldine de Gruyter, 1997).

22   Angie Beeman, Davita Silfen Glasberg, and Colleen Casey, "Whiteness as Property: Predatory Lending and the Reproduction of Racialized Inequality" *Critical Sociology* 37, no. 1 (2010): 27–45.

23   Nancy Denton, "Housing as a Means of Asset Accumulation: Good Strategy for the Poor?" in *Assets For the Poor: The Benefits of Spreading Asset Ownership,* (ed.) Thomas M. Shapiro and Edward N. Wolff (NY: Russell Sage, 2001): 232–266; Thomas M. Shapiro, "The Impor-tance of Assets," in ibid., 11–33; Edward N. Wolff, "Recent Trends in Wealth Ownership, From 1983 to 1998," in ibid., 34–73; Chenoa A. Flippen, "Racial and Ethnic Inequality in Homeownership and Hous-ing Equity," *Sociological Quarterly* (2001): 121–149.

PART 2

EFFECTS

"All oppression creates a state of war."
—*Simone de Beauvoir*

THE END OF MEANING, THE MEANING OF END

SOME THOUGHTS FROM GREECE

ANTONIS VRADIS

IN THE WESTERN PORT CITY OF PATRAS, THE LOCALS USE THE WORD *erēmēn* (erimin) a lot.[1] And yet, should you ask, most of them—yours truly included—would struggle to explain the word's actual meaning. "Erimin is just erimin," would be the most often encountered response; shrugged shoulders and an admission of something of a self-defeat, "There isn't really a meaning to it." This is precisely the wonderful thing about the word. The locals' inability to attribute a meaning to *erimin* might very well stem from the fact that the word connotes an event so strange that we can no longer fully comprehend or conceive it—an event, in other words, that lies outside of our existent system of logic.

"What just happened is erimin," we will say—the word meaning, literally, *in the absence of.* But what we omit from our own description is what is also omitted, what is missing from the scene that unfolds before us; no less than an element of logic, of rationality, some rationality that would allow us to extract meaning from what instead turns into a meaningless situation.

What is an erimin? Your favorite sports club winning against all odds is one. A friend acting in an unexpected way is too (only too often, this has a negative connotation, i.e. a friend behaving in a way that we wouldn't have expected them to). Running into a friend or an acquaintance somewhere far outside the city itself is also an erimin. In short, anything happening against the odds and usually also against our own desire for what should have happened instead. But much more than the improbable or the undesirable, erimin is the incomprehensible; it is what we fail to understand, what we cannot fully conceive, even though it may very well play out before us. It is the moment when our minds lack the cognitive ability to comprehend what we bear witness to.

With the above in mind, I want to make a proposition. What has been happening on the Greek territory over the past three to five years—the years of revolt, crisis, and austerity—is an erimin, and absolutely so. It is an erimin, first of all, in the oft-used, grammatically correct, yet cognitively botched, interpretation of the word. What has happened in these years has happened in an absence, in our own absence. But also, and much more crucially, it has happened in the absence of a system of logic that would allow us to assign meaning to the changes that have been taking place around us.

I will return to our inability to give meaning. But I want to begin with what is a brighter note: we are not alone—not by a long shot!— in not being able to fully comprehend what the spectacular trembling of global financial capital has brought about, or what it could further bring about.[2]

A SPECTACULAR END
TO MEANS AND MEANING

Let us look at the example of some of the most important, and at the same time devastating, financial news in Europe during the first quarter of 2013. After negotiations that lasted for about one week, the Eurogroup (the European Union finance ministers) reached a deal with the Cypriot government to rescue the small island's troubled economy. This single sentence serves as just one example of the dry, finance-related news that we have gotten used to being bombarded with, week in and week out, in recent years. Any such news, really, would do. Let's now take the key terms in the announcement that broke the Cypriot news. We have *negotiations*, we have a *deal*, and we have a *rescue*. They are all terms that have long since become a part of the vernacular despite their meaning being far from uncontested. Without blinking an eye, Eurogroup officials termed a rescue what is, effectively, the pushing of the island's economy over the brink of collapse. Only a few kilometers away, in Greece, the effectiveness of such rescue packages has been tried and tested in an economy which now ranks in the bottom third of the entire EU-27.

Even if we were to put the only-so-often bewildering world of financial terminology aside, a spectacular collapse of meaning is by now evident—and endemic. In the Greek case alone, the examples are seemingly endless: the Golden Dawn is reminiscent of the Nazi regime, but has steadfastly refused to use such identifiers in the public realm, opting instead for the comparatively harmless "nationalists"; the country's present coalition government, whose ever-increasing totalitarian turn is being taken in the name of protecting democratic values against political extremism; and in the smallest—but crucial—partner of the totalitarian-leaning government coalition, DIMAR. In a twist of meaning that goes much beyond irony, DIMAR confusingly translates as Democratic Left. Another example is the Greek police force's largest peacetime operation (with more than 70,000 individuals detained to date), meant to be part of the democratic plexus of power's self-protection against seething totalitarianism. By implication, therefore, totalitarian acts stem from a moderate and democratic system of power.

Seems paradoxical? It is so much more than that. Almost half a century ago, on the eve of the events of 1968, Guy Debord predicted the turbulence that was to come. In his magnum opus, *The Society of the Spectacle*, Debord pointed at the crucial separation between real life and its representation—the ultimate form of alienation.[3] And yet, Debord was talking about and during a time when the modern conditions of production, however alienated or exploitative, nevertheless still functioned: there remained a system of production that had the means to safeguard its own reproduction.

What happens now, in our own time? Take the dictionary definition for *means*, "an action or system by which a result is brought about," and you will realize that the same system Debord claimed had the means to keep going might have to, or is about to, stop doing so. As the crisis centered in the Eurozone (yet now stretching across most of the global North) deepens, there does not seem to be any action, let alone an entire system, that is bringing about a result. Reaction to an already rolling catastrophe has replaced action and achieving a tangible result has given way to a shoving of catastrophic repercussions into the future.

The financial world may no longer have the means to get itself out of the corner it has driven itself into. This crisis is no longer merely a financial one. By now, it is questionable whether the entire system of production Debord criticized possesses the means to reproduce itself any longer. And this possible inability makes itself evident in the world of words and of meaning. If, in Debord's time, the meaning of words was inverted, it has now flat-out collapsed. After all, meaning is defined as what we intend to convey, especially by language. It is, therefore, a system of words, by which a notion, an idea, is brought about and communicated. And so, the present system of order is unable to produce not only the means by which it will safeguard its own reproduction, but also the meaning that would explain this incapacity.

At the time of writing, we were only a few days into the Cypriot crisis—the latest national facet of a global financial hazard. The devastating effects of the Cypriot "rescue deal" were only just beginning to become apparent to a still-dazed local population. What will the near future bring to the island? Could it still become the cornerstone of a Eurozone collapse? Those who believe that the recent Eurogroup decision about Cypress is a small matter, or that the troubled Cypriot economy will find the means to resurrect itself, ought to think again: a collapse of meaning directly reflects a lack of means. And, in the present system of capitalist production, with capital accumulation as the running force, one would be hard-pressed to find a more acute sign of such collapse than in the breach of savings trust.

If anyone were still looking for an example of the collapse of finance capitalism's means to reproduce itself, or of the ensuing collapse of the meaning it had produced so far, the story of Greece would work well. Let us begin with the build-up to the Athens Olympics of 2004. From the early 2000s until 2010, the country was caught up in a frenzy of development. Its so-called modernization (*exygchronismós*) project carried all the usual marks of the "uninterrupted progress" discourse. Exygchronismós had assumed (a) a non-"modernized" past, (b) an ensuing process of "modernization," and (c) a new, "modern" economy and country, should the project actually come to fruition. In the run-up to the Athens Olympics, this modernization discourse dominated—it had arrived along with the golden years of Greek capitalism, the never-ending loans, the frenzied construction, and the new middle class springing up all around. Of course, it was a golden history written in the blood of the migrants entering the country en masse for the first time in its recent history, but these annoying footnotes mattered little at the time.

What then were the material conditions that could have possibly allowed for exygchronismós to play out? Looking back at the way in which Greek capitalism presented itself at the time, it is only too obvious that no one ever quite bothered to explain. The golden years came and went, with no sign of a rational explanation. A miracle-like boom was attributed to no one—except, perhaps, to the country's Eurozone entry (the irony) and to the passing of time. This was, after all, the arrival of the twenty-first century, and what more fitting way to welcome it, in science-fiction fashion, than for the country to be technologically advanced, developed, and prosperous beyond the locals' wildest imaginations?

If the rise of a loan-fuelled economy is attributed to nothing but time running its course, its fall can also be explained in the same way. The arrival of the IMF-EU-ECB (International Monetary Fund–European Union–European Central Bank) troika in May 2010 appeared in the public discourse, by and large, as something of a godsend—astonishingly, both in the sense that its appearance was supposed to be an immensely positive development for economy and society, but also in the sense that that this was a development coming completely from outside, as an intervention. It was something that lay beyond our own system of knowledge and something that should also remain beyond criticism. A sentiment that was, for example, expressed as, "The gods of the troika are here now, and they have decided this and that. What could we possibly do?" In the months and the years following May 2010, the troika would become the Greek version of a TINA (There Is No Alternative), because the troika said so.

So far, so neoliberal. There is little surprise in seeing the power apparatus tightening its grip to crush our own understanding, our own conceptualization of how things *are* and how they are *meant to be*. A tight grip, in other words, on our conceptualization of the framework within which we are allowed to think, and to act; the framework outside which action becomes an *erimin*.

ON MOVEMENT PROSPECT AND PERSPECTIVE

To CRITICIZE, so far, has been easy. Finance capitalism is hitting a dead end. It no longer has the means to reproduce itself. Its ideological apparatus can no longer make meaning. This should have been

music to the ears of a movement against it—that is, to the social antagonist movement, since it had focused entirely on highlighting how
exactly the world produced by finance capitalism makes absolutely no
sense. In the case of a territory like Greece, where the history of the
movement is so rich, one would expect things to take off. This, with
all the notable exceptions, *didn't quite happen.* And so it is time, five
years into this turbulent historical moment, for some criticism and reflection. If we were to look back at the entire social antagonist movement during the years of the crisis in Greece, it is possible to see that
the movement has been trying to read this "new world" with what are
entirely old tools.[4] Out of all the groups, collectives, and movements
that had existed before the troika's arrival, there was virtually no one
who had managed to foresee the impending collapse. Or rather, to be
more precise, no one who quite managed to foresee *and* to communicate this impeding collapse in a way that would have been effective
enough to make the movement central or even relevant.

What on earth happened? To put it very simply, the *movement
against* was a movement against a collapsing order, a collapse that it
had, to its credit, foreseen. But as a movement that would primarily
define itself in negation of the existent, the Greek antagonist movement suddenly and shockingly found itself to be an integral part of
the collapsing world that it had thought it was fighting against. And
so, the movement failed, in large part, to do anything much more
significant than add to the noise of meaning collapsing all around it.

From the "Democratic Left," to the "Xenios Zeus" (the god of hos-
pitality) operations *against* undocumented migrants, we have found
ourselves confronted with an utter collapse of the meaning of words
as we knew and understood them, up until yesterday. "Rescue packages" leading to social havoc are now a norm. A complete and utter
collapse of the meaning of words as we understood them, as we felt
them before, has taken place.

And yet, there is an immensely positive element to this banging
sound of collapse. The late financial capitalist model and the plexus
of power that has accompanied it have both failed to find the *means*
to perpetrate their existence in a way that would be uninterrupted
and *quiet.* Suddenly, the sheer force of the plexus of power has been
exposed, naked, as it knocked itself on the floor, collapsing. High
capitalism (or financial capitalism, or whatever other term one might
find appropriate) has dropped its consensual veil with a bang. This

collapse, in and of itself, has immense potential for all those who have been pointing at impending dead ends all along. At the exact same time that capitalist production and reproduction, and the plexus of power in which they rest, reach a limit, so do we, as an antagonist movement, both in terms of finding the language to describe this limit and to suggest ways to overcome it.

NOTES TOWARD A FORTHCOMING END

WHAT HAS BEEN happening in the world of finance and, by extension, to the social and political reality in Europe is the epitome of an er-imin—unexpected, mostly unforeseen, and incomprehensible by our old system of logic. But let us, for a second, take a closer look at one of the word's relatives: there is a cunning coincidence (or maybe not so much of one), in that erimin shares an etymological root with *erēmos*, the Greek word for desert or the space of (near) absolute absence.[5] An absence, that is, of nearly all elements that make up our everyday reality. *Erēmos* is the space of material absences; erimin, on the other hand, signals a situation of an absence of meaning. In the space of material absence, perspective prevails. To put it more simply: if we stand in a space with no material objects around us, there will be no hindrance to our perspective, like gazing at the vast horizon of an open sea. To find ourselves in a desert means there are no obstacles around us and it is for this reason that our perspective is maximized. But perspective, as John Berger tells us, is a *convention,* one that "centers everything on the eye of the beholder" and that makes, by extension, "the single eye the center of the visible world."[6] The biggest problem with this beam-like conceptualization is that it allows us no visual reciprocity, he concludes.

Now let us take this idea and see how it might work in the case of the *cognitive* absence, in the absence of meaning. Like the people who find themselves in the middle of a desert, we feel like we have nothing. We are not even able to grasp the situation that engulfs us, to understand, and then to decide how to act. Worse even, is that we lack the cognitive tools to put the situation in any bearably recognizable context. But of course, this is a schematic representation; a sketch of what life under extreme austerity feels like. One by one, peoples' familiar *objects* and *ideas* are taken away from them. From the assurance of shelter to the assurance of a system of values (an ideology) that not only predicts, but also counters a faltering system, the concrete blocks as they existed begin to vaporize. This is not an end, but it feels like we are heading for an end or, rather, heading toward a limit, a threshold. This is something that Giorgio Agamben discussed at some length in the closing words of *Homo Sacer*. The threshold represents the idea of drawing a line (in Agamben's case, a physical line, as he discussed the concentration camps of Nazi Germany) between a *normal state* and a *state of exception*: "only because the camps constitute a space of exception . . . in which not only is law completely suspended but fact and law are completely confused—is everything in the camps truly possible."[7] In much simpler terms, we need to cross a limit in order for things to become possible. This is an idea that crosses from humanity's darkest hours to its brightest ones. And in this sense, it is true that we might very well live in *erimin times*, during which most of us can make very little sense of what is going on around us, let alone what to do next. We are faced with an inability to conceptualize the present and imagine the future. But at the same time, this lack, this void, translates into an immense strength. An absolute lack of familiar objects of thought will eventually translate into immense potentiality. That is, the potentiality to go way beyond the understanding of the world as we have conceived it so far. Our perspective becomes clearest and most far-reaching in the desert, in the space of absolute absence. In an equivalent way, our cognitive perspective (our way of thinking) becomes clearer in a space of cognitive absence, in this *erimin world*, at these *erimin times*.

ENDNOTES

1   Pronounced er-im-in. As much as the great homogenisation project of the Greek state did away with many local dialects and idioms, a small but vivid collection of words that hold very local meanings still exists.

2   When using the first-person plural in this article, I mean the wider antagonist movement—alternatively called, as in the title of this collection, the movements against.

3   Guy Debord, *Society of the Spectacle* (Oakland: AK Press, 2005).

4   These "years of crisis," from the revolt of December 2008 to the arrival of the troika in May 2010, were approximately three to five years before this essay was written (in April 2013).

5   To accept that the desert is a space of absolute absence, a void, is of course incorrect, both in terms of indigenous populations, as in the Sahara and the desert's physical characteristics. Here, it only works schematically, as illustration.

6   John Berger, *Ways of Seeing* (London: BBC and Penguin Books, 1972), 16.

7   Giorgio Agamben, *Homo Sacer: Sovereign Power and Bare Life* (Stanford: Stanford UP, 1998), 97.

A FAILURE OF IMAGINATION

HUMAN RIGHTS THROUGH NEOLIBERALISM, THE ECONOMIC CRISIS, AND AUSTERITY POLICY

HARPREET K. PAUL

When Lehman Brothers filed for bankruptcy on Monday, September 15, 2008, the full extent of the financial crisis came to the surface and there was a sense that this signaled the end of the world, as we knew it. Financial institutions had deceived each other. Banks no longer trusted one another. Financial institutions stopped lending and investing. We entered a "credit crunch," followed by a recession with huge numbers of evictions, foreclosures, and prolonged unemployment. Yet, on Friday, October 3, 2008 (behind closed doors and without requirements to behave differently), the US government bailed out corporations "too big to fail," initially to the tune of $700 billion.[1] Having been bailed out, financial institutions did not lend and invest; instead directors and managers rewarded themselves with bonuses, compensation, and stock options. Unemployment continued. A sovereign debt crisis in Europe ensued, and in 2011, concerns also began to ring in the US over unsustainable debt levels.

A report on Wall Street and the financial crisis (issued on April 13, 2011 by the US Senate Permanent Subcommittee on Investigations) confirmed that the crisis was "the result of high risk, complex financial products, undisclosed conflicts of interests; and the failure of regulators, the credit rating agencies, and the market itself to rein in

the excesses of Wall Street."[2] Senator Levin noted, "institutions deceived their clients and deceived the public, and they were aided and
abetted by deferential regulators and credit ratings agencies."[3] Yet, the
popular narratives from governments continue to lay the blame with
vulnerable borrowers, often depicted as "unscrupulous" (unscrupulous people of color and women who took out subprime mortgages;
unscrupulous governments of Portugal, Ireland, Greece, Spain, Argentina, etc.). Balakrishnan and Heintz point out that this narrative
depicts the banks as the "victims," thereby justifying and legitimizing
huge bailouts.[4]

The narrative also implies that banks and borrowers (whether individuals or states) have equal bargaining power. Thirty years of deliberate legislative changes toward trade liberalization has resulted in
global restructuring that has eliminated state resources, which could
potentially be used to fulfill human rights obligations. The US eliminated many of the safeguards that had been put in place after the
Great Depression. The 1999 repeal of the Glass-Steagall Act ended
the separation between commercial and investment banking that had
existed for sixty-six years prior. And legislation such as the Financial
Services Modernization Act, 1999[5] enabled

> perverse incentives [that] encouraged lenders to exploit
> vulnerable borrowers while the government looked
> the other way…. reform of personal bankruptcy laws
> [were] pushed through. This made it more difficult
> for people suffering a catastrophic medical problem or
> prolonged period of unemployment to manage onerous
> levels of personal debt. An unexpected setback could
> lead to a loss of basic social and economic rights for the
> rest of a person's life."[6]

The past thirty years have seen a movement towards financialization, where profits are increasingly generated through financial activities rather than trade and production. New financial products have
allowed room for the maximization of shareholder value through financial manipulations.

For example, prior to 2008, financial institutions had been investing in various financial instruments whose ultimate value was linked
to the mortgage markets. Mortgages were bundled in a process called

"securitization" and then repackaged to produce new, innovative financial products. The complexities of these products prevented any accurate assessment of risk, particularly as regards subprime mortgages, and created an environment of economic fragility. The US Federal Reserve dramatically raised its key interest rate, the Federal Funds rate, from a low of 1.1 percent in 2003 to 5 percent by 2006 (over concerns of modest increases in inflation). The subprime mortgages were not fixed-rate mortgages. Instead, monthly payments were tied to market interest rates. When the Federal Reserve raised its interest rate by a multiple of over four times, monthly payments on subprime loans quickly became unaffordable.[7] Defaults became commonplace, and the housing market collapsed, creating ripple effects throughout the global financial sector.

A crisis with its origins in US financial markets had a global impact; between fifty-three and one hundred million additional people fell into extreme poverty, living on less than two dollars a day.[8] In 2009, the World Bank estimated that between 2009 and 2015, 200,000 to 400,000 additional children each year would die before their fifth birthday.[9]

In the US, unemployment, evictions, and foreclosures increased, as did the pressure to cut funding to public services. Many older persons in the US have had to postpone retirement, go back to work, or face homelessness due to reductions in the value of their pensions.[10] In the 1970s, economists promoted moving away from guaranteed defined benefit pension schemes to defined contribution (DC) schemes, which are subject to market fluctuation and risk. During the financial crisis, the value of DC pension schemes fell, leading millions to lose social security.[11] The shift to DC pensions was associated with shifting economic ideologies towards market-based, private sector solutions, in order to meet public social needs.[12]

An International Monetary Fund (IMF) report suggested that one cause of the ongoing financial crisis, as well as the debt crisis, was increased inequality.[13] Inequality had been rising since the 1970s. Through increasing access to credit, people in the US appeared to be experiencing an expansion in access to economic goods and services. Yet, hourly wages had been stagnant for decades; according to data from the US Bureau of Labor Statistics, the hourly wage of production and nonsupervisory workers was $18.08/hour in 1970 and $17.81/hour in 2007 (adjusted for inflation). Household incomes increased, even taking inflation into account, but this was due to longer hours worked by all household members, including women's increased labor force participation. Income inequality between households grew significantly during this period, but growth of consumer demand of low-income households was sustained by a rapid growth in household indebtedness.

It is in this context that some have argued that the US has not been complying with its human rights obligations, and that financial policy would look very different if it was; in demanding compliance with obligations to protect, promote, and fulfill economic and social rights, it is possible not only to encourage greater social assistance schemes, but challenge the very assumptions that the economy is based on.

HUMAN RIGHTS

Social activism and political rhetoric from the 1940s to the 1970s moved human rights from the hallways of the United Nations (UN) onto the global stage. Labor activists fought for the right to peaceful assembly, the right to strike, for better working conditions, and to forbid or regulate child labor, for example. National liberation movements called upon the right to self-determination, among others. The language of the civil rights movement highlighted systemic injustices and discrimination, and the discourse continues to frame many women's and girls, minority and indigenous, and lesbian, gay, bisexual, transgender, and queer rights movements today. The rhetoric of the morality of individual rights has achieved contemporary prominence. When states have attempted to carve out exceptions, in the name of "national security" or otherwise, the language of human rights has helped articulate concepts of social justice prioritizing the inherent dignity of each human being above abusive state exercise of power. And there have been attempts to extend rights concepts to communities and the environment.

International human rights law aims to elevate the fundamental rights of individuals above the absolute sovereignty of states. The idea of limited sovereignty was a motivating principle behind the adoption of the Universal Declaration of Human Rights (UDHR), which contains within it civil, political, economic, and social rights.[14] These rights are predicated upon the inherent dignity of all peoples.[15] Traditional human rights discourse speaks of rights arising out of agreements and commitments negotiated and entered into by states. Recently, human rights advocates have suggested that the neoliberal economic policies that led to the 2008 financial crisis violate basic human rights commitments and norms. Campaigns call for the US government to protect, promote, and fulfill obligations relating to the right to health, food, social security, and work. These campaigns outline the ways in which women and communities pay disproportionately for disinflationary monetary policies and public expenditure policies that are, in effect, discriminatory. US tax policies also impose a disproportionate burden on those with the least wealth (often women and people of color), who pay a bigger share in taxes than those with the most wealth and highest economic status. Advocates are thereby calling for a fundamental reenvisioning of economic policies, so that the economy is underpinned by a commitment to human rights principles.

At the same time, it is recognized that over the past thirty years, the US deliberately deregulated and reregulated markets and privatized public resources to the benefit of wealthier population groups and private corporations, withdrawing economic and social protections, while promoting individual responsibility and competition, disproportionately hurting low-income people and communities of color.[16] States have, in this way, been the primary violators of human rights. Using human rights language and norms can delegitimize the very notion that states are willing or able to respect, ensure, and provide fundamental dignities and freedoms to the populations they claim to represent.[17]

Armaline and Glasberg have suggested that the human rights enterprise can be seen as a pattern of struggle "from below" against powerful states and transnational corporations over access to limited resources and political voice (in decision-making).[18] Such grassroots movements seek to challenge, side step, and supplant abusive corporate and state practices in a decentralized and decentralizing movement towards self-government.[19] That human rights principles are based upon concerns for human freedom and dignity can cohere with understandings of freedom whereby, free *from* oppression, discrimination, exploitation, control, we are free *to* exercise our individual skills, capacities, and talents in socially valuable ways (autonomously and in community with others), and participate directly in decision-making that will impact upon our ability to do so, self-consciously creating new forms of social architecture that produce diverse but equal out-comes for all.

The UDHR includes the right to work, rest and leisure; adequate standard of living (including food, clothing, housing, medical care, social services, security); and the right to education.[20] The International Labour Organization's Declaration on Fundamental Principles and Rights at Work includes the freedom of association, the effective recognition of the right to collective bargaining, the elimination of all forms of forced or compulsory labor, the effective abolition of child labor, and the elimination of discrimination with respect to employment and occupation.[21] Two international covenants (one on civil and political rights and the other on economic, social and cultural rights) expand upon the rights contained within the UDHR and have facilitated the creation of committees that monitor state compliance with the covenants.[22] The US has not ratified the International Covenant on Economic, Social and Cultural Rights. However, it is arguable that (under customary international law), the US is responsible for respecting, promoting, and fulfilling the economic and social rights contained in the UDHR. It is worth mentioning that the US has also not ratified the Convention on the Elimination of all Forms of Discrimination against Women (CEDAW) or the Convention on the Rights of the Child (CRC).[23] Somalia is the only other country not to have ratified the CRC. However, countries are reviewed on their compliance with all human rights norms at their universal periodic review (which takes place every four years).[24]

Over the past thirty years, the US has instituted monetary and fiscal policy that has seen increasing impoverishment, exclusion, and criminalization of people, as public welfare services seeking to meet basic needs have been commercialized.[25] In a recent book, *Economic Police and Human Rights: Holding Governments to Account*, the authors seek to highlight that this is inconsistent with human rights law, principles, and norms. The right to work, and to decent work, provides further insight into the problem.

The Federal Reserve Bank has a dual mandate to have regard for inflation and unemployment, but has, since at least 1979, generally prioritized keeping inflation low.[26] Unemployment has been rising since 1979.[27] High wages are seen (by neoclassical economists) as potentially driving inflation up, while the same rationale is never provided for increasing profits[28] and research suggests that rates of inflation up to 20 percent have not done any harm.[29] Maintaining inflation in the very low single digits requires high interest rates, and more unemployment, and the costs of such a policy exceed any possible benefits.[30] In prioritizing disinflationary policies over employment, the Federal Reserve Bank policies have discriminatory effects on some of the most vulnerable segments of the population (i.e. people of color, women, LGBTQ people, etc.), since they are already disproportionately affected by both poverty *and* precariousness.

At the same time, consecutive governments have granted tax cuts for the very wealthy, reducing the pot of available resources for initiating job creation projects and for meeting basic needs through welfare provisions.[31] The state has continued to spend more than an estimated $624 billion on the military for fighting wars that many state advisors have said increase national insecurity, by fomenting further antipathy towards the US.[32] A study has found that "spending $1 billion on personal consumption, clean energy, healthcare, and education will all create significantly more jobs within the US economy than would the same $1 billion spent on the military."[33]

In addition, an astonishing number of people work low-wage jobs that would unlikely meet decent work standards. Decent work standards require opportunities for work that, among other things, delivers a fair income.[34] Between 1959 and 1979, wages for production and nonsupervisory workers (usually receiving lower pay) grew in close relation to productivity. But, between 1979 and 2008 the gap between pay and productivity widened.[35] Balakrishnan and Heintz suggest that the fruits of increased productivity are going to other groups, which does not seem consistent with the right to just and favorable conditions of work, particularly fair wages attached to that work.[36]

Half the jobs in the US pay less than $34,000 a year, and wages have been stuck since 1973 (increasing just 7 percent).[37] One quarter of jobs in the US pay below the official poverty line, which is set very low, for a family of four (less than $23,000 annually).[38] Families with two earners do better. But, poverty among families with children headed by single mothers exceeds 40 percent.[39] In December 2012, a report issued on single parenthood in the US and sixteen other high-income countries showed that the majority of single mothers in the US work more hours and yet have higher poverty rates than single mothers in other high-income countries.[40] In addition to families headed by single mothers, there is also persistent higher poverty among people of color. Around 27 percent of African Americans, Latinos and Native Americans are poor versus 10 percent of whites. At the same time, cash assistance welfare for low-income mothers and children has almost disappeared. Wealth disparities are even wider—and are heavily gendered and racialized.

Inequality may have been one of the causes of the ongoing financial crisis. Yet, in 2011, incomes rose more than 11 percent for the top 1 percent of earners, but not at all for everybody else. Excluding earnings from investment gains, the top 10 percent of earners took 46.5 percent of all income in 2011, the highest proportion since 1917. At the same time, family income has declined. In 2011, it stagnated for the poorest and dropped for those in the middle of the income distribution spectrum. Median household income, which was $50,054 in 2011, is about 9 percent lower than it was in 1999, after accounting for inflation.[41] A report issued by Pew Economic Mobility Project shows that, when it comes to wealth distribution (not income), the rich are getting richer and the poor are getting poorer.[42]

During the worst financial crisis since the Great Depression, rather than introduce policies that would reverse trends in inequality, US policy makers have watched corporations further exploit, as the majority of people are forced to sell their (increasingly productive) labor for ever-reducing pay checks. And, at the same time, states have introduced "right to work" legislation, negatively impacting the bargaining power of labor associations. In parts of Europe, businesses have been able to make employees redundant and then hire them back on worse conditions, including reduced pay. UK government officials have complained that labor laws (seeking to protect workers) are in fact obstacles to economic growth, suggesting the companies would be more likely to employ staff if they knew in advance that they could also dismiss them at will.[43] Such steps by US and European governments highlight ambivalence towards employment rights and, by extension, human rights.

Public expenditure has implications for the realization of many human rights, including the right to health and the right to access nutritiously safe food and drinking water, basic sanitation, and adequate housing and living conditions, which are the underlying determinants of health. 101,000 people are estimated to die each year in the US because of the way the health system is organized, and 45,000 deaths per year are attributed to the lack of health insurance.

The US has some of the worst health outcomes among high-income countries, despite spending more than twice as much on healthcare as any other country.[44]

The US has the fourth highest infant mortality rate in the OECD (Organisation for Economic Co-operation and Development) and the sixth highest rate of maternal mortality (although there has been a decline between 1985–2007, the mortality rates are particularly high for African-American women).[45] The US has the lowest life expectancy among major developed nations and the highest probability of dying before the age of five. At least twenty-five million people are underinsured. Hispanics, American Indians, and non-Hispanic blacks have higher rates of being uninsured than whites and Asians. Almost 50 percent of noncitizens are uninsured, while only 15 percent of citizens are uninsured. There have been no long-run declines in the percentage of people without insurance and the gaps between different racial and/or ethnic groups persist over time. In addition, women have persistently lower rates of being uninsured than men. Both white men and white women have higher cancer survival rates in comparison to their black counterparts, and the gap does not close despite improvements for both race groups over time.[46] Aydiner-Avsar and Elson assert that the US health system does not seem to comply with the obligation to guarantee the right to health on an equal basis, without discrimination.[47]

Accessing nutritiously safe food and drinking water is an underlying determinant of health. The legal right to welfare in US ended in 1996 and was replaced by the Temporary Assistance for Needy Families, and, since then, the number of recipients has decreased by a third to around two million. Data from 2008–2009 shows that food insecurity is more common in the most vulnerable segments of society, especially for female-headed single households, families with young children, and households of minority race and or ethnic groups.

Among single-mother families, 36.6 percent suffer from food insecurity, as do 22.9 percent of families with young children. 26.0 percent of Hispanic households suffered food insecurity in 2009; 24.9 percent of African American households were food insecure. Only 11.0 percent of white, non-Hispanic families suffer from food insecurity, which is below the overall rate of 14.7 percent of all households.[48] Human rights principles call for policies to be sensitive to these realities—particularly international covenants that call for human rights norms to end discrimination based on race and gender (such as the aforementioned CEDAW and ICERD—the International Covenant to End All Forms of Racial Discrimination).

Adequate housing and living conditions are also underlying determinants of health and yet US policies fail to provide safe and decent housing for everyone, a goal set by the Housing Act of 1937. Around 500,000 public housing units have been lost to demolition and privatization since 1995. The UN Special Rapporteur has called for an immediate moratorium on the demolition and disposition of public housing and explicitly condemned the disastrous impact of the demolition policy in New Orleans.[49]

US social spending policies do not have in mind the respect, promotion, and protection of human rights that seek to protect the inherent dignity of all peoples. They have often been in direct opposition to human rights obligations. Consecutive governments have supported tax cuts. Such cuts limit the available pot of resources to fund basic services. In the US, the share of revenue coming from corporations has fallen, and that coming from individuals has risen. However, tax on the incomes of the very wealthy has fallen, reducing the resources available to realize economic and social rights. At the same time, sales taxes are applied universally which means that poorer people pay higher proportions of their wages to consume goods. Balakrishnan believes that from this, we can infer that tax policy "has imposed an undue burden on those with the lowest economic status—in other words, women and people of color."[50] She proposes that the US government consider sales tax exemptions on items disproportionately consumed by poor racial and ethnic minorities.[51] Although, during the financial crisis, governments have suggested and, in the case of Greece, implemented the opposite (sales tax increases on such items).

UNWILLING AND UNABLE?

GOVERNMENTS SEEM UNWILLING to hold the human rights of their citizens as preeminent. Economic liberalization laws have enabled inequality to rise substantially over the past thirty years. During the "crisis," inequality has deepened. At the same time, Republicans have held the government hostage, calling for reductions in public social spending (rather than introducing higher levels of taxation for the rich) in response to the US debt crisis. For Nobel Prize-winning economists Paul Krugman and Joseph Stiglitz, the answer lies in increased public spending to meet peoples' needs and create jobs. Stiglitz has said cogently:

> The argument that the response to the current crisis has to be a lessening of social protection is really an argument by the 1% to say: "We have to grab a bigger share of the pie." But if the majority of people don't benefit from the economic pie, the system is a failure. I don't want to talk about GDP anymore, I want to talk about what is happening to most citizens…. The notion of the welfare of most citizens is almost a no-brainer.[52]

Yet, although there are important differences between them, consecutive governments have pursued relatively similar policies. One of the reasons for this could be that there is a revolving door between Wall Street and Washington. Two US Treasury Secretaries have come directly from Goldman Sachs.[53] While former Wall Street executives have direct access to shape economic policy and regulatory decisions in the US, most people are excluded from policy discussions. The Committee on Economic, Social and Cultural Rights[54] has indicated that the right of individuals to participate in the formulation, application, and review of national policies must be an integral component of any policy or practice that seeks to meet the state obligation to ensure the equal rights of men and women to the enjoyment of all human rights,[55] yet this is seldom done in practice (and the US has not ratified the International Covenant on Economic, Social, and Cultural Rights which the Committee oversees the implementation of).

Rather than comply with human rights obligations and call into question the very neoliberal economic policies that caused the crisis, states pursue austerity measures pushed by neoliberal economists that are in the interest of the wealthy and powerful. During the financial crisis, the percentage of the overall population living in poverty has steadily increased, up to 15.1 percent in 2010 from 12.5 percent in 2007.[56] At the same time, in January 2012, it was reported "U.S. corporate profits are higher as a share of gross domestic product than at any time since 1950."[57] The *Financial Times* said: "Call it the $1,700bn problem. Companies in the U.S. are flush with cash and are paying out a smaller proportion of their earnings as dividends than ever before. Much the same can be said for Western Europe. Governments and households on both sides of the Atlantic are meanwhile strapped for cash."[58]

In 2011, General Motors celebrated record profits of $7.6 billion, surpassing the previous record of $6.7 billion set in 1997, while underfunding its pension scheme and demanding greater and greater productivity of fewer staff.[59] In 2011, the US economy grew by 1.7 percent, but median wages fell by 2.7 percent. The pay gap between the average Standard & Poor 500 CEO and the average US worker, which was 42 times in 1980, widened to 380 times in 2011 from 325 times in 2010.[60] In 2011, German exports set a record of a trillion Euros; its trade surplus reached €158 billion, after a €155 billion surplus in 2010.[61] At the same time, the German chancellor worked to ensure that austerity measures were enforced in Greece, Spain, Ireland, and Portugal, resulting in increasing poverty and unemployment in those countries. In the years preceding the economic crisis, fast-growing southern European economies ran current account deficits that allowed for German export surpluses (while German workers' wages also stagnated). And, as Greek sovereign debt was devalued, Germany is said to have profited by more than €9 billion from the crisis, as investors fled Greece, highlighting the global nature of the obstacles.[62] On the basis of this information, it is certainly arguable that governments have "successfully facilitated socio-economic exploitation of [their] own majority population (workers and the unemployed) to the benefits of its powerful minority (owners)."[63] Those in power (across the right and center-left spectrum of the political parties) have remained unhinged by global movements against austerity measures. Consecutive governments in Greece and Spain have pursued largely similar austerity measures. There have been increasing calls for *real* democracy from movement spaces experimenting with horizontal forms of decision-making, as trust in the very mechanisms of representative democracy diminishes, particularly among youth.

States have other obligations besides complying with their human rights commitments. Yet, in the Vienna Declaration (1993), states undertook to give human rights their first priority.[64] However, the human rights machinery does not have strong enforcement mechanisms and states attempt to weaken the existing mechanisms further.[65] Armaline and Glasberg point out that the lack of enforcement mechanisms allows powerful and/or repressive states to simply ignore, discredit, or selectively recognize public international law.[66] At the same time, bodies governing private international law and international trade policies have very effective methodologies for settling disputes. Macmillan contends that the supremacy of trade liberalization in international law has been made possible by the World Trade Organization's effective enforcement mechanism (the Disputes Settlements Body).[67] There is no equally strong mechanism protecting the environment or human rights against abuses by states and other actors. And human rights and environmental protection are threatened by some aspects of the World Trade Organization agreement. For instance, the right to health is threatened by intellectual property rights protection under the Trade Related Intellectual Property Rights agreement; the General Agreement on Trade in Services may threaten the rights to water and education; and the Agreement on Agriculture jeopardizes food security. Trade liberalization has also been argued to have implications for the right to work, by increasing inequalities between skilled and low-skilled workers.[68]

Further, trade liberalization and massive bank deregulation in the US in the 1980s and 1990s resulted in a structurally cohesive and powerful private financial industry upon which many states are now dependent.[69]

> Global restructuring of private finance capital meant that the private industry was able to transcend individual states' ability to ensure the rights of citizens to food, clothes and shelter—let alone a living wage or healthcare to their populations. In sum, global restructuring simultaneously diminished states' sovereignty and autonomy in relation to private financial and corporate actors…As a result, even powerful states have very little of the political economic autonomy necessary to "choose" the protection of human rights when challenged by economic interests beyond their control.

When Dutch president of the Eurogroup of finance ministers indicated that a new approach to the "financial crisis" was needed, one that would put the full burden of future bank restructuring on creditors and depositors (rather than taxpayers), the *Financial Times* reported that this "rocked financial markets."[70] In effect, investors took their money elsewhere. Since the 1970s, through trade liberalization policies and deregulation, states have introduced policies that have made it easier for financial institutions to act as they please (moving money across national boundaries, impacting local economic situations)—making it more difficult for states to effectively protect the economic and social human rights of their citizens, even if they wanted to.[71]

Additionally, in the US, corporations are bound by law to act in the best interests of their shareholders, who seek greater returns on investments through profits, even when the pursuit of profits may result in violation of human rights and/or cause environmental degradation.[72] In the UK, companies must take the interests of stakeholders (employees, the environment, producers, and suppliers down the supply chain, etc.) into account. But the obligation to act in the shareholders' best interests remains. Governments have been slow to adopt regulations and implement policies that will prevent abuses, the UN Human Rights Council's guidelines on Business and Human Rights are unenforceable, and the World Trade Organization has found—on a number of occasions—that domestic environmental legislation acts as a barrier to trade.[73]

Grassroots workers' groups do seek to hold corporations accountable for violations of human rights. Groups have pressured companies to implement human-rights-based monitoring programs to assess whether produce is harvested under fair labor conditions and ensure that independent monitoring is conducted with the participation of workers themselves. United Workers, for example, a grassroots organization of low-wage workers in Baltimore, has fought with large private developers. They pressured developers to enter into a binding human-rights agreement, which requires their business tenants to pay a living wage and provide good working conditions for all workers.[74]

In this way, human rights norms can provide a discourse around concepts of social justice, a discourse that has become increasingly popular to fight for—and hopefully win—struggles in the short term. In the struggle to move to a wholly different social architecture (a long-term project moving away from authoritarian "representative" democracy, markets, private ownership of productive assets, disempowering work etc.), the broader human rights enterprise, as Armaline and Glasberg describe, would be conducive to highlighting a movement "from below" toward self-government.

SELF-GOVERNMENT

BEUYS HAS WARNED that if money becomes a full rights document in and of itself, so that those with more money have more rights, it will encroach on and ensure the decline of creativity, of the human soul, of the power of creation.[75] Authoritarian governance and forms of ownership will prevent self-determination, full expression, and the development of capabilities.[76] In the US, the Community Environmental Legal Defense Fund (CELDF) has pioneered the Community Bill of Rights, which is based on three essential elements: 1) the assertion of rights, including the right to self-government, 2) the banning of harmful activities, such as fracking, and 3) the assertion that the community will not tolerate companies that violate the community's rights through legally-granted privileges. The initiative has arisen out of recognition that corporate interests have become so embedded in our structure of law and are bestowed privileges which enable them to assault the rights of individuals, communities, and nature.

In relation to the right to food, grassroots organizations around the world have called for a move away from "food security" as a concept. The concept leads to the adoption of market-oriented rules governing food and agricultural systems, dispossessing smallholder producers, and creating environmental destruction. Instead, these groups call for a move to a "food sovereignty" framework. The food sovereignty framework advocates communities having control of their own food systems, including their own markets, production methods, and environments within democratic processes rooted in localized food systems.

The term "food sovereignty" was first made public following an international conference of La Via Campesina in 1996. On October 16, 2012, World Food Day, the International Network for Economic, Social, and Cultural rights (ESCR-Net) ran an article describing some of the initiatives that had been taking place. In Sri Lanka, the National Fisheries Solidarity Movement struggled to promote artisanal fishing against corporate fisheries and against land grabs for large-scale tourism projects. The Pakistan Fisher Folk Forum has engaged in similar struggles and sought to restore historical ownership rights relating to water resources and create a national sustainable fisheries policy. In India, Ekta Parishad has waged a long struggle for landless people and those living in extreme poverty to take control over livelihood resources. In the US, the Coalition of Immokalee Workers (CIW) has worked to improve the inequalities in the food system in Florida and beyond. The farmworker organization has challenged some of the biggest companies in the world and won concessions that have improved the working conditions and secured the living wage of Florida farmworkers—many of whom are immigrants and are among the most marginalized people in the US. In their long struggle against the degradation of their lands by oil extraction in Nigeria, the Movement for the Survival of the Ogoni People (MOSOP) has mobilized powerful grassroots demands for the right to their land, including adopting the Ogoni Bill of Rights.[77]

Rather than requesting that states comply with human rights obligations they are signatories to, Armaline and Glasberg argue that the strength of the human rights enterprise lies in its ability to challenge all authorities in power, states, banks, or corporations, and to highlight a pattern of struggle "from below."[78] I agree wholeheartedly with their conclusion that:

> The human rights enterprise is not only a useful concept to critique and move beyond formal human rights discourse; it is useful in evaluating the "legitimate authority" of states. Formal human rights discourse presents human rights as flowing from the agreements, protections and action of sovereign states that claim to represent populations within their jurisdiction or territory. In contrast the human rights enterprise presents human "rights" as flowing from the struggles of people: within, outside of, and against formal state structures and powerful global players such as banks or TNCs [Transnational Corporations]. When viewed through the lens of the human rights enterprise, the role and legitimacy of states ... can be tested against their ability to protect, ensure, and provide fundamental dignities and freedoms to the populations they claim to represent, and according to their supposedly binding agreements. [79]

In this way, grassroots struggles using the language of human rights can be seen as democratizing, decentralizing movements that challenge the very authority of states as primary social actors responsible for granting us a basic, dignified quality of life. In winning short-term improvements in the lives of people today, through struggle, we might hope to build deeper and larger movements that challenge current constructs of power, experimenting imaginatively with the creation of autonomous, democratic, prefigurative spaces that embody new structures and relationships along the way. The language contained within international documents can be discursive tools (whether or not states have signed up to the documents or comply with them) portraying concepts of social justice, but it is also necessary to move beyond them. In pursuit of a social and international order in which rights or needs and freedoms can be fully realized, "every person must be an artist in this realm of social sculpture, social art or social architecture."[80] Indeed, realizing human rights in the wake of crisis and austerity is tied to the construction of a different kind of society altogether. This requires imagination, which states—as stakeholders in the existing society—have failed to develop. But we might develop this social imagination collectively from below.

ENDNOTES

1   David Goldman, "Bailout tracker," *CNN*, http://money.cnn.com/news/storysupplement/economy/bailouttracker (accessed July 12, 2013).

2   Carl Levin and Tom Coburn, "Wall Street and the Financial Crisis: Anatomy of a Financial Collapse" (United States Senate Permanent Subcommittee on Investigations, April 13 2011), Homeland Security and Governmental Affairs website, http://www.hsgac.senate.gov//imo/media/doc/Financial_Crisis/FinancialCrisisReport.pdf?attempt-2 (accessed July 12, 2013).

3   Ibid.

4   James Heintz and Radhika Balakrishnan, "Debt, Power, and Crisis: Social Stratification and the Inequitable Governance of Financial Markets," *American Quarterly* 64, no. 3 (September 2012), 387–409.

5   Banking Senate, "Information Regarding the Gramm-Leach-Bliley Act of 1999," US Senate Committee on Banking, Housing and Urban Affairs website, http://www.banking.senate.gov/conf/ (accessed 13 July 2013).

6   The National Economic and Social Rights Initiative, Los Angeles Coalition of Immokalee Workers, et al. See also Radhika Balakrishnan and James Heintz, "Why Human Rights are Indispensable to Financial Regulation," *Huffington Post*, http://www.huffingtonpost.com/radhika-balakrishnan/why-human-rights-are-indi_b_517128.html (accessed July 12, 2013).

7   Four times the low rates that prevailed during the height of the boom.

8   Share the Worlds Resources, "Global Financial Crisis Pushing Millions into Poverty in 2009," STWR website, http://www.stwr.org/poverty-inequality/global-financial-crisis-pushing-millions-into-poverty-in-2009.html (accessed July 12, 2013).

9   UN Report, "Financial crisis to deepen extreme poverty, increase child mortality rates," UN News Centre website, http://www.un.org/apps/news/story.asp?NewsID=30070#.UVdPpBwqxJs (accessed July 12, 2013).

10   The National Economic and Social Rights Initiative, Los Angeles Coalition of Immokalee Workers, et al., "Toward Economic and Social Rights in the United States: From Market Competition to Public Goods" (Joint Submission to the United Nations Universal Periodic Review, Ninth Session of the Working Group on the UPR, December 3, 2010).

11   Radhika Balakrishnan, "Regulation: Pension Reform and Human Rights in the USA" in (ed.) Radhika Balakrishnan and Diane Elson, *Economic Policy and Human Rights: Holding Governments to Account* (Zed Books, 2011), 240.

12   Ibid.

13   Michael Kumhof, "IMF economist: Crisis begins with inequality," *Eurozine*, http://www.eurozine.com/articles/2012-03-09-kumhof-en.html (accessed July 12, 2013).

14   Scott Turner and David Miller, "Anarchist Theory and Human Rights," (Presented at the British International Studies Association Conference, St. Andrews, Scotland, 2005).

15   Universal Declaration of Human Rights, Preamble, United Nations website, http://www.un.org/en/documents/udhr (accessed July 12, 2013).

16   The National Economic and Social Rights Initiative, Los Angeles Coalition of Immokalee Workers, et al., Executive Summary paragraph 2.

17   William T. Armaline and Davita Silfen Glasberg, "What Will States Really Do For Us? The Human Rights Enterprise from Below," *Societies Without Borders* 4 (2009): 430–451, 448.

18   Ibid., 444.

19   Ibid., 447.

20   United Nations Documents, "Universal Declaration on Human Rights," UN Documents website, http://www.un.org/en/documents/udhr (accessed July 13, 2013).

21   International Labour Organization, "Text of the Declaration," ILO website, http://www.ilo.org/declaration/thedeclaration/textdeclaration/lang--en/index.htm (accessed July 13, 2013).

22   Treaties UN, "International Covenant on Civil and Political Rights," UN Treaty website, http://treaties.un.org/Pages/ViewDetails.aspx?mtdsg_no=IV-4&chapter=4&lang=en (accessed July 13, 2013); Treaties UN, "International Covenant on Economic, Social and Cultural Rights," UN Treaty website, http://treaties.un.org/Pages/ViewDetails.aspx?mtdsg_no=IV-3&chapter=4&lang=en (accessed July 13, 2013).

23   Treaties UN, "Convention on the Elimination of All Forms of Discrimination against Women," UN Treaty website, http://treaties.un.org/Pages/ViewDetails.aspx?src=TREATY&mtdsg_no=IV-8&chapter=4&lang=en (accessed July 13, 2013); Treaties UN, "Convention on the Rights of the Child," UN Treaty website, http://treaties.un.org/Pages/ViewDetails.aspx?mtdsg_no=IV-11&chapter=4&lang=en (accessed July 13, 2013).

24   UN Human Rights, "Universal Periodic Review," Office of the High Commissioner for Human Rights website, http://www.ohchr.org/EN/HRBodies/UPR/Pages/UPRMain.aspx (accessed July 13, 2013).

25   James Heintz and Radhika Balakrishnan, "Human Rights Dimensions of Fiscal and Monetary Policies: United States," in *Economic Policy and Human Rights*, 71.

26   Ibid., 16–18.

27   Ibid., 65–66.

28   Ibid., 60–61.

29   Ibid., 62.

30   Ibid., 60–62.

31   Ibid., 60.

32   Ibid., 60 (figures from 2008).

33   Ibid., 59.

34   The International Labour Organization's Declaration on Fundamental Principles and Rights at Work defines decent work as "work that is productive and delivers a fair income, security in the workplace and social protection for families, better prospects for personal development and social integration, freedom for people to express their concerns, organize and participate in the decisions that affect their lives, and equality of opportunity and treatment for all men and women." See the text of the Declaration.

35   Peter Edelman, "Poverty in America: Why Can't We End It?," *New York Times*, http://www.nytimes.com/2012/07/29/opinion/sunday/why-cant-we-end-poverty-in-america.html?_r=3&pagewanted=all (accessed July 12, 2013).

36   Radhika Balakrishnan and Diane Elson, 64

37   Peter Edelman, "Poverty in America."

38   Ibid.

39   Ibid.

40   Greg Kaufmann, "This Week in Poverty: US Single Mothers—'The Worst Off'," *The Nation*, http://www.thenation.com/blog/171886/week-poverty-us-single-mothers-worst#ixzz2YrEQwm1y (accessed July 12, 2013).

41   Annie Lowrey, "Incomes Flat in Recovery, but Not for the 1%," *New York Times*, http://www.nytimes.com/2013/02/16/business/economy/income-gains-after-recession-went-mostly-to-top-1.html (accessed July 12, 2013).

42   Catherine Rampell, "Richer Rich, and Poorer Poor," *New York Times*, http://economix.blogs.nytimes.com/2012/07/10/richer-rich-and-poorer-poor (accessed July 12, 2013).

43 Christopher Hope, and Robert Winnett, "Give Firms Freedom to Sack Unproductive Workers, Leaked Downing Street Report Advises," *Telegraph*, http://www.telegraph.co.uk/finance/jobs/8849420/Give-firms-freedom-to-sack-unproductive-workers-leaked-Downing-Street-report-advises.html (accessed July 12, 2013). See also Department for Business, Innovation and Skills, "Flexible, effective, fair: promoting economic growth through a strong and efficient labour market" (October, 2011), https://www.gov.uk/government/uploads/system/uploads/attachment_data/file/32148/11-1308-flexible-effective-fair-labour-market.pdf.

44 The National Economic and Social Rights Initiative, Los Angeles Coalition of Immokalee Workers, et al., 3.

45 Nursel Aydiner-Avsar and Diane Elson, "Human Rights and Public expenditure in the USA," in *Economic Policy and Human Rights: Holding Governments to Account* (Zed Books, 2011), 99–130.

46 Ibid., 116.

47 Ibid., 110–111.

48 Ibid., 112.

49 The National Economic and Social Rights Initiative, Los Angeles Coalition of Immokalee Workers, et al., pg. 5.

50 Radhika Balakrishnan and Diane Elson, 11, 167.

51 Ibid., 11, 172.

52 Joseph Stiglitz, "Politics Is at the Root of the Problem," *The European*, http://www.theeuropean-magazine.com/633-stiglitz-joseph/634-austerity-and-a-new-recession (accessed July 12, 2013).

53 William T. Armaline and Davita Silfen Glasberg, 438.

54 Radhika Balakrishnan and Diane Elson, Committee on Economic, Social and Culture Rights General Comment 16 (paragraph 37), General Comment 14 (paragraph 54), General Comment 15 (paragraphs 16(a) and 48), 11.

55 Ibid.

56 Poverty USA, "The Population of Poverty USA," Poverty USA, http://www.povertyusa.org/the-state-of-poverty/poverty-facts (accessed, July 13, 2013).

57 John Authers, "Hordes of Hoarders," *Financial Times*, http://www.ft.com/cms/s/0/4cd6cb8c-48e0-11e1-974a-00144feabdc0.html#axzz2OTrZJ22P (accessed July 13, 2013).

58 Ibid.

59 Rebecca Jarvis, Charlie Rose, and Erica Hall, "GM: No More Pensions for White-Collar Workers," *CBS News*, http://www.cbsnews.com/video/watch/?id=7398941n (accessed July 13, 2013).

60 Leslie Patton, "McDonald's $8.25 Man and $8.75 Million CEO Shows Pay Gap," *Bloomberg*, http://www.bloomberg.com/news/2012-12-12/mcdonald-s-8-25-man-and-8-75-million-ceo-shows-pay-gap.html (accessed July 13, 2013).

61 BBC, "German exports set record of a trillion euros in 2011," *BBC News*, http://www.bbc.co.uk/news/business-16941142 (accessed July 13, 2013).

62 Valentina Pop, "Germany estimated to have made €9bn profit out of crisis," *EU Observer* website, http://euobserver.com/economic/114231 (accessed July 13, 2013).

63 William T. Armaline and Davita Silfen Glasberg, 438.

64 Radhika Balakrishnan and Diane Elson, 13.

65 Through the so-called "Treaty body strengthening process."

66 William T. Armaline and Davita Silfen Glasberg, 432.

67 Fiona Macmillan, "International Economic Law and Public International Law: Strangers in the Night," *International Trade Law and Regulation* 10 (2004): 122.

68 Radhika Balakrishnan and Diane Elson, 200.

69 William T. Armaline and Davita Silfen Glasberg, 436.

70 Nicolas Véron, "With Cyprus, Europe Risks Being too Tough on Banking Moral Hazard," *Financial Times*, http://www.ft.com/cms/s/0/d3e2c5e6-97d0-11e2-97e0-00144feabdc0.html#axzz2PJpvlpkX (accessed July 13, 2013).

71 William T. Armaline and Davita Silfen Glasberg, 439.

72 Ibid., 434.

73 Richard W. Parker, "The Use and Abuse of Trade Leverage to Protect

the Global Commons: What We Learn from the Tuna-Dolphin Conflict," *Georgetown Environmental Law Review* No. 1 (1999): 86–100. Also published in Fiona Macmillan's *The World Trade Organization and the Environment* (London: Sweet and Maxwell, 2001), 105.

74 The National Economic and Social Rights Initiative, Los Angeles Coalition of Immokalee Workers, et al., pg. 7.

75 Joseph Beuys, et al., *What is Money?: A Discussion,* (Clareview, 2010), 31–32.

76 Ibid., 49.

77 International Network for Economic, Social & Cultural Rights, "Social movements claim the right to food and food sovereignty," ESCR-NET website, http://www.escr-net.org/node/364953 (accessed July 13, 2013).

78 William T. Armaline and Davita Silfen Glasberg, 446–447.

79 Ibid., 448.

80 Joseph Beuys, 16, 24–25.

MECHANISMS OF POWER
PRIVILEGE AND RACISM AS EXERCISED THROUGH ECONOMIC CRISIS

ERNESTO AGUILAR AND AYN MORGAN

THE INTERNATIONAL ECONOMIC DOWNTURN AND DEEPENING INCOME inequality will, in the writing of history, be a defining moment for many countries. Austerity protests across Europe, an insurgency in India brought on by ethnic and class divides, and clashes in China over working conditions are among the most famous flashpoints. In the United States, the specter of foreclosures and bleak unemployment figures regularly make headlines in every major media outlet; yet only tell part of the story.

For communities of color in the United States, the economic calamities of the first thirteen years of the new century proved incredibly challenging. Anti-immigrant upsurges in defense of jobs for citizens were among the uglier reactions to festering financial troubles—particularly their racial coding here in the US. Policing of youth and minorities, a problem over many decades, was exacerbated by economic problems, creating a situation where social anxieties could have deadly consequences. Today, there are disproportionate numbers of people of color in prisons, contributing to stunted employment opportunities as a result of prison records. Rental housing, community, and lifestyle options can also be shaped by background and credit checks. When hate and bigotry are no longer culturally acceptable, subtler methods for supporting dominant racial narratives flourish. As United for a

Fair Economy states, those promoting the idea of a post-racial society are all too eager to use tired, dog-whistle politics to exploit racial resentment among whites.[1] These political tensions endure in a post-Obama period; for example, as the Southern Poverty Law Center notes, militia and hate group organizing, resulting in part from the aforementioned anti-immigrant tensions, is cresting.[2]

This chapter seeks to explore the impact of the financial collapse on communities of color in the United States. Moreover, this examination will also explore the idea of socioeconomic rights as they relate to communities of color. While there are many contentious issues related to monitoring and access, the United States has a long established concept of political rights, such as freedom of speech and freedom of assembly, for its citizens. Within the context of this system, political rights are those the American public accepts as a guarantee. These rights are mythologized to a point of near caricature. A couple of quick examples of the ironies of these "rights" might include the right of corporations to influence elections as a function of "free" political speech, or the idea that the vilest of bigotry, even to the point of operating against people's own political and social interests, is to be treasured (again, as an example of the benefits of "free speech"). The existence of such dubious freedoms is one of the reasons "terrorists," the Third World, and indeed the rest of the planet is coming to hate the United States. Indeed, virtually all Americans have assimilated these ideas as fundamental to what makes the United States what it is and, in further irony, what makes it great.

A much more difficult conversation, one certainly germane to the US financial collapse and its tremendous impact on communities of color, concerns the absence of the right to live. Socioeconomic rights, such as the right to a job, the right to education, and to healthcare, are not generally acknowledged as needs in the United States, even though multiple surveys cite the primacy of such to the majority of Americans. The Obama healthcare debate, in which the most minimal coverage was sanctioned, demonstrated a deep conflict in society, in which a significant segment of the populace, including leadership, was firmly opposed to public healthcare options. States continue their slow retreat on public education, with many shifting resources to private industry, in the form of charter schools, under the rhetoric of "school choice." Inevitably, job creation conversations are almost exclusively centered on incentives for businesses, in the form of tax breaks, undercutting unions, and deregulation. As Fairness and Accuracy in Reporting notes, a bad economy is regularly regarded as impetus for a government to "do something"—meaning tightening budgets—rather than framing budget cuts in terms of what those policies may do to communities and workers depending on tax-funded programs to support basic services.[3]

The downturn, by most accounts, has impacted communities of color disproportionately. As the *New York Times* reports, education is doing less and less to help young people out of poverty, and more to preserve class divisions and economic inequality.[4] Several studies indicate that unemployment is particularly affecting African Americans and Latinos. Similarly, foreclosures (and a less examined, but noted, trend of bad loans, disadvantaging interest rates, etc.) impact racial minorities at rates exceeding the overall population (see Glasberg, Beeman, and Casey's chapter in this volume).

In the United States, people of color have faced the most difficult struggles over recognition of their political rights. In the current century, attempts to reduce African American voter participation through various forms of disenfranchisement and the dismantling of Affirmative Action have been among the most visible scandals affecting political participation and, by extension, economic disenfranchisement within the US. Yet these matters have an extensive history. The right to vote, freedom of speech, freedom of assembly, and so on have been contentious issues since the Black Codes and post-Reconstruction actions aimed at managing post-slavery political participation.

In the last one hundred years, the United States has seen, to varying degrees, a curbing of the robber baron entrepreneurship that resulted in rapid industrial progress alongside crushing mistreatment based on race, gender, and class, replaced by a system with some basic restrictions. But this has reverted slowly to a system in which corporations were given free rein to produce and look askance at issues of pay equity and human rights, particularly as "free trade" agreements such as NAFTA and CAFTA opened up global markets. Korkut Erturk argues that capital unraveled with the deregulation of the rules put in place in the 1930s to avoid another Great Depression.[5] With deregulation, borders became increasingly irrelevant to corporations, who saw in offshore blue-collar work an appropriate solution to boosting profits in a period of rising US labor costs. The post-World War II period, acknowledges Azizur Rahman Khan, was marked by more countries becoming openly willing to tolerate greater degrees of un-employment and, in all, more tolerant of inequality.[6]

The dominance of banks at the center of Occupy Wall Street and other protests stretches back more than half a century, with rapid expansion, domestically and internationally, of financial institutions following World War II. With the disintegration of public trust in authority during the Vietnam War era, crisis became the mechanism for power. Leo Panitch and Sam Gindin suggest that the labor strikes of the 1970s, in reaction to the reorganization of work, prompted cor-porate concern over maintaining workplace control. Thus, the specter of crisis was summoned to shore up larger inventories.[7] Correspond-ingly, banks and investment companies have transformed their busi-ness models over the last twenty years, away from taking risks on bond maturity and interest rates, toward high-risk deals that have hastened municipal indebtedness and facilitated processes of privatization.[8]

The civil rights movement redefined the struggle of economic equality, but, in the post-Jim Crow period, ideas of states' rights evolved into de facto defenses of racial segregation. Jason Morgan Ward remarks that nowhere was this more evident than in the Re-publican presidential campaign of Barry Goldwater, who argued that integration should not be regarded as a civil right accorded by the Constitution.[9] His coalition of "forgotten Americans"—those fearful of growing support for African American civil rights; those who op-posed the federal government in favor of a racially-coded advocacy for states' rights; and those worried about political and economic dispos-session by the social developments attached to the civil rights move-ment—became the model that united the Republicans for another twenty-five years. Federal statutes in 1964 and 1965 would deal blows to educational, social, and economic disparity, although, as Morgan notes, the political rhetoric of white supremacy at this time recast ob-structionist prejudice into a patriotic and moral crusade (in a process similar to contemporary right-wing rhetoric aimed at reclaiming a lost era of "traditional values" in the US—particularly attached to the Tea Party).[10]

In particular, high African American unemployment, through this lens, has been one of the most enduring, albeit dour, statistics. As Andy Kroll writes, the steady Black jobless rate of about twice that of whites has long been attributed to factors such as education and crime, yet these explanations have been discredited amid improving education and reduced rates of crime. Instead, Kroll notes, many studies show that unemployed African Americans often have added hardships finding work. Indeed, studies have clearly shown that racism, not a supposed African American propensity for crime, is at issue here, as whites with criminal records found themselves with better job prospects than equally qualified African Americans *with clean records*.[11] Racial discrimination has persisted, even as conservatives champion the notion that the racial bigotry of the US's past has vanished, and created a level playing field for finding and maintaining work.

While this history is crucial in understanding how the current crisis is affecting communities of color in the US, it is impossible to understand how the current financial crisis has damaged those communities without a clear analysis of the ascendance and internationalization of American empire in the present moment. Jodi Dean offers that capitalism has been successful at adapting to the crises it generates. Among its successes is the redefining of the public discourse around justice. Dean reminds us that the neoliberal ideal is one in which competition and money are seen as intimately connected to liberty and equality.[12] Implicit in this is capitalism's equating of money with the person—the idea that, through choices, funds, and resources, people are more free, more protected from prejudice, and better able to have brighter futures in a system of private ownership and market exchange. Taken to its natural conclusion, however, it stands to reason that only the wealthiest are relatively free from the power of the State and the limitations of want. These ideological underpinnings of contemporary capitalism are, of course, paired with commercial practices that benefit the wealthy. Although a close look at this ideology may seem abstract to some, how it has played out structurally for communities of color in practice is anything but vague.

However, white supremacy in the context of the economic downturn is one of the great unreported phenomena for our generation (and indeed many other generations). The racialized fight is a dying one, as the census estimates there will be no white majority in thirty years.[13] That statistic does not change the statistics of wealth and power, however, and suggests a real danger of power and force concentrated in the hands of what will become a numeric minority racial group. For this minority, a culture of fear is rooted in a loss of resources, typified, for example, in blaming unions and workplace organizing for the failure of businesses (like Hostess, to name one recent example).

Racial discrimination, on a host of platforms from housing to employment, says Steven Ramirez, is so deep and durable it can only be seen as pervasive social oppression, and it is upheld even at the cost of diminished national economic output. Whether the country is failing to harness the existing education of people of color, concentrating their employment in sectors that fail to utilize their talents, or under-investing in the economic and educational performance of communities of color, the United States continues to cultivate an economy driven by debt rather than the innovation that would accompany the unrestricted inclusion of communities of color in the economy.[14] Institutional corruption and racial privilege, applied in virtually every aspect of public life, cripple the idea of meritocracy. However, this is how American capitalism is designed to function and has only been exacerbated by the economic crisis.

Predatory lending practices are aimed at vulnerable communities, particularly communities of color (again, see Glasberg, Beeman, and Casey's chapter in this collection). The subprime debacle of 2006–2007, in which a lending population (half of which qualified for prime loans) was saddled with interest rates, on average, 3.5 percent higher, has been widely documented. Later audits confirmed suspicions that, even at the highest income level, African Americans were more than three times more likely to be steered toward subprime loans than equally qualified whites.[15] By 2007 federal estimates, banks pushed 54 percent of high-income African Americans into high-cost loans compared to 28 percent of *low-income* whites. The outcomes of such discriminatory activity were devastating. For instance, in Memphis, Tennessee, Ramirez notes that 43 percent of foreclosures by Wells Fargo were in African American neighborhoods, where only 15 percent of their loans were made. Racism by lenders suggests communities of color were targeted for short-term profits and bonuses for staff, at the cost of destroying the financial futures of many communities.

And the housing crisis has devastated many communities (see, for example, Burley's chapter in this collection). According to one report, more than three million people in the US have experienced a period of homelessness. Nearly half of that number are children. This is occurring while an estimated eighteen million housing units are vacant, often due to eviction. From 2008 to 2012, millions lost their homes due to failure to pay mortgages.[16]

Foreclosure-related disparities provided additional opportunities for racism exercised through the economic crisis. A 2012 undercover investigation by the National Fair Housing Alliance documented an alarming pattern in the maintenance and marketing practices of many of the banks, lenders, investors, and additional entities that manage Real Estate Owned (REO) assets and properties, i.e., foreclosed homes. REO homes in white neighborhoods were cared for in a substantially better manner than those in communities of color. While REO properties in predominantly white neighborhoods were more likely to have neatly manicured lawns, securely locked doors, and attractive "for sale" signs out front, homes in communities of color were more likely to have overgrown yards littered with trash, unsecured doors, broken windows, and indications of marketing as a distressed sale. REO properties in communities of color generally appeared vacant, abandoned, blighted, and unappealing to real estate agents who might market the unit to homebuyers. On the other hand, REOs in white communities generally appeared inhabited, well maintained, and attractive to real estate agents and homebuyers. [17]

The foreclosure explosion ran headlong into a national trend of housing privatization, notes Sasha Lilley, where public housing was simply bulldozed in cities like Miami. Economically disadvantaged communities lost large tracts of property through eminent domain and other methods, and people of color especially experienced political scapegoating as the economic crisis sharpened. The unemployment uptick that is a regular feature of capitalism's addiction to crisis was twisted, Lilley notes, particularly for workers of color, whose circumstances are considered a consequence of "personal or cultural dysfunction."[18]

The collapse has also created a financial ripple effect in the form of austerity cuts that are distinctly racialized in nature. For instance, in 2013, educational institutions like San Jose State University and North Carolina State University forecast cuts to ethnic studies departments, under the banner of balancing budgets and reducing classes that may not have widespread enrollment. In these scenarios, the value of disciplines which were previously considered bedrocks of learning, such as philosophy and art, or the spirit of inquiry and exploration embodied by ethnic studies and history, are sacrificed for the mass appeal of sports or marketing coursework. Educators are also subject to these pressures, which presume education should parallel market demands. Interdisciplinary and liberal arts professors at the University of Texas at Austin, for example, issued a letter to the administration with concerns about denial of tenure. One professor, speaking to *Inside Higher Ed* on condition of anonymity, complained UT-Austin recruited scholars when the economy was good, then cut their programs during leaner times.[19] Other instances mirror the projected steep tuition increases, course elimination, and additional streamlining techniques of the nation's largest community college, City College of San Francisco. For junior colleges and campuses serving working-class students, reliance on limited foundations, and other failed financial institutions produced difficult choices. Those decisions seldom mean cutting administrative salaries, but rather increase the burden on students. For students on the margins, disproportionately young people of color who see higher education as a ticket out of poverty, rising course costs mean taking fewer classes or none at all.

In the midst of the intense ideological and economic tumult, a number of movements are emerging in response. Protests of foreclosures and property seizures, such as Take Back the Land, sit-ins in Minnesota against evictions, and the reemergence of Homes Not Jails are among a few instances of resistance. A reinvigorated immigrants' rights movement has mounted an offensive against the demonization of immigrants with a multitiered campaign aimed at the DREAM Act (passed in Maryland in 2012), media use of the term "illegal" to describe undocumented workers, and pressing for more attention to hate crimes.

In 2006, the Take Back the Land Movement became a focal point in Florida, after its supporters seized government-held land and occupied it for a year. Shanty structures built on these properties for residence, as well as a means of popularizing the struggle, were christened in the name of revolutionary activists such as Fred Hampton and Mumia Abu-Jamal. As Max Rameau told the media, "This started because of the housing crisis in Miami and its particular impact on the Black community with gentrification. Groups have worked on these issues for years without any success. And it turns out that the elected officials and county government have been stealing the money slated for affordable housing. We couldn't go back to the government, since they were the problem. We had to take back the land."[20]

Each effort pushes against the effects of ongoing white racism and privilege, and increases public awareness by shifting the dialog from the dominant paradigm to tangible action through creative and constructive solutions. Antiglobalization protests remain a vibrant part of Third World struggle and should also be understood in this context. These international protests, when covered by mainstream or activist media, inspire further interest and illustrate the possibilities of reclaimed and renewed communities of color who have been systematically denied fair access to education, housing, and employment opportunities—and, ultimately, stripped of dignity and decent lives. These hardships are incrementally denied or removed by those of privilege by fostering continued and flawed perceptions, which become easier to exploit or more accepted during the pretense of economic crisis. Indeed, the ideology of white racism uses communities of color as convenient targets for austerity policy. But we are fighting back.

ENDNOTES

1   "Racism, Post-Racialism and Election 2012," United for a Fair Economy, http://faireconomy.org/enews/racism_post-racialism_and_election_2012 (accessed July 13, 2013).

2   Southern Poverty Law Center, "The Second Wave: Return of the Militias," http://www.splcenter.org/get-informed/publications/splc-report-return-of-the-militias (accessed July 13, 2013).

3   Fairness and Accuracy in Reporting, "Nancy Altman on Deficits and Social Security, Alfie Kohn on Education," Fairness & Accuracy in Reporting, http://fair.org/counterspin-radio/nancy-altman-on-deficits-and-social-security-alfie-kohn-on-education/ (accessed July 13, 2013).

4   Jason DeParle, "For Poor, Leap to College Often Ends in a Hard Fall," *New York Times*, http://nyti.ms/UYmYn7 (accessed July 13, 2013).

5   Korku Erturk, "An Essay on the Crisis of Capitalism—à la Marx?" The IDEAs Working Paper Series (February 2012), 3.

6   Azizur Rahman Khan, "Inequality in Our Age" Political Economy Research Institute Working Paper Series (January 2012), 16.

7   Sam Gindin and Leo Panitch, *The Making of Global Capitalism* (New York: Verso Books, 2012), 136.

8   Ibid., 175

9   Jason Morgan Ward, *Defending White Democracy: The Making of A Segregationist Movement and the Remaking of Racial Politics, 1936–1965* (Chapel Hill, NC: University of North Carolina Press, 2011), 169.

10   Ibid., 183

11   Andy Kroll, "The 60-Year Unemployment Scandal," *Counterpunch*, http://www.counterpunch.org/2011/07/05/the-60-year-unemployment-scandal/ (accessed July 13, 2013).

12   Jodi Dean, *The Communist Horizon* (New York: Verso Books, 2012), 92.

13   Michael Cooper, "Census Officials, Citing Increasing Diversity, Say U.S. Will Be a 'Plurality Nation,'" *New York Times*, http://www.nytimes.com/2012/12/13/us/us-will-have-no-ethnic-majority-census-finds.html (accessed July 13, 2013).

14   Steven Ramirez, *Lawless Capitalism: The Subprime Crisis and the Case for an Economic Rule of Law* (New York: New York University Press, 2012), 144.

15   Ibid., 148.

16   "The Absurdity of Capitalist Overproduction: A Glut of Homes in a Sea of Homelessness," *Liberation* (January 2013), 7.

17   National Fair Housing Alliance, *The Banks are Back—Our Neighborhoods are Not: Discrimination in the Maintenance and Marketing of REO Properties* (April 4, 2012), 4.

18   Sasha Lilley, *Capital and its Discontents: Conversations with Radical Thinkers in a Time of Tumult* (Oakland: PM Press, 2011), 13.

19   Carl Straumsheim, "Interdisciplinary and Out of a Job," Inside Higher Ed, http://www.insidehighered.com/news/2013/03/08/liberal-arts-instructors-rally-around-interdisciplinary-studies-after-tenure-denials (accessed July 13, 2013).

20   "United Action Can Stop Foreclosures, Evictions: The Growing Movement to Occupy Homes and Make Housing a Right," *Liberation* (January 2013), 2.

NO MANCESSION
CRISIS, GENDER, REPRODUCTIVE LABOR, AND THE COMMONS

GAYGE MAGGIO

CAPITALISM IS IN A CONTINUING CRISIS THAT SHOWS NO SIGNS OF BE-
ing resolved any time soon. Beginning with a global economic decline
that started in late 2007, marked by a financial meltdown in 2008,
and having failed to achieve a meaningful recovery, it has been utilized
for the acceleration of neoliberal policies and a hastened imposition
of austerity worldwide. In the US, the recession was initially characterized as a "mancession," with the assumption that male-dominated
employment sectors were hit the hardest. However, a more complete
view of the labor of capitalism, particularly one that recognizes the
centrality of unwaged caregiving work, reveals that austerity measures
are a major tool for reimposing and intensifying patriarchal social relations within the capitalist system. We can also term this caregiving
work, both waged and unwaged, reproductive labor—the work done
so that people can work and live the next day, week, or month, in addition to caring for the next generation of people. One of the keys to
both understanding crisis and austerity, and structuring our responses
to it, lies in the dual character of this reproductive labor.

Reproductive labor in capitalism both reproduces us as living, loving human beings and communities and as labor power that is sold
to capital for the wage. Crisis contains both serious threats to the self-
organization and strength of the working class and the opportunity

for responses that strengthen the position of the class or open the way for revolutionary responses. Thus, crisis can both further alienate our reproductive labor and intensify the patriarchal character of its organization, or it can provide opportunities for us to regain control and socialize caregiving as a space of resistance and a path to a new commons. To struggle for the latter and against the former requires us to both understand the crisis and be strategic in our responses to it. The first step in this process is to confront the myth of the "mancession."

THE MYTH OF THE MANCESSION

"Modern bourgeois society with its relations of production, of exchange, and of property, a society that has conjured up such gigantic means of production and exchange, is like the sorcerer who is no longer able to control the powers of the nether world whom he has called up by his spells."
—Karl Marx and Frederick Engels[1]

WE DO NOT have to look beyond the "progressive" media to find arguments that the idea of a mancession was a myth; however, the reasoning these sources use to draw their conclusion is fundamentally flawed. Their argument is to look solely at waged employment, map the sectors where job losses initially occurred, and examine how the recession continued to play out, in terms of employment in other sectors. While Alice O'Connor, for instance, is of course correct in pointing out that job losses shifted from construction and manufacturing to such fields as education and human services, signifying a shift from male-dominated to female-dominated fields, she does not examine the full scope of economic activity.[2] O'Connor rightly refers to the continuing inequities in household work, and the wage losses and increase in poverty rates experienced by women. However, the historical favoring of men by government programs, unions, and the private sector only enters into the discussion peripherally.

Capitalist logic separates society into political and economic spheres, and separates work into waged and unwaged, tending to invisibilize the unwaged work. The progressive viewpoint harkens back to Keynesianism, which states that the government can enact social policies to cushion the extremes of the market. The political will to accomplish this, of course, comes from individuals and lobbying groups, the analysis done by Keynesian economists, and from within the "progressive" wing of the Democratic Party. Our deeper critique, however, does not accept the idea of a separate political sphere that can shape the economic sphere in a limited way, but, rather, assumes the unity of politics and economics. The social programs threatened by austerity originate not from a benevolent state that is responsive to the voices of progressive-minded lobbyists, but from a state that maintains capitalism finding itself forced to create institutions to uphold capitalist social relations. These institutions were a mix of concessions and control, and were a response to heightened struggle that threatened the continuation of the capitalist system.

When we take an expansive view of how the crisis of capitalism affects every aspect of daily life, and not just employment, we see that even without a shift in falling employment from male-dominated to female-dominated sectors, the mancession would be a myth. The cutting of social programs, education, and all the other institutions that have been targeted by the neoliberal agenda, whose attacks have been amplified by the crisis, of course affect far more than just men. We should not see these cuts as part of a political sphere separate from, but capable of exerting an influence on, the economic sphere. Rather, these aspects of daily life under the intensified attacks of austerity are as fundamental to the economic activity of the working class—the daily reproduction of both the class as a collection of people and as a class—as the waged workplace.

We should also not be "mechanical Marxists" and place all things outside the immediate relations of production in the workplace as part of an overly determined superstructure secondary to the class struggle. Rather, we should, from the philosophical standpoint of the dialectical unity of base and superstructure, proceed to an understanding of how capitalist relations form a totality that pervades all of society.[3] This pervasiveness of capitalist relations is accompanied by a pervasiveness of class struggle. The class struggle is not only in the workplace or the landlord-tenant relationship, but exists also in relation to welfare programs, educational institutions, and social services. It exists in the struggle for the control over our bodies.[4]

Furthermore, the idea that the economic crisis consists solely of heightened unemployment and depressed wages, and that a combination of job creation and social spending can resolve it, is based on the idea that crises are rooted in "underconsumption" rather than "overproduction." This Keynesian idea rests on a flawed belief in a perfected, near-steady state capitalism, which can be achieved by the correct level of social spending, properly administered, to keep consumption levels high enough to keep the circuits of capital flowing at an optimal rate. However, crises are crises of overproduction—capital is constantly driven to increase the amount of constant capital (machinery, facilities, and so forth) involved in the production process, to decrease socially necessary labor time, and to increase the amount of absolute value. However, only labor can create surplus value, the difference between the value of commodities produced and the wages and constant capital consumed in their production. As the portion of constant capital in this process rises, the portion of surplus value falls. This leads to a falling rate of profit. When the rate of profit falls too low, capitalist investment slows, leading to a crisis.[5]

Neither social spending nor job creation can resolve this; only the devalorization of large amounts of capital can, either by its devaluation or destruction. Thus far, the crisis has not managed to do this. If we are not interested in defending capitalism, and also understand that social programs are not a brake on the intensified rate of the immiseration of the working class caused by the crisis, why do we defend social programs when they are attacked? The answer is simple: they, in very limited ways, help serve the immediate needs of the working class, and also serve as a springboard for larger struggles, which may have revolutionary potential, both in our analysis of them and in ways that struggles to expand the social wage can be organized.

We know that the burden of reproductive labor falls disproportionately on women, and that this is due to the patriarchal relations built into the very structure of capitalism. The struggle around the social wage has reshaped these patriarchal relations, and has also formed part of the impetus for working-class women seeing themselves as a set of castes within the class, further divided by race, sexuality, and so forth. The reshaping of reproductive labor from something done primarily in the nuclear family, into an activity performed in a combination of public and private institutions, networks of friends, and so forth, has contributed to its social character.

The attacks on schools, libraries, assistance programs, etc. in the name of austerity threatens to re-isolate more and more reproductive labor in the home, obscuring its social character, and also threatening its ability to be performed, as the family has been restructured by both earlier victories against patriarchal social relations and the demands of capital. While we certainly do not want to return to the days when divorce was difficult or impossible, or to greater reliance on a male wage earner, we must be worried about what austerity will do to further weaken our real ability to control our own lives and relationships, as there are less and less resources to do more and more work in the home. This reason alone would be enough to justify a defensive battle around the targets of austerity. Within defensive battles, there is potential to go on the offensive, and within every crisis, there are opportunities. And the current crisis of capital certainly means a crisis of reproduction for the working class.

THE CRISIS OF REPRODUCTION

"Finally, the law which always holds the relative surplus production or industrial reserve army in equilibrium with the extent and energy of accumulation rivets the worker to capital more firmly than the wedges of Hephaestus held Prometheus to the rock. It makes an accumulation of misery a necessary condition, corresponding to the accumulation of wealth. Accumulation of wealth at one pole is, therefore, at the same time accumulation of misery, the torment of labour, slavery, ignorance, brutalization and moral degradation at the opposite pole, i.e. on the side of the class that produces its own product as capital."
—Karl Marx[6]

THE NORM IN capitalist society, of course, has been for the reproduction of the proletariat to be in a constant state of precarity. Struggles during the postwar boom led to a situation, for certain strata of the working class in the overdeveloped world, in which the immediate means of survival were not in imminent question. However, even during this time period, this was not true for working-class communities of color, single mothers, queers, and other marginalized groups. We are now seeing the precariousness experienced by these groups in the overdeveloped world, and by the working class in the underdeveloped and developing world, re-extended to the uppermost strata of the working class in the overdeveloped world. It is a mistake to focus only on the reintroduced precariousness of certain sections of the class in the overdeveloped world (e.g. the "graduate with no future"); such a focus obscures the continuation of the precariousness of the rest of the class, and erases all the work, waged and unwaged, that does not fit the mold of the knowledge worker.[7]

In the overdeveloped world, this shift is leading to an expansion of struggle. In the US, the children of parents whose lives were marked by a lessening of precarity see themselves, despite their having racked up massive amounts of debt to get high levels of education, in increasingly precarious waged work. Sections of the class that have always led a precarious existence see the institutions and programs that provided partial assistance to their reproduction gutted and destroyed before their eyes, as they are simultaneously further criminalized and faced with an ever-expanding prison industrial complex. In the EU, we are seeing the destruction of social democracy, as the capitalist agenda destroys post-World War II social programs. In the the states of the EU's periphery, we are seeing the direct seizing of the resources of the working class to bail out banks and the states themselves, in a deepening quasi-imperialism.

In the underdeveloped/developing world, we are seeing environmental destruction on an ecocidal scale and the massive dispossession of the peasantry from the land, leading to the rapid growth of cities of slums, while some persist as landless agricultural laborers. In China, rapid proletarianization and construction of massive factories has fueled China's rise to the status of an world power, while creating a large industrial proletariat laboring in conditions reminiscent of the US or England during the nineteenth century. In Africa, we are seeing a new wave of imperialism leading to massive corporate land and resource grabs, fueling war and pandemic disease. In Latin America, there is both the continuation of US imperialism and strengthened movements against it. Simultaneously, indigenous people's land and ways of life are threatened by the projects of both Latin American states and multinational corporations. This massive imperialist grab for land and resources forms a set of "new enclosures," a pattern of capital accumulation that first emerged in England during the sixteenth century, during the transition from feudalism to capitalism.[8]

All over the underdeveloped/developing world, women are forced to leave their homes and families to work in the new factories, or to emigrate to the overdeveloped world, hoping to be able to secure sufficient waged work to send money home. Once there, they often labor as domestic workers or do the most physically demanding and poorly compensated work in healthcare. More and more, the reproductive labor needed by capital in the overdeveloped world has been globalized, relying on the imperialist conditions that force women of the underdeveloped world to emigrate, facing racist immigration policies and shattering the web of caregiving in their former homes.

All of these processes, while different, share an essential commonality, resulting from a continuous, global process: primitive accumulation. Primitive accumulation, in its initial stages, not only dispossessed the European peasantry from the land and enclosed the common land that was used for sustenance, but also restructured gender relations, creating the wage and excluding women from it, atomizing reproductive labor into individual homes. In addition, sexuality became heavily regulated, to guarantee the biological reproduction of the working class. It also included the colonization of the Western Hemisphere and Africa, and relied on genocide and enslavement on a massive scale. Capitalism was born via fire, disease, the sword, and the gun. Its methods have not changed.[9]

Ongoing primitive accumulation is not an externality to capitalism that can be reformed away. It is a process through which capitalism both expands and stabilizes itself during crisis, by expanding its markets, proletarianizing more people, creating and maintaining the gradients of development necessary for its function, and adding new pools of capital accumulation. Just as much as capital accumulates surplus value for itself, it also accumulates misery for the dispossessed of the world. The global intensification of this process first precipitated by neoliberal restructuring and changes in the global flows of capital, and further intensified by the current crisis, highlights capital's continual need to destroy our communities and jeopardize our ability to survive.

Capital depends on turning functional, collectively sustaining communities into collections of atomized individuals whose only choice to survive is to take part in the market, selling labor power or being dependent on others whose labor power they reproduce, and purchasing commodities, the products of labor. It has always accomplished these tasks through a great deal of violence, which it has variously naturalized or invisibilized. Often, this violence, integral to capital, has the surface appearance of being external to it. While it is important to note the current character and extent of this violence, and root its present form in the circumstances of the crisis and the particular ideology and policies of neoliberalism, we must also clearly put forward the analysis that structural violence is a fundamental feature of capitalism, essential to its functioning. It cannot be reformed away, either by returning to a prior permutation of capitalism or attempting to find a "friendlier" one.

The crisis has augmented processes already occurring, and those processes jeopardize the very reproduction of human beings and the possibility of lives worth living. The wholesale environmental destruction of capitalism, the commodification of nature through the patenting of the genetic code of living species, the divvying up of every bit of the world into privately exploited resources, is intimately linked with the crisis of our reproduction as human beings. Capitalism's logic has always seen reproductive labor and women—who are the primary performers of it in the capitalist division of labor—as natural resources to control and exploit. [10]

We should, however, while remaining conscious of how the crisis allows for an intensified attack on all forms of collective living, any possibility of living in harmony with ourselves and the earth, and the possibilities of our very survival as a human community, a species, and a planet, remember that the crisis was not intentionally created by capitalists. They are like the sorcerer that Marx referred to; they have, in fact, never been able to control the tremendous forces of full-fledged capitalism. The crisis presents both an opportunity for capital and a rapid increase of our immiseration by capital, and an opportunity for us to strike at capital while it is in jeopardy. Ultimately, the outcome of the crisis will be determined in struggle; capital does not control its crises, but neither will it collapse on its own.

REPRODUCTIVE LABOR: BLURRING THE LINE BETWEEN WAGED AND UNWAGED

"As Thatcher famously said, "Economics are the method, the object is to change the soul." One of the aims of neo-liberalism is to produce a new kind of social subject—one that is coldly rational and entrepreneurial; one that is totally responsible for their own care, education and reproduction and is morally judged on how they put their "freedom" to work. The processes of privatisation and marketisation that feature so heavily in

neo-liberal "reforms" are, as well as being part of a process of
accumulation by dispossession, a means to that end."
—Camille Barbagallo and Nicholas Beuret[11]

WHILE ALL FORMS of capitalism rely on social subjects who are atomized and reliant on capitalism for their survival, neoliberalism has a
particular form of social subject in mind, and its own particular way
that this social subject interacts and secures its continued reproduction. One lens through which the crisis can be seen is as an opportunity by capital to hasten the transition toward a more neoliberal social
subject, as well as bringing the contradictions of that social subject
into sharp relief. The aforementioned acceleration of austerity, allowing the capitalist class to hasten its program of attacks on the social
wage and on the web of reproduction, has hastened the development
of this social subject, while simultaneously making its survival less and
less likely. This contradiction at the heart of the neoliberal project is a
specification of the larger internal contradictions of capitalism.

Before examining the neoliberal subject and investigating what it
implies for the neoliberal view of reproductive labor, it is useful to
examine how women's participation in waged labor has changed over
the last several decades, and how that should reshape our demands
around the social wage. Participation in waged labor by women went
from 34 percent in 1950 to 60 percent in 2000, a year when women
made up 47 percent of the total number of waged laborers. The projected figure for 2010 included further growth of the participation
of women in waged labor, reaching 62 percent. The US Bureau of
Labor Statistics identifies the women's rights movement leading to the
option for women to remain single, increasing age of first marriage,
longer and more extensive education by women, delayed childbirth
and a lowered birth rate, and an increase in the divorce rate as contributing factors.[12]

However, based on US Census Bureau data, the ratio of female-to-
male earnings only climbed from 0.61 (sixty-one cents on the dollar)
in 1960 to 0.77 (seventy-seven cents on the dollar) in 2009. This is
caused both by continued gender disparities in various employment
sectors, where female-dominated sectors continue to be devalued,
and continuing unequal remuneration within professions, disparities
which vary by field. For instance, among personal care and service
workers, a sector marked by overall low wages, male and female wages

are equal. Among registered nurses, women earn ninety cents on the dollar as compared to men; among physicians and surgeons, they earn sixty-four. Such disparities cannot be accounted for by hours worked in wage labor alone. In 2010, men worked in waged labor an average of just under forty-two hours a week, while women worked an average of around thirty-seven. In addition, the wage ratio statistics given are for full-time wage workers, whom the Census Bureau defines as those who work in waged labor at least thirty-five hours a week, for at least fifty weeks of the year. A greater portion of women being "part-time" waged workers would not exaggerate wage disparities presumed to come from differences in hourly compensation in these statistics.[13]

Prior to the restructuring of the workforce that occurred in response to the women's movement, the denial of access of many women to the wage was one of the primary means to coerce women into supplying the reproductive labor necessary to maintain and reproduce the labor force. But the recomposition of waged labor and the drop in the real purchasing power of wages has changed the relationship of women to the wage. The "ideal" family was formerly one where a wage-earning man funds the household containing a woman whose work in the household— maintaining it, providing for the emotional, physical, and sexual needs of her husband, and raising the children—was utterly devalued. Now we see the image of a household of two wage-earners, purchasing as much of their reproduction—whether in the form of physical commodities or reproductive labor—as possible, and the uneven division of the labor that remains in the home is itself invisibilized. It should also be noted, once again, that the most demanding forms of this reproductive labor—housecleaning, childcare, nannying, preschool—fall to women, who are typically paid very low wages.

The factors that the Bureau of Labor Statistics identifies as increasing the waged workforce participation of women can be seen as the result of decades of a massive project of refusal of work by women. The denial or delay of marriage, increased rates of divorce, and later and less frequent childbearing are all ways that women have refused reproductive labor that is foundational to capitalism and which capital tells them is their natural role. The state has a vested interest in maintaining the birth rate; maintaining both a sufficiently large labor force and a large reserve army of labor is necessary for economic growth. Therefore, the hegemonic culture—that of capital and the capitalist class—continually tells us that being wives and mothers and finding ways to center the home, while also performing waged labor, is both personally fulfilling and toward the "common good." However, throughout the overdeveloped world, where birth rates have plummeted, women have seen through the "common good" and seen that it is what is good for economic growth, good for capital, and not what is good for women. In the overdeveloped world, women have access to the reproductive and contraceptive technologies necessary to control biological reproduction. Women have strongly demanded both control over their own labor and the process of biological reproduction, seeing control over the reproductive processes of women's bodies as a fundamental part of control over our labor and our lives.

However, as Dalla Costa states, "We could never have had children and then refused to take care of them."[14] The refusal of reproductive labor is a limited one, due to the dual nature outlined in the introduction to this essay. We wish to continue to reproduce ourselves as living, loving human beings, while denying capital our labor power and refusing to structure our reproduction via capitalist logic. For the first to occur while the second is resisted, a more positive project that is not just a simple refusal of work, as central as that may be, is necessary.[15] An earlier campaign, initiated prior to capitalism having restructured the waged labor force so completely, was Wages for Housework. While much of that movement's analysis still rings true, new sets of positive demands, which will be discussed in this article's conclusion, are necessary.

The neoliberal restructuring of reproduction takes advantage of this recomposition of the labor force. By this extension of the wage, it is possible for capital to characterize all aspects of reproduction as individual responsibility. This, along with "tough economic times," is justification for the privatization and cutting of all means of social support. While capitalism has always attempted to portray wage labor as free choice, hiding the structural violence and economics that determine that choice, this appearance of free choice is further extended into all spheres of life. Women supposedly freely choose whether to have a partner or not, to get married, when and how many children to have, what waged labor to work, and what resources to access for their children, and their moral character is judged on the basis of these choices.

Of course, women's wages are still much less than those of men, marriage is still coerced through both financial and social factors, the access of working-class women to reproductive technologies is constantly under siege, what wage labor can be accessed is still strongly affected by patriarchal relations incorporated into capitalism, and what women can provide for their children is heavily determined by financial factors. Wages for Housework emerged during an earlier social and ideological structuring of the labor force—while many women did work for a wage, many more did not than today, and more importantly, the ideal was the single income household, where the women did not participate in waged labor, and her unwaged work in the home was viewed as not really work.[16] While women still work a double shift, the changing nature of the patriarchal relations of the wage has gone from one where the woman is almost entirely dependent on the man's wage, to one where, to a great extent, single income families are no longer possible without the utter precariousness of poverty.

They are the most impossible for single mothers; the official poverty rate for people in single mother families is 42.2 percent.[17] Women are faced with a double bind—be dependent on a man, while working long hours both in waged labor and at home, or be independent of men, and be condemned with their children to poverty, with ever-diminishing social safety net programs and continually less-funded schools for children. And, of course, when we are poor, society will tell us that it is our fault. If we do "choose" to be with men, and we experience domestic violence and sexual assault, we can still expect that violence to not be taken nearly as seriously as other forms of violence. While there have been many laws passed around domestic and sexual violence, the state still withholds a great deal of its repressive apparatus against the perpetrators of this violence. When it does use its repressive apparatus, it often has far more to do with maintaining racial hierarchies than any true concern for women.[18] While we seek a solution to the problem of domestic and sexual violence outside of the state form, it is important to note the actual nature of the state's role in its perpetuation.

Wages for Housework's analysis is still particularly valuable. It posits that reproductive labor follows the logic of capitalism; it is capitalism's necessary foundation, and most of it is performed by women, a role that is not "natural," but rather structured by a form of patriarchal relations particular to capitalism. However, framing our demand for all work to be recognized, and attacking the logic of capitalism that declares certain work to not be real work, by insisting that wages are paid to those who do housework, is no longer as useful. With a far greater participation of women in waged labor, the question is no longer achieving the wage, but, rather, guaranteeing ourselves all the necessities of reproduction.

By fragmenting the labor of reproduction, and increasingly commodifying it, capital has blurred the distinctions between waged and unwaged reproductive labor. Increasingly, the lines between our unwaged and waged work are not clear. In healthcare, we are seeing the deployment of more and more advanced technologies both to deskill the healthcare workforce, and to have more and more healthcare occur in the home. Cuts in educational funding are leading to more and more demands on parents to both provide supplies for their children and to put more and more work into their children's education, which is increasingly more about metrics based on standardized tests than useful knowledge.

If we want the autonomy to form new collective forms of reproductive labor that are based on our needs, we must structure our movement not toward what has already been achieved, in a partial way, but rather demand that all will have full access to the necessities of life. This could mean expanding the demand for Wages for Housework into a guaranteed income for all, no matter what activities they may engage in. This is a demand that has been raised by autonomists for decades.[19] We can also, when we are expected to perform work to maintain institutions that are failing us, demand that we have true control over those institutions, and run them by our communities, for our communities' needs.

SELF-REPRODUCING MOVEMENTS, CENTERING REPRODUCTION, AND TOWARD A NEW REPRODUCTIVE COMMONS

"One crucial reason for creating collective forms of living is that the reproduction of human beings is the most labor-intensive work on earth, and to a large extent it is work that is irreducible to mechanization.... Shared responsibility and cooperative work, not given at the cost of the health of the providers, are the only guarantees of proper care."
—Silvia Federici[20]

If we hope to center reproduction, or even have movements not be condemned to perpetually peak and then dissolve away as struggle ebbs, continually losing the most experienced participants, we must, to use Barbagallo and Federici's term, create "self-reproducing movements."[21] These are movements that do not separate their political work from the activities that are necessary to reproduce our daily lives; rather than simply trying to provide some limited sort of services to enable participation, such as childcare at events, or occasional healthcare workshops, we must center the work of reproduction in our movements. Our movement must be capable of sustaining and supporting us, not just so that there is more diverse participation, but so that we are not forced to choose between the movement and our lives. Creating new, collective forms of reproduction, in how we care for each other, raise our children, and sustain ourselves is necessary. This will involve creating new, communal forms of life, where we will have an expansive definition of community, one that focuses on our collective responsibility and intertwined web of cooperation amongst ourselves, our planet, and all the other life on it. When collective forms of living remain isolated and exclusive, they present no challenge to capitalist logic or domination, and in fact remain externally governed by it. When they take place in the heart of our daily lives, and seek to expand their reach, they are brought into conflict with capital. It is only through these new forms of living that a new commons can be realized, one founded on cooperation rather than competition.

We need to create collective forms of child rearing, where we socialize the massive amount of work involved and provide for a place where children can live and grow into the people they, not capital, desire themselves to be. Providing collective places where this work is socialized also will prevent us from having to choose between potentially unwanted intimate relationships or poverty, or feeling that we can never have children while living the lives we want to live or remaining part of the movement.

Similarly, healthcare workers, the elderly, those with chronic illnesses and disabilities, and our families and communities as a whole—since we all at some point need healthcare—need to come together to collectively find a new form of healthcare and wellness. We must create spaces that we control as communities, where we focus on collective and egalitarian ways of maintaining our health and healthcare delivery. These new, true community clinics, will not only be places of care that focus on true wellness and happiness rather than the cost-efficient maintenance of the labor force, but also places where we spread the specialized knowledge and skills of healthcare amongst all of us. The historical experience of the Jane Collective in Chicago in the pre-Roe v. Wade era can provide a starting point that can be expanded beyond abortion and reproductive health.

When we struggle against cuts in social programs, education, and social institutions, we must be cautious of being reduced to providing volunteer labor for capitalism. If we occupy our schools, we must be careful to avoid a situation where we keep them running only by providing unwaged labor, while gaining no control. In addition to resisting cuts, we should attempt to take control of these social institutions, running them according to our needs, and not the state's. Concurrently, we should raise the demand for a true social wage—where all have a guaranteed income to secure all the necessities of life, just for existing. This is the only way, with the reconstruction of the labor force, to put forward a demand to be compensated for all the unwaged work we do for capital's needs.

As I, and others, have noted in the past, the queer movement is both an integral part of our struggle for a postcapitalist world and also suffers from co-option by capitalism and, at times, a self-isolating, inward focus.[22] The desire to love who and how we choose has been subverted into a reactionary campaign for same-sex marriage which, instead of providing a greater variety of ways to structure our lives and relationships, seeks to discipline queer people's relationships to be more fully incorporated into the patriarchal logic of reproductive labor within capitalism. Rather than constructing the desire for acceptance of queer relationships in opposition to our desire to not face the financial necessity of marriage, both struggle around the social wage and collective forms of reproductive labor support all sorts of relationships, not just those that serve the purposes of capital.

The trans and genderqueer movement has shown us that capitalism can be made to allow us some limited means to actualize ourselves and determine our gender, but only within binary options. Capitalism harshly polices the borders of gender, particularly those in groups already multiply targeted by structural violence—namely trans women of color. We have seen that it tries to renormalize trans bodies, coercing trans people's choices of medical options to force them to be embodied in "acceptable" ways for recognition, regardless of their own desires, while simultaneously providing very limited access to those medical options. The experiences of genderqueer people has shown us that we can identify ourselves outside the binary as much as we want—but our workplaces, communities, families, and the state will always put us in one position in the gender binary or the other. In addition to struggling alongside trans people against the structural violence they face in the workplace, society, from the state, and the prison industrial complex, we can also see our support for the gender self-determination of trans and genderqueer people to be an integral part of our struggle against the gendered division of labor.

To struggle against the racialized and imperialist relationships among women and within reproductive labor, we must recognize the racial stratification in waged reproductive labor, and form workplace organizations that do not accept the divisions in organizing imposed by the trade unions, which separate us by job role and educational attainment. Rather, we must all organize together with equal voices, finding ways to center the struggles of those most targeted and viewed as most expendable in the workplace, and refuse a differential valuation between mental and physical reproductive labor. For example, in the nursing field, RNs have much higher wages, more job stability, and perform a role that requires a greater degree of formal education compared to technicians and nurses' aides. The trade unions divvy up the different job roles amongst themselves, sometimes working together, sometimes infighting over the boundaries. Either situation keeps the struggle contained. Rather, we should all struggle together, collectively determining our action, and working together to confront the divisions caused by race, gender, and immigration status within the workplace. These organizations can then join up with the community, to expand the struggle, and address the needs of healthcare workers, patients, and the entire community.

We cannot wait for the revolution to come, and hope that it will do away with the gendered and racialized division of labor. Nor can we hope that a sole focus on productive labor in the workplace will lead to a future society where reproductive labor will be structured differently. To continue to reproduce ourselves as living, loving human beings who live in communities structured around cooperation rather than competition, we must make our movement one that both prefigures the new commons and actively expands new social relations in direct conflict with the logic of capital. If we do not center reproductive labor in our struggle, we have no hope either for a sustainable movement or a postcapitalist future. When we do, we open the path toward a future where we contribute according to our abilities and receive according to our needs. We have nothing to lose but our isolation, alienation, and devaluation, and we have a new community waiting to be born. Let us help its birth!

ENDNOTES

1   Karl Marx and Frederick Engels, "Manifesto of the Communist Party," in *Economic and Philosophic Manuscripts of 1844 and the Communist Manifesto* (Amherst, New York: Prometheus Books, 1988), 203–243.

2   Alice O'Connor, "The Recession's Hit Women Hard, but the Myth of the 'Mancession' Won't Die," AlterNet website, October 30th, 2010, http://www.alternet.org/story/148681/the_recession%27s_hit_women_hard%2C_but_the_myth_of_the_%22mancession%22_won%27t_die?page=0%2C0 (accessed March 18, 2013).

3   For an excellent discussion of this dialectical unity, see Eve Mitchell, "For Herself, and Therefore, for the Class: Toward a Methodological Feminism," Unity and Struggle website, March 11th, 2013, http://gatheringforces.org/2013/03/11/for-herself/ (accessed March 18, 2013).

4   For a superb introduction to this idea of capitalist relations being a totality that have incorporated and altered prior power relations, see Barbara Ehrenreich, "What is Socialist Feminism?" Marxists Internet Archive, http://marxists.org/subject/women/authors/ehrenreich-barbara/socialist-feminism.htm (accessed March 18, 2013).

5   For a far more detailed discussion of the tendency of the rate of profit to fall and its relation to the current crisis of capitalism, see Michael Roberts, "The Rate of Profit is Key," Michael Roberts Blog, July 26th, 2012, http://thenextrecession.wordpress.com/2012/07/26/the-rate-of-profit-is-key/ (accessed March 18, 2013).

6   Karl Marx, *Capital, Vol. 1* (London: Penguin Books, 1990), 799.

7   Silvia Federici, "Precarious Labor: A Feminist Viewpoint," In the Middle of a Whirlwind, http://inthemiddleofthewhirlwind.wordpress.com/precarious-labor-a-feminist-viewpoint/ (accessed March 19, 2013).

8   Midnight Notes Collective and Friends, "Promissory Notes: From Crisis to Commons," Midnight Notes, http://www.midnightnotes.org/Promissory%20Notes.pdf (accessed March 19, 2013).

9   For an in-depth discussion of primitive accumulation, and in particular its effect on women, see Silvia Federici, *Caliban and the Witch: Women, The Body, and Primitive Accumulation* (New York: Autonomedia, 2004).

10   Mariarosa Dalla Costa, "Capitalism and Reproduction," http://libcom.org/library/capitalism-reproduction-mariarosa-dalla-costa (accessed March 28, 2013).

11   Camille Barbagallo and Nicholas Beuret, "Starting From The Social Wage," The Commoner N. 15—Winter 2012—Care Work and the Commons, http://www.commoner.org.uk/wp-content/uploads/2012/02/07-barbagallo-beuret.pdf (accessed March 28, 2013).

12   Mitra Toossi, "A Century of Change: the U.S. Labor Force, 1950–2050," Monthly Labor Review, May 2012, http://www.bls.gov/opub/mlr/2002/05/art2full.pdf (accessed March 28, 2013).

13   "Women in the Workforce," United States Census Bureau, http://www.census.gov/newsroom/pdf/women_workforce_slides.pdf (accessed March 29, 2013).

14   Mariarosa Dalla Costa, "Reproduction and Emigration," 1974, reprinted in "Care Work and the Commons," *The Commoner*, n.15, Winter 2012, http://occupytampa.org/files/commons/commoner_issue-15.pdf (accessed March 28, 2013).

15   Mariarosa Dalla Costa, "Women's Autonomy & Renumeration of Care Work," "Care Work and the Commons," *The Commoner*, n.15, Winter 2012, http://www.commoner.org.uk/wp-content/uploads/2012/02/09-dallacosta.pdf (accessed March 28, 2013).

16   Selma James, "Wageless of the World," in *Sex, Race and Class: The Perspective of Winning* (Oakland: PM Press, 2012), 102–109.

17   Legal Momentum: The Women's Legal Defense and Education Fund, "Single Mother Poverty in the United States in 2010," National Center on Domestic and Sexual Violence, http://www.ncdsv.org/images/LM_SingleMotherPovertyInTheUS-2010_9-15-2011.pdf (accessed March 29, 2013).

18 For a discussion of the role of the state's withholding of its repressive apparatus in matters of domestic and sexual violence as a way of maintaining the position of women and patriarchal social relations within capitalism, see Giovanna Franca Dalla Costa, *The Work of Love: Unpaid Housework, Poverty and Sexual Violence at the Dawn of the 21st Century* (Brooklyn: Autonomedia, 2008). Also particularly refer to Mariarosa Dalla Costa's new introduction, discussing how the state responded to struggles around achieving formal legal recognition of the domestic and sexual violence faced by women.

19 Some history of this demand:

> The notion of a guaranteed income has long held an honoured place within Italian autonomist discourse. In the years immediately following the worker and student unrest of 1968 and 1969, the "social" or "political" wage was a central theme for Potere Operaio, a workerist group which would later supply many of autonomia's most prominent figures. Central to Potere Operaio's understanding of modern class conflict was the notion of a struggle within the immediate process of production which, in challenging the hierarchies of skill and command to be found there, sought to uncouple income from productivity.

And:

> A "social" wage was also demanded for those outside the traditional realms of paid work. Since, for Potere Operaio, capitalist society was now a social factory subject to the dictates of accumulation, a "political" wage was necessary for all those with nothing to sell but their ability to work... Apart from students and the unemployed, women as houseworkers were also seen as prime candidates for a guaranteed wage...

Steve Wright, "Confronting the Crisis of 'Fordism': Italian Debates Around Social Transition," Libcom.org, http://libcom.org/library/confronting-crisis-fordism-steve-wright (accessed March 30, 2013).

20 Silvia Federici, *Revolution at Point Zero: Housework, Reproduction, and Feminist Struggle*, (Oakland: PM Press, 2012), 138–148.

21 Camille Barbagallo and Silvia Federici, "Introduction," "Care Work and the Commons," *The Commoner*, n.15, Winter 2012, http://www.commoner.org.uk/wp-content/uploads/2012/02/01-introduction.pdf (accessed March 28, 2013). See also Silvia Federici, "On Elder Care Work and the Limits of Marxism," in *Revolution at Point Zero: Housework, Reproduction, and Feminist Struggle* (Oakland: PM Press, 2012), 115–125.

22 See Gayge Operaista, "Radical Queers and Class Struggle: A Match to be Made," in *Queering Anarchism: Addressing and Undressing Power and Desire*, (ed.) C.B. Daring, J. Rogue, Deric Shannon, and Abbey Volcano (Oakland: AK Press, 2012), 115–128. Also, Gayge Operaista, "A Critique of Anti-Assimilation," http://libcom.org/library/critique-anti-assimilation-gayge-operaista (accessed March 29, 2013); and JOMO, "Queer Liberation is Class Struggle" (Edmonton: Thoughtcrime Ink, 2010) http://gatheringforces.org/2010/01/08/queer-liberation-is-class-struggle/ (accessed March 29, 2013).

INTERVIEW WITH MIGUEL ÁNGEL FERNÁNDEZ ON THE CNT AND CRISIS IN SPAIN

INTERVIEW AND TRANSLATION BY DUSTIN SHANNON, SPRING 2013

Dustin Shannon: *Hello, Miguel Ángel. Thank you for giving this interview. Please, tell us a bit about the CNT. What are the differences between the CNT and other workers' organizations in Spain?*

Miguel Ángel Fernández: Founded in 1910, in Barcelona, from the union of workers' societies unconnected to social democratic currents, the CNT continues to follow anarcho-syndicalist principles, and is the heir in Spain to the spirit of the First International.

The CNT is today the only syndicate in Spain that is totally independent, in that it does not participate in the system of union elections and is completely against subsidies and the existence of union reps.

Union elections and works councils benefit companies and the administration, which, in the end, are those who finance them. With union elections, whose origin is found in the Francoist vertical syndicate, companies and administrations obtain interlocutors so as not to have to deal directly with workers. These legal interlocutors keep workers contained, submissive, and immobilized because they are the first people interested in maintaining their position, and they directly depend on subsidies and works councils.

Shannon: *What have been your different roles in the CNT? How do you currently participate in the organization?*

Fernández: Since joining around 1990, I have occupied different positions in the CNT. Due to my professional experience with the media, my positions have almost always been related to the area of social communication.

I was the director of the newspaper *CNT* from 2003 to 2007. Perhaps the most significant position I have held has been that of Press, Communication, and Propaganda Secretary, on the confederate level, between 2009 and 2012. Currently, I am the Organization Secretary of the Syndicate of Graphic Arts, Communication, and Spectacles of Madrid, with which I have been affiliated since comrades and I reconstituted it in 1998. (Before that, I was affiliated, first and as a student, with the Organization of Teaching and later in the Organization of Various Trades, both also of the Local Federation of Madrid.)

Shannon: *This book contains comments from people all over the world involved in workers' struggles against the policies of austerity enacted after the collapse of markets in 2008. Could you tell us a bit about what forms austerity has taken in Spain and how they have affected workers?*

Fernández: The truth is that since the transition in Spain [the shift from the Francoist dictatorship to the current constitutional monarchy, which took place from 1975 to 1978] and especially since the PSOE [Partido Socialista Obrero Español, or Spanish Socialist Workers' Party] came to power, workers' demands and struggles, which had entered a critical phase in the last years of Francoism, have suffered a progressive slowing, if not demobilization. This moment has logically been taken advantage of by capital, which has always been supported by the different governments in office, to enact a series of measures that have led to a constant loss of rights.

If this loss of rights has been, as I said, a constant for decades, it has become more noticeable with the appearance of the "crisis," when the workers' movement already had been severely weakened, and with the CCOO [Comisiones Obreras, or Workers' Commissions] and UGT

[Unión General de Trabajadores, or General Union of Workers] acting for decades as fire extinguishers.

So, we find ourselves facing one of the biggest offensives against the rights and living conditions of the working class. For years, they have put us in a situation of permanent crisis that serves to justify many types of aggression and elimination of rights. The ranks of the unemployed have swollen to include six million workers, and continue to grow as a result of the purposeful policies of work destruction carried out by the government at the dictates of owners and international financial institutions. Unemployment functions as permanent coercion to facilitate workers' folding in the face of wage and rights cuts that are imposed by owners.

An illegitimate debt, and one that we have not incurred willingly, is shaken in our faces by the European institutions to justify cuts and the dismantling of the most basic of public services. This debt constitutes a mechanism of permanent blackmail against the weakest sectors of society.

The political and economic system that has dominated us for the last thirty years is sinking in bankruptcy, demonstrating in an increasingly quotidian way its fierce class character and the conflict between policies that are more and more aggressive towards the popular sectors of society. These policies are practiced similarly by the different political parties when they form governments. Also, the "democratic" discourse that serves to justify these policies is similar from all the political parties.

Corruption, which forms an intrinsic part of this system, is spreading among the principal institutions. It is increasingly evident because of the difficulty in continuing the speculative dynamic that has greased the system for years and pleased distinct power groups, and because of an inability to generate new speculative bubbles that can be dangled like carrots in front of the working class so that we continue supporting the system. The government's intention is for this dark panorama to enmesh the popular sectors in desperation, fear, and paralysis—the staunchest allies of power.

Facing this situation, the CNT, sometimes alone and sometimes with other alternative or "combative" syndicates, is trying to organize an active resistance and to affirm the necessity to organize another way, fashioning tools to struggle and build a strong workers' movement from the unity of workers—a movement that is powerful, effective, and forceful in defense of the rights of the working classes, and that promotes direct action, solidarity, mutual aid, and self-management, on the basis of radical autonomy.

Shannon: *Can you enumerate the principal concrete measures that the governments have taken since the beginning of the crisis that have negatively affected workers?*

Fernández: In June 2010 the PSOE passed new labor reform legislation, in which the following general characteristics stand out:

- Severance pay was reduced and firing was subsidized. New contracts were allowed and the possibility of collective firings were maintained, simply due to poor administration (so that companies are not even required to argue that economic circumstance is to blame) or due to structural change. It is significant that if the company action is deemed incorrect, the collective firing is not declared null and void, but rather only unfair.

- The possibility of dismantling collective bargaining agreements only on the basis of circumstantial evidence has increased. On the other hand, more room for maneuver has been given to the official unions because in those companies in which "unitary representation" does not exist, conflict will be administrated directly by CCOO and UGT.

- Temporary work agencies have been converted into collaborating entities of the unemployment office without specifying the extent of this collaboration. Collective bargaining agreement vetoes of temporary work agencies have been tacitly prohibited. Additionally, temp agencies have entered sectors in which they were formerly prohibited, like the construction sector. These temp agencies are for-profit entities.

Afterward, the government agreed to terms with the principal unions to increase the retirement age to sixty-seven (from sixty-five) and to increase the computational period for pensions to twenty-five years, which has translated to an important decrease in monthly pension payments.

The PP [Partido Popular, or Popular Party], which won the general elections at the end of 2011 with a discourse centered on job creation, carried out new labor reform that tightened the screws even more than the reform that the PSOE had begun:

- A new reduction in severance pay: labor contracts were generalized with indemnities of thirty-three days' payment per year (whereas before they were forty-five days' payment per year) and a maximum of twenty-four monthly payments (the reduction in severance pay also affects ordinary contracts—even those that were signed before the reform in the epoch of the forty-five days). Additionally, firing for objective causes has been made easier and is now generalized.

- Getting sick is now punishable by firing: workers who are out of work on sick leave for two months can be fired with twenty days of indemnity and without the possibility to ask for the inadmissibility of the firing.

- The "dismantling" of collective agreements in "companies in difficulty" has been amplified. Additionally, business owners have the ability not to respect agreements reached during negotiation (a way to achieve greater internal flexibility).

- Employment Regulation Plans (EREs) [plans for mass layoffs] no longer require administrative authorization (they can be authorized merely by a judge and no longer does the employment council of the corresponding autonomous communities [Spain is divided into seventeen autonomous communities] need to authorize them). In this situation, only a judge can protect workers.

On the other hand, and apart from purely work-related aspects, there has been a continuous cut of budgets and personnel in key sectors, like education and healthcare (with the privatization of hospitals and services), the implantation of payment requirements for prescription pharmaceuticals, and so on.

The result of all this has been the impoverishing of society, a dismantling of the welfare state, and an increase in inequalities (the gap between the rich and the poor, with immense growth in the ranks of the latter group since the beginning of the crisis).

As far as unemployment goes, the policies implemented, just as the CNT foresaw and decried, not only have not done away with joblessness, but rather have contributed to breaking all previous records, so that today Spain has over six million people unemployed for the first time. This is 27.16 percent of the active population and has reached dramatic numbers (57.2 percent) among youths, who now see the only escape in fleeing abroad.

Shannon: *Can you enumerate the concrete reactions to each of the measures of the different Spanish unions, highlighting the differences in the reactions among the UGT, CCOO, and the CNT?*

Fernández: It can be said that the tandem of the CCOO and the UGT has turned into an apparatus dependent on the state itself, which has utilized them as "interlocutors" to sign everything that is placed in front of them upon their desks (for example, the increase in retirement age) until they have had no choice—due to a generalized discredit [among Spanish workers]—to call three general strikes (one against Zapatero and two against Rajoy). Yet they have not discussed alternatives, but rather have merely tried to save face. Also, paradoxically, there have been cases in which both unions have carried out layoffs among their own functionaries, in which they have applied measures from the same labor reforms that they had denounced when the various governments had implemented them.

The CNT has involved itself in the deepening, radicalization, and extension of struggles, with the intention of giving them greater content of demands. But it must be conceded that due to its limited size and influence, the CNT has obtained unsatisfactory results, though at least spaces for struggle have been opened that would have been unthinkable a few years ago.

Similarly, the creation of a combative syndical front has been promoted with other alternative and radical union organizations, which have been translated into various campaigns of struggle at the statewide level, but which have had unequal results in the different territories.

In parallel to strictly labor-related issues, the CNT has continued to explore more deeply one of the agreements of its last Congress—that of empowering the alternative economy and self-management as immediate measures to address the crisis. With this objective in mind, a conference was held in December of 2011, centered on the alternative economy, in which a potpourri of experiences and analyses focused on the strengthening of training, learning, and collective relationships were touched upon in this area—that of the self-managed economy. This is a field in which networked relationships and mutual support strengthen the viability and permanence of projects, as well as the progressive construction of a real alternative that allows us to move toward the rupture of imposed capitalist economic relations (production, distribution, and consumption) to widen and amplify their impact and participation on the premises of collectivism, self-management, and the anarcho-syndicalist and libertarian proposal.

Shannon: *How have the different governments reacted to these diverse forms of workers' demands? Have there been significant differences between the reactions of the government of the PSOE and the government of the PP?*

Fernández: It can be said that the differences have not been especially significant. The PSOE, now in opposition, has returned to its classic social democratic discourse, though when it was in power, it opened the way for the policies that the PP is now carrying out.

What is clear is that, up until now, the governments of the PP and the PSOE, obligated by external pressure from the EU, have continued to be inflexible in their dynamic of labor and social cuts. In fact, the confluence of both parties made constitutional reform possible in only two weeks without it being put to referendum (with the justification of limiting the state deficit). To give you an idea of the importance of this fact, it must be highlighted that the topic of constitutional change has been especially taboo since the transition.

Shannon: *Could you summarize the emergence of the Indignado movement in Spain?*

Fernández: Although there had already been sectoral mobilizations against unemployment and cuts, by students and so on, it could be said that the origin of said movement began on May 15, 2011, with the convocation by the platform *¡Democracia Real YA!* and other collectives of protests in fifty-eight Spanish cities. These protests gave voice to a wide and heterogeneous array of political, social, and economic demands. The demands centered on the desire of the participants for profound changes in the existing democratic and economic model. It is for this reason that afterward the press referred to the movement as the "15M" or "*Indignados*" (and also as the "Spanish Revolution" in social networks).

They are a series of normally peaceful citizens' mobilizations, spontaneous in origin and arising in great part from social networks that initially obtained the support of more than two hundred small associations.

Shannon: *What have been their most important achievements? What have been their weaknesses?*

Fernández: It could be said that spontaneity and lack of organization are relative weaknesses (though they were a positive aspect at first) that have led to a loss of energy after two years.

On the other hand, the heterogeneity of the movement (although sociologically it could be considered leftist in majority—even far leftist—extremely heterogeneous, and cross-sectioned) facilitated bringing in very diverse people, though it also made the demands intangible and diffuse to a certain extent. Although, certain erroneous concepts pertaining to assemblies and consensus made the assemblies never ending, which tired many people and led to reduced levels of participation.

Despite a loss of energy lately, the mobilization generated by 15M is enormously positive: it has gotten people out of their homes and into the street to show how fed up they are with the political class and corruption. Indeed, the system itself has begun to be questioned, its economic bases and irrational capitalism, that is leading us to disaster and that is a generator of so much death and suffering, not only in Spain, but also around the entire planet.

On the other hand, the movement has revived the demand for basic rights: housing, work, culture, education, free personal development, and the right to basic necessities. In this context, it could be said that a national debate has begun on the problems associated with housing and evictions (which in Spain has driven people to suicide, which has reverberated loudly in the press). This has forced the administrations to begin to take certain steps, even though they are certainly timid steps.

The truth is that such massive mobilizations had not been seen since the transition. It could be said that these protests have been bigger and more continuous than those against the war in Iraq or the entrance of Spain into NATO (which were also massive in themselves).

Shannon: *Has the CNT worked with the* Indignados? *If that is the case, how so? How would you characterize the relationship between the CNT and the* Indignados?

Fernández: Although the CNT has not worked as an organization with the movement (in theory, the 15M is unaffiliated with any party or union), a great part of its most active militants have become involved in mobilizations, different work groups, and assemblies, offering ideas and proposals, and participating in the organization of events and struggles. Additionally, the movement has always been publicly supported by the Confederation, through communiqués from the Permanent Secretariat of the Confederate Committee and also by writings in the CNT's official newspaper, website, and so on.

The relationship has been supportive and, though there was a certain friction in some assemblies of the 15M about the CNT (pertaining to "traditional" and historical organization), the common practice of popular, horizontal, participatory, and transparent assemblies has broken all the taboos that could have existed.

Shannon: *What do you see in the future of the movement?*

Fernández: I believe that it is still too soon to predict what the future could be, since the movement is changing so often. For example, certain entities of the press announced the end of the movement after the clearing of the plazas in the principal cities. But the truth is that, with its decentralization, the movement has been able to implant itself more closely in its own local reality in quite a few places.

I just do not know—it could continue to lose consistency, since it is difficult to maintain such a high level of activity over time. But, personally, and without trying to play fortuneteller, I think that it could resurface with the same strength that it had in 2011 at any moment. Let us not forget that the situation in Spain is extremely complicated for the most vulnerable. Even the middle class is seeing how it is losing rights and purchasing power (which is what hurts it the most).

On the other hand, it is also probable that the movement will lose its pacifistic character and become more socially offensive. The last protests in front of the parliament, for example, were already headed in that direction.

We will just have to see how things go from here.

Shannon: *Before, you mentioned the role of evictions in the Indignado movement. Could you tell us how the Plataforma de Afectados por la Hipoteca (PAH) [platform for those affected by the mortgage crisis] emerged? How would you describe the development of this group's activities since its inception? What have been the reactions of the authorities (governments, police, judges, and so on) to its demands? Has the CNT collaborated with the PAH? If so, how?*

Fernández: The PAH arose in Barcelona in February of 2009, in the context of a real estate crisis set off by the bursting of the real estate bubble. Thousands of people found themselves unable to pay their mortgages and were evicted from their homes. This association defines itself as horizontal, nonviolent, assembly-based, and unaffiliated to any political party. It also has obvious links with the 15M movement (the *Indignados*). In little time, the movement spread across all Spain.

The reactions of power have been repressive up to now. The PP, the current governing party, has even described them as pro-terrorist or close to the terrorist organization ETA [a Basque separatist group], in an effort to demonize and discredit them to an overwhelmed populace, who sees how the problem of housing has crudely exploded in the last few years.

The CNT does not collaborate as an organization with the PAH, although there are militants who participate in its different assemblies as individuals.

INSTITUTIONALIZING CRISIS

THE CASE OF DAYTON BOSNIA-HERZEGOVINA

JASMIN MUJANOVIĆ

THE POSTWAR PERIOD IN BOSNIA-HERZEGOVINA (BiH) HAS BEEN DE-fined by a political system of institutionalized crisis.[1] While this situation is the direct result of the dissolution of the Socialist Federal Republic of Yugoslavia (SFRJ) and the subsequent Bosnian War (1992–1995), its informative potential extends beyond so-called "post-conflict societies. "This institutionalizing of crisis has meant the end of politics as something other than the administration of crisis. In this way, BiH fits into the context of the newest mutation of the global neoliberal world order, as a kind of variation on the theme of institutionalizing austerity, currently definitive of the rearranging of societies across the global North and South.

However, the purpose of this chapter is to carry this analysis further. Though traditionally imagined, even within the Balkans, as a "backward" polity, contemporary BiH may represent the future of the nominally "democratic" world. I argue that the Dayton constitutional order is an exercise in the institutionalizing and formalizing of violence, fear, and dispossession within the context of parliamentary democratic practice, and that this represents a vision of contemporary austerity policies brought to fruition.

The chapter begins with a set of definitions: namely, of what I understand as politics and crisis. I will then explain the historical emergence of the contemporary constitutional order in BiH. I will expand this discussion through examining supposed "reform" efforts in BiH, and argue that these illustrate precisely the institutionalized nature of crisis in BiH. I will conclude by examining efforts at dismantling rather than reforming the Dayton order, and what these attempts might indicate about the prospects of saving the ideal of participatory politics.

POLITICS & CRISIS

WHAT I UNDERSTAND by *politics* is referred to in academic literature as *the political*. Sheldon Wolin defines the political as the "expression of the idea that a free society composed of diversities can nonetheless enjoy moments of commonality when, through public deliberations, collective power is used to promote or protect the well-being of the collectivity."[2] In Wolin's conception, the political is different from politics, which he understands as "legitimized and public contestation, primarily by organized and unequal social powers, over access to the resources available to the public authorities of the collectivity. Politics is continuous, ceaseless and endless."[3] To him, the political is an open, participatory exercise, full of potential, while politics is institutionalized, managed, and dominated by the elite. Simply put, the idea of the political defines politics as being *about something*, rather than strictly the theatrical, partisan exchanges that occur between elected officials within established parliamentary democracies.

Yet it is doubtful whether a truly participatory political culture can *ever* exist within the confines of the state. When Mikhail Bakunin remarked that "the people will feel no better if the stick with which they are being beaten is labeled 'the people's stick,'"[4] he was anticipating Max Weber's definition of the state as the one social entity characterized by its monopoly over the "legitimate use of violence." In other words, "that with regard to the use of force the state is always a dictatorship,"[5] no matter if it is a liberal-democratic or authoritarian socialist state. In short, the state is organized and systemic violence; the state itself is violence.

Nevertheless, the idea of the political is a useful one because it allows us to think about crisis in an illuminating way. Here, crisis is understood as a period of panic, in which questions of what *ought* to be are replaced exclusively by questions of sheer survival—both individual, biological survival and the survival of broader political arrangements.[6] Yet this "period" has become institutionalized, so that however narrow and hollow democratic exchange may have been within the confines of parliamentary democracies or the state in the past, contemporary policies in BiH and beyond have all but ended even this pretense.

THE DISSOLUTION OF THE SFRJ & DAYTON BIH

The dissolution of the SFRJ had its origins in a narrow, conservative, antidemocratic reaction against the move towards decentralization and democratization that began with the 1974 constitutional reforms. These reforms seismically decentralized the Yugoslav state; the new order itself a result of lasting liberal-conservative tensions within the Federation.[7] Conservative elements within Yugoslavia's ruling establishment resented these reforms as an "anarcho-liberal" turn.[8] Liberals, on the other hand, were frustrated by the strictly institutional nature of the reforms. Ever the strategist, Tito's precarious balancing act between the two sides had lasting consequences: "While Tito ended the reforms, he retained the decentralization of power to the republics (and two autonomous provinces of Serbia). The result was eight unreformed republic-level economic and political systems with institutional interests in the maintenance of their institutional bases of power."[9]

The emergence of Slobodan Milošević in 1987 was a coup for the forces of reaction in Yugoslavia. Fundamentally, Milošević accomplished his meteoric rise to power by marrying the visions of authoritarian Yugoslav Communists and Serb nationalists. While the authoritarians resented the reformers merely for fracturing Belgrade's central authority, the nationalists insisted on the presence of a vast anti-Serb conspiracy. To the nationalists, the 1974 constitution was an attempt to divide the Serb nation across republican borders, thus reducing the Serbs to a systematically marginalized and discriminated minority. The 1986 publication of the so-called *Memorandum of the Serbian Academy of Sciences and Arts* (SANU) proved to be the ideological manifesto—invoking the specter of an impending "genocide" of the Serb nation—on which Milošević relied in his initial confrontations with Serbian reformists in 1987, and then later across the Federation.[10]

The subsequent war in BiH was almost entirely the product of the wider dissolution of the SFRJ and had its origins in Belgrade (and Zagreb) rather than Sarajevo. As Milošević's attempt to recentralize the Federation was rejected by the republican cliques in Slovenia, Croatia, and BiH (and unlike in Serbia, Kosovo, Montenegro, and Vojvodina, he was unable to topple them in turn) his strategy shifted. Having become a patron of the listing, post-Tito Yugoslav National Army (JNA), Milošević turned to carving out of Yugoslavia, at least, a "Greater Serbia."[11]

The ensuing maelstrom of violence Milošević unleashed is ideologically chauvinist, yet practically characterized by abject criminality and profiteering. Peter Andreas refers to the emergence of a "patriotic mafia" across the region—smugglers, hit men, thugs, and gangsters—whose objectives masqueraded as "national liberation" and the "defense of our people," while in reality pursuing simple plunder.[12] The use of ethnic cleansing and genocide in this process is critical to understanding postwar BiH.

The postwar BiH state that emerged is an exercise in "apartheid cartography."[13] Through the internationally brokered/imposed 1995 *General Framework Agreement for Peace in Bosnia and Herzegovina*, generally known as the Dayton Accords, peace in BiH has come through institutionalizing the effects of Serb (and Croat) nationalist ethnic cleansing and genocide. Contemporary BiH is an administrative quagmire—characterized by isolated, ethnic enclaves that have replaced once-thriving multicultural cities, towns and villages.

Present-day BiH is comprised of two highly autonomous entities—the Bosniak-Croat Federation of BiH (FBiH), itself further divided into ten cantons, and the Serb Republika Srpska (RS), as well as a jointly administered Brčko District. There is then a nominal central government in Sarajevo, headed by a three-member Presidency, though final authority resides in the internationally appointed Office of the High Representative (OHR). Finally, the state is composed of "three constitutive peoples" (Bosniaks, Serbs, and Croats), while the "Others" (persons identifying simply as Bosnian, Roma, Jews and/or other minorities) are constitutionally barred from many public offices.[14]

The representatives of the constitutive peoples are further able to monopolize their hold on power through a "vital national interest" veto. This veto is meant to protect the respective ethnic groups from systemic marginalization by larger ethnic communities but is, in practice, used as a crutch by nationalist political parties to block dilution of their hold on the levers of power. Asim Mujkić refers to this as an "Ethnopolis," a system whereby "[u]nder cover of the legitimacy conferred by free and fair elections, citizens as individuals are stripped of any political power."[15] In other words, the concern becomes one of biological survival as embodied by the state, rather than a deepening of the "the political": *we, the Bosniaks/Serbs/Croats, need our state/entity/canton to consolidate its authority and secure territories in order that they, our historic ethno-national enemies, will not exterminate us as individuals and as a group.* The official political discourse is thus dominated by a cartel of "competing" (or rather, electioneering) ethno-nationalist oligarchs and a facile, disinterested supervisory echelon of international observers and representatives.

"REFORM" AND THE DAYTON CONSTITUTIONAL ORDER

As David Chandler suggests, the Dayton period is one marked by the "faking [of] democracy." In other words, Dayton-era BiH has all the classic liberal-democratic institutions, titles, offices, and even the "efforts" at improving and reforming the system. Yet for elites, the incentives of preserving these arrangements are such that there exists an incredible reactionary inertia to the Dayton constitutional order. In short, the only people *capable* and with an *interest* in reforming (or better yet, dismantling) the Dayton constitutional order, are precisely those individuals excluded from its operational logic: ordinary Bosnians and Herzegovinians.

From the perspective of official "reform" efforts, the postwar period in BiH can broadly be divided into two policy regimes—one from 1996 to 2006, and one from 2006 to the present. While the first period was no less beset by the glaring inadequacies of the Dayton Agreement, it was also a period marked by significant transformation. Among these transformations: the ending of armed conflict; the granting of the so-called "Bonn Powers" to the OHR in 1997, allowing the High Representative to sack uncooperative local politicians and suspend any state or entity laws viewed as comprising the peace agreement, in conjunction with the establishment of the jointly administered Brčko District; the creation of a stable single currency regime and Central Bank; and wide-ranging security, police, and military reforms. One optimistic observer argued that the combined thrust of the reform efforts in BiH meant that the country was then truly on its way "from Dayton to Brussels."[16]

In 2005–2006, buoyed by their decade of success, the international community, namely the US and EU, launched the first of two (at the time of writing, three) serious constitutional reform efforts. The idea then, as it has remained throughout every subsequent round of reform negotiations, has been to simplify the political decision-making process, primarily by strengthening state-level institutions and reigning in the powers of the entities. The so-called "April Package" (AP) came within two votes of passing in the state parliament. It was primarily defeated because of a last-minute effort by the prominent former wartime Foreign Minister and Prime Minister of the Republic of BiH Haris Silajdžić's Party for Bosnia-Herzegovina (SbiH),[17] "which refused to approve any 'cosmetic' constitutional solution that did not envision the elimination of both [the] RS and entity voting. The second reason for the rejection of the AP was the belief that the adoption of the [AP] would imply ratification of Dayton's constitution, which was never voted on in the Bosnian Parliament."[18]

The SBiH's concerns were not entirely without merit: by 2009, a second round of constitutional negotiations began that would again put the question of ethno-national territorialization at the center of debate. Paradoxically, though the period after the 2006 negotiations marked one of increasing belligerence and obstructionism on the part of the Serb nationalist leadership, headed by then Prime Minister and later President of the RS Milorad Dodik, it was also marked by significant international withdrawal from BiH, which largely continues into today.[19]

Dodik, ostensibly frustrated by the failures of the 2006 round, began arguing that the RS had been illegally stripped of its constitutionally enshrined powers and status between 1996 and 2006, and that any future reforms would have to be premised on respect for the letter, rather than the "spirit," of Dayton. Of course, given the RS' authorities intransigence on the question of Annex 7 of the Dayton Agreement, concerning the right of return of displaced persons, among numerous other points of obstruction, it is difficult to take Dodik seriously as a defender of the constitution.[20] Nor has Dodik's "constitutionalism" expanded to respect the decisions of the courts, as "the Constitutional Court concluded...that the entities were under the sovereignty of Bosnia-Herzegovina and that the Bosnian Constitution had supremacy over the constitutions of both the FBiH and the RS."[21] If anything, Dodik has used every available opportunity to declare the "inevitability" of the dissolution of BiH on a nearly weekly basis and advance his own fictitious understanding of the country as a so-called "state union."

The irony is that politicians have, in the past, been sacked for far more minor transgressions than Dodik's day-to-day behavior. Yet as incoherent EU and US policies have floundered, Dodik's posturing has only grown—posturing that is widely understood to be a front for his government's actual policy objectives: kleptocracy and the pacification of the social resentment arising out of such practices.[22] Considering the man's documented origins as a war profiteer and smuggler, the only shock in any of this is that he was once believed to be a progressive, practical political moderate, by the Americans in particular.[23]

In 2009, the EU and US once again convened a series of talks, dubbed the "Butimir Process," that essentially presented the relevant parties with a virtually identical package as in 2006: "to empower the prime minister within the council of ministers at the expense of the presidency council; to disempower the House of Peoples by making it (effectively) an appointed committee of the House of Representatives; and, to empower the BiH-level government in order to allow it to meet the conditions necessary to further BiH's journey toward NATO and EU membership."[24] However, the talks in 2009 were marked by a far greater level of disagreement among local elites, on the one hand, and the makings of a renewed alliance among the nationalist Croat and Serb blocs on the other, which pushed for the creation of a "third entity" to be carved out of the FBiH.[25] The alarmist rhetoric on all sides was only further ratcheted up by the impending 2010 general elections, which would bring about a level of institutional gridlock unseen in the country since the end of the war that seems set to continue well into the 2014 election season. Tellingly, even at the time, Nerzuk Ćurak, of the University of Sarajevo Political Science Department, was able to characterize the efforts at Butimir not as the beginning of a substantive reform process but precisely the opposite. Ćurak noted that the meetings were a concerted effort on the part of local elites to institutionalize their oligarchic rule, by attempting to "change the Dayton constitution without changing the Dayton Accords."[26]

Traditional accounts have taken almost at face value the idea that the various (nationalist, especially) parties authentically represent the interests and opinions of the various communities in BiH. This is the same warped logic that led that to the disastrous response of the international community to the dissolution of Yugoslavia in the first place. Yet despite its catastrophic failure, this logic remains an integral part of the EU's approach especially, to the country and its peoples. Severely marginalized remains the understanding that all previous (and subsequent, I contend) approaches to constitutional reform in BiH have been strictly elite-dominated, consciously premised on excluding "nonestablishment" actors for the supposed sake of efficiency and expediency, thus creating what is tepidly referred to as a "democratic deficit." Yet time and again, the international community has found itself confronting the reality that "installing the right elites" is absolutely no guarantee of success in building a "rationalized" state or conciliatory elite culture—to say nothing of a broader, participatory democratic culture.[27]

The international community seems unwilling or unable to confront the elementary problem arising out of this reality, which is that reform is simply not in the interests of the majority of the main political actors in BiH, who were established largely as a result of the international community's explicit and implicit legitimation in the first place. Nor should this be a surprise: BiH's main political actors virtually all operate as criminal syndicates, with individual party leaders and associates having made millions over the course of the war and postwar period through various profiteering and privatization schemes.[28] Electoral politics and parliamentary negotiations, especially since the 2010 elections, have shifted overtly into the realm of score settling, division of spoils (with the lucrative state company posts as prime targets), and extrainstitutional tit-for-tat agreements between the ruling "seven" (formerly "six") political parties. As such, the collective strategy of the ruling oligarchs in BiH is to maintain just enough of a pretense of competence and reform-mindedness to keep their international partners and donors relatively satisfied, and ordinary Bosnians from rioting in the streets.

The insidious character of the Dayton order is such that, even in arriving at moments where change seems inevitable (or even just possible), the parameters of this change seem strictly curtailed by the reactionary inertia of the present arrangement. By insisting on creating a climate of perennial crisis, and reifying and institutionalizing it through criminal and/or ethnic territorialization, local elites are able to derail or postpone, virtually indefinitely, any official reform efforts. Indeed, this "derailment" is so clearly a result of the parameters of the Dayton Agreement itself that it cannot even correctly be referred to as such. After all, from the beginnings of the Yugoslav dissolution crisis, the "solutions" offered by both domestic and international elites in the region as a whole, but BiH in particular, were fundamentally premised on *excluding* ordinary people from the political decision making-process. While this is not a unique feature of BiH political life, the transparency and overt reactionary nature of these efforts there is paradigmatic.

DISMANTLING DAYTON

A NEW APPROACH seems necessary then, one that recognizes that "it is undeniable that most episodes of major reform have not been initiated without major disorders and the rush of elites to contain and normalize them…structural reform has rarely been initiated by decorous and peaceful claims."[29] In short, the kind of change necessary in BiH cannot come from another elite-dominated, constitutional convention. An opening of the constitutional reform process may indeed, produce favorable results—but these efforts too will be insufficient. What is necessary is a liberation of politics, of the political, of the people's autonomous power to organize themselves and their society. This conception of politics, of the political, if it is to exist, must exist in opposition to the state—it must be in the process of becoming *the anarchic*, I suggest. "This is democracy without the state," Wayne Price writes and "[any] other program, such as staying within the limits of the existing state but making it 'more democratic' ('democratic socialism' or 'radical-liberal democracy') capitulates 'democracy' as an ideological cover of the rule of a minority," an elite.[30]

I should like to give some indication now of where the potentialities for such a turn exist in BiH.

The slogan of the 2001–2002 Argentinean uprising that forced out four presidents in three weeks was "*¡Que se vayan todos!*"—all of them must go. A similar sentiment has been circulating in the region for some time. Recently, at massive protests across Slovenia, frequently held up as the most prosperous and democratic of the former Yugoslav republics, participants have been calling for the wholesale resignation of the entire political establishment; "Ne diskriminiramo, vsi so gotovi!" or "We do not discriminate, you're all finished!"[31] In 2012, a wave of antiausterity and antigovernment protests also took place against the Montenegrin strongman Milo Đukanović, the highest-ranking regional holdover and erstwhile ally of Slobodan Milošević. Similar protests in Croatia in 2011 led to the collapse of the long-time HDZ government; the sentiment all too familiar, "Twenty years is enough, [the] political oligarchy has to go." Meanwhile, perceptions of unaccountability and corruption have likewise fueled protests in Macedonia—where opposition and government representatives have engaged in physical confrontations in the Parliament and activists have organized massive convergences in the streets.

The situation in BiH is economically, politically, and socially many times worse than in any of the above states. Yet the purposefully divisive and fragmented character of the constitutional order in BiH has meant that the kind of collective, mass mobilizations necessary to upset the status quo have been especially difficult to organize. Still, resentment grows, suggesting that when it finally does boil over, it is unlikely to simply fizzle away. Apologists for the Dayton order have continued to advance essentialist logics that maintain that political negotiations between elites are the only possible means of change and that advocating for popular mobilization is inviting a return to the violence of the 1990s.[32] I have already explained why this is a horrendous misrepresentation of the causes of the dissolution of the SFRJ and the origins of the war in BiH; yet in the context of a polarized postwar environment, the point deserves attention. Whatever the causes of the war in BiH, it is an undeniable truth that the fighting, ethnic cleansing, and genocide has, at the very least, created three increasingly homogenized, isolated, frightened, and suspicious communities. Is it unreasonable to suggest then, as critics do, that in a scenario where the legitimacy of the state definitively breaks down, these communities will (again) turn on another?

The problem with this narrative is twofold: one, it assumes that the contemporary BiH state has any legitimacy to begin with and two, it ignores the growing body of evidence that suggests that while mutual suspicion is by no means a non-factor in the country's social relations, neither is it all consuming. It is worthwhile to cite some of these recent manifestations.

One of the less discussed dimensions of the successful creation of the unified BiH armed forces was the forced retirement of thousands of professional soldiers above the age of thirty-five in 2010. The move was both an attempt to rejuvenate the forces, as well as a cost-cutting measure. The laid off soldiers, many of them war veterans, were promised severance. Unsurprisingly, few of the unemployed men were ever to see any of these monies. After two years of failed pleading and negotiating with the government, in January and February of 2012, the veterans organized a days-long, sit-in protest in front of the government buildings in Sarajevo, demanding officials address their concerns. With no state government in place at the time, the somewhat functional government of the FBiH set aside some token funds for veterans of the ABiH and HVO.[33] The government of the RS, ever the paragon of Serb nationalist interests, refused to do the same for veterans of the VRS.[34] In a remarkable gesture of solidarity and mutual aid, the veterans from the ABiH and HVO collected funds to send to their peers in the RS who had been left without any government or state aid whatsoever. "When we were sixteen, politicians gave us guns and forced us to kill each other. Now their ignorance is forcing us to help each other," one man remarked, while another commented, "I am now helping the people who shot at me so they can feed their children."[35]

Nor are the soldiers the only ones who have reforged bonds after the war. Concentration camp survivors have created a unified organization, comprised of members from all ethnic communities, and begun a legal process to attempt to win restitution for the crimes they suffered during the war. The President of the Federation of Camp Detainees, Zijahudin Smailagić, explains that this "is the only way forward for those people who have been stripped of their rights. Politics are the reason we do not have a common detainee association. If we want reconciliation this is our only chance. You should see our members from all sides; they all have the same stories, whether they are Bosniaks, Croats, or Serbs. They understand one another."[36] As of October, 2012, Smailagić's organization, numbering over seven thousand individuals, has won all thirteen cases brought before state courts—though, unsurprisingly, cases in the RS have been tougher going. Smailagić and his associates remain defiant, insisting that they merely want "the truth to be known."[37]

While elites attempt to mitigate radical changes to their preferred state arrangements, this apartheid regime, in a country where "difference" cannot be identified other than through names, invites resistance. Azra Hromadzic has documented how, in the segregated schools of Mostar, "bathroom mixing" between Bosniak and Croat pupils has opened spaces, however small, for authentic, renewed interethnic dialogue, friendship, and romance.[38] Similar sentiments were on display in the summer of 2012, after another instance of hooligan violence gripped the city, following which local students organized a "Chocolate Mess"—an informal gathering of the city's residents to share chocolate and to demonstrate that Mostar is "not a hooligan city."[39] Attendees from Mostar, Sarajevo, Banja Luka, and neighboring Croatia came out and, in a show of cheeky optimism, raised a banner reading "Boulevard of the Chocolate Revolution" from a large, gutted, shrapnel-marked structure whose imposing and depressing visage has come to symbolize the city's "frozen" status.[40]

In Banja Luka, an attempt by city authorities to bulldoze a local park met with a storm of controversy. In a matter of days, regular "walks" began occurring, attended by hundreds, to save the park, progressively growing in size.[41] Local organizers were careful not to refer to the events as "protests," as local elections were around the corner and, in the past, many attempted protest movements had been hijacked by political opportunists or had otherwise been painted as the work of paid rabble-rousers by the various oligarchs. Instead, the organizers demanded the city disclose why the park, one of the city's last green spaces, had been marked for demolition, and to meet with municipal representatives, as well as representatives of the company slated to begin construction on the lot. It was a conservative gesture, but it was one of the first consistent civic movements in postwar BiH. Activists from all over the country organized solidarity actions and sent representatives of their own to attend the gatherings. Within a few weeks, the group's Facebook page included nearly 40,000 members.

While only a fraction of these attended, and city and entity representatives refused to meet with the organizers, the interest and the conceptual framework developed in Banja Luka were significant. In a "Declaration," the organizers made their position clear: "When fear disappears, tyrants, dictators, autocrats and false authorities fall.

The authorities have shown that they are afraid of 'the walkers' and we insist that they have reason to be: we are Change because we are the voice of every citizen whose rights have been denied."[42] The text builds to a crescendo, making it clear that whatever its conservative origins, bigger ideas were in mind:

> We are in a time when the ruling oligarchy confirms that we, the ordinary peoples, are the biggest losers of the war and the transition. This oligarchy puts profit above people under the banner of national interest, personal interest above justice, and terror in place of equality.
>
> We have peacefully assembled, which is our right, that we might declare the following facts: We walk because we desire a normal life!
>
> The park is ours, this country is ours, these bodies are ours!
>
> Our bodies matter, they are our weapons and non-violence our method!
>
> We citizens declare that we are not irrelevant, that the authorities are afraid of "the street!"
>
> We are in solidarity on the basis of the differences by which they mean to divide us![43]

CONCLUSIONS

THE EU HAS threatened that unless major constitutional changes go through ahead of the 2014 General Elections in BiH, the results will not be deemed legitimate and the Union, along with the US, the IMF, and the World Bank, will cut off funds for the country's political and social institutions. As a result, yet another round of constitutional changes is being debated by experts and politicians on the front pages of BiH's newspapers and magazines. The evidence already suggests, however, that any "reforms" will be spun in the most conservative and reactionary way(s) possible.

The institutionalized crisis of the Dayton regime is a warning. While its origins are in great violence, its perseverance is rooted in its legitimation of apartheid and kleptocracy through nominally democratic mechanisms. In this, Dayton represents the logic of neoliberal capitalism and austerity taken to their extreme conclusions: a society held hostage through the fabrication of supposedly antagonistic differences, masking the operation of the existing political economy—utter dispossession.

In BiH, the exit(s) from this trap are being timidly felt out and they bear a striking resemblance to the realities activists elsewhere are embracing: no part of this structure can be preserved, we must dismantle it entirely. In this process, ordinary people have only themselves to rely on, to create the kinds of assemblies and networks that will produce societies and economies of substantive participation and equality.

ENDNOTES

1   Portions of this discussion appear also in my chapter, "Nothing Left to Lose: Hip-Hop in Bosnia-Herzegovina," in the forthcoming anthology *Hip-Hop in the East of Europe.*

2   S. Wolin, "Fugitive Democracy," *Democracy and Difference: Contesting the Boundaries of the Political,* (ed.) S. Benhabib (Princeton: Princeton University Press, 1996), 31.

3   Ibid.

4   Mikhail Bakunin, "Statism and Anarchy," *Marxist Internet Archive,* 1873, http://www.marxists.org/reference/archive/bakunin/works/1873/statism-anarchy.htm (accessed April 28, 2012).

5   M. Hardt & A. Negri, *Multitude: War and Democracy in the Age of Empire* (New York: Penguin Books, 2004), 29.

6   In the case of BiH, it is indeed *biology* that is stressed as being of the utmost concern, although the emergence of overtly *racialized* and *racist* discourse is hardly unique to the Balkans. We need only cast our attention toward the rhetoric in the US and Western Europe on undocumented migrants from Latin America and Africa or the reghettoization of the Roma across Europe.

7   V.P. Gagnon, *The Myth of Ethnic War: Serbia and Croatia in the 1990s* (Ithaca and London: Cornell University Press, 2004).

8   Dennis Rusinow, *The Yugoslav Experiment: 1948–1974* (Berkeley and Los Angeles: University of California Press, 1978), 156.

9   Gagnon, *The Myth of Ethnic War*, 59–60.

10 Josi Glaurdić, *The Hour of Europe: Western Powers and the Breakup of Yugoslavia* (New Haven & London: Yale University Press, 2011), 65–66.

11 Jasminka Udovički and James Ridgeway, *Burn This House: The Making and Unmaking of Yugoslavia* (Durham: Duke University Press, 2000), 180–181.

12 Peter Andreas, *Blue Helmets, Black Markets: The Business of Survival in the Siege of Sarajevo* (Ithaca & London: Cornell University Press, 2008).

13 David Campbell, "Apartheid Cartography: The Political Anthropology and Spatial Effects of International Diplomacy in Bosnia," *Political Geography* (1999): 395–435.

14 Lucy Claridge, "Discrimination and Political Participation in Bosnia and Herzegovina: Sejdic and Finci vs. Bosnia and Herzegovina," *Minority Rights Group International*. March 12, 2010, http://www.minorityrights. org/9773/briefing-papers/discrimination-and-political-participation-in-bosnia-and-herzegovina.html (accessed November 14, 2011).

15 Asim Mujkić, "We, the Citizens of Ethnopolis," *Constellations* (2007): 113.

16 Marius Søberg, "Empowering Local Elites in Bosnia and Herzegovina: The Dayton Decade," *Problems of Post-Communism* 53, no. 3 (2006): 55.

17 From its independence in 1992 to the end of the war in 1995, BiH was known as the Republic of Bosnia-Herzegovina (RBiH). Since the signing of the Dayton Accords, the country is referred to as Bosnia-Herzegovina (BiH).

18 Sofía Sebastián, *Leaving Dayton Behind: Constitutional Reform in Bosnia and Herzegovina*, (Madrid: Fundación para las Relaciones Internacionales y el Diálogo Exterior, 2007), 6.

19 Steven Woehrel, *Bosnia: Current Issues and US Policy* (Washington, DC: US Congressional Research Service, 2012).

20 Oslobođenje. *Srušit ćemo aparthejd u RS-u*. 2012, http://www.oslobodjenje.ba/vijesti/bih/koalicija-1-mart-srusit-cemo-aparthejd-u-rsu (accessed December 26, 2012).

21 Igor Štiks, "'Being Citizen the Bosnian Way': Transformations of Citizenship and Political Identities in Bosnia-Herzegovina," *Transitions* 51, no. 1–2 (2011): 256.

22 Maja Bjelajac, "Dodikove vjetrenjače: Ugroženost maska za neuspjeh," January 4, 2013, http://www.slobodnaevropa.org/content/sta-se-krije-iza-dodikovog-spinovanja-javnosti/24815689.html (accessed January 9, 2013).

23 Dragan Čavić, *Traktat o Miloradu.* 2013, http://slobodanvaskovic. blogspot.ca/2013/01/traktat-o-miloradu.html (accessed January 11, 2013).

24 Liam D. Anderson, *Federal Solutions to Ethnic Problems: Accommodating Diversity* (New York: Routlegde, 2013), 40.

25 Wikileaks, *Bosnia and Herzegovina,* 2009, http://wikileaks.org/gifiles/ docs/1698820_bosnia-and-herzegovina-.html (accessed December 26, 2012).

26 BHT 1 Dnevnik, "BHT 1 Dnevnik: Nerzuk Curak," October 12, 2009, http://www.youtube.com/watch?v=ZGtDxeE6Was (accessed December 31, 2012).

27 Carrie Manning, "Political Elites and Democratic State-building Efforts in Bosnia and Iraq," *Democratization* 13, no. 5 (2006): 725.

28 International Institute for Middle-East and Balkan Studies, *The Vicious Circle of Politics, Mafia and Crime,* 2010, http://www.ifimes.org/default.cfm?Jezik=En&Kat=10&ID=548 (accessed 2012 26, December).

29 James C. Scott, *Two Cheers for Anarchism* (Princeton, New Jersey: Princeton University Press, 2012), 20.

30 Wayne Price, *The Abolition of the State: Anarchist & Marxist Perspectives* (Bloomington: AuthorHouse, 2007), 176.

31 The slogan "You're all finished" is also a reference to the slogan "Gotov je!" ("He's finished!"), popularized during the overthrow of Slobodan Milošević in October of 2000.

32 Jasmin Mujanović, *Another Bosnia and Herzegovina is Possible,* 2012, http://www.transconflict.com/2012/06/another-bosnia-and-herzegovina-is-possible-116/ (accessed January 11, 2013).

33 The RBiH Army and the Croatian Defense Council.

34   Army of the Republika Srpska.

35   The Associated Press, *Bosnian Bailout: War Vets Send Cash to Former Foes,* 2012, http://www.ctvnews.ca/bosnian-bailout-war-vets-send-cash-to-former-foes-1.761455 (accessed January 12, 2013).

36   Denis Džidić, *Bosnia Ex-Camp Detainees Join Force,* 2012, http://www.balkaninsight.com/en/article/bosnian-ex-camp-detainees-coming-together (accessed January 12, 2013).

37   John Hooper, *Bosnian Man Leads Compensation Campaign for War Victims on All Sides,* 2012, http://www.guardian.co.uk/world/2012/oct/09/bosnian-man-compensation-campaign-war (accessed January 12, 2013).

38   Azra Hromadzic, "Bathroom Mixing: Youth Negotiate Democracy in Postconflict Bosnia and Herzegovina," *Political and Legal Anthropology Review* 34, no. 2 (2011): 268–289.

39   Elvira Jukic, *Chocolate Mess Helps Mostar Solve Town's Own Mess,* 2012, http://www.balkaninsight.com/en/article/chocolate-unites-mostar-in-solving-town-s-messes (accessed January 12, 2013).

40   Katie McCraw, *Chocolate Riots Uniting Mostar,* 2012, http://katieinbih.blogspot.ca/2012/06/chocolate-peace-revolution-in-mostar.html (accessed January 12, 2013).

41   Buka, "Masovni protesti u Banjaluci : Svi su na ulicama!" September 7, 2012, http://www.6yka.com/novost/28109/masovni-protesti-u-banjaluci-svi-su-na-ulicama (accessed January 24, 2013).

42   Građanska inicijativa, "Park je naš!." "Građanska inicijativa "Park je naš!" Deklaracija." *PARKZin!* no. 2 (2012): 4.

43   Ibid.

THE PUERTO RICAN EXPERIMENT

CRISIS, COLONIALISM, AND POPULAR RESPONSE

JORELL A. MELÉNDEZ BADILLO

> *"Economics cannot understand the depth of the crisis, because below the crisis of financial exchange there is the crisis of symbolic exchange"*
> —Franco "Bifo" Berardi[1]

FOR RADICAL THINKERS IN THE NINETEENTH AND EARLY TWENTIETH century, especially in the classical Marxist tradition, it was a matter of time until capitalism finally collapsed. Their teleological analysis of its historical development, along with the study of its cyclical crises, fueled their positivist conviction that its dialectic nature would inevitably lead to its own dissolution.[2] Yet we are once again stranded in the middle of another crisis. This lets us affirm that "capitalism is not in crisis, capitalism is the crisis."[3] Its incoherence lays in the fact that "on the one hand, capital posits labor as the source of all value and attempts to absorb as much of it as possible; on the other hand, it employs labor-solving technologies which expunge living labor from production."[4] Thus, in order to exist, capitalism must keep expanding, while bearing in its depth a continuous necessity to delimit the physical elements that construct its existence. Also, as Murray Bookchin noted in 1968, the expansive nature of capitalism threatens the very survival of humanity because "the contradiction between the exploitative organization of society and the natural environment is beyond co-optation."[5] These continuous contradictions, which have mutated and diversified themselves in different Keynesian, neo-Keynesian, state capitalist, and neoliberal manifestations, beat deep in the core of the capitalist system.

Meanwhile, it has developed a "deterritorialized financial class [that] has no interest in long-term survival."[6] This class understands the chaotic nature of capitalism and "in a world that seems to hold together only through the infinite management of its collapse,"it has embodied the crisis as a paradoxical means of governing.[7] In order to maintain this set of conjoined relations, while trying to restrict any social upheaval as a response to it, the state created "a vast apparatus of armies, prisons, police, various forms of private security firms and police and military intelligence apparatus, and propaganda engines of every conceivable variety."[8] Through coercion and domination, capitalism transgressed the physical plane and presented itself as a totalizing reality to which there was no outside. In this way, market ideology came to represent the only real option and was internalized over time, transforming our social relations and interactions along with the construction of our social imaginary. This is nothing new. Bakunin understood that the relations set forth by capitalism transcended the material scope when he argued: "the vexations and oppressive conditions of the contract...*turn the worker into a subordinate, a passive and obedient servant,* and the employer into a nearly *absolute master.*"[9]

So, in order to be assimilated, capitalism commodifies our social relations, our emotions, and every single aspect of life with a set of values that is used to construct (hetero)normativity. It transcends the economic sphere and becomes intertwined in the social fabric, giving meaning to the set of symbols we use to interpret reality. On this particular aspect, Eduardo Colombo argues "the *structure of domination* is a *socio-historical construction* that reproduces the perverse effects of power and inscribes every human relation in the 'dialectic' between master and slave."[10] Thus, even though capitalism is not synonymous with ideas of superiority of one individual or group over another—such as patriarchy, sexism, colonialism, white supremacy, and imperialism—it has created a symbiotic relationship with them.

These interrelations of domination have been historically legitimized and protected by the state.

Yet, despite the fact that capitalism reproduces its incoherence on a global scale, we have to take into consideration the structures it creates in different geographical contexts, for they are not identical. Joel Olson understood this when he argued that, given the historical development of the United States, any revolutionary organization in that country should address, and attack, white supremacy. His arguments were clear:

> The system of global capitalism, we believe, is the root source of exploitation, oppression, and alienation in this society. It must be abolished and replaced with a free society in which people are able to fully develop their capacities without hurting others to do so. But how to do this? Ruckus believes that in the United States, the key to abolishing capitalism is to attack white supremacy. In a nation whose economic and social structure has depended on slavery, segregation, genocide, and reservation, to attack whiteness is to strike a blow at the pillars of American capitalism and the state.[11]

Taking time and space into consideration, Olson developed his critique around the reality of the United States's geographical context. This does not mean, however, that capitalism manifests itself the same way around the globe. We must understand that its chaotic nature creates a heterogeneous representation. Hence, when we take Puerto Rico as a case study, even though white supremacy is present as a form of oppression among others, historically the capitalist system embedded itself into society, with the help of the state, through other manifestations, specifically colonialism. It is for this reason that we find necessary a brief analysis of the historical reproduction of capitalism and colonialism in Puerto Rico in order to understand how the latest crisis of capitalism affected the island. When we try to analyze the capitalist system, its crises, and its different manifestations, we are doing so in order to understand how to attack it because we are seeking its total destruction. We throw away any sense of false objectivity and burn our intellectual drags to the ground. We do not seek to orchestrate a grand theory but instead we want to understand the various hierarchical layers of domination that embrace our social relations in order to break with them.

ONGOING COLONIALISM

"Our constitution was made by a civilized and educated people.... To give...the ignorant and lawless brigands that infest Puerto Rico...the benefits of such immunities... would, of course, be a serious obstacle to the maintenance there of an efficient government."
—Simeon E. Baldwin, Yale Law School[12]

AT THE CUSP of the nineteenth century, the United States projected itself as a global superpower. Craving to expand its imperial project, it used the Caribbean and the Pacific Ocean as theaters of war, thus engaging against the decaying Spanish empire in what became known as the "Spanish-American War." In the midst of this conflict, Puerto Rico was militarily occupied on July 25, 1898. This set forth yet another layer of domination on an island that had been seized from its original inhabitants four centuries before by the crown of Spain; it also entangled the complex relations that had been fostered in a turbulent and incomplete process of collective identity construction.

The United States's occupation reverberated in various aspects of the island's social life. Not only did it implement a capitalist mode of production, thus proletarianizing the workforce and industrializing the economy, but it set forth a series of institutions that were in charge of "consolidat[ing] their control (and claim[ing] moral legitimacy) by training the racialized 'primitive' through the ideological apparatus."[13] A project of Americanization was instituted using the school system, censorship, and propaganda. It came to the point of changing the official language of the island to English and even the name to Porto Rico because Puerto Rico was too difficult for the new masters to pronounce. Yet, it was through a collective resistance, anchored on the discourses of Puerto Rican culture and national affirmation, that this forced transculturization process was aborted.[14] The penetration of US culture on the island is an undeniable fact but it did not become a holistic element.[15]

In the legal and judicial framework, Puerto Rico became a territory *of* the United States but it *was not part* of it, as the Supreme Court dictated. Even though it was granted Commonwealth status in 1952, everything stayed pretty much the same. In fiscal matters, the island became an appendage of the United States's economy.[16] Hence, "the specific form taken by the long-term fluctuations of capitalism within Puerto Rico cannot be divorced from the framework imposed by US colonial rule and shifting state policies within that framework."[17]

Beyond the judicial scope, the island served as fertile ground for social, political, physical, and fiscal experimentation. In her analysis of colonialism, Maia Ramnath argues: "A restive or insurgent colony was even better than a pacified one as a *laboratory for states to develop their military, bureaucratic, disciplinary, policing, and surveillance capabilities.* Here administrators tested new techniques for future application to domestic security in the metropole."[18] Even though we recognize the juxtaposed particularities of each geographical space, in accordance with its own historical development and individual manifestations, we hold this to be true in Puerto Rico. It might not come as a surprise that the US government tested chemical weapons in the mountains of El Yunque, used peasant women as guinea pigs to test means of contraception,[19] used novel techniques of torture on radical leaders,[20] used Vieques and Culebra as a military testing ground, and experimented with fiscal policies that were to be later implemented in the metropolis.

But we need to take into consideration that not only was the island physically occupied but there was also an ongoing process of symbolic occupation. Five hundred years of colonialism have created a deep crisis in our social imaginary and in the way we perceive ourselves. Having internalized most of the racist notions that have paved the way for the institution of capitalism and accepting our role as the *other*, the majority of the people on the island have tolerated the present situation, and have legitimized the State and the spectacle of representative democracy. This has also affected the way we perceive the past and our collective memory. So, in order to maintain a certain status, some people have adopted the customs and values of a westernized consumerist mentality, in which property and individualism are venerated. All of these elements have created a process of chaotic collective decomposition of society.

THE ONGOING CRISIS

"Chupamos la leche que brota de las tetas de la estatua de la libertad y lloramos como un niño cuando nos dicen que ya pronto se secarán."
—La Experiencia de Toñito Cabanillas[21]

BY THE 1970S, it was becoming clear that the government-oriented Operation Bootstrap, which could be considered Puerto Rico's take on the New Deal and was considered an economic miracle, had failed. The original project had encouraged a massive industrialization model loosely based on Keynesian policies; it made the State the biggest employer on the island, thus making the government a huge bureaucratic apparatus. It subsisted dialectically through external investment, which did not encourage a local integrated economy. During those years, the great commercial agricultural sector Puerto Rico had heavily depended upon disappeared, and left hundreds of thousands of people without any type of income. Thus, industrialization meant nothing for the subaltern classes of the island that lacked adequate housing, food, or any means of subsistence.[22] This encouraged the creation of a welfare state that promoted a predatory populist policy.

By then, the New Right in the United States "fostered the adoption of antiwelfare, privatization, free trade, monetarist and neoliberal policies."[23] It was only a matter of time until those ideologies were implemented on the island. The time came in the early 1990s under the administration of Governor Pedro Rosello, who sought to implement a mixed model that promoted public welfare with "the gospel of entrepreneurial initiative, competition, deregulation, and privatization."[24] Following the populist rhetoric that had marked past colonial administrations, the government carried out a series of welfare programs while it set forth the privatization of institutions such as the Puerto Rico Telephone Company and "the management of agencies, [as well as] subcontracting, outright sale of facilities, construction of private installations parallel to public facilities, private operation of toll bridges, and, in the case of education, financial autonomy for schools and school vouchers."[25] The dialectic of this mixed program could be seen in the health reform "that implied the privatization of public facilities and the creation of a government health insurance for those not covered by private plans."[26]

In 2000, after the opposing party won the elections, things went unchanged. In order to deal with the island's situation, the government started to use debt to finance the deficit.[27] The ongoing crisis was taking its toll and by 2006 the economy went into recession, after government agencies "ran out of funds two months before the end of fiscal year 2005-06."[28] An impasse between the two ruling parties of the island, one controlling the executive branch and the other the legislature, forced the government to shut down, which caused "a two week layoff of close to 100,000 public employees."[29] This was the local situation before the global crisis of 2007. Hence, when the crisis hit the United States, it had a devastating effect on the island. Luis G. Fortuñoas was elected governor of Puerto Rico by an overwhelming majority on November 2008. His victory not only represented a triumph for the financial elite but it also concretized the hegemony of his conservative New Progressive Party in the legislature, townships, Supreme Court, and even in the University of Puerto Rico. In order to analyze and create a series of recommendations in relation to the island's situation, he created a group called *Consejo Asesor de Reconstrucción Económica y Fiscal* (CAREF), which was composed of representatives of the island's bourgeoisie. The group organized a series of austerity measures that included massive layoffs, freezing collective bargaining, and eliminating many other workers' rights.[30] The materialization of these measures came on March 9, 2009, when he signed a law entitled *Ley Especial Declarando Estado de Emergencia Fiscal y Estableciendo Plan Integral de Estabilización Fiscal para Salvar el Crédito de Puerto Rico, Ley Núm. 7.* Along with it came the layoff of around 22,000 government employees. This triggered a resistance movement, deeply rooted in the island's rich history of struggle, which opted for various mechanisms to counteract the State's power.

Nonetheless, even though most of our analyses up until now have been rooted in an economic discourse, we need to take into consideration other effects of the crisis on the island. The neoliberal policies and austerity measures implemented caused a deepening effect in the ongoing crisis. Unemployment reached a staggering 16.1 percent in 2010,[31] while the island's debt was approximately $51.9 billion dollars, with $14,000 per capita (89 percent of personal income).[32] These are important facts if we accept Guy Debord's argument that "the satisfaction of primary human needs is replaced by an uninterrupted fabrication of pseudo-needs which are reduced to the single pseudo-need of maintaining the reign of the autonomous economy."[33] The construction of these artificial wants is essential to the smooth function of the capitalist system. Hence, in order to satisfy these fabricated desires, society created a series of mechanisms that in turn gave way to underground economies, which did not challenge the economic system but merely emulated all of its hierarchical structures and power relations. This can be seen in the local drug war, in which "conflicts over the sales territories (*puntos*), the collection of debts, the silencing of witnesses and informers, and the financing of drug purchases produce deaths on a daily basis."[34] This chaotic situation is counteracted by State repression, thus creating a symbiotic relationship, furthering its collateral effects. The lack of a concrete identity and colonial mentality pushed many Puerto Ricans to pursue the American Dream. From 2004 to 2010, more than 176,000 individuals migrated outside the island, actively looking for jobs.[35] Also, we've seen a rise in the homeless population, which increased in 2008–2009 by 3.11 percent in the United States, and by 35.11 percent in Puerto Rico.[36]

Fortuño's economic plan was hailed in the conservative forums of the United States as a "miracle,"[37] and a "godsend to the GOP."[38] Even though he significantly reduced the budget deficit, he did so by putting all of its weight on the shoulders of subaltern sectors of society and creating a huge crisis in our symbolic exchange, by deepening the huge gap between classes and sectors, by creating institutions that subsist through racism, xenophobia, and sexism, and by benefitting a small elite.

THE ONGOING RESISTANCE

"Naturally, because of our colonial status, there exists a double interpretation of history: the colonial and the history of anticolonial struggle. In reality, colonial history does not belong to us. It belongs to the colonizer."
—Filiberto Ojeda Ríos, revolutionary nationalist assassinated by the F.B.I.[39]

PUERTO RICO HAS a rich history of struggle against colonial domination that can be traced back to the seventeenth century. Yet, when we write about, analyze, or interpret it, we need to be careful because we can easily reproduce discourses of victimization that hurt our radical aspirations and liberalize our revolutionary struggles. As bell hooks noted in her analysis of racism and white supremacy, when individuals acquire a victim identity, it may bring concerns into greater visibility but at the same time "they are acting in complicity with an assaultive structure of racist domination in which they invest in the absence of agency."[40] Victimization reproduces longstanding notions that are anchored in the womb of colonialism and also constructs the idea of the colonized as the *other*. Instead of developing strategies that will transform the situation, it encourages subjective inertia. The State has taken advantage of this and has offered cosmetic solutions to the problem in the form of "Status Referendums" that do not necessarily project the collective desire of the inhabitants of the island. They only serve as a way of pacifying the anxiety produced by the decomposition of reality through domination, and as a mechanism for manufacturing consent.

Another question surfaces: what are we fighting for? As an anarchist, I fight against any form of oppression and domination, but this simple argument becomes more complex when entangled in the historical situation of the island. Nationalism assumes that "in order for a people to be recognized as holders of collective rights and freedoms, it must be constituted as nation duly manifested in a state: an exclusive institution defined by its monopoly on sanctioned force and revenue extraction."[41] Even though I recognize that creating an independent nation will only change the foreign ruling elite for a national one, I also recognize that colonialism is the most explicit expression of reactionary violence and domination, and you cannot simply look the other way. You have to resist and attack it.

Yet resistance does not always take the most obvious form. When the United States imposed the English language as official and the school system had to change their classes accordingly, teachers would simply memorize one lesson in English and they would continue to impart classes in Spanish. When the supervisors would drop into their classrooms, they would simply give the only lesson they knew in English as a decoy. Such elements of resistance can be traced throughout our history. So, when the imposition of culture in order to assimilate the *other* becomes a colonizing factor, cultural and ethnic expressions become revolutionary elements in the struggle. All of this does not mean that revolutionary violence has not been part of the equation, for it has been a crucial element in the struggle since its origins. Thus, taking the massive strike at the University of Puerto Rico and the land occupation movement on the island as case studies, we will try to briefly analyze contemporary resistance to the ongoing crisis.

The University of Puerto Rico has been fertile ground for radical ideas since its origins.[42] We can trace conflicts between students and the administration all the way back to 1919, and the first strike to 1931. This defiant attitude was vindicated throughout time. Recent history is no different, for the center of studies had enormous strikes in 1973, 1981, 2005 and the most recent in 2010–2011. The latter will be our focus.

On October 15, 2009, hundreds of thousands of people marched to protest the unpopular Law 7. Plaza Las Américas, the biggest shopping mall in the Caribbean, was the point of convergence for the massive event. It seemed like yet another peaceful demo until a group of students decided to occupy the main highway on the island, obstructing the way for thousands of drivers. After a few hours, the police, and the distant voices of bureaucratic labor leaders on the main stage, tried to dissuade the students of their actions but were unsuccessful. This crystallized a symbolic split. The reformist labor movement wanted to keep chanting songs in front of Plaza Las Américas, hoping to convince the government through the power of the convocation they held, while the students armed themselves with spontaneous organization. This contradiction grew even deeper when Rafael Cancel Miranda, a nationalist who fired some shots in the US Congress in 1954, went over to the students and persuaded them to stop their protest and the inevitable clash with a greater number of police officers. A ghost from the past came to pacify a movement that was barely starting to burn. The students gathered in an improvised assembly and decided to march back to the University of Puerto Rico (UPR).

Barely six months after these events, the students at the UPR started a massive strike that would be one of the most important acts of rebellion against the government in recent history. Taking into consideration that students "confront the crisis of reproduction directly, as the cost of job training (tuition) increases, and as the value of such training decreases,"[43] they adopt a class consciousness through a process of proletarianization that is loosely based on the denial of a middle-class future and their "huge debt before they have begun to even earn a wage full time."[44] These conditions create what the Situationists called "an imaginary present," and it is of utmost importance in the construction of the student identity. At the same time, they are submerged in a misery decorated with false prestige, inside an institution that reinforces the State and polices their actions, ideas, social relations, and even their bodies.[45] It was precisely the protection of the illusion that radicalized the student movement, when it was announced that their privileges were going to be challenged by a cut of more than $180 million dollars to university funding under Law 7.

The strike, which can be divided into two different phases—one that consisted of the student occupation of ten of the eleven campuses for more than two months, and the second, which was distinguished by the seizure and militarization of the campuses by the police—marked a really important breakthrough in the way people imagined and created a revolutionary movement on the island. Influenced by the major struggles against the US Navy in Vieques and a kaleidoscope of events that fills the annals of collective resistance, the students redefined the way people envisioned strikes by experimenting with new forms of struggle. They replaced the inactivity and the modus operandi of traditional labor unions with a proactive attitude that was the product of direct action, democratic assemblies, and occupation of physical space, which inevitably led to the questioning of capitalism and the State. After an intermittent strike of almost a full school year, the struggle not only radicalized a generation through the process of creating street art, barricades, organic gardens, lovemaking under the stars, and even physical confrontations with the police, but it also served as a lodestone for a wide range of social movements that were fighting against the austerity measures imposed by the State.

Another important militant movement was taking place among the subaltern classes of the island: *los rescatadores de terrenos* (land rescuers). Even though we can trace land occupations to the seventeenth century, there was a sharpening of the movement during the last four decades of the twentieth century.[46] Also, these classes were greatly affected by the imposition of harsh neoliberal policies implemented during the last couple of years. It was thanks to a process of defying colonial intersubjectivity, through self-management practices and cultural reaffirmation,[47] that these communities resisted austerity measures and set forth radical practices without necessarily reproducing any type of political discourse. Driven by necessity and recognizing the inefficacies of the government, thousands of families have decided to take over lands collectively, redistributing them and creating complex communities. Out of the dozens of occupied communities that were active during the last few years, we have concrete information about five of them: Villa Esperanza: Tierra para Todos (Hope Village: Land for Everyone), Comunidad El Sol (The Sun Community), Villa Cañona (Cannon/Cannoned Village),[48] Barrio Boca (Mouth Village), and Central Cortada (Cortada Central).[49]Altogether, the aforementioned communities house around five hundred families and some of them, such as Central Cortada, do not have access to electricity or potable water. In some cases, land has been distributed equally and the construction of houses is a collective effort by the community. In all of them, the occupied or rescued land, as they like to call it, was unused and abandoned. Some pieces of land were being used for clandestine garbage dumps or as popular sites for drug users, yet the government has been trying to expropriate each one of them. Some of the communities are built on privately owned land (whatever the fuck that means), others are located near archeological sites with potential for tourism, and others are designated as dangerous because of potential floods. Even though all of the communities have tried to negotiate with the government through legal means on several occasions, they have been ignored. They are intimidated by the police on a daily basis and live in constant fear of being forcefully expropriated, as has been the case in other occupied communities. In Villa Esperanza, in January 2011, four houses were demolished without due eviction process before the community got together and fought back against the police and the workers in charge of the demolition. As time goes on, the community members' demands are becoming more political in nature and, instead of absorbing the same old political narrative, they're radicalizing it with their direct action and participatory democracy.

THE PERPETUATION OF THE CRISIS

Your heart is a muscle the size of your first,
keep on fighting, keep on loving, and hold on.
Hold on for your life.
—Ramshackle Glory[50]

THE FUTURE LOOKS bleak. During the 2012 elections, the Popular Democratic Party won using a heavily liberal discourse that appealed to grassroots sectors disenchanted with the past administration. Some elements in the struggle gave their vote so they could "punish" Fortuño for his actions. The result of representative democracy is the perpetuation of the crisis and the domestication of the left. During the first four months, the new administration has already privatized Luis Muñoz Marín International Airport and continued with the same neoliberal agenda that got us here in the first place. Yet, the future is still unfolding. Perhaps we will begin learning from the direct actionists in the student movement and among the land rescuers. It is within these antiausterity movements, connected in spirit to opposition to capitalism and the State, that we might find seeds from which to grow a qualitatively different future, free of the constraints of austerity—and capital itself. But that will require a definitive turn away from electoral strategies and reliance on state tinkering.

ENDNOTES

1   Franco "Bifo" Berardi, *After the Future* (Oakland: AK Press, 2011), 143.

2   As an example, Rosa Luxemburg analyzed the periodic crises of capitalism in her excellent critique of Bernstein's reformism. She argued that, in 1898, we were "at the start of the end, the period of the last crises of capitalism." See Rosa Luxemburg, "Reforma o revolución," in Rosa Luxemburg, et. al, *Manifiesto: Tres textos para cambiar el mundo* (Havana, Cuba: Ocean Press, 2006), 92.

3   We have stolen this analogy from the Michael Truscello's documentary, *Capitalism is the Crisis: Radical Politics in the Age of Crisis,* 2011. See www.capitalismisthecrisis.net (accessed January 12, 2013).

4   Jasper Bernes, "The Double Barricade and the Glass Floor," in *Communization and its Discontents: Contestation, Critique, and Contemporary Struggles,* (ed.) Benjamin Noys (Brooklyn: Minor Compositions, n.d.), 157–158.

5   Murray Bookchin, *Post-Scarcity Anarchism* (Oakland: AK Press, 2004.), 7–8.

6   Franco "Bifo" Berardi, *After the Future,* 73.

7   The Invisible Committee, *The Coming Insurrection* (Los Angeles: Semiotext(e), 2009), 14.

8   David Graeber, *Debt: The First 5,000 Years* (Brooklyn: Melville House Printing, 2011), 382.

9   Mikhail Bakunin, "The Capitalist System," http://dwardmac.pitzer. edu/anarchist_archives/bakunin/capstate.html (accessed January 12, 2013), our emphasis.

10   Eduardo Colombo, *El espacio político de la anarquía* (Montevideo, Uruguay: Editorial Nordan-Comunidad, 2000), 137, our translation.

11   Joel Olson, "Movement, Cadre, and Social Dual Power," in *Perspectives on Anarchist Theory 13,* no. 1 (Fall 2011): 34.

12   Cited in: Mario Murillo, *Islands of Resistance: Puerto Rico, Vieques, and US Policy* (New York: Seven Stories Press, 2001), 27.

13   Maia Rammath, *Decolonizing Anarchism: An Antiauthoritarian History of India's Liberation Struggle* (Oakland: AK Press and Institute of Anarchist Studies, 2011), 18.

14   For some examples: Fernando Picó, *Historia general de Puerto Rico* (Río Piedras: Ediciones Huracán, 1990), 245, note 49.

15   For a more rigid analysis, see José Luis González, *El país de los cuatro pisos y otros ensayos* (Río Piedras, Puerto Rico: EdicionesHuracán, 1989), 11–42.

16   Movimiento Socialista de Trabajadores, "¿Qué es y porquélucha el MST?," *Bandera Roja, http://www.bandera.org/documentos/documentos-históricos/¿qué-es-y-por-qué-lucha-el-mst* (accessed February 3, 2013).

17   Rafael Bernabe and Cesar Ayala, *Puerto Rico in the American Century: A History Since 1898* (North Carolina: University of North Carolina Press, 2007), 337.

18   Maia Rammath, *Decolonizing Anarchism,* 18, our emphasis.

19   Rafael Bernabe and Cesar Ayala, *Puerto Rico,* 113, 202, and 207.

20   Pedro Albizu Campos suffered chemical attacks while he was imprisoned. See Pedro I. Aponte Vázquez, *¡Yo Acuso! Tortura y asesinato de Don Pedro Albizu Campos* (San Juan: Publicaciones René, 1992).

21   Translation: "We suck the milk that springs from the tits of the Statue of Liberty and we cry like a baby when they tell us it will soon dry out." Lyrics from the song "La perla del caribe" by La Experiencia de Toñito Cabanillas, *Idiotós fera* (San Juan: Tenet Records, 2001).

22   See Fernando Picó, *Historia general de Puerto Rico,* 287.

23   Rafael Bernabe and Cesar Ayala, *Puerto Rico in the American Century,* 291.

24   Ibid.

25   Ibid.,192.

26   Ibid.

27   Joanisabel González, "Alerta roja a la economía Boricua," *El Nuevo Día,* April 26, 2012, http://www.elnuevodia.com/alertarojaalaeconomiaboricua-1243822.html (accessed February 2, 2013).

28   Rafael Bernabe y Cesar Ayala, *Puerto Rico in the American Century,* 341.

29   Ibid.

30   See "Informe al gobernador de Puerto Rico sobre la reconstrucción fiscal: Resumen ejecutivo," *Consejo Asesor de Reconstrucción Económica y Fiscal.* *http://www.gdb-pur.net/spa/communications/documents/2009-01-08-Inf.ReconstruccionRESUMEN_000.pdf* (accessed February 2, 2013).

31   "Employment and Unemployment Puerto Rico, 2011 Average Calendar Year," *Government of Puerto Rico: Department of Labor and Human Resources,* http://cce.estadisticas.gobierno.pr/Documentos/ FD0F53DC-B605-4565-893F-64109B98F937/EMPLEO_Y_DE-SEMPLEO_EN_PUERTO_RICO_PROMEDIO_ANO_NATU-RAL_2011.pdf (accessed February 23, 2013).

32   Global Credit Research, "Moody's downgrades Puerto Rico general obligation and related bonds to Baa3 from Baa1 and certain notched bonds to Ba1," *Moody's Investors Service,* http://www.moodys.com/ research/Moodys-downgrades-Puerto-Rico-general-obligation-and-related-bonds-to--PR_262231 (accessed February 23, 2013).

33   Guy Debord, *The Society of the Spectacle* (Detroit: Black & Red, 1983), 51.

34   Rafael Bernabe and Cesar Ayala, *Puerto Rico,* 313.

35   Inter News Services, "Secretario del Trabajo afirma que sin medidas duras del gobierno la fuga de talento sería," *Primera Hora,* January 5, 2012, http://www.primerahora.com/secretariodeltrabajoafirmaquesinmedidasdurasdelgobiernolafugadetalentoseriapeor-599396.html (accessed February 23, 2013).

36 Oscar J. Serrano y Elis Acevedo Denis, "PR sufre un dramático aumento de deambulantes," *NotiCel,* April 25, 2011, http://www.noticel. com/noticia/103758/pr-sufre-dramatico-aumento-de-deambulantes-serie.html (accessed February 23, 2013).

37 Christopher Ruddy, "Fortuño's Puerto Rico Miracle," *Newsmax: Independent, American,* http://www.newsmax.com/Ruddy/fortuno-puerto-rico-taxes/2010/04/07/id/355060 (accessed February 3, 2013).

38 Tom Squitieri, "A Godsend to the GOP," *Newsmax Magazine,* http:// w3.newsmax.com/a/mar10/fortuno/ (accessed February 3, 2013).

39 Filiberto Ojeda Ríos "Los macheteros y la lucha revolucionaria por la independencia en Puerto Rico," in *En busca de una estrella vol. 1: Antología del pensamiento independentista en Puerto Rico desde Betances a Filiberto,* (ed.) Juan Mari Bras (Mayagüez, Puerto Rico: Causa Común Independentista, 2007), 478.

40 bell hooks, *Killing Rage* (New York: Owl Books, 1996), 58.

41 Maia Rammath, *Decolonizing Anarchism,* 19.

42 "Breve historia de las luchas estudiantiles y laborales en la Universidad de Puerto Rico—Parte I," *Abayarde Rojo,* January 25, 2011, http:// abayarderojo.org/index.php/breve-historia-de-las-luchas-estudiantiles-y-laborales-en-la-universidad-de-puerto-rico——parte-i/ (accessed February 25, 2013).

43 Jasper Bernes, "The Double Barricade and the Glass Floor," in *Communization and its Discontents: Contestation, Critique, and Contemporary Struggles* (ed.) Benjamin Noys (Brooklyn: Minor Compositions, n.d.), 164.

44 Ibid.

45 Members of the Situationist International and Some Students at the University of Strasbourg, *On the Poverty of Student Life: Considered in its Economic, Political, Psychological, Sexual, and Particularly Intellectual Aspects with a Modest Proposal for its Remedy* (Detroit: Black & Red, 2000), 5.

46 Juan Llanes-Santos, *Desafiando el poder: Las invasiones de terrenos en Puerto Rico* (Río Piedras: EdicionesHuracán, 2001), 55.

47 See: Alejandro Cotté Morales, et. al. *Trabajo comuntiario y descolonización* (San Juan, Puerto Rico: n.e., 2012).

48 We need to point out that "cañona" is colloquially used for processes or things that require hard work and bravery.

49 We would like to thank Yamil Corlaván for letting us use the data recollected through a series of interviews and very intense research.

50 Lyrics from the song "Your Heart is a Muscle…" by Ramshackle Glory, *Live the Dream* (Bloomington, IN: Plan It X, 2011).

PART 3

THE RESPONSE OF THE DISPOSSESSED

"The workers want no lying."
—Mikhail Bakunin

INFILTRATING THE MYTHOLOGY OF AMERICAN EMPIRE

MEDIA, HISTORY, AND OCCUPY WALL STREET

MARK BRAY

Occupy Wall Street (OWS) was a lot of things to a lot of people, but to a large extent, it was a battle over competing interpretations of the decline of American Empire. In the immediate context of the worst economic crisis since the Great Depression, and the larger context of the end of the "American Century" and the rise of China and India, the fears, aspirations, uncertainties, and anxieties of the entire political spectrum were projected onto Occupy. For years, conservatives bemoaned the decline of the idealized mid-twentieth century work ethic of the "Greatest Generation," which defeated fascism and solidified the country's superpower status. They lamented a lack of religious devotion and traditional values, complaints which are often thinly veiled commentaries on America's shifting demographics, which will make the country predominantly people of color by 2043.[1] In their eyes, OWS was an especially egregious manifestation of a spoiled, soft, entitled, ungrateful generation that cried in the face of adversity, as opposed to earlier generations that supposedly understood the need for stoic perseverance. Echoing the arguments of turn of the twentieth century proto-fascists, conservatives essentially interpreted OWS as a potentially fatal particle of societal decadence writhing its way through this generation's American inheritance. Rather than sleep in a park, they advocated the same kind of collective sacrifice (austerity) that past generations endured to pull the country out of tough times.

For liberals, America's problem stemmed from letting Wall Street run amok and failing to keep up internationally in terms of education and green technology. Given the fact that the already right-wing Democratic Party had drastically shifted further rightward over the past thirty years, many liberals welcomed OWS as an opportunity to reconnect to their imagined self-image as the American "Left," and feel like they were living out this generation's great social movement. That's why liberals initially flocked to a movement that many of them hoped would awaken America's conscience from its *recent* hibernation. However, once it became clear that OWS wasn't going to be the liberal Tea Party that they craved, interest waned.

Although most democrats agreed that the leftist renaissance of Occupy was in part about resisting Republican austerity measures, in practice the debate between the Democratic and Republican leadership wasn't about *whether* to impose austerity, but rather how much. After all, Obama's 2011 debt ceiling deal cut $570 billion over ten years in "nondefense discretionary spending," reducing America's nondefense spending from 3.3 percent of GDP to 1.7 percent, the lowest it's been in fifty years. It was only slightly less severe than Paul Ryan's plan, which would have lowered it to 1.5 percent of GDP.[2] These cuts reduced funding for increasingly vital programs like clean drinking water funds, FEMA assistance for disasters, nuclear waste cleanup, and low-income heating assistance for the poor.[3]

Common to both liberal and conservative interpretations was an unwavering, modernist, capitalist faith in the irrepressible forward march of "Progress." Growing up in the 1990s, it was simply understood that the United States was head and shoulders above all other countries and that its vast power would be a given into the foreseeable future. But after September 11 and the economic crisis of 2008, political books about the decline of American Empire flew off the shelves because their narratives so fundamentally challenged the traditional American self-image. It was akin to the popularity of apocalyptic blockbusters.

However, in order to craft their bizarre populist rendition of the unbroken upward slope of American history, politicians have inevitably smoothed over some "nasty rough patches" and marinated some horrible eras in vats of disinfectant. After all, it's political suicide to speak about the genocide of the indigenous population or the fact that many of the "founding fathers" were slaveholders, for example. When atrocities such as slavery or Jim Crow are briefly mentioned, they are merely referenced as points of contrast against the inevitable triumph of the inherently righteous American spirit, which had to shed some oppressive baggage over the years, but whose essence is truth and justice.

Popular discourse about history tends to frame progress in terms of the hackneyed axiom "those who ignore history are doomed to repeat it."[4] It's a way for teachers to try to convince their students that studying history matters, in order to prevent another genocide; however, it's a thoroughly ahistorical premise. The notion that there are certain transhistorical "lessons" that apply equally across time and space, which must be learned to redirect the torrent of history away from essentially identical cycles of brutality, ignores the specificity of historical context. Our most cherished values of family, community, society, labor, gender, merit, sexuality, time, space, and even history itself have drastically shifted over the centuries in ways that we can only partially understand from our vantage point. That's not to say that we can't learn from history. After all, if there were nothing from that past that could be made useful today, then it wouldn't be more than a curiosity. But whereas the popular "doomed to repeat it" school of thought tries to boil off the context of an event, to morph it into a transhistorical "lesson" out of Aesop's Fables justifying the current status quo, more radically historicist approaches delve deep into the context of history to understand the vast differences that separate us from those who came before.

The historicist approach may sound disempowering because it emphasizes the chasms of time that separate us from those we study, but it's actually far more liberatory. Whereas the "doomed to repeat it" outlook emphasizes continuity with the past and a timeless interpretation of order, born out of a premodern worldview that saw history as a cycle of decline (the "dark ages") and grandeur (Rome), the historicist approach emphasizes change and difference. It allows us to study history to understand how we got where we are today, and to use that information to develop concepts and ideas that fit our current circumstances, rather than chain ourselves to past conventions. Of course, nothing ever emerges out of the blue, there's always an overlap between past forms and innovative breakthroughs, but a historicist approach shows us that if things were so different in the past, then inevitably they will be unfathomably different in the future.

The "doomed to repeat it" school of history is undergirded by the concept of the *idea as motor of history*.[5] When we think about popular historical examples of social change, the kind of changes that we should learn lessons from to avoid repeating our nation's past errors, who do we think of? When the civil rights era is brought up, you don't hear a lot about the Southern Christian Leadership Conference, but you hear an awful lot about its most famous leader, Martin Luther King Jr., who is portrayed as an individual whose brilliant idea, or dream if you will, instantaneously changed hearts and minds once it passed through enough ears. Groups like the Student Nonviolent Coordinating Committee (SNCC), or even the National Association for the Advancement of Colored People (NAACP), are sidelined in favor of supposedly isolated individuals like Rosa Parks. Parks is portrayed as a visionary woman with an "idea" that caught like wildfire, rather than a dedicated political activist who had worked with the NAACP for a decade. Acts of civil disobedience on buses had been carried out for years prior to Parks's famous trip to the front of the bus, which wasn't the first bus action she had staged either.

Groups are sidelined, political conflict is at worst maligned or at best relegated to another era, activists and organizers are atomized, and their supposedly unique ideas are presented as the products of personal genius and foresight, rather than especially notable variants of wider collective outlooks with deep histories. This individualistic outlook has roots in Christian theology, which posits the irresistibility of hearing the "Good News" about Christ and the immediate salvation that can be attained by embracing the idea of Jesus as personal savior. The practical implication of the concept of the idea as motor of history is that the way to improve society is supposedly to express an idea as an individual and hope that it's good enough for a lot of people to agree. If you actually study history, however, you'll realize that ideas are never enough on their own. They have to fit into the right political, economic, and cultural context and ride waves of popular upheaval to gain any traction. After all, most of us who organized

Occupy Wall Street had been making the same political arguments for years before the Fall of 2011 without getting much reaction.

Therefore, when the opportunity came for Occupy Wall Street organizers to express our ideas to a previously disinterested public, we tried to make the most of the opportunity. In order to make our ideas as intelligible and accessible as possible, we realized that we needed to take popular narratives, belief systems, and common sense outlooks seriously. As my fellow Press Working Group organizer Michael Premo wrote, we need to engage with popular "myths" that structure our belief systems because all too often "our messaging…instead of persuading, often assaults and repulses the very people we seek to reach."[6] A strategic presentation of our politics was so important for OWS because the vast majority of organizers were not interested in propping up American Empire, preserving "American values," or competing against the rest of the world as if we were living in some gigantic sports metaphor. Although liberals and conservatives projected their interpretations of the decline of American Empire onto Occupy Wall Street, OWS organizers themselves were predominantly anticapitalist, antiauthoritarians. As I explore in my book *Translating Anarchy: The Anarchism of Occupy Wall Street*, based on 192 interviews I conducted with the most active organizers of the movement in New York and my experience as an OWS organizer, I found that 39 percent self-identified as anarchists and another 33 percent had "anarchistic" politics (anticapitalist, antihierarchical, direct action-oriented) that were largely indistinguishable from anarchism.[7] When combined, this shows that, overall, 72 percent of OWS organizers had explicitly anarchist or implicitly anarchistic politics (78 percent of organizers were anticapitalist). Nevertheless, most of us involved in framing messages to the general public agreed that directly calling for the immediate abolition of capitalism and the state, and its replacement with directly democratic federations of worker and community councils that would prioritize fulfilling human need and attaining environmental sustainability, might not resonate easily with many people who would otherwise be receptive to ideas of economic justice and a true democracy, but have negative associations with their ideological trappings.

Rhetorically, we faced a challenging dilemma: in a society that has so thoroughly discarded leftist politics, the only way that we could express our politics was to infiltrate some of the myths, symbols, axioms, ideas, and narratives of the dominant political culture, in order to exploit their polyvalent elements for subversive purposes. If arguments for austerity, economic exploitation, and American Empire pervade the minds of many Americans and perpetuate themselves through these discourses, then many of us felt it necessary to engage with them in order to drain them of their meaning and resignify them. This was often a messy process. At times, some Occupy groups or organizers wandered too far in the direction of adopting mainstream tropes and mimicking reactionary behaviors. Nevertheless, our strategic messaging afforded us a rare and valuable opportunity to articulate a politics that was essentially anticapitalist and antiauthoritarian to a wide public and bring a lot of new people into radical organizing.

For the remainder of this essay, I will touch upon four significant myths of popular culture, or ideas supposedly learned from history to avoid being doomed to repeat it, faced by OWS organizers who dealt with messaging: "Shining City Upon a Hill," "Living Within Your Means," "A Fair Day's Wage for a Fair Day's Work," and "You Will Always Have the Poor Among You." I hope the rhetorical strategies implemented by Occupy Wall Street organizers to address the wider public will encourage activists to put more thought into how their radical arguments are interpreted, as we continue to fight against austerity, the latest front in the ongoing struggle against state and capital.

SHINING CITY UPON A HILL

Since at least the twentieth century, American politicians and patriotic Christians have spoken of the United States as a blessed "shining city upon a hill" based on Jesus's Sermon on the Mount (Matthew 5:14), where he is purported to have said, "You are the light of the world. A city that is set on a hill cannot be hidden." Through its invocation by politicians such as JFK and especially Ronald Reagan, it has become one of several famous phrases used to emphasize "American exceptionalism": the idea that the United States has had a unique national history, distinct from that of other countries, which has produced a distinctly freedom-loving and justice-promoting culture, and that it's destined, in many cases, to lead the way internationally. This outlook is a distant echo of the interpretation that many early Christian settlers made, that God had set North America aside for the creation of a truly Christian society, one that could divorce itself from European social ills.

Many Americans may not realize it, but our country's patriotic fervor is really far more pervasive and rabid than in many other countries. For example, if you visit Paris on the national day, *la Fête Nationale* (known to English speakers as Bastille Day), you wouldn't know what day it was, unless you happened to bump into the military parade. After the horrors of twentieth century nationalism, many Europeans have toned down their love of country. In contrast, if you go to any American town on the Fourth of July, you can't escape the day's festivities. Every politician and mainstream public figure has to agree that America is, and will always be, Number One. Once in a while, you'll see public service announcements on TV about how the US is slipping behind a dozen other supposedly lesser countries in math scores or science education. I have no doubt that this is true, and that the American educational system could be a lot better in a number of ways, but why not watch those commercials and say, "Hey, good job Finland!" Why see success in terms of competition rather than cooperation? Don't we ideally want all students in the world to do well? Many patriotic Americans would rather have global educational achievement lowered so the USA can be Number One than feel inferior to Japan.

Like it or not, this was the patriotic political culture that we had to engage with, if we hoped to spread our message beyond the confines of the radical left. OWS organizers did this in several ways. First, it was common to argue that, given America's wealth, we should be doing a better job of taking care of each other. The resources clearly existed to have a better healthcare system, eliminate poverty, etc., but it wasn't happening. If the United States was really the greatest country in the world, then it should act like it. By associating living standards with patriotism, we tried to harness jingoistic fervor for social justice purposes. The following is an example of the kinds of points we made:

> Family income has fallen by $4,000, but health insurance premiums are higher, food prices are higher, utility bills are higher, and gasoline prices have doubled. Today more Americans wake up in poverty than ever before. Nearly one out of six Americans is living in poverty. Look around you. These are not strangers. These are our brothers and sisters, our fellow Americans.

The only thing is that this quote is from Mitt Romney's speech at the 2012 Republican National Convention and, in his eyes, these problems were all caused by the Obama presidency. The fact that Romney had to continually defend himself from critiques of his vast wealth and incorporate Occupy-style messaging says a lot about how we helped to shift the country's political terrain. But rather than get caught up on the electoral merry-go-round, we sought to shift the blame toward the bankers, CEOs, and financial institutions responsible for the crisis to begin with. Therefore, a second tactic that many took was to portray banks and corporations as anti-American. Common OWS talking points included points about how bankers and corporations wrecked the economy, how they continued moving jobs out of the country, how the upper class paid lower taxes than everyone else and hid their money from taxes in offshore accounts, how free trade agreements lowered environmental and labor standards, and how most major corporations didn't pay taxes at all.[8] Although many of the sign-holders lining Liberty Square (formerly known as Zuccotti Park) were liberals, progressives, or conspiracy theorists, most of the organizers were anticapitalists whose goal was not simply to adjust rates of taxation but to abolish economic exploitation entirely. For those of us working toward that goal, the idea was to exploit the tensions between neoliberalism and statist nationalism, and veil our radicalism with a healthy dose of populism. In that vein, some OWS organizers tried to funnel conservative distrust of the federal government and traditional affinity toward an American "rugged individualism" toward antiauthoritarian arguments for decentralized community and workplace self-management. By diverging from the standard liberal playbook of "big government," we managed to tap into the American love affair with an apolitical, "nonpartisan" orientation. In the fall of 2011, I met a woman from the Spanish 15M movement who harshly criticized our focus on domestic issues at the expense of internationalist messaging. I completely understood her perspective and sympathized with her priorities, but I tried to explain how Americans are so focused on what's going on in their country that language about austerity in Europe or third world debt or *campesino* movements in Latin America usually doesn't feel directly relevant to many Americans. In fact, such comparisons often run the risk of sounding grandiose and head-in-the-clouds, as opposed to discussions about immediate local issues like police harassment, foreclosures, and unemployment. Certainly it wasn't uncommon for someone to reference our solidarity with Tahrir Square in Cairo or Puerta del Sol in Madrid, but such international acknowledgments weren't what made the majority of New Yorkers and Americans agree with our message.

LIVING WITHIN YOUR MEANS

A KEY COMPONENT in the popular narrative of the American success story is "living within your means." Whenever you hear a politician giving a convention speech, they usually briefly refer to their youth in the context of having to make do with less. Mothers are frequently lauded for their ability to balance the household budget and fathers are cherished for their work ethic in the face of scarcity. For all of the American reverence for capitalist wealth, those who make up the "real America" are imagined as hardworking, "middle-class," rather than working-class, people who get by with a modest standard of living and don't complain when they hit hard times.

This conservative praise for working-class stoicism plays an important ideological role in maintaining class rule. The underlying argument is that if you have it better than anyone else, you shouldn't complain, because if it weren't for capitalism or your government you might be in their position. This logic was in action on FOX News in 2011, when Robert Rector of the conservative Heritage Foundation argued that there actually aren't really any poor people in the United States because apparently 99.6 percent of poor families have a refrigerator, 81.4 percent have a microwave, and 54.5 percent have a cell phone. From this perspective, it's shortsighted to complain about living conditions that have improved since the nineteenth century and are far better than those in other countries.

However, not only has the minimum wage drastically declined when adjusted for inflation, since its peak at $1.60 in 1968, which would be $10.56 in 2012, and not only does that outlook ignore the thousands of Americans who are drowning in debt and don't have affordable access to basic healthcare, but it's a rhetorical tool to bring us all down to the lowest common denominator. This potential danger was on display when Charles Kenny wrote the nauseatingly class-collaborationist article "We're All the 1 Percent" in *Foreign Policy*, which argued that Occupiers should "stop whining" because Americans are more affluent than most of the world.[9] While it's true that working-class Americans have it better than their counterparts in the global South, the only way to end class oppression is through international organizing and mobilizing. If every group that had it better than someone else just shut up and turned to their rulers, like Kenny suggested, we'd remain mired in subjugation.

Historically, the ruling class has implemented this basic rhetoric to divide resistance in all its forms. Bosses have told skilled workers to "stop whining" since they have it better than the unskilled, and imperial rulers encouraged white, working-class settlers to see themselves as superior to indigenous populations and be thankful that they weren't in their position. Most recently, this argument has been mobilized to support austerity.

In the context of the economic crisis, the myth of meritocracy, economic remuneration based on production, and the divine wisdom of the market were all called into question. Conservative commentators responded to the assaults on meritocracy by pinning the blame on "entitlement." In their eyes, the problem boiled down to too many individuals and governments "living beyond their means," who had come to feel entitled to goods and services they hadn't earned in the old-fashioned way. Southern European countries like Greece and Spain supposedly collapsed because they had erected unmanageable "nanny states" that enacted "all sorts of lavish benefits for government workers" and sapped the population of their incentive to innovate and produce.[10] If the United States was to avoid "ending up like Greece," conservative pundits claimed, then the country needed to fall back on the tried and true values that made her great, and limit spending to what the budget could tolerate. In an absolutely asinine article entitled "In Defense of Austerity," Steve Tobak argued that finance works the same for "individuals, families, companies and nations," and that the same lesson that people teach their children, "that money doesn't grow on trees," applies across the board. For Tobak the entire debate boils down to this "simple fact": "you can't live perpetually beyond your means. You just can't."[11]

Therefore, the only "whining" that was tolerable was directed toward homeowners who had made "reckless" purchases or government workers, like teachers, who "mooched off the system." FOX News made a big deal out of the Heritage Foundation report that teachers are "overpaid."[12] Although the study's quantitative evidence demonstrates that, on average, those who become teachers see their salaries increase about 9 percent, while those who leave teaching see them fall by 3 percent (which sounds plausible), the conclusion drawn by conservatives was that any group making even slightly more than minimum wage workers is "overpaid." They certainly don't apply that metric to the upper class. Moreover, this argument encourages working class people to try to pull down those around them who have made slight gains, and think of economic justice as a force that pulls workers down rather than pushing them up.

There are other essays in this collection, such as Spannos's examination of Greece or Bowman's analysis of the origins of the crisis, that do a great job of delineating the fallacies behind the argument that the economy crashed because working people were living in luxury (although it's true that, under a capitalist system, the market imposes limits on the potential satisfaction of human need through the welfare state). Here, I'll spend a moment talking about how those arguments grafted themselves onto Occupy Wall Street. From the very start, our detractors portrayed the movement as a bunch of lazy people who were either rich (and therefore hypocrites) or unwise with their money, had fallen into debt, and/or lacked the individual wherewithal to help themselves. Just as conservatives tried to blame the collapse of the housing market on the "reckless" purchases of homeowners who could no longer keep up with their payments, rather than the criminal bankers and their fraudulent system (see Silfen Glasberg et al. in this volume), Occupy Wall Street was thought to be emblematic of a wider tendency of irresponsible Americans to blame others for their personal financial misfortune/errors. To counteract this individualization of economic exploitation, the OWS group Strike Debt put out "'The Debt Resistors' Operations Manual," which situates consumer, medical, and student debt within a larger movement of debt resistance.[13] The popular OWS slogan said, "You Are Not A Loan."

When responding to the press, Occupy organizers routinely pointed out that appeals to tighten our belts are always directed at the working class. Despite the heinous destruction of the financial sector, bankers and CEOs were still getting ridiculous holiday bonuses, while the families that they put out on the street had nothing. Rather than dispute the notion that groups, families, or governments should "live within their means," more often we pointed out the hypocrisy of the notion that the upper class was living according to their own rhetoric. This position was neatly summarized in the popular OWS chant: "Banks got bailed out/We got sold out!"

A FAIR DAY'S WAGE
FOR A FAIR DAY'S WORK

A PIVOTAL ELEMENT in the myth of American freedom and liberty is the idea that hard work is adequately rewarded, while "laziness" is not. The United States is imagined as a country (or, in many cases, the *only* country) where a sufficiently motivated person can go from rags to riches without outside interference. As opposed to more socially democratic countries, imagined as soft and entitled, the United States has managed to maintain its ethos of social Darwinist market meritocracy.

It's interesting, however, that "a fair day's wage for a fair day's work," or the notion that people should receive proportional remuneration for their labor, has been used to support both capitalist meritocratic positions and labor struggles. In the Occupy context, it was often used as a "common sense" standard to vilify us, but its conservative interpretation was destabilized by the economic crisis. On the one hand, critics patched together the worn-out argument that homeless and unemployed people should just try harder to get a job and that without putting in a fair day's work, it was spoiled of Occupy protesters to be asking for handouts. On the other hand, those arguments failed to resonate in an economic situation where hardworking people had been dispossessed by a bunch of suits who pushed around imaginary derivatives, who not only failed to contribute anything tangible to society but actually destroying the economy, and were being paid hundreds of times more than the workers they left jobless and homeless. It was a clear example of "a fair day's work" being rewarded with economic ruin while far more than "a fair day's wage" was being paid to a bunch of criminal bankers.

Therefore, many of us used the popular concept of a fair day's wage for a fair day's work to evade right-wing redbaiting. When speaking with journalists, I'd often say things like, "The Occupy message isn't radical at all. We're just saying that working people should have what they need to meet their needs and live a meaningful life. The bankers have taken the radical step of rewarding hard work with destitution, while they line their pockets with taxpayer money." Part of Occupy's success stemmed from our ability to tap into popular perspectives on justice to portray Wall Street as a deviation from American values.

But as my sound bite indicates, many Occupy organizers tried to push beyond moderate slogans and phrases like "a fair day's wage for a fair day's work" toward a more radically anticapitalist stance. Therefore, it was more common to hear organizers saying that we need to build an economy that meets our needs, than to hear rhetoric about raising the minimum wage. As the Liberty encampment indicated, a large percentage of OWS organizers advocated the traditional communist slogan, "From each according to their abilities, to each according to their needs" (although the vast majority of those in favor of this slogan came to it from a *libertarian* communist direction, rather than the more well-known authoritarian Soviet-style communism, which has amounted to little more than exploitative, authoritarian regimes operating under the guise of a workers' state). By pushing for an economy that meets our needs, we managed to address the obvious fact that capitalism was not sufficiently rewarding work, while subtly reorienting popular criteria for assessing an economy. Ultimately, the first step toward inculcating an anticapitalist consciousness is helping people realize that the highest priority for an economy is meeting our (as in the global population's) individual and collective needs in an environmentally sustainable fashion. Once those criteria are in place then it becomes plainly evident that the market consistently pushes in the opposite direction.

When journalists asked me whether I was an anticapitalist (which actually happened rather infrequently), I liked to use a line I first heard from Noam Chomsky, but was also said in one form or another by Martin Luther King Jr. and others, "What we have is socialism for the rich and capitalism for everyone else," when the government gives the banks a second chance, while throwing homeowners and the unemployed out on the curb. This angle provided an easy way to dissociate capitalism and fairness, and encourage people to focus on the material reality in front of them, rather than the discourse of a supposedly "free" market.

However, neither I nor other anticapitalist OWS organizers were opposed to speaking openly about the evils of capitalism or the American government. For those of us working to articulate the politics of OWS to a mainstream audience in short sound bites on TV, short articles on Occupy websites, or in periodicals (what I refer to as the first layer of OWS communication with the public), we tended to focus on bringing people into the movement based on where they were at, while pushing their politics in the direction of prioritizing human need over profit, understanding the charade of electoral politics, and gaining a greater appreciation for tactics of direct action. Once we managed to gain people's attention and bring them in, the second layer (more long-form and explicitly radical periodicals and media) and the third layer (actually speaking with radical and anarchist organizers and radicalizing through participation) of OWS communication turned many liberals into anticapitalist antiauthoritarians.

YOU WILL ALWAYS HAVE THE POOR AMONG YOU

POLITICALLY, POVERTY GETS far less attention than it deserves. In the American popular consciousness, the only people who say they want to end poverty are adorably naive children or hippies. In part, this is because poverty is thought to be the fault of the poor and no one can make someone else sufficiently "responsible" and "hardworking," but also because grandiose political goals were politically sidelined long ago in favor of small "practical" tweaks and adjustments in a system thought to be imperfect but far better than the "fanaticism" of ideology. Therefore, the generally unspoken attitude in mainstream political culture can be summed up in the oft-quoted biblical passage, "You will always have the poor among you." Poverty's just part of the landscape of political life, we are told, so we need to contain it, rather than undertake the foolhardy task of tackling it head-on.

The economic crisis, and subsequently Occupy Wall Street, gained media attention because the havoc of the market extended beyond its usual confines to affect many middle-class people who previously considered themselves exempt from the fear of destitution. Debt, unemployment, and homelessness even haunted "kids that did everything right...they went to school, they graduated and then they faced this very problematic labor market."[14] Once you boil it all down, the media narrative was pointing to the fact that the market failed to reward merit according to the traditional equation. One could follow the rules of the game and still end up poor (or lower than one's earlier class position).

While doing press work for OWS, it was also clear that this media narrative was about race. Journalists salivated over the opportunity to interview respectable-looking, white college students who had fallen on hard times, or a formerly middle-class, white father of two who had lost his job and was fed up. Often we would present a reporter with several interview subjects and they would end up only using the scandalous riches-to-rags story of a young white person, while ignoring a person of color's testimony about resisting long-term oppression. On election night, Bill O'Reilly mourned the decline of the "white establishment" and clarified the conservative perspective that, whereas white people are hardworking and self-motivated (and therefore deserving of what they have), people of color "want stuff" without earning it and, according to O'Reilly, that's why they voted for the "enabling" Barack Obama.

We found ourselves in a situation where much of the attention being generated by OWS was materializing for the wrong reasons. The challenge we faced was how to capitalize on the media frenzy, while thoroughly refuting the capitalist and white supremacist notion that the proper state of affairs entails a stable underclass primarily composed of people of color.

The OWS Press Working Group worked to foreground voices of color in the media (though not quite as much as we should have, in retrospect) and compiled a long, diverse list of spokespeople, organized by race, job, and economic situation. In terms of rhetoric, I often started speaking with journalists about the fact that this would be the first generation in a long time to have it worse than their parents. Given the liberal and conservative obsession with progress, this statement really seemed to chill many people to the bone. Pointing out the ineptitude of the market allowed us to destabilize the popular assumption that there is a clear path to material comfort. Essentially, I tried to acknowledge the reporter's inclination to see the post-2008 period as a bizarre aberration, in order to leverage that opening into a few comments about how working-class people and communities of color had been facing their own economic crisis for a long time before 2008.

* * *

Many Americans like to think of their political system as an open field of political self-expression, where the best ideas rise to the top and the rest sink to the bottom. Although elections are often framed in the hyperbolic language of war and conflict, most Americans actually become rather queasy at the notion that politics is fundamentally about conflict rather than individualistic free expression. Even OWS tapped into the American identification with the *idea as motor of history* with the popular slogan "You Can't Evict an Idea Whose Time Has Come," drafted by our Press Working Group for our press release in advance of the anticipated eviction of Liberty Square.

When it comes to government spending and cuts, the differences between the Republicans and Democrats are framed as philosophical differences to be determined by the voters, rather than manifestations of an ongoing class war being waged by the rich against the working class. In fact, the term "austerity" is rarely used in the American context; it is almost always applied to the European situation. If you google "Occupy Wall Street" and "austerity," you only find articles from Occupy and radical sources. "Austerity" as a distinct economic entity doesn't come up in the American mainstream media because politicians don't want to portray their policies in that light, and because the term implies a grand shift in historical eras, from a time of plenty to a time of hardship. Instead of portraying an era of reduced government spending as a new phenomenon reflecting global, neoliberal trends germinating since the 1970s, American politicians describe the situation as an age-old philosophical disagreement about "the role of government."

In the wake of Romney's defeat, the Republican Party was forced through a painful process of introspection. His reputation as the candidate of big money, evident in his infamous "47 percent" comment, clearly damaged his electoral potential. As rising star Bobby Jindal phrased it in a post-election Republican National Committee meeting, "We must quit 'big.' We are not the party of big business, big banks, big Wall Street bailouts, big corporate loopholes, or big any-thing…We are a populist party." While he added that the Republicans "must not become the party of austerity," Jindal made massive cuts to Medicaid programs in Louisiana that "provide behavioral health services for at-risk children, offer case management visits for low-income HIV patients and pay for at-home visits by nurses who teach poor, first-time mothers how to care for their newborns," while proposing tax increases on the poor.[15]

It's clear that Occupy Wall Street sparked enough popular indignation to force politicians to mitigate their rhetoric, but usually not enough to significantly alter their policies. Over the coming years, we'll have to experiment with new organizing forms and practices to take that next step toward constituting ourselves as a formidable obstacle in the path of capitalist destruction. But, for the moment, I hope readers will come away from this article thinking about how the first step toward shifting popular consciousness on a large scale must occur at the point of ideological and political mythological production.

ENDNOTES

1   Walter Hickey, "CENSUS: Whites Will Become A Minority in the United States by 2043," *Business Insider*, Dec. 18, 2012, http://www. businessinsider.com/census-whites-will-become-a-minority-in-the-united-states-by-2043-2012-12 (accessed July 14, 2013).

2   Andy Kroll, "Welcome to the United States of Austerity," *Mother Jones*, Aug. 2, 2011, http://www.motherjones.com/politics/2011/08/united-states-of-austerity (accessed July 14, 2013).

3   Carl Gibson, "'We Pay More': US Austerity Well Underway," *Common Dreams*, Oct. 26, 2012, https://www.commondreams.org/view/2012/10/26 (accessed July 14, 2013).

4   This saying is derived from philosopher and poet George Santayana, who said, "Those who cannot remember the past are condemned to repeat it," from his 1905–1906 work, *The Life of Reason*. See George Santayana, *The Life of Reason* (New York: Prometheus Books: 1998), 82.

5   The "doomed to repeat it" understanding of the relationship between ideas, history, and progress is different from a Hegelian interpretation, though they share some common intellectual ancestors.

6   Michael Premo, "Unlocking the Radical Imagination," in *We Are Many: Reflections on Movement Strategy from Occupation to Liberation*, (ed.) Kate Khatib, Margaret Killjoy, and Mike McGuire (Oakland: AK Press, 2012), 315–317.

7   Mark Bray, *Translating Anarchy: The Anarchism of Occupy Wall Street* (Winchester, UK: Zero Books, 2013).

8   Right now, about $32 trillion is kept by the extremely wealthy in tax-free overseas accounts, more than the national debts of the USA and EU combined. See Gibson, "'We Pay More.'"

9   Charles Kenny, "We're All the 1 Percent," *Foreign Policy*, March/April

2012, http://www.foreignpolicy.com/articles/2012/02/27/we_are_all_
the_1_percent?wp_login_redirect=0 (accessed July 14, 2013).

10 Quote from Stephen Moore of the *Wall Street Journal* on Fox News'
On the Record with Greta Van Susteren. See Albert Kleine, "Right-
Wing Media Falsely Compare U.S. with Greece to Support Spending Cuts," *Media Matters*, Jan. 2, 2013, http://mediamatters.org/
research/2013/01/02/right-wing-media-falsely-compare-us-with-
greece/191976 (accessed July 14, 2013).

11 Steve Tobak, "In Defense of Austerity," *CBS Moneywatch*, May 8,
2012, http://www.cbsnews.com/8301-505125_162-57429583/in-
defense-of-austerity/ (accessed July 14, 2013).

12 Ben Smith, "Conservative Think Tanks: Teachers Are 'Overpaid,'" *Po-
litico*, Nov. 1, 2011, http://www.politico.com/blogs/bensmith/1111/
Conservative_think_tanks_Teachers_are_overpaid.html (accessed July
14, 2013).

13 The Debt Resistors' Operations Manual, http://strikedebt.org/The-
Debt-Resistors-Operations-Manual.pdf (accessed July 14, 2013).

14 Colin Moynihan, "In 'Occupy,' Well-Educated Professionals Out-
numbered Jobless, Study Finds," *New York Times City Room*, Jan. 28,
2013, http://cityroom.blogs.nytimes.com/2013/01/28/in-occupy-well-
educated-professionals-far-outnumbered-jobless-study-finds/ (accessed
July 14, 2013).

15 Sy Mukherjee, "Louisiana Will Eliminate Health Benefits for HIV Patients, Poor Children, and First Time Moms this Week," *ThinkProgress*,
Jan. 29, 2013, http://thinkprogress.org/health/2013/01/29/1510161/
louisiana-will-eliminate-benefits-for-hiv-patients-poor-children-and-
first-time-moms-this-week/?mobile=nc (accessed July 14, 2013).

UNDOING THE REASONABLE MIDDLE

SEXUALITY AND GENDER MOVEMENTS IN THE AGE OF CRISIS AND AUSTERITY

ABBEY VOLCANO

"Seems shit's happening again."

An older comrade shared this dubious insight in early 2012. At this point, we were deep in the economic crisis. We watched the Arab Spring revolts topple dictators (and install new ruling classes). We'd seen a group in Spain calling themselves *Indignados* (the indignant ones) occupy Puerto Del Sol in Madrid. News of neighborhood assemblies were popping up all over the world, as people began experiments in public participation and collective decision-making. Students in London had stormed Conservative Party headquarters. And, to give the comrade credit, things were even popping off in the US with the Occupy movement. Though, to be fair, the police were also kicking our asses quite a bit (I don't want to paint too rosy a picture).

A common theme, a steady murmur, among a lot of radicals variously involved in these uprisings has been talk of a sort of battle over the character of the movements. In many instances, the primary divisions within these formations have been between, on the one hand, liberals, who saw this as their Great Opportunity to do things like "speak truth to power" or "be the change," and reform our ruling institutions to make them nicer, kinder, a little less glaringly miserable.

On the other hand, radicals saw this as a time to push these formations as far as they could go—to magnify the contradictions in our
institutions and to make a break with present society. I call the liberal
loyal opposition in this chapter the "reasonable middle": those folks
who view the contemporary rebellions with an eye toward managing
them and channeling them into politics. We might juxtapose that
reasonable middle with radicals: those who push at the seams of the
possible, refuse to be controlled, and see possibilities beyond attempts
at reining in our horrific institutional relations.

Anytime throughout history that "shit's happening," there are elements of struggle around gender and sexuality. Part of this is because
these moments of collective action are about how power is organized in
our daily lives. Gender and sexuality are two major, socially constructed
sites of power where some segments of society wield power over other
segments. At certain historical moments, we have greater cycles of struggle around power (in Marxist phraseology, the "material conditions" are
ripe for conflict). Thus, during the great revolutionary movements of the
early twentieth century, we saw the rise of groups like the Mujeres Libres
in the Spanish Revolution, who argued that their revolution must also
liberate women.[1] We heard calls for "free love" (as if love—if it has any
meaning at all—could be anything but) and denunciations of marriage;[2]
and radical calls for seeing same-sex desire and love as legitimate, rather
than an aberration to be cured.[3] Similarly, when the global social spark
was lit during the late 1960s and early 1970s, we saw the rise of many
kinds of feminist radicalism (admittedly, some more radical than others),
the Stonewall Riots, the rise of groups like the Gay Liberation Front and
STAR (Street Transgender Action Revolutionaries), and so on.

Today, if one takes a glimpse at this global wave of unrest, one
can likewise find struggles centered on gender and sexuality. Within
these struggles, there are conflicts over whether our task is to create
kinder and gentler social relations around gender and sexuality, or if
we should abolish what exists. In this chapter, I'd like to highlight and
describe some of these struggles. And I'd like to conclude with some
analysis for those of us unwilling to settle for reforming the existent.

ANTI-RAPE SQUADS IN CAIRO

"OP ANTI–SEXUAL HARASSMENT/ASSAULT" has developed in Cairo as
a response to the increased prevalence of sexual harassment and sexual

assault against women who have joined in public protests, most notably in Tahrir Square. Street harassment and sexual harassment are not
new to women the world over, but instances of attack and gang rape
have heightened in Cairo since the transitional period (which also
saw an increase in public sexual assaults). The response of the young
women involved in Op Anti–Sexual Harassment/Assault has not been
to avoid Tahrir Square or stop participating on the frontlines. Similarly, these young women have not turned exclusively to the state for
protection. Instead, the women in Op Anti–Sexual Harassment/As-
sault have refused to leave the squares or the streets and have insisted,
and rightfully so, that a woman's place is wherever the revolutionary
struggle might be, including the squares, the streets, wherever.[4]

In Cairo, thousands of women have marched against sexual assault and sexual harassment—insisting that it's not individual men
who are the problem, but rather that it is society that assaults women,
and it is the state that condones it (or even encourages such attacks).[5]
Many women in these protests have carried large knives, gripped
with their fists in the air, insisting that women will free Egypt, not
the other way around. Hundreds of men have volunteered to help
protect groups of women in the squares, and during protests especially. The volunteer men have gone as far as using flamethrowers
against groups of sexual harassers and sexual assaulters.[6] The women
and men involved with Op Anti–Sexual Harassment/Assault have
taken on the task of turning the squares into places where women
are just as able as anyone else to participate in revolutionary struggle
(a good starting point, at least). The streets and squares aren't safe,
and women are being raped *for being women* in Tahrir Square—the
response, then, has been to address these assaults directly and not to
simply ask for state mediation or "protection."

One reason to take direct action against the rape, assault, and harassment of women in the squares and on the streets is because of the
belief that the state has a stake in the sexual assault of women in revolutionary struggle (and of men as well, but most notably women this
time around). But another reason, like the old Wobbly slogan says,
is because direct action gets the goods—when women aren't able to
maintain bodily autonomy during revolutionary struggle (or in calmer
social times, for that matter) for fear of being raped and assaulted, one
response is for people to band together and turn this fear around, so
the harassers and the assaulters become the ones under attack. Again,

this was not a symbolic action meant to eventually have an effect. Rather, the direct action in this struggle *protected women in the streets.* With the masses of volunteers attacking men who assault and harass women for being women, we see that the overwhelming response has been to take direct action on the streets and in the squares. Part of revolutionary struggle is reclaiming the commons, and part of that wider struggle is making the commons (and their acquisition by the people) a place where women can struggle, without being stripped of their clothing and their autonomy by the state, the police, or other so-called "revolutionaries." Rather than "the protection of women" being the pursuit of specific *activists* who place pressure on the state to respond to social unrest, the people responding to these attacks are the people in Cairo who want to struggle *against* the existing state, and, for some, against class society and patriarchy. They are finding the best way to do so is through self-organization of the working class, supporting each other and fighting their enemies, outside and within the class. Similar actions have taken place in the United States, where some women are not seeking state mediation or protection from sexual assault and harassment. Instead, these "girl gangs" are directly providing protection (defensive and offensive) for themselves and their communities.

GIRL GANGS IN THE BAY AREA AND CRITIQUES OF PRIVILEGE THEORY

In the United States, feminism has often been based in movements that are largely middle-class, white, academic, etc. But post-crisis, not everyone is rallying around the category of the monolithic "woman," demonstrating the limits of identity (this was also true pre-crisis but seems to be spreading since 2008, as a reaction to the effects of austerity). In the fall of 2012, "women, queers, rebels, and allies" organized a "feminist vigilante gangs" march in Oakland, California.[7] One of the reasons for this march was to bring women, gender outlaws, and queers together to start planning an *offensive* against the violence they all experience. The break here is with a narrow conception of the identity "woman," as well as a shift toward an offensive strategy rather than a state-centered, defensive approach to addressing the myriad effects experienced by those on the receiving end of gendered violence in all its various forms. The organizers of the march reported that these feminist vigilante gangs were to take the place of the state where it fell short in response to gendered violence against people of the working class (that is, in nearly all cases).

The police and the criminal "justice" system have *clearly* failed at eradicating gendered violence. But we need to be honest with ourselves and admit that they never had the capacity to do so in the first place. The state and its institutions *are* gendered violence. Understanding this reality helped shape the organization of these self-identified "girl gangs." Rather than relying on the state, they are self-organizing, not only to protect each other, but to be on the offensive toward entities that commit gendered violence, whether they are individuals, institutions, conceptual understandings, or cultural forms. The gangs have said their aim is to "Bash Back"—a tactic already in use by a former group of the same name.[8]

Another departure from the reasonable middle in the United States can be seen with some current critiques of "privilege politics." Some of the dynamic aspects of these newer movement experiences are the rejection of various forms of "privilege theory" and the ways it has managed to kill movements and movement groups.[9] These critiques of privilege politics are directly related to the gendered and sexualized components of these movements, as much of the criticism is coming from women, queers, and people of color within organizations and mass movements.

Will argues that privilege theory fails when put into practice within social movements. "Privilege theory's main weakness [sic] are a tendency towards reformism, a lack of politics, and a politics of retreat."[10] He claims that reformism in the context of privilege theory often tells us the most oppressed are at the most risk, and therefore should not be at the forefront of struggle, because they have too much to lose. In turn, privilege theory is often used to justify "less oppressed" people fighting on behalf of the oppressed, since the former can afford to get arrested without losing their homes or facing deportation, for example. But it has been demonstrated, again and again, that the oppressed must take their struggles into their own hands, and the movements that succeed in actually building capacity among those most affected are the ones that do this. Informed by (some interpretations of) privilege theory, reformism argues the opposite and turns the oppressed into "helpless victims," who can be "saved" by tinkering with our institutions instead of abolishing them. In many ways, this peculiar situation reifies white supremacy and other structures of domination, and also produces a situation where professional "activists" manage struggles rather than the self-organized working class struggling in solidarity.

By "lack of politics," Will refers to a lack of analysis of structures of power and domination, while putting the most effort into making sure that individuals somehow "check" their own privilege within social movements. In effect, this strategy depoliticizes movements and turns revolutionary potential into simple individual attempts to "check" one's own privilege within personal settings. Checking one's privilege can surely be helpful and is often appreciated, but the question remains as to what those attempts *actually do* to destroy current structures of power and domination. Will also argues that privilege theory is a politics of retreat because it thrives in depoliticized times when mass revolutionary movements are hard to find. Again, Will's critiques of privilege theory come from his time spent organizing in mass movements that use privilege theory as a filter through which to make decisions and inform strategies and tactics. The reasonable middle often thrives on these manifestations of privilege theory and, in effect, depoliticizes struggle. Departing from this reasonable middle means critically assessing tactics and strategies, and preventing the *management* of struggles by professional, often self-appointed activists who typically rely on the state for change. Instead, we might rely on those most affected, through direct action strategies.

On the Bay of Rage website, CROATOAN critiques privilege theory by arguing that it tends to conceptualize white privilege, for example, as a mainly psychological problem created by the attitudes of individuals, and that this view fails to address power and structures of domination in society, let alone change them.[11] Many critiques of privilege theory similarly argue against this point—the idea that privileges manifest in individual behaviors, which, in turn, require a simple change in such individual behaviors to eradicate complex structures of power, such as white privilege, patriarchy, heterosexism, cissexism, ableism, etc. The critique here is that abolishing patriarchy, heterosexism, cissexism, white supremacy, class society, etc., requires, among other things, militant and radical social movements to replace our old structures of oppression and domination with new structures, ones that might foster a classless, egalitarian, participatory, and, hopefully, vastly less boring society. CROATOAN writes, "We argue that prevailing discourses of personal privilege and political representation in fact minimize and misrepresent the severity and structural character of the violence and material deprivation marginalized demographics face." So, not only do privilege politics, deployed in this manner, miss the point, but the politics actually *set back* militant class-struggle movements, by removing an analysis of how political economy creates crises, and relying on abstract notions of shared identities, removed from structural context, as the basis for organizing.

If we struggle only in the name of a shared, broad identity like sexuality, gender, or race, we have to think about what that means for our goals (short- and long-term). Some emergent shifts in the agendas of queer struggle highlight what it means to move from organizing around a shared (imagined) identity, such as "queer," ignoring material differences, beyond "we are queer, so we therefore have common goals," and toward a more materialist understanding of not only identity, but of strategy, goals, and possibilities. More concretely, these shifts bring back an important part of liberation, one that often seems lost in academic settings, and certainly has seemed lost for decades in the United States; a *method* that is perhaps back on the agenda with the rise of the Occupy movement: class struggle.

SHIFTING QUEER AGENDAS

In the United States, a shift in queer organizing as response to austerity measures can be seen, as a number of queer movements have begun to coalesce not simply around a shared identity of "being queer and having that in common," but toward a shared position vis-à-vis power and access to the material needs required to live worthwhile lives—a position that is not exclusive to *only* queer people, nor relevant to *all* queer people.

Standing on the shoulders of queer organizers/writers (like Jerimarie Liesegang), John D'Emilio argues that we've come upon a "new era" in queer organizing, although it looks quite similar to previous eras of radical queer struggles. "Instead of thinking, 'AIDS funding,' we should think, 'national health insurance.' Instead of thinking 'same-sex marriage,' we should think, 'security for all families and households.' Instead of 'queer studies programs,' why not, 'affordable public higher education for everyone'?"[12]

This "new queer agenda" has been argued for in various forms and demonstrated in a variety of movements and struggles.[14] Although not technically new, class struggle has become a *central method* of contemporary queer organizing once again.[15] The single-issue politics of organizations such as the Human Rights Campaign, the National Gay and Lesbian Task Force, and Lambda Legal (all part of the "reasonable middle"), are becoming less popular with working-class queer people who aren't necessarily part of the radical milieu. What's being recognized now is that "being queer and having that in common" is not a good basis for politics. Rather, working-class queer people are situating their obstacles and demands within the class. Rather than solely demanding liberal notions of "recognition," demands are shifting and, to a greater extent, becoming based on material needs and desires, rather than liberal and insufficient demands of recognition within structures ultimately organized to cage and discipline the working class. As Gayge Operaista argues, "The task is for radical queers to become class struggle militants."[16]

Richard Blum argues that queer organizers need to start focusing on the erosion of the welfare state and the collective power of the working class and our demands, not just the specific demands of queer people in the workplace:

> If we think we can make a separate deal for our protection and not participate in the larger effort to give workers a meaningful voice in the workplace, we will fail for all but a few. It is and will remain cold comfort for a queer worker that she or he is being let go into a failing economy along with straight coworkers in order to increase company profits and not because she or he is gay or trans.[17]

These types of shifts demonstrate a trend toward organizing as *queers in class struggle*, rather than as queers who seek the same recognition and access as wealthy, white, and otherwise normative and dominant nonqueer people, within the utterly destructive and deplorable structures under which we currently suffer. This is a clear shift from the "reasonable middle" toward more radical politics. And again, we can see a shift toward direct action strategies around gender and sexuality.

In Sydney, Australia, earlier this year, queer radicals began organizing against police brutality.[18] Property laws and police systematically target queer youth, since many of them are living in poverty and engaged in sex work, often performed in public due to a lack of adequate private space. In addition, violent, homophobic attacks are prevalent and often go unreported for a variety of reasons. Queer radicals in Sydney have made a call to form self-organized queer and women's militias to combat gendered and sexual violence, instead of relying on police and laws to "protect" them (police and laws *are* gendered and sexual violence, and we need protection *from* them, not *by* them).

CONCLUSION

In Cairo, hundreds of people, often using Black Bloc tactics, are attacking those who assault and harass women in the street—they are struggling and organizing to protect female organizers and demonstrators. This is but one example of a clear break from the liberal ways of "speaking truth to power" (idealist), toward direct action with the intent to *act on and alter existing society* (materialist) in its particular context, not just talk about it, or ask someone else or a bureaucracy to do it for us (as though they even could). This is the undoing of the reasonable middle—it's a refusal to ask the state and its lackeys for things we might be taking, creating, changing, or destroying in the here and now, initiated and carried out by ourselves. Not only does direct action in this sense "get the goods," but it also fosters (and is a product of) the self-organization of the working class, rather than management of social change in the hands of professional leftist activists.

Part of the project of undoing the reasonable middle is to recognize the limits of identity politics—not to dismiss identity or the importance of standpoint, but to recognize their limits. Contemporary shifts in queer organizing demonstrate a politics not limited by identity, but rather a materialist politics that recognizes the importance of class struggle, creating classlessness, and the ways in which queer liberation is directly tied to this endeavor. It has been argued that there's been a retreat from class struggle within feminist and queer organizing—not because class is dropped from the analysis, but because class is treated as just one other form of oppression to add to the laundry list.[19] This transformation of class into "just another oppression" has the effect of divorcing class from the political economy that creates it, while also ignoring the uniqueness of exploitation under capitalism. A politics that recognizes the importance of meaning and subjectivity, as well as abolishing capitalism, the state, and political economy, might be a politics that can actually foster a world that is not just organized differently in terms of quantitative measure, but one that produces *qualitatively* different experiences of daily life, with social relations of our own creation.

These struggles outlined above demonstrate the difference between the desire to self-manage the existent and the desire to break with (negate) it. This undoing of the reasonable middle might seem, understandably, "unreasonable" to those who still think we can rearrange capital and the state differently so that everyone will have their needs and desires met. But for those struggling to undo the reasonable middle, "reason" isn't their ultimate goal. After all, many people consider the state, capital, and the various forms of social inequalities we live with on a daily basis, to be reasonable, and just in need of tweaking. To me, *that* is what's entirely unreasonable, and we need only to look at history to see this.

ENDNOTES

1   Martha Ackelsberg, *Free Women of Spain: Anarchism and the Struggle for the Emancipation of Women* (Oakland: AK Press, 2005).

2   For example, see Voltairine de Cleyre, "They Who Marry Do Ill," in *Anarchy! An Anthology of Emma Goldman's Mother Earth*, (ed.) Peter Glassgold *(Washington D.C.: Counterpoint, 2001),*103–113.

3   Terrence Kissack, *Free Comrades: Anarchism and Homosexuality in the United States 1895–1917* (Oakland: AK Press, 2008).

4   "This Is A Mass Sexual Assault . . . We Will Resist (Video)," *Jadaliyya,* February 4, 2013, http://www.jadaliyya.com/pages/index/9972/this-is-a-mass-sexual-assault-.-.-.-we-will-resist (accessed March 31, 2013)

5   Jihan Hafiz, "Sexual Harassment of Women is State Sponsored Say Egyptian Women," *The Real News,* February 9, 2013, http://thereal-news.com/t2/index.php?option=com_content&task=view&id=31&Ite mid=74&jumival=9658#.URg7UKXXak3 (accessed March 31, 2013).

6   Sallie Pisch, "Flamethrowers Used to Protect Women from Tahrir Mob Assault," *Demotix,* January 25, 2013, http://www.demotix.

com/news/1750555/flamethrowers-used-protect-women-tahrir-mob-assault#media-1752911 (accessed March 31, 2013).

7   Yael Chanoff, "Feminist Vigilante Gangs to March on Oakland Friday," *San Francisco Bay Guardian Online*, October 3, 2012, http://www.sfbg.com/politics/2012/10/03/feminist-vigilante-gangs-march-oakland-friday (accessed April 9, 2013). **Don't read the comments**

8   For example, see the Bash Back book *Queer Ultraviolence* http://ardent-press.org/bashback/

9   Will, "Guest Post: Privilege Politics is Reformism," *Black Orchid Collective*, March 12, 2012, http://blackorchidcollective.wordpress.com/2012/03/12/guest-post-privilege-politics (accessed April 10, 2013).

10   Ibid.

11   CROATON, "Who Is Oakland: Anti-Oppression Activism, the Politics of Safety, and State Co-optation," *Escalating Identity*, April 2012, http://escalatingidentity.wordpress.com/2012/04/30/who-is-oakland-anti-oppression-politics-decolonization-and-the-state (accessed April 10, 2013).

12   John D'Emilio, "Creating Change," in *The Scholar & Feminist Online*, "A New Queer Agenda," http://sfonline.barnard.edu/a-new-queer-agenda/ (accessed April 4, 2013). See also Jerimarie Liesegang, "Tyranny of the State and Trans Liberation," in *Queering Anarchism: Addressing and Undressing Power and Desire*, (ed.) Daring, et al. (Oakland: AK Press, 2012), 87–99.

14   For example, see *The Scholar & Feminist Online*, "A New Queer Agenda," http://sfonline.barnard.edu/a-new-queer-agenda/ (accessed April 4, 2013).

15   Liesegang, "Tyranny of the State and Trans Liberation."

16   Gayge Operaista, "Radical Queers and Class Struggle: A Match to Be Made," in *Queering Anarchism: Addressing and Undressing Power and Desire*, (ed.) Daring, et al. (Oakland: AK Press, 2012), 115–127.

17   Richard Blum, "Equality with Power: Fighting for Economic Justice at Work," in *The Scholar & Feminist Online*, "A New Queer Agenda," http://sfonline.barnard.edu/a-new-queer-agenda/ (accessed April 4, 2013).

18 "Queers Against Cops Respond to Attacks," Indymedia, http://indy-media.org.au/2013/03/10/queers-against-cops-respond-to-attacks (accessed April 4, 2013).

19 For example, see the (excellent) introduction to Rosemary Hennessy and Chrys Ingraham (ed.), *Materialist Feminism: A Reader in Class, Difference, and Women's Lives* (New York: Routledge, 1997), 1–14.

ARGENTINA'S MOVEMENTS AGAINST AUSTERITY AND THE POLITICS OF SPACE

MARIE TRIGONA

"QUE *SE VAYAN TODOS! QUE SE VAYAN TODOS!*" SHOUTED HUNDREDS OF thousands of protestors who took to the streets banging pots and pans to protest the austerity measures imposed during Argentina's financial crisis in 2001. By that year, the South American country had imploded into a total economic collapse. Businesses had gone bankrupt and thousands of factories were closed. More than half of the population was living in poverty, as unemployment rates soared above 27 percent. The protesters, shouting, "All of them must go!" forced out four presidents in less than three weeks following the December 20, 2001 demonstration. Police killed thirty-one people over the course of two days of popular rebellion.

Argentina's 2001 crisis was one of a myriad of contemporary global financial crises. Capitalism, however, has utilized these cycles of crisis as part of its survival mechanism. French philosopher Henri Lefebvre argues that capitalism has been able to resolve its "internal contradictions for a century…by occupying space, by producing space."[1] The shift toward austere neoliberalism has been a global phenomenon; global austerity's structures reflect how capitalism has survived crisis through the production and occupation of a fragmented, homogenized, and hierarchically structured space. The current contemporary phase of neoliberal capitalism occupies space through its ability to pick up and move production, and create a physically divided and temporary workforce, while ripping apart social safety nets and expanding the ranks of the poor and unemployed. The question now is: how do we resist this spatial exploitation, when capital tries to make all these changes seem objective and natural and therefore not worth challenging?

Edward Soja notes that the political challenge for the postmodern left,[2] in the face of the constant respatialization capitalization undertakes to resolve its crises, must be to directly confront capitalist politics with an informed postmodern politics of resistance and demystification, "one that can pull away the deceptive ideological veils that are today reifying and obscuring, in new and different ways, the restructured instrumentalities of class exploitation, gender and racial domination, cultural and personal disempowerment, and environmental degradation."[3] Soja's postmodern lens provides us with tools to analyze the system-wide crisis affecting contemporary capitalist societies and ways to resist. We must adapt a radical postmodernism of resistance, according to Soja, one that aims at taking control of the production of space.

Michel Foucault also suggests that we live inside a set of relations—spaces of relations. He also saw the connection between space and the exercise of power. With each crisis, we must confront new approaches to organizing the economy, and the expansion of the exercise of power into our everyday lives. The geography of capitalism attempts to discipline our bodies and our relations. We remain in a period of prolonged global crisis. And we must face that, at every stage of life, the spatial organization of society has been restructured to meet the urgent demands of capitalism in crisis.[4] Through their territorial resistance, nonhierarchical forms of organizing, occupations of the means of production and public space, Argentina's social movements provide insight into how to challenge the "objective" processes of structural change associated with capitalism's ability to develop and survive in the form of austerity.[5] Following Soja's and Foucault's analyses, these social movements have questioned capitalism's ability to reproduce social relations of production despite debilitating crises. Human rights groups have challenged the space for justice. The unemployed workers movement has questioned the formation of post-Fordist industrial organization and technology. The occupied factory movement has challenged the vertical reproduction of social relations in capitalism. These movements have begun to tear away the layers of contemporary capitalism's ideological mystification, which presents the capitalist regulation of space as an objective and necessary project.[6]

In this piece, we will examine Argentina's social movements' resistance to austerity and crisis. More pointedly, we will explore how this struggle focused on the production of space and the territorial structure of exploitation and domination.[7] This resistance helps us understand the transformations that have allowed capitalism to thrive, despite its own internal crises. All of these experiences unveil the guise of the objectivity of space. They also provide insight into strategies for anticapitalist struggle. Soja reminds us that the "power-filled social production of space under capitalism has not been a smooth and automatic process in which social structure is stamped out, without resistance or constraint, onto the landscape."[8] His thesis is correct. As we are in a permanent period of crisis, capitalism's mechanisms are facing a growing antiausterity movement seeking to challenge the hegemonic social relations of space and time with direct actions, occupations, and solidarity projects.

A SPACE OF TERROR: THE 1976–1983 MILITARY DICTATORSHIP

Neoliberalism was accomplished in Argentina, as in other parts of Latin America, through a US-backed coup. Austerity in the Southern Cone was rooted in the bloody 1976–1983 Argentine military dictatorship that disappeared more than 30,000 people, mostly labor and social activists.

Prior to the dictatorship, the radical left had regained momentum, with growing unrest culminating among union activists and students. A year after the French upsurge in May 1968, rebellion hit Argentina, in the city of Cordoba. The military took on the task of repressing the inevitable social conflict with their decision to do away with traditional politics through the institutionalization of state repression. The left implemented guerrilla tactics to resist this state repression and US hegemony.

The political conflict created instability and an opportunity for the military to launch a coup to suppress the left. Argentina's 1976 junta was capitalism's response to growing resistance. During the late 1960s and early 1970s, the United States and Latin American military governments developed Operation Condor as a transnational, state-sponsored terrorist coalition among the militaries of South America. As a result, in Argentina alone, some 30,000 people were disappeared; leaving loved ones to seek justice decades later. In his "Open Letter from a Writer to the Military Junta," published on the first anniversary of the coup, March 24, 1977, journalist Rodolfo Walsh described the abuses that occurred during the first year of Latin America's darkest chapter. He also connected the abuses to structural changes in Latin America's economic policies. The military dictatorship used a complex structure of terror to transform Argentina's economic space, open the markets to foreign investors, cease national policies of import substitution, and rack up debt with foreign lending institutions.

Rodolfo Walsh's letter, which would be one of the most important literary records of the dictatorship's economic strategy, described how economists trained by the conservative Chicago School implemented the core neoliberal policies after the advent of the military government, and exposed the abuses carried out by the junta, as part of a regional plan to wipe out opposition to an economic model that created widespread inequality.

> The real salary of workers has dropped 40 percent.
> They are freezing salaries with the butts of rifles while
> prices are soaring at the point of a bayonet, destroying
> any form of collective bargaining, prohibiting union as-
> semblies, making work hours longer and raising unem-
> ployment to record levels. When the workers protest,
> the dictatorship calls them subversive, kidnaps entire
> union assemblies. In some cases, the bodies turn up
> dead and in other cases they never turn up.[9]

This model, touted by the IMF and "Washington consensus" as a phenomenal success, was synonymous with unimaginable methods of terror imposed upon society. At the Ford Motor plant, twenty-five union delegates were detained and disappeared inside the plant's very own clandestine detention center for days, weeks, or months, until they were secretly transferred to the local police precinct, run by forces that had been transformed into a military cartel. Pedro Troiani was a union delegate for six years in the Ford plant in the Greater Buenos Aires district of Pacheco, until the 1976 coup. "The company used the disappearances to get rid of unionism at the factory," said Troiani. The Mercedes-Benz plant was also transformed into a clandestine torture and detention center. The exact number of workers who were disappeared from the Mercedes-Benz plant in Argentina is still unknown. Estimates say at least thirteen, but the number is most likely close to twenty. Many times, workplaces and government buildings turned into clandestine detention centers were situated in the middle of barrios.[10]

Through terror, the junta accomplished the restructuring of the institutional, financial, and economic landscape. Within this lexicon of terror, Argentina's labor force was terrorized into accepting new labor practices. Resistance and labor activists faced being kidnapped in the middle of the night by commando groups, driven away in green Ford Falcons. But the junta didn't accomplish this restructuring without intense resistance from a group of women who, from within the space of motherhood, became the new opposition to the status quo.

The Mothers of Plaza de Mayo would become one of the most respected human rights organizations as a result of their relentless demand for justice for crimes committed during the dictatorship. The Mothers of the Plaza de Mayo began protesting on April 30, 1977. Having visited police stations, prisons, judicial offices, and churches, but finding no answers, the Mothers began to hold weekly vigils in the plaza in front of the Presidential Palace, wearing white head scarves to symbolize the diapers of their lost and disappeared children. At the time, the military prevented groups of more than three people from gathering. So the mothers slowly walked around the plaza in small groups. Their actions brought international attention. The Mothers transformed the Plaza de Mayo, a public plaza, into a space of nonviolent resistance against the bloody military dictatorship.

The Mothers faced violence for not keeping silent. A church they were using as an organizing space wasn't safe from the grasp of terror of the military dictatorship. In 1977, three of the founding Mothers and two French nuns who supported the efforts of the Mothers also became part of "the disappeared." On December 8, 1977, the Mothers—Esther Ballestrino de Careaga and Maria Eugenia Ponce de Bianco—were forcefully taken by military officials, along with eight others, as they attended a meeting at the Santa Cruz Church in Buenos Aires. Just days later, Azucena Villaflor, another founding Mother, was kidnapped outside her home.

Two weeks after the secret raid on the Santa Cruz Church, and only one week after the Mothers of Plaza de Mayo afternoon march on December 15, five dead female bodies washed up on the shore of the Río de la Plata, a wide expansive river bordering Argentina and Uruguay that empties into the Atlantic Ocean. On December 8, 2005, twenty-eight years after the founding Mothers themselves "disappeared," the remains of Azucena Villaflor, Maria Ponce de Bianco, and Esther Ballestrino de Careaga were cremated and their ashes buried in honor at Plaza de Mayo, Buenos Aires.

The Mothers of Plaza de Mayo transformed resistance for a generation of radical activists into the realm of motherhood. They created a legacy in defending human rights as they walked steadily together around the plaza, showing the world they had not forgotten what happened to their loved ones during Argentina's "Dirty War."

THE 1990'S:
SPACE OF NEOLIBERALISM AND IMPUNITY

The junta needed to disappear a generation of activists in order to have enough influence to gain consent for the neoliberal model, which the leaders of the 1990s continued to use. But by the 1990s, US hegemony in Latin America had shifted, so the neoliberal revolution could be carried out through democratic means.[11] According to Manuel Gonzalez, who, since the age of nineteen, suspected that his military parents abducted him as a baby, the dictatorship used disappearances not just to terrorize the opposition but also to put the current neoliberal economic model in place. "It has been 30 years since a bloody dictatorship took power in our country. Where thirty thousand men and women were tortured, shot, killed, and disappeared—and also five hundred babies. The military junta used the sinister mechanism of terror to implement the neoliberal economic model in our country. And this is why they needed to disappear our parents."[12]

Impunity was a cornerstone of the economic model further implemented during the 1990s. The transition to democracy came at the cost of impunity for human rights abuses, granted under the Due Obedience and Full Stop Laws, which prevented members of the military from facing criminal prosecution. During the 1990s, military officials who had tortured and assassinated so-called dissidents during the junta were often spotted at nightclubs, vacation spots, and high-profile restaurants. With all roads to justice blocked in the courts, Argentina's human rights organizations transformed the streets into a space for popular justice, and to fight impunity and austerity.

Even with judicial roadblocks, human rights groups continued to push for investigations into the disappearance of tens of thousands. Founded in 1995, H.I.J.O.S. (Sons and Daughters for Identity and Justice against Forgetting and Silence) developed the *escrache* or "exposure" protest, held at the home or workplace of an unpunished criminal, as a method to deliver justice. They transformed the streets and neighborhoods of military leaders who carried out crimes into spaces of popular justice. During the trial of ex-Navy Captain Alfredo Astiz, also known as the Blond Angel of Death, H.I.J.O.S. attended the trial camouflaged as members of the public. With national television cameras focusing on Astiz, infamous for infiltrating the Mothers of the Plaza de Mayo and disappearing two of their leaders, the H.I.J.O.S. surprised the nation by yelling "murderer" and throwing rotten tomatoes at Astiz, who asked to be excused to go to the bathroom.

The Grandmothers of the Plaza de Mayo have also continued to demand that the kidnapped children be returned to their families. The Grandmothers have recovered the true identities of 107 of the estimated 500 missing children, who are now in their thirties. Events to mark the thirty years since Argentina's military junta kicked off with an *escrache* protest against the coup's first dictator, Jorge Rafael Videla. Over 10,000 people participated in the protest in front of Videla's home, where he was held under house arrest, in connection with numerous charges of human rights abuses. H.I.J.O.S. brought a crane and gave closing remarks directly in front of Videla's fifth floor apartment. Nora Cortiñas, one of the founders of the Mothers of the Plaza de Mayo, said that the same leaders responsible for illegally detaining, torturing, and killing activists during the military dictatorship, were now benefiting from state-sponsored impunity. She said,

> We are here because we don't forget, we don't forgive, and we don't reconcile. The struggle will continue for as long

as necessary. Until they tell us what happened to each
one of the women and men who were disappeared. Until
all the children who were snatched from their detained
mothers find out their true identity. Until all the killers are
put in regular jails with life sentences. Until those murder-
ers responsible for this genocide are truly punished. Until
the dreams of the disappeared and everyone who continues to fight today for social justice come true.[13]

The Mothers of Plaza de Mayo did not forget, and did not forgive.
They continued their weekly vigil in the Plaza de Mayo. They carried
on the struggle of their children, to demand justice for the crimes
committed under Plan Condor, and resist the rippling effects of the
neoliberal model that their disappeared sons and daughters risked
their lives to resist.

Human rights groups were successful in reversing the decision
granting impunity for military involvement in abuses. A 2003 Supreme Court order overruled the Due Obedience and Full Stop Laws.
According to the Center for Legal and Social Studies, 379 cases involving disappearances and torture were under judicial investigation
or being tried in court as of October 2011. Of 1,774 alleged perpetrators, 749 were facing charges for these crimes, and 210 had been
convicted.[14] Criminals like Jorge Rafael Videla and Alfredo Astiz have
been sentenced to life in prison for their participation in the state-
supported genocide of activists. In Latin America, these groups have
exemplified the regional struggle for democracy and sovereignty, in
a hemisphere plagued in the 1970s and 1980s by dictatorships that
disappeared over 90,000 people, according to the Latin American
Federation of Associations for Relatives of the Detained-Disappeared
(FEDEFAM).[15] Thanks to the endless work of human rights groups,
Argentina is paving the way for other countries to revisit their painful
past. Without justice for crimes committed in the past, the military
and repressive forces in the region will have the power to act with
impunity, as we are seeing with an active coup in Honduras, military
in the streets of Chile, and US military bases in Colombia. Militarization remains a risk for the region, and with long-standing impunity
for military crimes, Latin America could lose another generation.
However, a new generation of human rights advocates in Argentina is
trying to use the legal system to break this wall of impunity.

DECEMBER 19/20, 2001:
SPACE OF REBELLION

OVER THE COURSE of a decade, Carlos Menem implemented one of the most intense and drastic structural reforms in the region. To solve hyperinflation in 1991, Menem, with the blessing of the international financial community, masterminded a radical economic plan. He dismantled the public sector and privatized and liberalized the economy, opening it up to free trade. Menem's administration also invented the system of convertibility to strangle exports by fixing parity between the dollar and peso. This process resulted in the closure of thousands of factories. Corrupt union leaders and politicians balked at the deindustrialization of the economy, while the IMF touted Argentina as a South American success. What ensued in the 1990s would result in crisis.

Argentina followed the global wave in transforming the organization of work. It adopted policies in line with the Washington Consensus: privatization of almost all state enterprises, opening of the economy to international investments and goods, and deregulation of markets as a method to resolve its economic crisis.[16]

In his analysis of neoliberalism, David Harvey argues that there is an interconnection "between technological dynamism, instability, dissolution of social solidarities, environmental degradation, deindustrialization, rapid shift in time-space relations, speculative bubbles, and the general tendency toward crisis formation within capitalism."[17] Argentina is a case study for this theoretical tendency. Argentina's rapid shift took place with deindustrialization, but also with new forms of production. These policies were coupled with the breakdown of the nation's formally strong safety network and shift towards flexible production standards.

During the Fordist period, Argentina had a highly organized and combative labor movement. Following the military dictatorship's decimation of labor organizers, new forms of capitalist production further weakened the labor movement. Unions were replaced by "open door" policies, and businesses began to compete with the social benefits and protections offered by unions. Capital not only transformed the physical space of production but the "one big family" of business invaded other spaces in workers' lives, such as the home, family life, and bodies.

Foucault provided many illustrations of surveillance in contemporary capitalist spaces. The production of power rests on capitalism's ability to precisely supervise processes of production. These power relations produce our space and reality. His idea that "the individual and the knowledge that may be gained of him belong to this production" couldn't be truer as a description of how capitalism extracts labor and workers' knowledge.[18] During the 1976–1983 dictatorship, capital literally terrorized bodies in the factory. Whereas in contemporary capitalism, this control of our bodies has been democratized and intensified through workers' participation in management.

One of neoliberalism's prime achievements has been the breakdown of the labor movement. Workers' engagement and participation in the decision-making process and a disconnected global production structure have removed the function of labor unions in the work force—except as mediators between labor and capital. In a nation with a strong labor history and industrial base, global austerity policies forced Argentina's industrial workers to suffer a profound deterioration in their work conditions and saw the value of their salaries drop. This concentration of capital resulted in the breakdown of Argentina's industrial base, causing more than 15,000 factories to close between 1973 and 1993.[19] By 1998, the austerity model unleashed a crisis without precedent. In 1998, unemployment surpassed 20 percent. Infant mortality rates rose to 20.4 percent.[20] The nation no longer had a social safety net or welfare programs to help the poor subsist.

Collaboration, open-door management, reduction of hierarchy, work in groups, and decentralized decision-making have become pieces of the new model of production for twenty-first century industry.[21] This model has also idled labor unions' role in the workplace, with labor unable to influence managers, make demands, or strike if necessary.[22] The productive logic of capitalism has transformed to extract greater productivity, but also the intellectual know-how of the workers. This is the context in which Argentina's unemployed workers movements rose.

The unemployed were shut out of the factory—the arena of production—and denied access to the labor union to resist from within. The industrial landscape had been respatialized to convert full-time jobs into temporary jobs, while leaving millions unemployed. Droves of unemployed no longer had access to the factory, while corrupt union structures ignored deindustrialization or profited from it. The unemployed movements rose up from the streets and the neighbor-hoods, as a cry for sustenance and a cry for the right to work.

At the height of the crisis in 2001, the *piqueteros* or unemployed workers' organizations (MTDs) spread throughout the nation, es-pecially around the suburban rust belt of Buenos Aires, Cordoba, and Rosario. The MTDs, not a party or a union, took direct action to put public pressure on the government to obtain food supplies, basic necessities, social policy measures, and improvements in infra-structure. They took their name from their method, the *piquete*, or road blockade. As unemployed workers, they lacked the strike as a historical tool for the working class. They developed the road block-ade as a way to tangibly disrupt capitalist production, by disrupt-ing commerce in transit. The *corte de ruta* (road blockade) became the national buzzword, which spread to areas such as Cutral-Co in Southern Neuquen and Tartagal-General Mosconi in Northern Salta, where the oil industry had been privatized and restructured under Menem's administration. The government responded to these protests with violent repression. Since 1995, more than sev-enty people have been killed in protests. The repression peaked in 2002, with the police killing two *piquetero* activists during a road blockade.

The MTDs grew out of necessity, and represent a struggle for work, while transforming contemporary notions of organizing the working class. The unemployed shifted organizing efforts from spaces of production (the factory) to the street with direct action and in the neighborhoods with horizontal methods of organizing. Many MTD practices were underpinned by concepts such as autonomy, direct ac-tion, solidarity, and direct democracy. The MTD slogan of "work, dignity, and social change," and tactics of disrupting urban econo-mies, challenged the new economic order dependent upon a reserve of unemployed.

Edward Soja provides an outlook of how social movements have challenged capitalism's ability to advance by reproducing space. He asserts that when social movements struggle against the imposed spa-tial organization of advanced capitalism, they demystify this spatial-ity. The MTDs focused on territorial liberation and taking control of the production of space within the global structure of capitalism. By 2001, these movements made it clear that Argentina's neoliberal model had failed the peripheral region of Argentina's shantytowns, as well as the middle class. Movements against austerity, like in South Africa and Spain, have in many ways replicated Argentina's unemployed workers' organizing model.

SPACES OF SELF-MANAGEMENT

Within the spontaneous combustion of reclaiming popular power in December 2001, another tactic of workers' resistance emerged: the factory occupation. Argentina's occupied factory movement has directly challenged our notions about the nature of production and the organization of social relations in space. After a decade, Argentina's occupied factories have become one of the longest-lived laboratories of self-management of the millennium. Today, there are 300 recuperated enterprises up and running in Argentina, employing over 13,000 workers.

Argentina's worker-controlled enterprises were occupied to find a solution to joblessness, in a period of crisis when factory closures were rampant. Andres Ruggeri's thesis suggests that the process of deindustrialization is what led workers to take over the means of production, as a partial and defensive solution to the threat of unemployment. He considers that this activity is the "least heroic in the process of the worker occupied factories," as it was fear of the stigma of mass unemployment that motivated the occupations. More than 49 percent of the occupations took place between 2002 and 2004, when unemployment was at its highest.[23] Many enterprises followed the slogan "Occupy, Resist, Produce," the logic of the methodology they used. According to Esteban Magnani, sociologist and author of *El Cambio Silencioso*, fraudulent bankruptcy was a common practice for Argentine entrepreneurs: "You can sell the factory to someone else before going bankrupt. That person would go bankrupt and then you could buy the factory back with no debts."[24]

Bosses abandoning their workplaces and failing to pay workers' unpaid salaries were a common impetus for workers' occupations. The occupations were also a defense mechanism against the hide-and-seek model of flexible capitalism, where you close a factory to open up another plant in another space, with fewer full-time workers, less personnel costs, better technology, and higher productive output. The acceptance of flexible capitalism is rooted in the currents of technological change and rapid economic growth that have been associated with powerful revolutions in social conceptions of space and time.[25] The workers of the recuperated enterprises have questioned the social construction of the concept of space, as they develop new modes of production and social relations inside their workplaces.

Argentina's crisis deepened, as its entrepreneurs had perfected the underpinnings of the new global manufacturing model. Many businesses used fraudulent bankruptcy to wipe out debt and later reopen production with flexibility and scale at rock-bottom prices, as did Ford or Toyota in very different times and places. The factory in the era of modern globalization serves as a location for manufacturing that can disappear and reappear across borders. This is the game of hide-and-seek developed in the era of post-Fordism.

Hide-and-seek was the name of the game at Crometal (ex-Acrow), a metal factory producing industrial shelving.

Management withheld the workers' salaries for over six months, sparking a conflict in mid-2001, at the height of the crisis. "We started with a strike, we wanted to reach an agreement. We just wanted to work," says Javier Gómez, a member of the Crometal worker cooperative.[26] "One day they arranged with the police while we were outside to try to empty the factory of materials that were stored in the factory to sell them. These were materials that we had already produced and we had not been paid for the labor. The boss wanted to take it all, as well as the machinery." The workers occupied the plant on February 6, 2002, to demand their back pay. A few days later, the bosses sent them telegrams to inform them that they had been fired for usurpation. While in the process of bankruptcy, the original owners opened another factory with better technology and fewer personnel, hired as part-time workers.

The first violent eviction came in June. "There was no electricity. We were living in an abandoned bus at the plant's entrance so they wouldn't empty out the machinery," explains Gómez. The workers asked for donations on Highway 2, which runs in front of the factory, to survive. In October 2002, with the support from neighbors from the popular assemblies, workers from IMPA and other occupied factories, as well as representatives from OUM, the local metallurgical union, the workers decided to pass through the plant's gates and occupy.[27]

After eighteen months of occupation, the five remaining workers began production as a self-managed workers' cooperative.

The workers proved that they wouldn't be so flexible as to allow the plant where they had spent years selling their labor go to ruin. Since starting up production at the recovered plant, the workers have expanded production, bought new machinery, and hired new workers. Everyone is paid the same wage and managerial decisions are made democratically in a regular assembly. The workers haven't forgotten their commitment. "The owners thought we would give up, but it's just the opposite. The work here is for collective benefit. It's not just for us, it's for our families and community. The factory is for us, if we gain the title, it won't be just 30 of us, we'll be 200 or 300 working here" explains Sergio Capragas.[28] Through their resilience and social projects, the Crometal workers have proven they are not only a strategy of defense but are also challenging the structures of the capitalist model.

In his postmodern analysis, Foucault conceived the factory as a point of discipline and surveillance, which rests on the functioning of a network of relations from top to bottom. Capitalism's complex spaces are hierarchical, indicating values, obedience, and an economy of time and gesture.[29] Flexible capitalism is ever more disciplinary, in that it functions on the self-discipline of the worker and the increasing fragmentation of production that relies on the appropriation of workers' know-how.

Argentina's self-managed enterprises have challenged the organization of space based on hierarchy, obedience, and fragmentation. They have replaced surveillance with cooperation, mutual solidarity, and community projects. One of the most emblematic spaces within the occupied factor movement is Zanon, renamed FASINPAT (Factory without a Boss) by the workers. As Latin America's largest ceramics manufacturer and with more than five hundred self-managed workers, it is one of the largest long-living experiences of self-management in the twenty-first century.

Zanon's road to self-management began with the grassroots effort to recuperate rank-and-file representation within the ceramists' union, which had represented businessmen. Luis Zanon built his factory, deemed a prototype of Argentina's neoliberal miracle, with austerity funds from the World Bank. The layout and internal organization of the 80,000-square-meter plant was meant to keep workers from socializing and organizing. Alienation went so far as management enforcing a rule that employees from each production line had to wear a specific colored uniform, so they could easily be identified and marked if they were speaking with workers from another production line. "The company had a very repressive system. They couldn't see you in another sector, talking with fellow workers, or even using the bathroom freely. Many times we had to communicate by passing notes under the tables in the cafeteria or make secret times to meet. We found ways to evade the boss' and bureaucratic control," says Carlos Villamonte.[30] Prior to the workers' occupation, conditions led to an average of thirty accidents per month, due to the level of production, lack of security measures, and disdain for the workers' well-being.

Self-managing their union struggle provided the workers with a sense of the power of collective action and worker solidarity. This experience helped them declare the plant under worker control. And it was through worker control that the FASINPAT collective has converted the plant that resembled a modern-day prison into a liberated space. Julian Rebon has noted, "In many cases there is a reorganization of space and its uses. On occasion, the function of the machinery is modified with the objective of adapting them to the needs of the workers. Also, there is free circulation of the workers through the entire business."[31] The transformation of space has gone beyond the physical space, aimed at taking over control of the production of space in which social relations are formed.

The workers at FASINPAT replaced the hierarchical, disciplinary gaze of management with horizontal and democratic practices for organizing production. "For the workers, the decisions should be decided by the assembly as the only authority in the factory," says Carlos Saavedra, a Zanon worker who has labored inside the plant for almost twenty years, ten of which have been spent working under worker self-management.[32] Workers receive the same pay. They have a coordinator system to organize production. They have democratized disciplinary measures for workers who break codes of conduct. In one case, the worker assembly voted that, instead of firing a worker who missed work because of a substance abuse addiction, he should receive treatment and come back to the cooperative on a probationary period.

FASINPAT has challenged the very notion of privatized space. The workers cooperative fought for legal recognition under the slogan "Zanon es del pueblo" (Zanon belongs to the people). The FASINPAT cooperative has recognized the importance of community support in their long struggle for the expropriation of the ceramics factory. In 2013, the courts put into effect a law that handed over the Zanon plant and machinery to the FASINPAT worker cooperative to manage indefinitely. "This is an enormous step forward that was carried out with the support of the Neuquén community, and many organizations around the world. It has value not only for the ceramist workers, but for other workers in the nation and around the world as a concrete alternative to the crisis and to the capitalists who close factories," says Raúl Godoy, a former union delegate and long-time activist in the FASINPAT struggle.[33]

The workers have opened their factories to the community. They have fostered community programs and cultural spaces. By 2008, twenty-three adult education programs were functioning within recuperated business and factories.[34] Some type of solidarity or cultural activity happens in 57 percent of the recuperated enterprises, with 39 percent of the two hundred occupied enterprises dedicating a permanent space to community projects, such as cultural centers, community radios, education programs, or work internships inside the plant or enterprise.[35]

The trajectory of these experiences is rooted in a long legacy of emancipation struggles. Argentina's occupied factories have contested the tyranny of capitalist space, but they must do so within the spatial confines of the market (which, as Foucault noted, carries with it its own internalized disciplinary mechanisms, even in a self-managed space). Hector Trinchero argues that Argentina's occupied businesses reflect the very core of capitalism's contradiction, the contradiction between work and capital.[36] Nevertheless, the factory occupation as a method of resistance is not a new phenomenon. Argentina's factory occupations are rooted in Latin America's long history of working-class resistance. In Cuba, the revolution experimented with worker self-managed industry. In Chile, in response to the industry-wide boss lockout against the popular government of Allende, workers coordinated self-management in the industrial belts.

FUTURE OF SPATIAL RESISTANCE

THESE SOCIAL MOVEMENTS' resistance to capital's neutralizing effects is the common thread that binds together the past forty years of resistance to austerity in Argentina. As Foucault noted, capitalism is constantly trying to neutralize the movement's ability to build counterpower because "capitalism with its social production of power... forms a resistance to the power that wishes to dominate it—anything that may establish horizontal conjunctions."[37] During the 1970s and 1980s, capital used the junta to neutralize the counterpower that was brewing regionally. Capital utilized impunity for the junta's crimes and the seemingly unstoppable offensive against the public sector and full-time employment as a way to neutralize labor unions and civil society during the golden era of neoliberalism. State-supported repression, hunger, and co-optation helped to neutralize the rebellion of the unemployed worker organizations and popular assemblies. And workers continue to face violent attacks, and even disappearances, while fighting against subcontracting and the decimation of public safety nets. Public school teacher Carlos Fuente-Alba and political activist Mariano Ferreyra were two victims in this neutralization process. In an attempt to silence torture survivors and human rights activists testifying in the junta trials, Jorge Julio López was disappeared for the second time on September 18, 2006, the evening before he was scheduled to testify against his perpetrator, who was later sentenced to life in prison for genocide.

The Bauen Hotel, a nineteen-story hotel in the heart of Buenos Aires, serves as a metaphor for this decades-long trajectory of social movements resisting austerity. The hotel was built in 1978 with public credit from the dictatorship and private loans. When Argentina's national soccer team took the 1978 World Cup, the military used a media campaign around the world championship to cover up gruesome human rights abuses occurring at the time. Guests at the hotel, among whom were high profile military and government reps, chanted the counter human rights slogan: "Somos derechos y humanos" (We are right and human). With the Argentine flag in hand, they cheered, as thousands of women and men cried in terror while undergoing indescribable torture sessions, and as the military drugged prisoners, dropping their bodies into the Atlantic Ocean on the *vuelos de muerte* (death flights). During the 1990s, the hotel served as an election bunker for Carlos Menem and as a popular hangout for the beneficiaries of neoliberalism.

All this changed with the crisis in 2001. The alleged owners at the time, Grupo Solari, who had acquired the hotel in 1997, filed for bankruptcy in 2001. Leading up to the hotel's closure, the rooms and facilities deteriorated and the bosses began laying off workers. The remaining workers were fired in December 2001, despite the fact that the hotel was functioning and lucrative up until the closure. The bosses abandoned the hotel, located on a major avenue in downtown Buenos Aires, boarding it up and allowing it to become an eyesore, reminding the city of the impending financial crisis and wide-spread unemployment the nation faced.

The owners didn't count on the workers breaking the chains and converting it into a modern day Paris Commune. In the same manner that the Parisians, rebelling against empire, destroyed symbols of an alien power, Argentina's social movements have redefined the meaning of space. Workers at the Bauen Hotel decided to occupy in 2003, two years after the initial closure. Nearly thirty workers, along with supporters from other occupied factories and workers' movements, participated in the action. Aside from transforming the productive space of the hotel, employing 150 workers with no boss or legal owner, they have also transformed the social definition of the space of the hotel. In the past decade, human rights groups, assemblies of worker delegates, social justice coalitions, workers from other occupied factories, and environmental groups have utilized the hotel's facilities to organize resistance to austerity. In 2012, the theater in the hotel was ceremoniously renamed "Grandmothers of Plaza de Mayo."

Argentina's social movements have modified the productive use of space and time, transforming the verticalization of time and space into horizontal conjunctions, as a consequence of the new practices of material reproduction. As with the Paris Commune, the workers in the Bauen Hotel cooperative and at the FASINPAT factory have not only questioned the capitalist organization of production, but they have also reformulated the social qualities of the geographic sites of production and territory into a nonhierarchical and communitarian structure.

As the financial crisis has spread around the globe, worker occupations have spread. Even though these experiences are isolated within the geography of capitalism, they have successfully resisted the neutralizing effects of the market and have inspired workers around the world to take matters into their own hands. Occupations have continued into the new millennium: workers occupied eight enterprises in 2013, including four restaurants in Buenos Aires. In Chicago and Greece, workers occupying their plants have cited Argentina's occupied factories as an inspiration to fight joblessness and increasing inequality. For many in the global activist community, Argentina is now known for its grass-fed beef, the tragedy of tango, and the occupied factory movement as a viable alternative to the capitalist model.

The popular rebellion of December 2001 left long-standing transformations of Argentina's landscape, challenging the geographic transformations of capitalism. Neighbors gathered in popular assemblies, workers took over their factories, and unemployed workers staged massive road blockades, all rebelling against austerity and demanding an end to impunity for crimes against humanity, while employing horizontal and democratic organizing methods. These social movements challenged the nature of unemployment, production, neighborhood participation, and organizing. They also changed the political terrain of economic policies in the Southern Cone.

For nearly four decades, social movements have resisted the economic model that Jorge Rafael Videla's military junta left behind, along with the open wounds of thirty thousand forced disappearances, while social movements have shifted the political terrain of economic policies in the Southern Cone. Argentina's economy has made a miraculous recovery since 2003, thanks mostly to the boom in transgenic soy exports. Economic policies allied with the Washington Consensus have shifted toward an extraction economy exporting to the BRIC (Brazil, Russia, India, and China) markets. The cultivation of soy and the destructive mining in the Andes has led to a violent displacement of indigenous, campesino, and rural communities from the land, as transnational corporations poison their air, soil, and water. Social movements have adapted and their future may involve a resistance of this occupation of space that focuses on food sovereignty and territorial resistance in the rural landscape. This brief and partial history of crisis, austerity, and particularly the working class response in Argentina may provide us with insights into how we might resist the current global imposition of crisis and austerity.

ENDNOTES

1   Henri Lefebvre, *The Survival of Capitalism: Reproduction of the Relations of Production* (London: Allison & Busby, 1976), 21.

2   We are using a postmodern perspective because we live in postmodern times. But the analysis here does *not* reject class struggle, as some postmodern academic theory does. Rather, it is rooted in an understanding

that class struggle changes form throughout space and time.

3   Edward Soja, *Postmodern Geographies: The Reassertion of Space in Critical Social Theory* (New York: Verso, 1989), 5.

4   Ibid.,35.

5   Ibid.,26–27.

6   Ibid.,73.

7   Ibid., 72.

8   Ibid.,27.

9   Rodolfo Walsh, "Carta Abierta de Rodolfo Walsh a la Junta Military," March 24, 1977, http://archivohistorico.educ.ar/sites/default/files/VIII_09.pdf (accessed April 28, 2013).

10 Marie Trigona, "30 Years Since the Coup," *IRC*, March 29, 2006.

11 David Harvey, *A Brief History of Neoliberalism* (New York: Oxford, 2005), 39.

12 Trigona, "30 Years Since the Coup."

13 Escrache a Videla, produced by *Grupo Alavío* (Buenos Aires, March, 2006), DVD.

14 Human Rights Watch, *World Report 2012: Argentina*, http://www.hrw.org/world-report-2012/argentina (accessed April 28, 2013).

15 Marie Trigona, "Argentina Revisits Dictatorship: A Year of Human Rights Trials," *Toward Freedom*, March 31, 2010.

16 Daniel Aspiazu and Martin Schorr, *Hecho en Argentina* (Buenos Aires: Siglo XXI editores, 2010), 143.

17 Harvey, *A Brief History of Neoliberalism*, 65.

18 Michel Foucault, *Discipline and Punish* (New York: Random House, 1977), 194.

19 Aspiazu and Schorr, *Hecho en Argentina*, 158.

20 Ibid.,187.

21 Hernan Harispe, "Trabajo y Sindicalismo," in *La Economia de los Trabajadores: Autogestion y Distribucion de la Riquesa*, (ed.) A. Ruggeri (Buenos Aires: Ediciones de la Cooperativa Chilavert, 2009).

22   Ibid.

23   *Las Empresas Recuperadas en la Argentina: Informe del tercer relevamiento de empresas recuperadas por sus trabajadores,* (ed.) A. Ruggeri (Buenos Aires: Ediciones de la Cooperativa Chilavert, 2010).

24   Esteban Magnani, *The Silent Change* (Buenos Aires: Editorial Teseo, 2009), http://www.elcambiosilencioso.com.ar/wp-content/uploads/2008/08/silent-change-2.pdf (accessed May 1, 2013).

25   David Harvey, "Between Space and Time: Reflections on the Geographical Imagination," *Annals of the Association of American Geographers* 80, no. 3 (1990): 418–434.

26   Claudia Acuña, Sergio Ciancaglini, and Diego Rosemburg, ed., *Sin Patron* (Buenos Aires: La Vaca, 2007), 100.

27   Ibid., 104.

28   "People & Power," from YouTube video, produced by *Al Jazeera,* May 23, 2007.

29   Foucault, *Discipline and Punish,* 192.

30   Carlos Villamonte (FASINPAT worker), in discussion with the author, May 2006.

31   Julian Rebon, *La Empresa de la Autonomia* (Buenos Aires: Ediciones Picaso, 2007), 153.

32   *Zanon Construyendo Resisten*cia, Produced by *Grupo Alavío* (Buenos Aires, 2003), DVD.

33   Adriana Meyer, "Zanon a Manos de los Trabajadores," *Página* 12 (2012).

34   Laura Vales, "Con útiles a la fábrica," *Página* 12 (2008).

35   A. Ruggeri (ed.), *Las Empresas Recuperadas en la Argentina: Informe del tercer relevamiento de empresas recuperadas por sus trabajadores* (Buenos Aires: Ediciones de la Cooperativa Chilavert, 2010), 122–123.

36   Hector Hugo Trinchero, "De la Exclusion a la Autogestion: Innovacion Social Desde la Experiencia de las Empresas Recuperadas por Sus Trabajadores," in *Las Empresas Recuperadas en la Argentina: del Segundo Relavamiento del Programa,* (ed.) Andres Ruggeri (Buenos Aires: Facultad de Filosofia y Letras, University de Buenos Aires, 2005).

37   Foucault, *Discipline and Punish,* 219.

AUSTERITY AND UNIONS

A CASE STUDY OF THE CANADIAN UNION OF POSTAL WORKERS

NICK DRIEDGER

"Austerity" is a strange word. An austere existence is not generally seen to be a bad existence, it just means to live more simply and with less. Of course, the question is less for whom. The answer is still simpler: less for those who work and not those for whom work is done. The other important question is how to make the transition to a more austere existence. The answer is again a simple one: by force, if necessary, by other means, if possible.

In June 2011, several labor struggles came to a head in Canada, as the governing Conservative Party intervened in several strikes on behalf of employers. The intention was to weaken unions in Canada and transfer wealth from those who generate it to those who own and manage several large businesses in Canada. We will look at one particular labor struggle, the conflict between the Canadian Union of Postal Workers (CUPW) and the Canada Post Corporation (CPC).

Canada Post has been a crown corporation for over thirty years. It essentially runs as a stand-alone business—it is owned solely by the Canadian government and hands its profits over to the government. The Canadian Union of Postal Workers is the union that represents most of the workers at Canada Post. In the case of the Canada Post, "austerity measures" meant two things: first, it meant the renegotiation of the urban and rural collective agreements; second, it meant that CPC was going to implement massive technological changes to the post office in order to increase efficiency. This program is called "The Modern Post" and is ongoing.

The Canadian Union of Postal Workers has a history of being a militant, radical, and largely democratic union. The union is on the forefront of feminist and antiracist struggles, and has caught a lot of negative press lately for vocal support for international solidarity campaigns around the struggles in Palestine. In the past, the union has engaged in nationwide wildcats and innovative direct action like the boycott of the postal code campaign, and has led several strikes that made inroads for other workers across Canada, such as collective bargaining rights for public sector unions and paid maternity leave.

CUPW started official job actions in mid-May, with no-uniform days, button campaigns, and some grassroots organizing on the floor. By June 2, the union decided to turn up the heat by implementing rotating strikes that effectively slowed down the mail and made the lives of senior management miserable, as they tried to make sure that mail traveling between cities would arrive in a place that was not being struck. It also had the advantage of most of the workforce still collecting a paycheck while certain cities struck against the employer by taking turns.

On June 14, the Conservatives legislated Air Canada back to work. Emboldened by that move, the Canada Post Corporation moved to lock out its CUPW Urban Operations bargaining unit the same day, effectively putting about 45,000 workers onto picket lines. While there is no proof that the government and CPC were coordinating their actions, it would be naive to assume that their lockstep movements were the result of anything other than very close communication and a common plan. In this chapter, I will investigate the interplay between the union, the corporation, and the government, and how attempts at imposing austerity measures unfolded through disciplinary techniques of *conditioning*.

JOB CONDITIONING

"It is a matter of course and of absolute necessity to the conduct of business, that any discretionary businessman must be free to deal or not to deal in any given case; to limit or withhold the equipment under his control, without reservation.

Business discretion and business strategy, in fact, has no other
means by to work out its aims. So that, in effect, all business
sagacity reduces itself in the last analysis to judicious use of
sabotage."
—Thorstein Veblen, *An Inquiry Into the Nature of Peace, and
the Terms of Its Perpetuation.*

Once upon a time, long, long ago, a militant union called the
Wobblies had a plan for dealing with bosses that they liked to call
job conditioning. Job conditioning wasn't a tactic, it was more of
a strategy. Just like one would "condition" a dog not to pee on the
rug, workers would try and get the working conditions they wanted through threats and incentives. When bosses paid well, workers
would do their best to work hard; when bosses paid poorly, the quality of the work would suffer. When treated with respect on the job,
respect would be returned; when treated with disdain, the workers
would return in kind.

A lot of terms were used by the Wobblies to describe what they
did. Some workers would refer a lot to the French word "sabotage,"
others would leave stickers with the IWW logo on them that said
things like "The Cat Likes Cream" or "Bad Pay Leads to Bum Work."
The message and the approach were clear. The workers would try
collectively to not just assert control over the job, but also limit the
choices the employer had available to them to deal with the problems
they created. So, the workers put a dilemma forward to the employer:
one choice would lead to a reward (the work getting done well), the
other to a punishment (lower profits or even a loss of money).

Sometimes, as radicals, we tend to think of ourselves as fighting
a stationary target. In hindsight, we are always skilled fencers and
our opponent is simply a wooden dummy. Of course, class struggle
means a real struggle, not between a dummy and a fencer; instead, it
involves two parties who have agency and cunning, access to a power
base, and who can both be creative. Just as workers will engage in job
conditioning, so too can the upper class. In fact, this is the essence of
governing, and key to any legislative intervention in social struggles.
Thorstein Veblen observed that sabotage is not the exclusive domain
of workers, and while workers may be able to do without bosses, neither workers nor bosses can live without the means of subsistence that
our economy provides. As long as the bosses have control over the

social context beyond the workplace, they can manipulate all sorts of factors to bring the workers in line. I will take a look at the various terrains on which the Canadian Union of Postal Workers struggled with Canada Post Corporation, as both workers and bosses engaged in processes of conditioning.

The essence of any social struggle is to drive a wedge between your opponents. The employer tries to break trade union unity by putting forward policies that benefit some workers at the expense of others. This dynamic is simply explained by the prisoners' dilemma, whereby two prisoners are separated under questioning. If they both keep their mouths shut, they get off for the crimes they have committed. If only one speaks about what happened, the other suffers and the one who talked is rewarded. However, if they both speak, they both suffer. In other words, social solidarity depends on the confidence of the actors. The goal of the employers, and the means by which they condition the job, is to attack social solidarity and undermine it.

BACK-TO-WORK LEGISLATION

ON JUNE 20, 2011, the Conservatives introduced "back to work" legislation into the House of Commons. There were several aspects to this legislation that were unique—the first being that the new wage scales were written into the legislation, wage scales that were lower than those being discussed during negotiations. This act alone sent a clear message: continued noncompliance would lead to punishment.

Aside from that, the other details included punishing fines: $100,000 per day for CUPW, $50,000 per day for any officer of the union, and $1,000 per day for any union member who disrupted production. This had the effect of putting a tremendous burden on anyone who spoke out in favor of defiance. They could, in the matter of a few days, have whatever paltry assets most workers had, whether a house, a car, or some small investments, seized. Many union officers pointed out that the union could also be bankrupted, though it would take a few weeks for the fines to bankrupt CUPW, given where their assets were at during the rotating strikes and lockout.

Another important part of the back-to-work legislation was the practice of "final offer selection." Essentially, this means that the arbitrator is instructed to choose between the two offers, each of which is taken as a complete whole, instead of picking parts of each and cobbling together a compromise. This, combined with the fact that the legislation required the arbitrator to pick based mostly on economic concerns for the employer, meant that the government all but legislated an outcome in favor of the employer, at the expense of the workers. However, there was one important point: if CUPW didn't want to face this stacked game, they could settle before it got to arbitration. The employers' plan was to put forward an outrageous "final offer," in order to bring CUPW to heel. They offered a starting wage of $17 per hour and a tiered benefit and pension package that was less substantial than the pension plan the more senior workers already had.

In effect, these measures drove a wedge between more militant elements in the union and the majority of union officers, who were justifiably concerned about losing their houses and savings. It's easy to think of this in terms of cynical bureaucrats manipulating the rank and file, but ultimately there was a tremendous burden placed on individuals for a reason. These measures incentivized a certain outcome. They created an environment where a solution that, in the long term, collectively punishes workers, would lead to fewer short-term, punishing outcomes for individual workers.

These measures also created a desire on the part of the union officials to "sell" a settlement over the following year and a half. The union headquarters in Ottawa used automated voice recording phone calls, or "robo calls," to encourage a yes vote to a tentative agreement; national office sent many national officers on speaking tours across the country; and it worked hard to limit debate on the agreement that was essentially written by CPC and forced onto CUPW by the government. Arguably there was more thought, work, and creativity put into the push for a yes vote for the tentative agreement, which no one felt was just, than went into preparation for the rotating strikes. It is entirely predictable that people will fight much harder to save their own finances and livelihoods than for a tradition of militancy no one has done more than pay lip service to for fifteen years.

SOCIAL DEMOCRACY, ANTI-AUSTERITY, AND THE STATE

LENIN ONCE REMARKED that socialism was merely all of society being run like the Prussian post office. Lenin clearly never worked at a post office. An important aspect of the struggle between the Canadian government and CUPW was the relationship between the New Democratic Party of Canada (NDP) and the union during the lockout. Some in CUPW had been privately told a year before the negotiations really heated up that NDP support would be dependent on the perception of our struggle by society at large. That perception would be gauged largely by polling the NDP regularly does. In other words, support would be tacit, but the NDP was not going to risk popularity to help anyone win a strike. Yet as soon as Bill C-6, the back-to-work legislation for CUPW, was proposed, the newly minted NDP official opposition drew a line in the sand and made a decision to filibuster, or hold up the bill for as long as possible, using every procedural trick at their disposal, often giving long, impassioned speeches that were televised across the country.

One criticism the conservative and liberal governments both brought to bear against the NDP was that they had not been above using back-to-work legislation when they were the Ontario provincial government facing recalcitrant workers. Much of the NDP's argument was one of principle, the position being that back-to-work legislation was unjust in and of itself and undermined free, collective bargaining. The Conservatives' criticism is undeniably true: it is much easier to support striking workers as the opposition than it is to support striking government workers when you *are* the government. The New Democratic Party does have strong ties to the labor movement; the Canada Labor Congress (CLC) is a member of the NDP, with designated positions in decision-making bodies. The Canadian Union of Postal Workers is also a member of the Canada Labor Congress, so part of the per capita they pay goes to CLC political projects that lean heavily in an NDP direction.

So it shouldn't be terribly surprising that there was strong support from these Members of Parliament. After all, they were newly elected, so the political risk was low. The labor movement as a whole helps write policy for the NDP; so party members, to a certain degree, are obliged to back a component member; and the workers managed to strike minimally before a full-scale lockout, so it didn't appear aggressive or out of line. In other words, everyone was playing by the rules, and going through the appropriate channels, so NDP support was politically expedient and forthcoming.

The logic of job conditioning isn't just a characteristic of the Conservative Party; in this case, we merely see the rewards side of the equation at work, instead of the punishments. The Conservatives and Liberals are also correct in pointing out that the NDP has legislated workers back to work. Austerity measures are also hardly exclusively characteristic of conservative political parties. Currently, in Spain, Italy, and Greece, the social democratic cousins of the New Democratic Party are implementing harsh austerity measures where massive amounts of wealth are transferred from working-class communities into the bank accounts of the rich. Like the struggles at the post office, this is all under the guise of contracting work out, undermining public sector workers' wages and working conditions, and "modernizing" work methods in order to intensify the rate of work.

The problem is that these relationships of conditioning each others' behavior have a chain effect, where international markets condition governments, governments condition unions, and unions condition workers. If the markets don't profit, the losses are passed to the governments; if the governments take losses, they make up the difference by going after the workers. In this instance, workers often resist by trying to disrupt the social discipline of society (demonstrations, riots, etc.), withdraw their labor (strikes, boycotts, blockades), or engage on the political terrain open to them in capitalist society (electoral activity and legal action). Some of these methods are legitimate because they are more conducive to the existing social order, and others are discouraged because they disrupt the existing social order, and allow, for a brief time, the working classes to act on a large enough scale from a position of strength to condition their unions, who condition the governments, who condition the international markets. During times of revolution, all mediating hierarchies are threatened with total displacement, as the struggle becomes one between the workers and the international markets (i.e. between labor and capital).

In this case, the workers were rewarded with NDP support, not because their cause was just, but because their timing didn't interfere with NDP strategy. So, CUPW is institutionally a part of a major political party, through its membership in the Canada Labor Congress. This party was created to advocate in Parliament on behalf of the workers. In many ways, their parliamentary filibuster was one of the high points of the strike and ensuing lockout. It was high profile and made news across the country. It also brought a lot of sympathy to the plight of postal workers, who were not only facing government repression, but seeing their working conditions deteriorate under technological change. It was most notable, however, because it failed, for which it also probably gained some respect and sympathy.

RUNNING THE GAUNTLET

Aᴛ ᴛʜᴇ ʀɪsᴋ of sounding quaint, one might say struggle is what you make of it. After the return to work, CUPW defeated several arbitrators in a row, through the legal appeals process. All of these arbitrators were chosen to stack the odds against the union. While the union was working hard to keep its workers at work, and struggling through the appropriate channels, in order not to bring the fines that came with legislation down on their heads, eventually it ran out of tricks. The union was now worried that it couldn't throw out any more arbitrators, couldn't stall anymore, and had labored under punitive back-to-work legislation through the rest of 2011 and most of 2012. Eventually, the CUPW national negotiating committee, under direction from the national executive board, recommended a contract that contained many of the provisions that the postal workers had gone on rotating strikes to resist. The national executive board almost unanimously, with two exceptions, voted in favor of the new collective agreement.

All of the official channels had been exhausted and the penalties were too severe for the officers to continue. The last official channel available was the threat that postal workers would turn up at the polls and oust the Conservatives in a distant election, as well as a Supreme Court challenge against the back-to-work legislation. In the meantime, the New Democratic Party continued to gain popularity, to the point that, by early 2013, many polls had them tied with the governing Conservatives for the first time in the party's history. The court case could take years to sort itself out. In early 2013, the International Labour Organization also issued a statement condemning the back-to-work legislation.

Of course, in the meantime, workers were being injured, bullied into quitting, and retiring as soon as possible, to be replaced by new workers earning $19 an hour. Even the best possible outcome would see the damage already done.

After this defeat, a strong current aimed at union reform developed, the limits of which are obvious, if one takes into account the layered discipline of the union bureaucracy. If you change the union leadership, the relationship between the union as an institution and the corporation stays the same, not to mention the relationship between the union and the government, as well as the market. All of these levels are designed to deal with (i.e. condition) each other. However, workers are the most effective when they seek to disrupt business directly (for example, with a wildcat strike), disrupt the business of governing directly (like the Quebec student strike), or attack the market directly (like when the Occupy movement targeted West Coast ports for blockades). Union reform can, no doubt, play a role in this process, but in order for unions to become a force for change, and not merely another institution at the mercy of the markets, they need to go off script and find new roles for themselves.

CONCLUSIONS

I HAVE ANALYZED how the international markets discipline the government, the government disciplines employers, employers discipline the unions, and finally, the unions discipline the workers. At every level, the pressure is applied downwards, to keep discipline on the job and profits flowing from workers to business owners, either through providing a service that businesses in the second largest country in the world must use (and often), or through profits paid directly to the Canadian government to offset tax revenue. After the lockout, Canada Post reported its first losses in nearly two decades. The jury is still out as to whether this is due to declining revenue, the massive loans taken out to finance the Modern Post project, or just simply business lost to competitors during the lockout.

Ultimately, it's clear that, in the case of the CUPW struggle, a conventional strike timed during the legally permissible period for striking, aimed strictly at bringing forward workplace-based demands under conditions of austerity, was not successful. Some say that under a different government, it could have been. However, if that were the case, why was the outcome so similar to the 1997 strike under a Liberal government? It's important to look to the resistance that CUPW mounted. However, the positive lessons were learned more on the boss's side of the conflict, and negative lessons on the workers' side. But in the global struggle against austerity—and in generalized struggles against capitalism—analyzing our failures is just as important as analyzing our victories.

NO EXIT

TRANSFORMING HOUSING THROUGH SOLIDARITY AND RESISTANCE[1]

SHANE BURLEY

LEONARD SPEARS ISN'T LEAVING HIS HOME. AFTER WORKING HIS whole life, and raising several children, Leonard decided it was time to own his own home. "It was like the American dream, to own your own home, so I was very excited."[2] He purchased a house that was nearly condemned and decided to fix it up. He put in new floors, insulation, and plumbing, deciding to do most of the work himself. From the ground up, it looked like the kind of stories conservatives love to cite, along with a catchphrase about bootstraps.

Then Leonard got hurt on the job and found himself unable to work. While he was waiting for the lumbering process of a disabilities claim, he began to come up short on his mortgage payments to Wells Fargo. He tried explaining the situation to them, usually unable to even get through to a person who could make any kind of decision. Finally, Leonard received a foreclosure notice telling him that he was going to have to leave his house after three years of hard work to make it livable, to make true a dream he had always had as he was struggling to raise his sons. He received additional paperwork, including one piece in particular stating that he was thereby served his foreclosure documents in person. Not only was this a fabrication, but also the physical description of him was of someone several inches taller than he was, with blond hair. There must have been some confusion, since Leonard has alopecia and cannot grow hair on his head. As he explains:

> I'm like about to be homeless, and I've worked all my
> life since I was sixteen. I'm fifty-seven years old now. I
> just don't understand why they didn't want to sit down
> and negotiate with me. And then I come to find that
> they sell it to Freddie Mae or Freddie Mac for $500.
> I'm kind of like disappointed with that. I mean, I'm the
> one that needs somewhere to live, and I was willing to
> pay way more than $500. I mean, what kind of justice
> is that?[3]

Some people from Take Back the Land Rochester stumbled upon Leonard's home when canvassing homeowners potentially going through foreclosure; by that time, Leonard was already moving his belongings out, not knowing there was anything he could do. It was then he decided he was going to stay in his home "by any means necessary." Like thousands of others pressed against the barrel of foreclosure, he made a choice, but only when he saw there was a community to stand alongside him.

GETTING LOST IN A CRISIS

The cause and effect of the financial crisis seem relatively obvious to most people, either from looking at the effects of deregulated capitalism or from direct experience as a victim of its mass destruction. One of the common tendencies, when discussing a depression like the 2008 financial meltdown and the subsequent foreclosure crisis of 2010, is to discuss it strictly in terms of wealth inequality, which is natural, since this is at its core. This can end up being somewhat misguided, however, distracting people from where the battle is actually being waged and, therefore, what kind of social movement can actually confront the effects of the crisis in a meaningful way. This is especially common when discussing movements against austerity, since a broad-based economic attack on poor and working people is taking place, with specific cuts being incidental to a larger system of financial ruin. The recent financial crisis has had a specific effect that seems somewhat generalized: the loss of people's homes. Mass foreclosure can be addressed as a relatively isolated effect of this crisis, instead of trying to counter the financial collapse as a whole.

This logic is clearly demonstrated by the special place that housing has in the US economy among working people. Elaine Bernard notes that homes have often been one of the two ways that working people actually hold wealth, making it vulnerable to a financial class seeking to undercut their losses and monetize the property of the rest of society:

> If you think about it, for working people, there are two forms of personal wealth. For the vast majority, the 99%, what's their personal wealth? Well, their personal wealth is the money they've saved, either through a company or individually towards their pension, their retirement. The second is the value, the equity, in their home. And now both of those are under attack. Both of those have been declining. So what we've seen is a tremendous inequality. America's always been a fairly unequal society, but now what we are seeing is a tremendous growth in inequality.[4]

While this may be the reason that houses were taken from their homeowners through foreclosure, houses are not just units of wealth that people would like to get back because of their value. These are homes that people live in. When homes are taken, it is not just putting the residents in financial turmoil; it very often leaves them homeless. For many people, this situation is not just one of "starting over," it can leave them in a type of debtors' prison, where they cannot regain the stability they need to function nor have the benefit of actually addressing the initial debt.

The problem we face in the discussion about housing is that the issue as a human rights catastrophe has been almost entirely lost in the world of market capitalism. As is the basic function of capitalism, items are separated from their functional use and transformed into commodities. This abstraction of value changes the perception, and indeed the functionality, of a home into a piece of property that is bought and sold. Instead of the basic function of a house to be the creation of a home for a family, its primary purpose has become a way to hold and trade wealth.

HOUSING AS WEALTH

AFTER YEARS OF increasing liberalization of the market, especially as commercial banks began to take the same kind of frightening risks as investment banks, the housing market began to function like the stock market (for more on the rise of risky lending practices in the housing market, see Silfen Glasberg, Beeman, and Casey in this collection). A fully free market policy allows for all property to be converted into units of wealth management without any human connection. It is in this format that a mortgage, the tool that is used so that working people can become homeowners, comes to be treated like any complex financial instrument. The difference is that most people would never involve their most basic assets in a risky financial investment, especially if losing meant that they would no longer have one of their most basic means of survival. Sam Levine, of the foreclosure legal defense organization Project No One Leaves, points out that there are fundamental differences between houses and other items that have been labeled commodities:

> The temptation on the right... has been to treat a
> house, like it's the price of wheat.... But a house isn't
> a bushel of wheat, houses are part of communities.
> When a house in a neighborhood goes into foreclo-
> sure it can bring down the whole block. That can
> drive more homes in that neighborhood into foreclo-
> sure, and once that block goes the whole neighbor-
> hood can go.[5]

Neighborhoods work like complex organisms, with a lot of different factors determining their success, but a single failure can be catastrophic. That the lowering of housing prices will mean that people will begin purchasing the empty properties in large numbers has not been proven true, especially in any way that would represent the original character of those communities.

The fact that housing is a maintainer of communities creates an incredible amount of social instability. Hannah Dobbz, in her book *Nine-Tenths of the Law*, deals with the history of the squatting movement in America, and notes that it is this very *perception* of housing as a commodity that creates a permanent flux:

We are all accustomed to talking about the "housing
market" as if it is actually a thing, and we are able to do
this because we have universally accepted that property
is a commodity that, as such, can be bought and sold
on a market. It is this common agreement that gives
the arrangement power. Liken this to money markets,
in which the users of currency universally agree that it
has value. Money is able to grow or shrink in a market based on the universal contract that money is real
and that is guaranteed. But when you take away that
guarantee, people lose faith that money has value…
The same can be said for the housing market, similarly invented as a fictitious system of measurement:
Property stands in for money in an elaborate game
of appreciation and depreciation based on arbitrary
criteria—that is, based on the level of faith that the
general public has in a neighborhood or region, or in
the market as a whole. When a house is assessed, rarely
is its worth based on *use* value, but is instead based on
the expectation that the market worth may grow. This
is why the housing market, as any market, is unstable
and perpetually poised to fail: Investments are gambles,
and there is not always enough money to back artificial
claims of value.[6]

These are not the kind of market ups and downs that we have
come to expect, but waves that are so profound that use value can
be entirely undercut. As we saw heading into 2009 and 2010, the
institution of commercial mortgage lending became so overwhelmed
with its own failure that its function reversed. Instead of being a basic
tool to increase home ownership, it became an efficient way to clear
out neighborhoods entirely, further driving down home values and
undercutting the working class's ability to maintain wealth.

One of the key elements of the housing crisis from 2010 onward
has been the massive level of fraud that has marked the mass exodus
from neighborhoods. A recent study commissioned by San Francisco's
assessor-recorder found that with 84 percent of mortgages, the bank's
actions were fraudulent, and found at least one major irregularity in
99 percent of the loans.[7] For anyone who has worked in foreclosure

defense, the level of fraud is so apparent that it is the first thing looked for; rarely can you find a case of straightforward eviction simply because someone cannot afford their payments. This illustrates the inability to deal with the massive number of foreclosures, leading to foreclosure mills that process them in such a massive sweep that legality is an afterthought to efficiency. The complexity of the mortgage securitization and sale process has led to difficulty in discerning who even owns the mortgages or the note; and with the Mortgage Electronic Registration System (MERS), there is often the question of whether or not the payments are even being received. What has been created is a monster that is so unstable that the format traditionally associated with home mortgages is no longer dependable, and yet home ownership is still critical to most communities. Through this process, we are seeing an increase in some of the classic forms of discrimination, with communities of color experiencing the most egregious forms of mortgage fraud. This includes the lack of mortgage modifications available to communities of color, which often has little connection to their financial circumstances (again, catalogued in Silfen Glasberg, Beeman, and Casey's contribution to this collection).

The details of the mortgage crisis are important because they determine where the point of struggle will be. The difference between a house and other assets that may be lost in a financial crisis is that people need houses to survive and are already occupying them. With the instability of the housing market, especially to the point of almost complete collapse, it is then easy to say that this is not an issue of reform but one of systemic change. The demand here should not be that the market must recover and become more equitable, but that housing must be separated completely from the rest of the market. People fundamentally deserve the right to a home by virtue of being human. This can only come from community control, as we have seen capitalism's inability to maintain access to housing for all people and the state's inability to ensure equitable distribution through periods of austerity. This is a fundamentally different approach than that of the majority of progressive activists, who instead simply demand more subsidies for public housing and tighter regulations on the housing market. While both of these are positive gains that are worth fighting for, the transformative demand is to pull housing out of the market and, in the process of raising this demand, to create community-based power that has the ability to confront attacks by the banks.

DIRECT ACTION AS STRATEGY

TAKE BACK THE Land, first made famous in Miami in 2008, has been on the ground, using direct action as a strategy to confront the foreclosure crisis head on. There is a certain common sense to what Take Back the Land (and similar groups such as the many Occupy Our Homes locals) does. Direct action seeks to meet people's needs directly, without relying on the state to provide services as an intermediary. In our current housing situation, there is a desperate need to both defend homes that are being taken by banking predators, and to find homes for people who are without them. By finding solutions directly, and through the creation of community solidarity, the direct action strategies of Tack Back the Land fundamentally challenge the ways that housing works in market society.

There are essentially two core tactics that those of us in Take Back the Land use and they both have community organizing and direct action at their core. The first, and often most sensationalized, is housing liberation. While communities are being decimated by mass foreclosures and the homeless populations of major cities rise, streets are littered with empty houses. The simple answer to address this problem is just to move people into the empty homes. Take Back the Land checks the foreclosure records to find bank foreclosures that have happened within an appropriate window of time, to ensure no previous owners are still attached to the properties, and so they have not been vacant long enough to become decrepit. Scouting missions are done to potential houses to see the conditions, paying special attention to essentials like windows and plumbing. During the process, we observe the buildings to see if property management companies are checking in regularly. This is not always a problem, however, because these companies are often so disconnected from the banking records that they do not see anything irregular when new residents move in.

From here the property is fixed up and made habitable, and we assist a homeless family moving in to take it over. This is not like a traditional squat, as the utilities are turned on, the family moves in regular furniture, and they become a part of the surrounding community. When the bank comes back to check on the house, they often become confused, as the new residents appear as though they could be the new owners. Neighbors are usually happy to have someone caring for the previously abandoned building.

The second piece of the Take Back the Land strategy is to support people who are looking to resist foreclosure and stay in their homes. There are a lot of pieces to a defensive framework, which often involves legal strategy. While this is critical to success, it is not always the aspect that organizers want to be engaged in. Instead, we treat these individual cases as on-the-ground organizing efforts, with a focus on direct action. A case can include an escalation campaign that may start with petitions and letter drop-offs, protests at the bank or city offices, and finally eviction blockades, where civil disobedience is used to physically stop the removal of the family. If they are finally removed from the house, we can then jump to the first strategy and move people back into their home.

The purpose of having this two-fold strategy is that it provides a countertactic to two relevant issues in the new nightmare of housing. Various service models have been available for decades to address homelessness (particularly run by state agencies and nonprofits), but they have failed to eradicate home insecurity. Perhaps more importantly, from an anticapitalist point of view, they fail as an avenue for building up community power and solidarity between neighbors. Rather, direct actions in their best manifestations can lead to cultures of autonomous resistance and support within neighborhoods.

THE SPARK OF A MOVEMENT

THE QUESTION THAT comes up about Take Back the Land is whether or not it will develop into a social movement. This question is particularly salient now, given the context of austerity and the disgustingly high rate of foreclosures following the burst of the housing bubble. Indeed, the current incredible growth of Take Back the Land seems to indicate its natural development, in light of the necessity for this type of resistance in communities. Dozens of Take Back the Land and Occupy Our Homes organizations have sprouted across the country, with on-the-ground defense and community organizing at their core, rather than traditional charities or nonprofit service organizations. The reason for the growth of these groups is that the need for housing has become so shockingly obvious that it cannot be ignored. When disparity is so apparent, and the tactics are so public, it is easy for direct action strategies to become a common sense approach to a social problem.

The other reasons behind the explosion of these groups as a social movement are more complicated. With the foreclosure crisis of 2010, we began to see a phenomenon that has been less common over the last two decades: white, middle-class home foreclosures. In poor communities of color, where unemployment rates are staggering in comparison to in their white counterparts, predatory loans and gentrification have been regular elements for almost fifty years. Mass displacement, evictions, and discrimination are not new elements for many of these people. In a report by the Center for Responsible Lending, 21.6 percent of African American homeowners were at imminent risk, while only 14.8 percent of white families faced the same.[8] What was unique about the crisis coming out of 2010 was that it finally began to trickle into the rest of the housing market. This was a clear sign of the growing instability of the housing market—precarious housing has always existed in poor communities of color, but finally began to be true of housing as a whole. This is not, however, a cross-class phenomenon in the larger sense. Instead, the foreclosure crisis began to unite working-class people because the only people who seemed to be immune from this were the people who had the power to fund mortgages, not those who purchased them. It should be noted, however, that racial disparity is still systemic in foreclosure and is not going to simply disappear simply because white working communities are increasingly affected.

Additionally, it is easy to trace the housing justice campaign's expansion into a social movement, as it is simply a piece of the larger anticorporate movement, which began swelling after it became clear the TARP bailout wasn't going to extend to homeowners as originally promised. Though the housing struggle, in practice, should be located in the neighborhoods, the context still remains the larger failure of global capitalism. The economy sank dramatically, companies laid off thousands before going on hiring freezes, pensions were gone, and the largest upward transfer of wealth in history, from workers to the rich, happened. This not only created moral outrage after the criminal element was bailed out, because of their "too big to fail" insurance plan, but people's lives were at stake. The money they had saved was gone, in many cases. We now risk seeing an entire "lost generation" of young people who played by the rules, yet may not be able to find the jobs they are qualified for. One of the reasons this angst has flowed directly into the housing movements after Occupy left the parks is the success it has had at being visual with direct action, and resting its praxis on the common sense of its actions, in response to the stark imbalance in housing.

Today, the housing crisis still causes fear, as it represents one of the major factors in the overall personal debt crisis. In the US, household debt has skyrocketed; in 2007, it was up to 127 percent of annual disposable income, as compared to 77 percent in 1990.[9] As of 2011, household debt hovered at around $13.2 trillion, a number that is increasing.[10] The private debt of the U.S was 290 percent of the GDP at the beginning of the crisis in 2008, which is a massive increase from 123 percent in 1981.[11] As we head into a "new normal" in the post-crisis American landscape, debt is no longer something that people can escape. As the property values dropped, people found that they owed more on their homes than the houses were worth. This created a complete failure in refinancing and modifications, and they were saddled with loans that are not representative of the assets they own. Debt is becoming a permanent part of life for many people and, with recent "reforms" (like the almost complete elimination of the option to declare bankruptcy), it seems easy enough to imagine a massive debt could remove people from consumer society completely. This heads us in an almost feudal direction, where a ruling elite begins to acquire large tracts of land and property and then saddles the rest of the population with perpetual work due to crushing debt.

This debt lies in the abstract, where avenues for resistance seem difficult and disconnected from the enormity of the thing itself. It is much easier to tackle a social issue with a distinct face, though this is scarcely found in economic justice. One of the clear exceptions here is in housing justice, where resistance to the repossession of property has a clear tactical approach and gains moral sympathy from the public because of the irresponsibility of the banks.

The explosion of this neighborhood militancy came from a mix of all of these elements, from the obviousness of the problem to the public nature of the possible solutions. No working-class community has remained untouched by this crisis. All homeowners and, in reality, renters have been forced into a state of constant fright, wondering how permanent their housing situation is. Everyone knows somebody going through a foreclosure. In this way, it is literally impossible to ignore because it is one of the most clearly definable aspects of the financial crisis. Since one house can affect the rest on a given block, the victimization of your neighbor could lead to you becoming collateral damage.

MAINTAINING NEIGHBORHOOD POWER

THERE ARE A number of political orientations among people involved in the housing justice movement, which has added depth to the discussion about what success might look like. On the more traditionally progressive end, there is an attempt to continually appeal to the powers of the state to essentially interfere with capital and provide a larger social service infrastructure. A dual strategy—of direct action efforts connected to legislative efforts—has been a particularly important part of the integrated housing campaign in Rochester, New York. Here, Take Back the Land Rochester focuses on direct action in a "case-by-case" approach, while connecting with the local social justice nonprofit, Metro Justice, which works on policy. In the Metro Justice Housing Committee, the focus is on a moratorium campaign, demanding that the city cease participation in the execution of foreclosure-based evictions. This means that the police will "stand down" when the marshal's office issues an eviction, rendering the eviction useless, because the force of the state is no longer present to give it authority. The logic provided to the city is that, with the substantial rate of fraud that is literally removing the functionality of neighborhoods in Rochester, the city can no longer be certain that its police force is executing legal eviction orders. For large-scale actions, marches, protests, and "speak out" sessions, Take Back the Land Rochester and Metro Justice work together. There is an acknowledgment that each group takes up a different, yet complementary, role in the struggle. Both groups share a number of members.

A multitiered strategy has been at play in a number of communities, and it has had a dramatic influence on the nonprofit culture that had been perceived as much more standoffish when it came to direct action. In Portland, Oregon, We Are Oregon, a nonprofit funded by SEIU Locals 503 and 49, has ended up taking the lead on foreclosure defense after interactions with groups like Unsettle Portland (a Take Back the Land local) and the Portland Liberation Organizing Council. In Boston, the nonprofit City Life/Vida Urbana has been using a foreclosure defense model for almost forty years.

While it is key to have the policy-focused movement support direct action, it is important to note the limitations of demands on the state right from the start. Gains that are given by the state are an important component, but they are not permanent and do not always build power on the ground. We can look to the antiausterity movements in Europe as a reminder. Whatever the state bestows on you, it can take away in times of crisis.

This paradox was at the heart of the Troubled Asset Relief Program (TARP), one of the earliest attempts at responding to the subprime crisis, involving the federal government's purchase of $475 billion in "troubled" assets. The intent was to protect the banks from collapse, as well as provide support to the public lied to by a corrupt financial sector. As Noam Chomsky pointed out, half of this promise was completely neglected:

> Basic human rights are being taken away by social and economic systems that have no real legitimacy. I mean, take foreclosure. Take a look at the legislative history. When the bank bailout was legislated by congress, the TARP bailout actually had two components. One was to bail out the banks, essentially the people who created the crisis. The other half was to do something to help their victims. Of those two components, only one was implemented. The first one. [12]

The TARP bailout was not a moral treaty on the part of the government, but a purely functional one. In an attempt to stave off impending doom, there was a financial outpouring intended for both the public and the financial sector, as a way of undercutting the damage on both ends. The demand from the banks ended up being too high and distribution among those with the underwater mortgages was never fully realized. The reasons for this are complicated or simple, depending on how you break it down, but the core is that those in the driver's seat have more in common with those in Goldman Sachs's towers than they do with your neighbors who are losing their homes and life savings. On its own, the state cannot be expected to act as anything other than a military force to maintain the status quo—a violent system that extracts wealth from the rent and labor of working people. As early as 2004, the FBI was being made aware that we were entering an era of mass fraud, as hundreds of billions of dollars in risky, mortgage-backed securities were being written down.[13] Without the power of regulation and the transparency to see what was happening, the mechanisms nominally intended to help were left impotent. Such is the nature of state tinkering.

This kind of "in name only" legislative policy is seen incredibly clearly in the Universal Declaration of Human Rights, a document that was adopted by the United Nations and approved by the US, outlining what people deserve just by virtue of being human. Article 25, Section 1, addresses housing specifically, as well as many other services that are by no means guaranteed in twenty-first century America:

> Everyone has the right to a standard of living adequate
> for the health and well-being of himself and of his family, including food, clothing, housing, and medical care
> and necessary social services, and the right to security
> in the event of unemployment, sickness, disability, widowhood, old age or other lack of livelihood in circumstances beyond his control.[14]

In this document, we have a tool for consistently making demands that the state has no intention of meeting. The largest legal entity in the world has declared housing to be a human right, and the United States has agreed; yet it has never materialized. We can demand legislation and language that reflects this sentiment, but those with the purse strings are not going to give up these resources unless there is a movement that gives them no choice. Benevolence is not a feature of the state, so a transformative movement for housing must stand opposed to the state and its methods of austerity.

This same logic—of demands that the state has no interest in meeting—is present in the movement rhetoric of housing as a "human right." Human rights as a concept typically presumes something bestowed on us by the state. Periods of austerity undercut this logic, so it is important to note that state measures do not guarantee anything. Social movements do. Short-term solutions can be put in place in terms of state concessions, but the long-term solution is the inspiration of people to come together and fight for the change we want to see, without relying on politicians. This solidarity, the willingness to come together in the interests of the working people of the world, is going to be the real force of permanent change and the only thing that can ensure the permanence of things we consider to be "human rights."

Some of this is simply stating the obvious, but it is important to clearly identify what can be expected of state demands. The state is an arbitrator of property rights, whose stake is in those who control the resources. While it can be forced into responding as a tool of redistribution, this is not its natural position. It is important then to move away from state-centered demands as a long-term strategy.

The power of people in an organized mass movement is what forces the state to build the social safety net, but this cannot be the final frontier. Progressive organizing has always attempted to create mechanisms within the state that would see injustice as it occurs and counter it; yet even at points of extreme victimization, the banks get what they need, while the mass of people are left without any options. A permanently just system of housing does not solely come from gifts from the state, but rather by forcefully taking it out of the state's purview. This would be a revolutionary movement, one that seeks to create a new path, different from what we have grown accustomed to. For this process to be complete, it has to move far beyond housing and into all areas of social life; in building counterinstitutions in the here and now, we force the state into giving us the protections needed for our neighborhoods to just survive. This is done to lessen our discontent, but when our method is direct action, we create power in communities to demand more, and eventually overturn the system that still allows homelessness while there is an overabundance of empty houses. True success is not in appealing to the morality of those in power, but instead giving them no choice but to concede.

The Portland Liberation Organizing Council, a short-lived housing offshoot of Occupy Portland, puts it thus:

> Ultimately, home defense results from the recognition
> that the economic and legal systems are used to take
> advantage of and manipulate working people for the
> gain of banks and financial institutions. This recogni-
> tion, that there is no justice in the system, builds belief
> and power in the principle that the only thing we can
> count on to meet our needs are our communities,
> neighborhoods, natural and created families.[15]

Direct action cuts through the myths of bureaucracy and shows us a world where we can take control of our lives, by going directly to the sources of the problem and by coming together as a community in mutual aid.

To combat the logic of austerity, you must find ways to completely demolish the power that ruling institutions have to determine the future of communities. This is not a simple proposition that can be done just by "retreating from capital." Acting directly on our own behalf can build dual power, where the process of abolishing one system gives rise to a new one. Late capitalism is failing all around us. Economic inequality is at an all-time high, international finance is in ruin, research and development is dropping. Today, the answers will not come by just reinstating Glass-Steagall. A system built for failure from the start has a shelf life. The heart of the new institutions that are forming in our neighborhoods is the solidarity between neighbors that develops into class power to contest the robbery of their most basic human rights. When successfully creating a surge of grassroots participation, this develops a new form of property relationship that sees housing as more than a product to be distributed to the richest bidder. Once housing is taken off the auction block, then the forces of austerity will lose their power, since they have to contend with the great majority of people who simply refuse to accept the meager crumbs they have been allowed.

THINKING BEYOND AUSTERITY

ONE THING THAT is difficult when thinking about housing in terms of the crisis is that these struggles are not *reducible* to the collapse of the housing market and the subsequent crisis. Poverty, homelessness, and evictions were here long before the recent crisis, even in periods of perceived prosperity. When the response to housing issues is framed strictly in terms of austerity or recession, then it can lose its longevity, as well as its possibility to challenge the core logic of capitalism. The crisis is attempting to normalize precarious living circumstances and create a new world where security of any sort is only afforded to the rich. As capitalism attempts to recover, it will do so at the cost of working people, not the rich. We will not simply return to where we were before austerity because this period of sanctions is permanent, which means our target must be transformation, rather than

just reversal. Our movements must not remain simply against austerity. Under capital, power remains with those who have the ability to
determine our futures. A powerful movement should seek to strip
them of this power entirely.

A CALL FOR SUCCESS

The housing movement, like most social movements, is messy. Often, a great idea is enough to spark a great movement marked by high
profile actions and romantic defiance, but that does not take it past
the initial fireworks. To give the movement longevity, there needs to
be clear self-reflection and an analysis of successes and failures.

For one thing, this means high levels of organization that cen-
tralize education and democratic decision-making. The process of
research, legal study, and outreach that is required to do things like
locate appropriate houses for liberation and involve affected people
is extensive. It is easy for certain people to end up taking on more
authority in movements because knowledge is unequally distributed,
undercutting the ability to become a real movement "by the people,"
as there will be unequal levels of possible participation.

At the same time, many of the people who have the time and
energy to organize do so less because they are directly affected, and
more often because they have a moral and intellectual impetus for it.
This can often lead movements like Take Back the Land to simply be a
"radical charity," where some benevolent anarchist superheroes break
into houses and deliver them to needy people. While this may be a socially positive thing for an afternoon, and does present an element of
mutual aid, it is by no means the seed of a movement that will extend
beyond itself and change the ways neighborhoods operate. Here it is
critical to keep the movement focused on the people who are actually
in situations of foreclosure and homelessness.

If growth is going to be successful, it means moving beyond working only with homeowners, to whom which these movements are often limited, since the avenues to dealing with foreclosure evictions
are a little easier to follow. This means working with renters, public
housing tenants, and people in unconventional housing situations. It
also means moving past the "case-by-case" approach and beginning
to look at tenant syndicalism in large rental properties. For tactical
inspiration, we can look to sectors where principles like solidarity and

direct action have been used successfully, such as employing radical union strategies in housing complexes.

We might also include looking toward counterlegal institutions to provide as tools in the box. One of these tools is the land trust, which is essentially a legal entity that has the ability to hold land. When a homeowner is going through foreclosure, the community can negotiate with the bank to donate to the property to the land trust, legally a nonprofit organization, for a tax write-off in the amount of the market value of the house. As these properties begin to accumulate in the land trust, they can then be held for the community, allowing neighborhood councils to form, to make decisions collectively. This is, again, not a final solution, as land trusts can also be opened up to developers and used against homeowners, though bylaws can be established as protections. Instead, this is simply a tool that can be used to enhance a community organizing effort. The social movement must always remain the heart of the battle, no matter what legal tools are employed alongside it.

Similarly, a legal claim like adverse possession allows an occupant to apply for legal ownership of a property after a certain amount of time and, if the legal owner does not contest it, may provide some legal protection. In states like Arizona, this period is as brief as two years, though the numbers in most states range between seven and twenty years.[16] This is more ammo in a war, and here the logic of property can often be turned against elites.

THE PRECARIOUS OPPORTUNITY

TODAY, LEONARD SPEARS is still in his home. His campaign began by writing up a demand letter, to be accompanied by a petition signed by people from all over his community. A large protest was arranged at a local Wells Fargo office for delivery of the letter, but it shut down in fear, and a local police officer had to act as an intermediary and deliver the letter to the office. They refused to read it at first, stating that the mortgage department was separate from the divisions that particular office dealt with. That was fine, as the group who had amassed immediately headed to the mortgage office, stormed in, and demanded the letter be read. The next day, Wells Fargo called Leonard and said there was a good chance of getting his house back.

It turned out that there was a lot more legal wrangling to be had and he eventually went to court. After presenting the information that not only had Wells Fargo falsified documents in the delivery of the foreclosure papers, they did not even own the mortgage nor the note at the time of foreclosure, the judge ruled that this was fine and that it could not be reversed this late in the game (though she noted that she simply did not have legal grounds to go after Wells Fargo in an appropriate way).

Leonard has committed to staying in his home, a decision everyone at Take Back the Land intends to support until the end. It is not clear how soon Freddie Mac, the current owner of the property, will take action to remove Leonard from his home. Leonard says his decision is steadfast, even though the process can be humiliating and demoralizing:

> I'm determined to stay here. I feel like I deserve to stay here. I mean, to me it's my life staying here, but to them it's just another piece of land. The neighborhood has a lot of condemned houses that have been sitting around here for a long time. And as we look going down the street all we see is boarded up houses, vacant houses, and that's deteriorating the neighborhood. You see a lot of homeless people, you know, sleeping outside. Sometimes you'll see them just lying on the porches of abandoned houses just covered up, and I'm like, what is going on with this world now? Why can't we just let them live in there? I mean, is it all about money? What happened to humanity? What happened to the love for people?[17]

Whenever they come to take Leonard's home from him, we will stand in solidarity to physically blockade the house, along with neighbors and friends. If we are unsuccessful, it may mean that we will liberate his house, but since both are on the table, there is always a way in. We are defining this neighborhood as an eviction-free zone and, in that simple act, we stand together as a community to say that we will no longer accept a status quo that does not ensure a safe home for everyone.

ENDNOTES

1   I would like to dedicate this chapter to my parents, Neil and Bonnie Burley, whose inspiration and support made this work possible.

2   Leonard Spears, interviewed by Shane Burley, May 15, 2012.

3   Ibid.

4   Elaine Bernard, interviewed by Shane Burley, November 8, 2011.

5   Samuel Levine, interviewed by Shane Burley, November 12, 2011.

6   Hannah Dobbz, *Nine-Tenths of the Law: Property and Resistance in the United States* (Oakland: AK Press, 2012), 3.

7   Phil Ting, "Press Release: Assessor-Recorder Phil Ting Uncovers Widespread Mortgage Industry Irregularity in San Francisco Foreclosures," Office of the Assessor-Recorder San Francisco, http://www.sfassessor.org/modules/show-document.aspx?documentid=1019 (accessed March 25, 2013).

8   Debbie Gruenstein Bocian, Wei Li, and Keith S. Ernst, "Foreclosures by Race and Ethnicity: The Demographics of a Crisis," Center for Responsible Lending, http://www.responsiblelending.org/mortgage-lending/research-analysis/foreclosures-by-race-and-ethnicity.pdf (accessed March 28, 2013).

9   Federal Reserve Statistical Release, "Flow of Funds Accounts of the United States: Flows and Outstandings Fourth Quarter 2012," Board of the Governors of the Federal Reserve System, Washington D.C., http://www.federalreserve.gov/releases/z1/current/z1.pdf (accessed March 28, 2013).

10   Debbie Jeffries, "The End of the Affair," *The Economist*, http://www.economist.com/node/12637090?story_id=12637090 (accessed March 28, 2013).

11   Colin Barr, "The $4 Trillion Housing Headache," *Fortune*, http://money.cnn.com/2009/05/27/news/mortgage.overhang.fortune/index.htm (accessed March 28, 2013).

12   Noam Chomsky, interviewed by Shane Burley, March 27, 2012.

13   Richard B. Schmitt, "FBI Saw Threat of Loan Crisis," *Los Angeles Times*, http://articles.latimes.com/2008/aug/25/business/fi-mortgage-fraud25 (accessed March 31, 2013).

14 General Assembly of the United Nations, *The Universal Declaration of Human Rights*, Palais de Chailot, Paris France, December 10, 1948.

15 Heidi Whipple, Taran Connelly, and Kari Kock, "Home is Where the Heart Is," *Perspectives on Anarchist Theory* 14, no. 1 (2012): 11.

16 Dobbz, *Nine-Tenths of the Law*, 257–260.

17 Spears, interview.

CIRCUMSCRIBED BY CONDITIONS THEY DID NOT CREATE[1]

THE ENGLISH RIOTS OF AUGUST 2011

CHRISTIAN GARLAND

BURNING AND LOOTING TONIGHT...

THE EVENTS OF AUGUST 6–10, 2011 APPEARED—AS REBELLIONS FREquently do—"from out of nowhere," although the original spark in Tottenham, London on that Saturday night was itself beyond question: the death of another black man at the hands of police. As widescale rioting and looting subsequently spread in a matter of hours across the capital, and then to almost every major city across the country, as well as outside of urban centers—literally like wildfire—events seemingly overtook analysis, with a few notable exceptions. At the time, much was made of the extent of "criminality" and "lawlessness": besides direct engagement with the police, mass looting—alternatively understood as the direct and immediate appropriation of commodities—became a recurrent feature of the disturbances.

Such outbreaks of "disorder" in a society such as the UK can be seen as indicative of a situation in which an increasingly significant section of the population is materially excluded, meaning that its labor is not required because it cannot be usefully exploited, and so the means for reproducing the material conditions of existence themselves are put out of reach. However, the products of consumerism remain mockingly ever-present to all, even as the bad conscience of actual material poverty and social deprivation reminds late capitalist society that they never went away.

This chapter will seek to contribute to a better critical understanding of the disturbances of Summer 2011 in England, with the clarity of two years passed and greater empirical evidence confirming that they were indeed an explosion of accumulated social misery and not the "opportunist" activities of a "criminal underclass." Indeed, the recognition that the trinkets and baubles of consumer capitalism are put beyond the reach of the majority, and that section of people who day-to-day are effectively rendered invisible, returned as the repressed for four nights in England at the beginning of August 2011. The use here of the phrase the "return of the repressed" is meant in the same way Marx and Engels referred to the "specter haunting Europe," that being *communism*, always present as the *communist tension*, forever threatening capital with its own historical becoming.[2] That such a tension is so explicitly and visibly made manifest in such imperfect and uneven events as these can be seen as the imperfect and uneven nature of *class struggle;* and, in this specific instance, where labor is dispersed, atomized, and rendered surplus by capital, one such manifestation of the apparently hamstrung agency of the revolutionary social subject is urban rebellions such as the English riots of August 2011.

HOW MANY MORE BRIDGES MUST WE CROSS...BEFORE WE GET TO MEET THE BOSS?

As HAS BEEN noted elsewhere, the events of August 2011 were, in many ways, unlike previous disturbances in the UK, some of which had a more clearly defined "social" character, in that they were, however haphazardly, an attempt at materially articulating rebellion against unbearable conditions. It has been contended from many different "critical" standpoints (in addition to the requisite agonized hand-wringing that tends to go with these standpoints) that August 2011 was much more "nihilistic," and offered little in the way of actual contestation of the conditions from which these events emerged. The hysterical denunciations and media narratives have been dealt with elsewhere, and so we will concentrate here on a more considered, *materialist* analysis.[3]

The destructive force of attacks against the immediate and most visible symbols of day-to-day misery (cars, shops, the police) is an immediate material expression of an imminent rupture of the class relation, frequently made most forcefully by those excluded from wage labor. This is what the 2011 English riots mean, and meant. No left or ultra-left pretense needs to be put forward, suggesting that the "violence" of those four nights in August was "justified" or, alternatively, "excessive," though the latter was unsurprisingly true of the state's response. The inchoate and imprecise acts carried out by the unwanted and superfluous subjects excluded from the wage relation and rendered as nothing by capital was a hesitant and temporary redress: an uneven and imperfect expression of class struggle.

The distinct lack of discernible "social" character to that year's disturbances has been thus explained:

> The chaotic and convulsive character of the August unrest, its huge distance from what could be normatively called a proletarian struggle, the impossibility for it to fit in a longed-for movement for working class empowerment, provoked a certain nostalgia for the early '80s. More than a few hurried to belittle the summer riots to something like a social defecation, as compared to the '80s riots that advanced beyond anger and frustration, into affirming a communal spirit and endorsing a political aspiration. This time, rioters fell behind as they are perceived not to have pursued what they could have ideally done, namely seek to lay the first stones for re-creating a strong, autonomous proletarian movement, through self-organisation and class solidarity. It is in the last instance a matter of the consciousness of the proletarian Subject to realise the forever given revolutionary Practice for the best. [...][4]

The absence of this *collective project*, which is indeed the weakness of agency, might be identified as the seeming fragmentation of social subjects; if we speak here of plural subjects, it is not to celebrate the postmodern condition, the cultural logic of late capitalism, but to try to explain how this leaves a social vacuum in its wake, one that makes the *singular* revolutionary social subject, the proletariat rejecting and ending both its own role and the class relation in revolution, far more difficult to approximate. The 2011 August riots, of course, began with a localized and very clearly defined combustion of anger at the state's killing of another black man, and his killers' callous refusal to have any contact with his family or supporters. But as this "localized" incident in Tottenham, north London, rapidly escalated into actual rebellion and riots, the disorder spread outward across the capital to include more than forty areas of the city,[5] and began to spark in Birmingham and the urban conurbation of the West Midlands, in a matter of hours.

By Monday night, August 8, riots had spread across the whole of England, including virtually every major city, though not to the other countries in the UK. Birmingham, Bristol, Leeds, Liverpool, Manchester, Nottingham, Salford, and many smaller places all saw disorder and what has frequently been termed "looting." This looting, which was also truly *mass looting*, and its "asocial" and "opportunistic" nature, has been one of the most repeated problematics of the events of that year. But the looting can also be seen as one of the most indicative acts of the fragmentary, individualized, asocial terrain of late capitalist society. Mass appropriation of the products of overproduction that must be consumed at all costs under normal circumstances, even though the material relations of "production" (i.e. work) become more and more removed from the experience of an ever-growing segment of the population, and that such consumption has only ever been made possible through credit and debt, means that the breaking of shop windows and the removal of goods without payment (i.e. looting) were some of the keynote features of last year's events.

This chapter is certainly not an attempt to simply cheerlead the disorder as being a rebellion for its own sake, overlooking the limited and specific historical context. The events themselves were one very specific and ephemeral manifestation of *class struggle*, even if there was no apparent revolutionary social subject in evidence. That the riots involved such mass looting, on such a scale, can be seen as merely one eruption of the ever-present tension of class relations; a totality that cannot be exited from, nor one in which "actually existing" social relations can be decontextualized or, conversely, *particularized* in ahistorical and severely limited terms:

> Taken this way, the August unrest was a historically
> specific event belonging to the totality that has the con-
> tradiction between classes at its core, as it exists today
> (restructured capitalism and its crisis).... The rioters
> attacked, in what they are, the proletarian situation
> now, namely the precarisation of labour power. In the
> absence of demands and in their concrete practices,
> namely looting, arson of commercial and public build-
> ings, attacks at the police and police stations, the wish
> to become an "ordinary proletarian"—a worker with a
> fair day's pay for a fair day's work—was made obsolete.[6]

The English riots were a material expression of labor that has long since been rendered surplus and obsolete. The immediate recognition by the rioters that no "normal" social situation exists for them, now or in the future, was also apparent the immediate destructive manifesta-tion their activity took, i.e. vandalism, rioting, looting, and arson. The thirty-five- to forty-year period of capital's continuous recomposition and restructuring—sometimes rightly or wrongly referred to as "neo-liberalism"—aimed at creating optimal conditions for its renewed ac-cumulation, has indeed rendered the wage relation a fragmentary and precarious privilege, which becomes harder and harder to secure and retain for an ever-growing number. The previous apparent homogene-ity of wage labor of the proletariat has also been superseded by capital, and the nature of "work" in the era of globalization is indicative of this. Production, "off-shored" many thousands of miles to new poles of accumulation, is primarily the *production of value*, and the discon-tinuity between capital accumulation and the production of value and extraction of profit can be seen in class relations in countries such as the UK and those of the EU as the *subsumption* of labor.[7]

This is not the place for a long excursus into the merits of the concept of subsumption, or the known and unknown nature of rela-tive and absolute forms, but it can certainly be observed that, "the labour process becomes the instrument of the valorisation process, of the process of capital's self-valorisation—the process of the creation of surplus value."[8] In Continental Europe, the contestation of class society, which is more or less visible in different countries, frequently takes the form of strike action, an example of a section of labor using "the only weapons currently available"—or at least known. A section of labor because it is heavily unionized and sectional labor, something that has been rendered basically defunct by capital, but, in the dynamic of class struggle, remains at least a partial threat—if not to capitalism, then at times to individual capitalists.

For all those not "lucky" enough to be included in this obsolescent segmentation of the workforce of advanced capitalist countries, there is simply *precarity*—ceaselessly, it would seem. The only certainty is that wage labor will become harder to secure, wages will be lower, and hours fewer. Such flexible or precarious and insecure conditions of employment, with the onus always shifted onto the individual to retrain and constantly update their skills as they are rendered obsolete, can be viewed as a twenty-first century degradation of labor.[9] To borrow Braverman's concept, there should be no misunderstanding that a vulgar Marxian rendering of the loss of a previous form of "skilled" work is intended. What is meant here, in applying the seemingly overlooked concept, is the accelerated process of capital producing more surplus value than it needs to extract from living labor in the form of the wage relation. Based on this premise, existing forms of work, in which labor is made as interchangeable—and thus dispensable—as possible, can be seen in the intensifying, all-pervasive demand to "always be on" (for work) intensifies, the scarcer and more precarious work becomes, just as unemployment and underemployment become the responsibility of the individual and not society. Indeed, as more and more work is seen to assume performative demands, in which workers are expected to give of themselves and always be on call, all employment—however temporary, insecure, or disagreeable—is seen to define the employee, through total, existential affect.

The "precariat" has been defined as "the new dangerous class." It might reasonably be contended that this is not, in fact, a "new class," but rather the scarred face of the recomposing proletarian class, and its "danger" is the scarf or ski mask concealing its identity.[10] The proletariat, or the side of labor, is always the dangerous class, because it is the diametric contradiction of capital. The living labor of active human subjects has been turned into the dead, abstract labor of objects, accumulated as value; such is the capital-labor relation. The surplus labor generated by the process of accumulation—observable in the UK, US, and EU—is the distance between capital and the actual production of value by this unwanted "unproductive" surplus. Such a fact is not overlooked by the state, which has, while remaining what it always essentially was (the legal monopoly of violence), undergone restructuring that makes it unrecognizable in comparison to thirty or so years ago. At the same time, the capitalist economy has entered paroxysms of crisis unseen at any time in the second half of the twentieth century; it has already remade and recalibrated its functions to be solely punitive. This process, which has taken place—especially in the UK—in virtual perpetuity during the same time frame as capital's recomposition and restructuring, can be seen in the habit of "tendering" and "contracting out" many, if not all, of its functions to private capital (including the repressive powers of prisons, and less successfully [so far] the police), from the provision of very basic public services to the removal of all but the most minimal "welfare" provision, through a transformation into "workfare" (i.e. forcing people to work for free, ostensibly preparing them for available work), in an effort to discipline the growing reserve army of surplus labor.

While the relative downward trend of capital accumulation on labor can be said to play a part in the creation of fragmented, separate subjects, ill-equipped to assert themselves collectively against their objectified and reified material categorization as abstract surplus labor, an uneven and somewhat haphazard collective assertion of labor-valorizing-itself-against-capital is nonetheless apparent. Labor as object and capital as subject is reversed, so labor becomes subject and capital object. As such, in countries where collective action is still possible in the older way, where organized labor still exists, the more insurrectionary form of contestation of the unwanted surplus of capital appears: riots. In Greece, Spain, and Portugal, but also France, a growing labor surplus is visible in the vast percentages of unemployed youth, just as unemployed and employed youth make themselves visible in the glare of burning cars and the flames of shattering molotov cocktails.

In the UK, as on the continent of Europe, the "possession of a permanent paymaster in the shape of the capitalist" is an increasingly elusive and temporary reality for a growing percentage of the population, and one with which many of those involved in the events of August 2011 have little, if any, experience.[11] The irony of coincidence of the 2011 events occurring almost thirty years to the month since a previous wave of urban disorder swept the country was not lost. However, it appears, with relative hindsight or perhaps the ongoing dynamic of class struggle that the ten days in July 1981,[12] in which the UK, not just England and not just in urban centers, combusted,[13] should have occurred at the very start of a decade of intense class conflict, at the end of which the side of capital would emerge victorious.[14] "Victorious" meaning the ever temporary, always fleeting, and uncertain "victory" of capital against labor, and in this decades-long process of capital restructuring and recomposition, what might be termed the "subsumption" of labor. It is this self-same process of capital recomposition, to become that much more fluid and assume that much more "liquidity," which fragments labor into plural subjects. While labor is still the contradictory producer of value and the inescapable, infernal necessity for capital's reproduction and valorization, it is (nearly) impossibly difficult for labor to materially articulate itself as subject (singular). As such, "flexible subjects" are left to compete ceaselessly with each other for formerly "guaranteed" wage labor, albeit frequently in diminishing amounts, the hours of work nearing zero.

THE "FORETASTE OF THE FUTURE" THAT IS OUR UNRAVELING PRESENT[15]

WITH ALL THIS in mind, it is possible to discern a definite "political" context and character to the August 2011 riots, and it should be restated that the English rioters acted from a class location of social deprivation, material exclusion—mass unemployment being the most obvious example—and the resultant subjective impotency of powerlessness. This observation can be further clarified, to avoid any left or liberal agonizing over such "issues." The UK riots disappointed nearly all of what remains of the left with their "apolitical nihilism"—the fact that they were seemingly about indiscriminate destruction on an epic scale. Destruction and "looting" of unattainable consumer goods were straightforward explanations of the "selfish and acquisitive" nature of capitalist society, and while not without some truth, this is a horribly simplistic account of what happened. The following is an edited transcript of a television news interview with four participants from the days that followed the riots:

> **Sky interviewer:** *Have any of you felt any kind of bad feelings or remorse since you did what you did?*

> **Rioter:** No, coz I'm watching my Plasma that I just got…It feels like Christmas came early! So, no.

Interviewer: *A lot of people wouldn't see any sense in what you were involved in. It was outrageously wrong in a lot of people's eyes. The government is saying that it is utterly unacceptable, that there is no reasoning behind it. Do you think there is any reasoning behind it?*

Rioter: Every time I go hand out my CV, I dress the smartest I can, talk the politest I can, but nah, they ain't noticing me, so obviously, if they ain't noticing me from that, man have to start doing it a different way.

Interviewer: *Generations of people have worked hard to get what you just went out and took. Do you not think that that's a better way to get it?*

Second rioter: We work hard, but they're not giving us no jobs. They don't wanna give us that chance. They don't wanna give us that chance.

Third rioter: Right now, it looks like there ain't a future for young people, that's how I see it innit? Because the government, they're not helping no one out except for the rich people. They don't care for us; they just leave us on the blocks to do whatever we do.

Interviewer: *There's a lot of wealth in this city, I mean you've only got to look over there there's Canary Wharf behind us, and in this city, there's a real focus on celebrity, and money and materialism.*

First rioter: And that's who the government look out for, them people up there—look at the flats, look at the flats—they're not thinking of us, they're thinking about that one pocket up there, that one pocket.[16]

"Apolitical" and "nihilistic" riots are one material articulation of the crisis of the class relation, as well as an expression of class violence. Indeed, there is surely the "foretaste of the future" with which the authors of *Like a Summer with a Thousand Julys* concluded their text on the 1981 events.[17] The "future" that was glimpsed thirty years ago is our present, but so too an unknown and uncertain unfolding of the near future from this vantage point. One such aspect of this unfolding present is the emerging recognition that class struggle is an irremovable dynamic of capitalist social relations, however much it may appear in uncertain and indeterminate forms. Marx's original formulation of revolution is one in which the proletariat will *negate the class relation* and in so doing, as the revolutionary social subject, *negate itself.* This "negation-of-the-negation" cannot ever be exactly determined, nor can the events and temporalities of "how and when" it will occur, but that is not to say it cannot be approximated, any more than it cannot be observed in different ephemeral and partial forms—riots are one such contemporary example, and a common one the world over, as the current crisis in capitalism continues to set in.

ENDNOTES

1   A paraphrase of Marx's "The productive forces are the result of man's practical energy, but that energy is in turn circumscribed by the conditions in which man is placed by the productive forces already acquired, by the form of society which exists before him, which he does not create, which is the product of the preceding generation." Karl Marx, 1846, *Letter to Annenkov*, http://www.marxists.org/archive/marx/works/1846/letters/46_12_28.htm (accessed July 15, 2013). A much shorter conference paper of the same name was presented as part of the "Resistance Today" stream at the Historical Materialism Ninth Annual Conference, "Weighs Like a Nightmare" SOAS, University of London, 8–11 November 2012.

2   Karl Marx and Friedrich Engels, *1848 Manifesto of the Communist Party*, http://www.marxists.org/archive/marx/works/1848/communist-manifesto/ch01.htm (accessed July 15, 2013).

3   Christian Garland, "Simulating Events as They Happen: Media Spectacle, Ideology, and Readymade Boogeymen," talk given at "Hot Analysis—The Streets of London," August 16, 2011), http://academia.edu/1088899/Simulating_events_as_they_happen_media_spectacle_ideology_and_readymade_boogeymen (accessed July 15, 2013).

4   Eustraum, "The Feral Underclass Hits the Streets: On the English Riots and Other Ordeals," *Sic: International Journal for Communisation,*

http://sic.communisation.net/en/the-feral-underclass-hits-the-streets (accessed July 15, 2013).

5   Vikram Dodd and Caroline Davies, "London Riots Escalate as Police Battle for Control," *The Guardian*, http://www.guardian.co.uk/uk/2011/aug/08/london-riots-escalate-police-battle (accessed July 15, 2013); Martin Wainright, et al., "Lockdown in London, While Trouble Flares in Nottingham and Manchester," *The Guardian*, http://www.guardian.co.uk/uk/2011/aug/09/riots-salford-wolverhampton-west-bromwich (accessed July 15, 2013); Paul Lewis, et al., "English Rioters Warn of More to Come," *The Guardian*, http://www.guardian.co.uk/uk/2011/dec/05/more-english-riots-to-come (accessed July 15, 2013).

6   Eustraum, "The Feral Underclass." But see also, Ricardo Reis, "The August 2011 Riots in Britain," http://www.revoltagainstplenty.com/index.php/recent/1-recent/183-ricardo-reis (accessed July 15, 2013).

7   Screamin' Alice, "The Breakdown of a Relationship? Reflections on the Crisis," http://endnotes.org.uk/articles/15 (accessed July 15, 2013).

8   Karl Marx, "Formal Subsumption of Labour under Capital," *Capital* vol.1. https://www.marxists.org/archive/marx/works/1864/economic/ch02a.htm#469 (accessed July 15, 2013).

9   Harry Braverman, *Labour and Monopoly Capital: The Degradation of Work in the Twentieth Century* (New York: Monthly Review Press, 1998).

10   Guy Standing, *The Precariat: The New Dangerous Class* (London: Bloomsbury, 2010).

11   Marx, "Formal Subsumption of Labour."

12   "Riot Comms: From Chalk, to CB Radio to Blackberry," History is Made at Night: 1981, blog, http://history-is-made-at-night.blogspot.com/2011/08/riot-comms-from-chalk-to-cb-radio-to.html (accessed July 15, 2013); "The 1981 Riots in South London," Libcom.org, http://libcom.org/history/1981-riots-south-london (accessed July 15, 2013); Jerry White, "The History of Riots in London Shows That Persistent Inequality and Injustice is Always Likely to Breed Periodic Violent Uprisings," British Politics and Policy at LSE website, http://blogs.lse.ac.uk/politicsandpolicy/archives/16492 (accessed July 15, 2013); Tracy Shildrick, "The Riots: Poverty Cannot be Ignored," http://sociologyandthecuts.wordpress.com/2011/08/23/

the-riots-poverty-cannot-be-ignored-by-tracy-shildrick/ (accessed July 15, 2013).

13   See also Evan Calder Williams, "Open Letter to Those Who Condemn Looting," Part 1 http://socialismandorbarbarism.blogspot.co.uk/2011/08/open-letter-to-those-who-condemn.html and part 2 http://socialismandorbarbarism.blogspot.co.uk/2011/08/open-letter-to-those-who-condemn_10.html (accessed July 15, 2013); L. Kettle and J. Hodges, *Uprising!: Police, the People and the Riots in Britain's Cities* (London: Pan Macmillan, 1982).

14   A decade after the events of July 1981, rioting took place across the UK, in the summers of 1991 and 1992. See: Beatrix Campbell, *Goliath: Britain's Dangerous Places* (London: Methuen, 1993); "Hot Time- Summer on the Estate," Libcom.org, http://libcom.org/library/hot-time-summer-estates-riots-uk-1991-2 (accessed July 15, 2013); "Summer 1992 riots in England-European Counter Network," Libcom.org, http://libcom.org/history/summer-1992-riots-england-european-counter-network (accessed July 15, 2013).

15   W. Smith, Tucker Speed, and June, "Like a Summer with a Thousand Julys…and Other Seasons," Libcom.org, http://libcom.org/library/summer-thousand-julys-other-seasons (accessed July 15, 2013).

16   "An Interview with London Rioters," http://www.youtube.com/watch?v=pbq6GdJXHFc (accessed July 15, 2013). See also "London Riots" interview http://www.youtube.com/watch?v=Zmo8DG1gno4 (accessed July 15, 2013).

17   Ibid.

SOLIDARITY NETWORKS AS A MEANS OF BUILDING RESISTANCE TO AUSTERITY

MATTHEW ADAMS

"It isn't just a bunch of starving people that are going to make a revolution. It's gonna be a people that have been asserting themselves."
—Fred Thompson

INTRODUCTION

WE ARE LIVING IN INTERESTING TIMES. TAKING A LOOK BACK AT THE last few decades, with a particular focus on the English-speaking world, the strike waves and crises of the 1970s gave way to the 1980s market confidence of the yuppies, and the assault on unions by Thatcher and Reagan. In the 1990s, the slow decline of the left continued and prospects for some kind of fundamental change in society seemed to recede into the past. There was no alternative. With the fall of the Soviet Bloc, the end of history was proclaimed. Instead of a battle between rival ways of dominating the world, we saw the expansion of capitalism into new markets and the removal of any obstacles to this growth: neoliberalism.

The late 1990s and early 2000s saw some spectacular resistance to what is now known as globalization, but it was ephemeral, never seeming to produce any lasting opposition. Finally, in 2011, things seemed to start boiling over in different corners of the world: Tunisia, Egypt, Greece, and even Wall Street. The mood has changed.

The long-term reasons for the economic crisis that started in 2007 are up for debate: has capitalism been in agonizingly slow death throes for the past half-century or more? Is this the inevitable result of the tendency of the rate of profit to fall? Whatever the case, most analysts agree its immediate cause is the collapse of the US housing market bubble (see chapters in this book by Glasberg, et al., and Burley), setting off a chain reaction through the absurdly complex and fragile international financial system.[1]

Over the past few years, the capitalist press has repeatedly proclaimed that we are well on the way to recovery, only to see markets slump again. The US does seem to be entering a period of at least temporary recovery (as of the writing of this chapter, in May of 2013), but the same can't be said of much of the rest of the world. It remains to be seen whether the crisis is over or whether the recovery being observed in some countries is only a temporary relief. In any case, the crisis is continuing to severely affect people's lives in many ways—foreclosures and layoffs continue; city, state, and federal budgets are still being cut; in fact, major austerity measures are only beginning to be implemented in parts of the US. In Washington State, for example, despite already having made $6 billion in cuts in 2011, the state government is planning more. The federal government intends to continue several more years of budget-balancing cuts. The effects of the crisis in our daily lives are unemployment for some, more work for less pay for others, foreclosure, homelessness, restricted access to healthcare, bigger class sizes, higher tuition costs, lack of public transport, and so on.

Even in the unlikely case that an extended period of recovery and prosperity is around the corner, capitalism will run up against severe limits within two or three decades—the coming climate and energy crises will result in much worse attacks by the state and the employing class.

So, for those of us who are interested not only in our basic survival but in ending a social system of extreme inequality, drudgery, wasted lives, and planetary destruction, for we who seek to destroy this social order and replace it with a world of freedom, the question is what can we do to build movements to not only defend ourselves from the worst effects of the crisis, but which we can build upon, to increase our collective power and bring about a final break with capitalism?

In an attempt to partially answer that question, this chapter will examine a few of the movements that have sprung up in response to the crisis, in terms of their strengths and weaknesses. I'll talk about the kind of organizing I'm most familiar with: small-scale but effective direct action to win back things like unpaid wages and stolen deposits, as practiced by the Seattle Solidarity Network (SeaSol). I'll look at various examples of organizing against austerity that have SeaSol-like features. Then I'll attempt to analyze what qualities in this kind of organizing are advantageous for antiausterity resistance, how to move from small scale fights to bigger ones, and, beyond that, which features are needed (and which should be avoided or minimized) for successful revolutionary movements to end the boom-bust cycle and generalized misery that capitalism creates once and for all.

MADISON

ONE OF THE first large popular explosions in the US, in reaction to the economic crisis, was in Madison, Wisconsin in February 2011. It occurred in response to the "budget repair bill" being introduced by Republican Governor Scott Walker, whose main purpose was to greatly restrict or remove 280,000 public employees' bargaining rights. In response, crowds of tens and then hundreds of thousands demonstrated and occupied the capitol building for three weeks, before peacefully leaving when ordered to do so by a judge. Predictably, the unions wasted all their energy in a failed electoral strategy to get the governor recalled, and that was that. The movement to resist the bill had been defeated by its own impotent tactics.

Only direct action disrupting the state's economy and functioning could have stood a chance of preventing the passing of the bill. One of the few actions that had any potential in this respect was when large numbers of teachers called in sick—40 percent of teachers in Madison alone—causing classes to be canceled across the whole school district, with many students joining the demonstrations. Threatened with losing their jobs, the teachers were supported by doctors who wrote them sick notes.[2] Any independent initiative by workers in other sectors to move beyond harmless symbolic protest was strongly discouraged by union officialdom's insistence that it had the situation under control, and that the only valid way to oppose the bill was through legal and electoral channels, as expressed by Jesse Jackson's delusional cry, "When we vote, we win!"[3]

Although the local Industrial Workers of the World (IWW) branch agitated energetically for a general strike, a call widely taken up by protesters and endorsed by the South Central Labor Federation (SCLF), this could only manifest with the consent of the SCLF's affiliated unions. It is illegal for public sector workers to strike in Wisconsin, so despite the vast numbers and widespread anger, this was certainly not going to happen without a much more militant and confident union membership, able either to force their will through the bureaucracy or take independent, unauthorized action.

In the opinion of one IWW member present during the events, a general strike was not in the cards for the following reasons: inexperience and fear of illegal tactics; seeing a general strike as something that would just happen; lack of clarity about the relationship to formal union structures; faith in an electoral solution; and inability to involve broader strata of the population, beyond the public sector workers, who were also affected by Walker's agenda. Despite the defeat, there were positive signs: "both the protests and the endorsement of the idea of a general strike are significant developments."[4] The occupations and wildcat strikes were the widest ranging in the US in years, and the occupation of the Capitol building was soon to inspire many more takeovers of public space.[5]

The situation in Wisconsin illustrates universal problems that movements against austerity are likely to face. In most parts of the US, there is much less in the way of working-class organization or militancy. The only organizations big enough to challenge austerity in Wisconsin were the unions, but they are committed only to retaining the ability to represent their members, and will typically not stray from the electoral path. They are adept at deploying vast numbers of staff to make sure things go the way the leadership wants, with little regard for the wishes of the workers to whom the union supposedly belongs.

We find ourselves in a situation where few workers in the US have any experience of, or will for, workplace struggle. The remaining few who possess the skills to organize effectively are often isolated and unable to share their knowledge. We operate in an environment of demobilization, defeat, and demoralization. In previous eras, large numbers of workers enthusiastically took up the fight to build a new world, but as the old Wobbly Fred Thompson said in the 1970s, "Today there is a sense of powerlessness, of fatalism, that has been growing from the '30s. Then, we just felt we didn't have the power, the organization. We never felt we were *inherently* incapable of achieving it."[6] This fatalism, this apathy, could be described as "ideological fatigue"—a justified cynicism given the oversaturation of spectacular and exaggerated claims, the decades of failures and betrayals of every working class movement, the irrelevance of disembodied ideologies to our daily lives. And yet, we seem to have passed through the darkest years of apathy and submission—strikes, occupations, sabotage, uprisings, and resistance of every form worldwide are on the rise.

THE SEATTLE SOLIDARITY NETWORK

FIVE MEMBERS OF the Seattle IWW started SeaSol in 2007. The situation on the activist left that year was one of low activity. Many anarchists had left the city and a large portion of those remaining retreated into inward-focused cooperative housing projects. Eight years had passed since the famous WTO riots—protests which had generated an initial flurry of organizing in the city—for example, campaigns against CitiBank, supporting locked out steelworkers at Kaiser, the development of Indymedia, and more. The early 2000s generated short-lived attempts to form anarchist collectives or federations, initially energetic but increasingly anemic antiwar organizing, and projects associated with food justice or ethical consumption in one way or another. Within the Seattle IWW itself, there had been a burst of organizing efforts in the early 2000s, within ACORN, at a gas station, and at a cooperative market (which was the only permanent organizational victory).[7] Unfortunately, the IWW suffered from problems similar to the broader scene—most of the key organizers of those previous efforts had moved on to other places, or became involved in International Longshore and Warehouse Union (ILWU) officialdom, and were either unable or unwilling to pass on their skills and knowledge to current IWW members. The currently active members had varying degrees of experience in the antiwar and antiglobalization movements, made attempts at union organizing by salting Starbucks, had been employed as union organizers, and had participated in formal anarchist federations (producing newspapers and propaganda).

SeaSol was created in reaction to many of the perceived deficiencies of the anarchist movement and activist left that we had participated in during the "antiglobalization era" of the late 1990s to mid-2000s, deficiencies I shall return to later: excessive preoccupation with symbolic protest against war or capitalism which lacked clearly defined targets, ritualized a-to-b marches, and a preoccupation with personal behavior (diet, ethical consumption, cooperative living), resulting in an inward-looking scene that did not have any motivation to interact with the population at large or ability to communicate with people effectively.

As an attempt to avoid these problems, we discussed more promising movements: the "direct action casework" of the Ontario Coalition Against Poverty[8] and Canadian interunion solidarity "flying squads"[9] seemed to be appealing forms to imitate. Unfortunately, there wasn't a great amount of detail on how those groups operated, so we looked at our own experiences. A friend in Chicago had worked at a restaurant for one day, only to be told it was a "training day" and she wouldn't be paid. She resolved this problem by walking into the restaurant with a large group of friends and refusing to leave until the issue was settled. We were looking to create something with characteristics opposite to the flaws we perceived in the movements we had emerged from: a focus on the immediate issues caused by capitalism in daily life as experienced by the general population of Seattle and ourselves, not as activists (specialists in social change) but as workers in precarious employment or living conditions; a focus on effective strategy rather than moral force; realistic opposition to targets we could actually overcome; and an approach that placed us in direct conflict with the powerful interests in society, rather than one that sought to create an alternative but coexisting culture. SeaSol is itself partially a product of the crisis—without the low pay, unstable jobs, landlords trying to cut corners, and high unemployment, perhaps the group would not have generated the interest and momentum to keep going.

"Propaganda of the Deed without Explosives"

By taking on a project of manageable size, and starting with a few small victories, we hoped to boost our morale and confidence, increase our experience and strength in numbers, and act as a sort of "propaganda of the deed," demonstrating the usefulness of direct action, and that workers and tenants in today's society are not totally powerless. It would also serve to illuminate the true nature of society as one divided between workers and exploiters, tenants and landlords.

This would act as a stepping stone to bigger projects and reinvigorate the flagging Seattle IWW branch.

To launch SeaSol, we created a website, a contact list of a few dozen people, a phone number, and posters that said things along the lines of "Problems with your boss? Problems with your landlord? Contact us!" After putting up several hundred of these posters, calls started coming in. In contrast to the IWW, which had a well-established system of rules and procedures, we took a more ad hoc approach. Our first few contacts were dead ends, the most promising one resulting in a short-lived postering and leafleting campaign at a shipyard, in support of one worker's attempts to galvanize his co-workers to react to management abuses and their union's indifference. A few politically inclined friends joined the group, which started operating independently of the IWW branch meetings.

The first fruitful campaign came a few months into 2008, when we met with dissatisfied tenants of the Greenlake Motel, which, despite its name, was used as long-term housing for people who could not obtain standard rental accommodation, due to bad rent history, bad credit, criminal records, or similar problems. The residents paid well-above average rent to live in small rooms with leaking roofs, malfunctioning washing machines, unreliable electricity, and rat infestations. After some discussion and research, a crowd of thirty or so people descended on one of the landlords' more upmarket hotels one sunny February morning to present to the management a list of repairs to be made to the motel. Unfortunately, all but one of the tenants were too afraid of potential eviction to participate in this demand delivery, but nonetheless it scared the owners enough to get them to make repairs within a few days, despite muttering to tenants, "Don't listen to those communists." During the following five-and-a-half years, SeaSol engaged in thirty-six fights against recalcitrant business and property owners, and won twenty-eight of them outright. In some of the rest, at least partial victories were attained, one case resulting in the permanent closure of the business. Typical fights have included getting unpaid wages, tips, or overtime for a fired worker at a restaurant, or forcing a landlord to return a deposit, make repairs, or cancel an eviction. More unusual fights have involved forcing Chase Bank to return money they shortchanged a SeaSol member, getting a company to pay for an employee's car smashed by a crane at work, and preventing a 50 percent rent increase for a group of a dozen tenants in low income housing.

SeaSol has also occasionally engaged in solidarity and strike support actions, and joint actions with other solidarity networks, or groups such as Casa Latina, an NGO for Latino immigrants that sometimes uses direct action in wage theft cases. The group has several levels of commitment: there are three hundred people on the phone tree, of which 120 are "members" who have said they are interested in participating frequently in actions; another eight hundred or so are subscribed to the action announcement email list; and there are currently twenty-two people on the "organizing team," who have committed to attend meetings, answer phone calls, and mobilize people using the phone tree.

The Life Cycle of a Typical Fight

After receiving a call or email from someone who has seen one of our posters or heard about SeaSol from a friend, a few SeaSol members will meet with them, find out if they have a grievance that falls within SeaSol's broad scope, and explain how the group works—through the direct action of the people affected by the problem themselves. If the new person is amenable to playing a leading role in their own fight and supporting other people's actions, research is conducted into the situation, to assess the landlord or boss's background, properties, customers, funds, social, and political connections—anything that could be used to pressure them if the fight is taken on.

A fight proposal is then brought to the weekly meeting, where it is discussed by the group and assessed in terms of "winnability": can we effectively hurt the target by causing economic or reputational damage, or disrupt the functioning of their business in other ways, such that giving in to our demands will be the rational thing to do? We also consider whether the person with the grievance is likely to remain involved and help others.[10] If we decide we have the means and capacity to take on the fight, the next step is the "demand delivery": a crowd of twenty to fifty SeaSolers will support the person with the grievance, and turn up as a large group to deliver a letter demanding that the issue be resolved within a short time period (usually two weeks). The purpose of the demand delivery is twofold: to show the boss or landlord that the person they have wronged has a large and active group of supporters, and to energize participants in a collective exercise of power against the class enemy, gaining their interest and commitment to the coming campaign. Demand deliveries are often fast-paced and fun trespasses onto the territory of the powerful.

Escalation

There is a chance that the landlord or boss will give in before the deadline expires, but more often they choose to ignore the demand letter. In that case, a campaign of escalating direct action begins. Escalation is one of the key principles of SeaSol. The idea is to start with small, low-cost tactics, such as postering and leafleting, and over a period of weeks increase the intensity and variety of tactics used against the target, perhaps with an increasing frequency of louder and more annoying pickets at more locations, eventually expanding to the company's other shop fronts, and/or the owner's house. Creativity in tactics is highly encouraged. We have found that it is often not the current tactics that the bosses or landlords are facing that cause them to give in, but the fear of what will come next. The appeal of trying to wait out the campaign disappears, as they realize that we are a persistent and increasing threat. Escalation allows us to conserve our forces and use just the right amount of pressure to make them give in.

Other Solidarity Networks

Within a year of SeaSol's creation, our procedure for waging campaigns was more or less fully established, and we started giving trainings (inspired by the IWW's widespread and effective organizer trainings) to members on organizing, research, and tactics. We also publicized our activities online, announcing our victories on various anarchist sites. Some members, myself included, felt that our methods would be a boon to anarchist groups worldwide, many of which were stuck in a rut of activism and propaganda activity, lacking the experience and power to launch effective workplace or community organizing. As well as improving our capacity locally, it was necessary to take a global view and broadcast what we believed was an effective strategy as widely as possible. The training was adapted into a shorter presentation format that outlined the key ideas and, over the next two years, presentations were given in over thirty cities in the US, Canada, England, Scotland, and Spain. More extensive trainings were also given to local groups that requested it, sometimes via Skype to remote locations such as New Zealand and Lithuania, and a "Build your own Solidarity Network" guide was produced and distributed online and eventually in print, in English, Spanish, and Slovakian. Detailed descriptions of an organization's activities and processes can be quite hard to find, and it would be great if other groups started circulating

more extensive accounts of their activities with more of a technical focus on the specifics of mobilization and tactics and so forth, to enable
their worldwide reproduction.

Thanks to local initiatives by anarchist-communists, anarchosyn-
dicalists, IWW branches, and insurrectionary anarchists, at least forty
groups have sprung up across the world—Steel City Solidarity in
Hamilton, Ontario may be the most successful of these, having just
won its seventh fight, for unpaid tips at Seven Windows restaurant.[11]
Unfortunately, a significant fraction of these groups disband within
a year of their creation, and some have only been able to maintain a
low level of activity. In some cases, this is because the organizers are
too busy with multiple projects and are unable to devote the amount
of time needed to keep a solidarity network functioning; in other
cases, organizers leave town, or there is a lack of response to postering
campaigns, or the issues encountered are too difficult to frame as a
simple demand. It is possible that we understated the amount of effort
required to launch a solidarity network, made it seem too easy and too
much of a quick fix. Nonetheless, solidarity networks have become
a popular and successful way to get local organizing off the ground.

OCCUPY ALL THE THINGS

Occupy Wall Street emerged from a call by *Adbusters* to shut down
the financial center in September 2011, to protest the bailout of the
banks, corporate influence on democracy, increasing wealth inequality, or any comparable permutation of buzzwords. There are dozens
of similar international calls to action put out by activist groups every
year; so why did this one become so popular compared to others?
Clearly it resonated with masses of people whose living conditions had
worsened thanks to the economic crisis, whether they had lost their
homes through foreclosure, their jobs through layoffs, or were facing
furloughs or restricted access to social services thanks to recent cuts.
The influence of previous events in 2011 was clear—the idea of occupying public spaces was now familiar to many, thanks to Madison and
the "movements of the squares" (the *Indignados* in Spain, Syntagma
Square in Athens, and the much more extensive revolts in the Arab
world focused around Tahrir Square in Cairo and similar locations).
Indeed, according to David Graeber, "One thing that helped a lot was
a smattering of people from Spain and Greece and Tunisia who had

been doing this sort of thing more recently. They explained that the model that seemed to work was to take something that seemed to be public space, reclaim it, and build up an organization headquarters around that from which you can begin doing other things."[12] Several rounds of mobilization from the unions and NGOs, and the brutal police reaction, combined with reluctantly increasing media coverage, added to the momentum. Soon hundreds of localized versions of Occupy Wall Street sprang up around the US and the world.

Occupy Seattle

Occupy Seattle followed the same trajectory of many other Occupies around the country, though it was more active and radical than most. Its first few days in late September saw a few libertarians and conspiracy theorists handing out leaflets about chemtrails outside the Federal Reserve Building. Something struck a chord, perhaps the increasing coverage of Occupy Wall Street combined with the effects of cuts and crisis, and soon there were nightly gatherings in Westlake Plaza, downtown Seattle's commercial center. The power struggle in the daily general assemblies between the liberal-pacifist wing and the radicals (a temporary anarchist-socialist alliance) resulted in a consistent series of victories for the radicals—the Mayor's attempt to neutralize the movement by hosting it in City Hall was defeated, and a "night of 500 tents" to start the permanent occupation of Westlake was launched. The police soon forced the campers out of the downtown square, displacing them to the Seattle Central Community College campus. It was notable how many liberals became radicalized after experiencing a police beating. Enthusiastic general assemblies continued, as did the interminable debate about violence and nonviolence. As the weather worsened, the uneasy coexistence of downwardly mobile urban professionals, homeless youth, the long-term unemployed, and students degenerated.[13] Hard drug dealing led to small-scale, nightly, internal violence. By mid-December, the encampment at Seattle Central was no more, and without this central focus, Occupy Seattle scattered into separate projects. A little over a year after the dissolution of the camp, only a few of these projects survive—the problem of ephemerality familiar from the antiglobalization years.

But before it disappeared, Occupy Seattle gave birth to the greatest confrontations in the city since the WTO: the day of action on November 4, in solidarity with the Oakland general strike, where, after a pepper spray-filled day of demonstrations against banks, angry crowds surrounded the hotel where Chase Bank CEO Jamie Dimon was speaking; the West Coast Port Shutdown action on December 5, intended to show solidarity with longshoremen and port truckers (again marred by union legalism and control of turf); and a series of occupations of vacant buildings, one of which lasted for three months.

One of the few material gains of Occupy was accidental—banks backed down on a wide range of fees they wanted to introduce, but that isn't where the importance of Occupy lies.[14] It created space outside the normal political system in which a surprisingly wide range of people could interact. For all its faults and limitations, it was a significant break from the norm of US politics, displaying an unusual degree of mass involvement, and a challenge to the legitimacy of power of the "1%" and of capitalism in general.

SeaSol and Occupy

Despite being one of the most active social struggle groups in the area, SeaSol's efforts to intervene and engage with Occupy Seattle were fairly lacking. SeaSol is very focused on its organizing activity and some SeaSolers were skeptical, since Occupy seemed to display all the loathed activist features. Beyond the participation of individual members and a drive to mobilize for the December port action, we hosted a "Direct Action Workshop/Discussion," whose purpose was to clarify the meaning, and encourage the use, of direct action—returning the phrase to its original anarchist definition of unmediated action by the people affected by a problem, in contrast to the confused, modern interpretation that it means some kind of militant, aggressive stuntism. Discussion ensued about potential ways Occupy Seattle could use direct action. We intended this to be the first of a series of workshops, and began work on a proposal for Occupy to start a direct action campaign around foreclosures. Unfortunately, we did not follow through with this plan, due to demoralization and worsening conditions at the Occupy encampment.

Several months after Occupy, some SeaSol members started an antiforeclosure group in Seattle. Stand Against Foreclosure and Eviction (SAFE) is closely based on the City Life/Vida Urbana NGO in Boston.[15] It follows a different model than the decentralized, direct-action-based groups that are the subject of this article, being more amenable to paid staff and negotiations with banks, but SeaSol is supporting its actions and it will be interesting to see how it develops.

EAST BAY SOLIDARITY AND A
FORECLOSURE-FREE OAKLAND

The East Bay Solidarity Network started in mid-2011 and engaged in several SeaSol-like fights before changing gears. Many of the East Bay Sol organizers were heavily involved in Occupy Oakland and noticed that the home occupations they participated in during Occupy were supported by lots of people and generated media interest. The time seemed ripe for a direct action campaign against foreclosures:

> We thought that the time would be now to start defending peoples' houses because we could get people to come out and support, the media was eating it up, and the narrative that big banks were screwing people out of their homes was widely accepted. As Occupy Oakland faded away, we saw that we could channel some of that energy into this campaign.[16]

East Bay Sol started brainstorming on how to build an effective campaign. Their research revealed that Oakland was one of hardest hit cities in California: over 1000 foreclosures in a city of 400,000 people. According to East Bay Sol, "In a city that was majority people of color and low income folks, this didn't come as much of a surprise."[17] The potential profit to be made from ongoing gentrification meant that banks were facing pressure from real estate developers to go through with foreclosures. Just Cause and Alliance of Californians for Community Empowerment (ACCE), the two nonprofits fighting foreclosures before Occupy started, could each only take on one to five foreclosures a year.

The plan was to form a coalition of four groups (Just Cause, ACCE, East Bay Sol, and Occupy Oakland Foreclosure Defense), focus on the areas most heavily hit by foreclosures, and build neighborhood assemblies intended to encourage neighbor-to-neighbor mutual support for antieviction defense, shifting the emphasis away from the four groups arranging pickets on behalf of foreclosed families to a more self-organized model, one that had the potential to build longer term, sustained activity.

A campaign of extensive door knocking in the Maxwell Park neighborhood was carried out by the coalition during the summer of 2012, but according to East Bay Sol, "After a few months of really trying, we realized that we all had *very* different ways of actually doing this work and how we developed and helped new people become organizers."[18] There was a tension among the groups in the coalition, between support for the typical NGO, staff-driven, service- oriented model and East Bay Sol's nonhierarchical model that emphasized developing local organizers.

The coalition dispersed and East Bay Sol members decided to focus on their own neighborhood in West Oakland instead and fight against all evictions, renters as well as homeowners. This new project, called FEFO (Foreclosure and Eviction Free Oakland), is currently in its initial phase, with flyering, door knocking, and one big community meeting having happened as of the penning of this chapter. It is still taking on normal SeaSol-style "micro-fights" as well.

ANTI-WORKFARE IN THE UK

In 2011, the British government introduced workfare—forcing people to work without pay, in order to receive meager unemployment or disability benefits—its stated purpose being something along the lines of "helping the long term unemployed back to work." The imposition of workfare is another effect of crisis and austerity. Politicians benefit by being seen to be doing something about high levels of unemployment; welfare can be cut; businesses benefit from unpaid labor; and if the workfare scheme is successful in the long run, they also benefit from the downward pressure on wages and working conditions[19].

The Solidarity Federation (SolFed) sees workfare "as part of a long term re-structuring of the labour market towards more temporary, lower paid jobs and with poorer conditions and fewer benefits."[20]

SolFed is the UK section of the anarcho-syndicalist international, the IWA (International Workers Association). It shares SeaSol's commitment to direct action and opposition to bureaucracy, while having more explicit political aims and industrial strategy and not being limited to just one city. SolFed locals have used direct action tactics partially inspired by Sea-Sol[21]—first, to get unpaid wages for a member who was employed by the temp agency Office Angels, using their international links to target Office Angels's parent company in several countries,[22] moving on to tackle other cases of wage theft, and also targeting landlords. They then applied a similar strategy in their campaign against workfare.

While the idea for the campaign came from SolFed members on workfare schemes, reaching out to other claimants via leafleting efforts outside Job Centres has proven difficult. According to SolFed, "Claimants are generally kept isolated from each other and approach the benefits systems as individuals which makes bringing them together quite difficult."[23]

The principal form of action has been noisy pickets outside the companies using workfare, turning away their customers, and damaging their reputation. As with SeaSol, the idea is to hit companies in the pocket, making their continued participation in workfare unprofitable. By focusing primarily on one company at a time, until they pull out, the intent is to trigger a domino effect, resulting in the eventual collapse of the workfare system.[24] One idea proposed within SolFed was to run wage-theft campaigns, to get current or former workfare employees the money they should have been paid, building on those initial victories to gain momentum and power in a similar vein to SeaSol's strategy.

Aside from standing outside shops, communications blockades and social media campaigns have proved quite effective, tactics that SeaSol should consider imitating. On May Day 2012, SolFed organized a "quite large roving picket of companies using workfare which had around 150–200 people participating and was supported by Occupy London."[25]

The withdrawal from workfare of the health food chain Holland and Barrett can be directly attributed to SolFed's pickets. SolFed and Boycott Workfare, a more activism-oriented network, together with various anarchist and activist groups, have targeted Poundland, Argos, HMV, Haringey County Council, Superdrug, Tesco, Oxfam, Homebase, and multiple other companies and charities. Their actions, combined with negative public opinion, unfavorable media, legal, and logistical issues have resulted in the withdrawal of an increasing number of companies.[26] The campaign against workfare continues to operate successfully. Hopefully, workfare will only last a few more months before being scrapped by the government as unviable.

USEFUL CHARACTERISTICS OF MOVEMENTS: DEFICIENCIES AND PROBLEMS

IN THIS SECTION, I'd like to summarize what I believe to be the most advantageous features of the various projects I've described, contrasting them with their opposites. This may come across as an over-simplification—in reality, I realize that all movements contain contradictory aspects; the movements I've looked at have many weaknesses, and these characteristics overlap and can't really be separated so neatly. For example, sometimes symbolic action *is* useful—in inspiring people, raising awareness, and acting as a focal image for a movement—but it's of secondary importance and should not be prioritized as it has been until now.

Direct Action vs. Symbolic Protest

In my personal experience, there was no better illustration of the weakness of symbolic protest than the 2003 march in London against the Iraq war. Millions marched, saying "Not In Our Name," and the government did not change a thing about its foreign policy. At times, one of the greatest weaknesses of Occupy was its dependence on and orientation towards the mass media. The default assumption is that we can persuade the powerful to see the error of their ways through protest or argument. Power does not care when people speak truth to it. This is rooted in a moral, "magical thinking" conception of the world, where being in the right will automatically lead to righteous outcomes. In the place of "speaking truth to power," we propose directly interfering with the ability of businesses and governments to function or make profits.

Collective Action vs. Personal Behavior

A capitalist society individualizes social problems and prevents collective solutions. It's automatic to assume the solutions to problems in your life are individual. Everyone is out for themselves, it seems. Hence the interest in personal solutions: changes in diet and lifestyle. The individual way out of problems caused by crisis and austerity is to spend less and work more. SeaSol and related movements illuminate another way out: collective conflict against the common enemy.

Alienated Activism vs. Struggle Based in Daily Life

Many of the problems of modern day movements are characterized in the article "Give Up Activism," written shortly after the "Carnival Against Capitalism" (also known as J18) in 1999.[27] Since then, the term "activism" has sometimes been used to critique these tendencies, which can become confusing, as it has broader uses. When I've referred to "activists" in this chapter, I do not necessarily mean they display all the negative features of activism. "Activism" as obstacle to authentic mass participation has been conveniently summarized as:

1. Activist identity (identifying primarily as belonging to an "activist community," " to think of yourself as being somehow privileged or more advanced than others").

2. The subsequent substitution of an activist group for wider struggle, "a division of labour implies that one person takes on a role on behalf of many others who relinquish this responsibility."

3. An opposition to abstract nouns, "the bizarre spectacle of 'doing an action' against capitalism—an utterly inadequate practice."

4. Ritualistic activity which serves only to reinforce the activist martyr identity, "dull and sterile routine—a constant repetition of a few actions with no potential for change."

5. A focus on saving others, struggling on behalf of some oppressed group (animals, Palestinians, or indeed, "the workers"…) as opposed to for ourselves: "revolutionary martyrdom goes together with the identification of some cause separate from one's own life." [28,]

In contrast, SeaSol, East Bay Sol, and SolFed's activities are "for ourselves"—they are based on our own experiences as workers, tenants, and benefit claimants. If I don't get paid at work, I know I can rely on SeaSol to back me up. Beyond this, revolutionary ideas suddenly become much less abstract in the context of collective, practical struggle: "instead of making the case for self-organisation, direct action, solidarity in the abstract, you can just ask people to come along to a picket."[29] It's difficult to make a complete break with activism though, and solidarity networks still retain some features of it.[30]

Mass Participation vs.
Professionalized Social Management

Far more serious than the problem of activism is the related tendency for movements to bureaucratize, and for a layer of experts to become the permanent leadership of a movement, disempowering their followers, and inevitably warping the movement away from its original purposes for their own benefit, intentionally or not. This is one of the key reasons anarchism broke from socialism—it recognized the universal tendency for power to corrupt, for any movement to fall back into the hierarchical and commodified modes of behavior of the society it springs from. In a world based on wage labor, everything decays toward "service" or work. This is alienation again; the tendency towards separation of all activities into distinct realms, moving from self-interested direct action toward doing things on behalf of abstract, distant causes. Representation dominates self-management.

For the sake of "efficiency," paid organizers are brought in and the organization starts to resemble a business, accruing nonprofits, integrating into the system, becoming dependent on grants and relationships with politicians and sponsors, diverting energy into useless dead ends like elections and harmless protests. This tendency is very established, omnipresent even. NGOs and union bureaucracies were some of the principal barriers in Madison and major obstacles for self-organized movements against austerity to overcome.

This is why solidarity networks emulate anarcho-syndicalist groups, in minimizing bureaucracy and spreading decision-making, participation, initiative, skills, and knowledge as widely as possible throughout the group. This entails direct democracy in meetings, rotating positions, and frequent training and education. While anarcho-syndicalist unions show an important workplace organizing practice, SolNets could very well be considered a form of community anarcho-syndicalist organizing—or a form of *community syndicalism.*

Adaptation to Contemporary Conditions

"Permanent work has been abolished. Part time and flexible work, long periods of unemployment following short periods of work are now the rule."[31] This quote refers to the situation in post-austerity Greece, but precarious and flexible employment has been a reality in the US and UK for some time, particularly for youth. If crisis and austerity continue, the situation will only worsen.

Solidarity Networks emerged due to the difficulties of organizing inside a workplace. While the intent is certainly not to remain an external force, organizing only with those who have already left their employment or living situation, it is an easier point to start from. One former SeaSol organizer put it in terms of "organizing the worker, not the job." It might also be termed "diffuse organizing"—anyone who has been through a SeaSol fight will be much more likely to initiate collective direct action in future situations in their life, opening up multiple opportunities for inside organizing within a city where Solidarity Network type activity is widespread.

Winnability and Escalation

Lacking a shared pool of experience from which to draw and used to what some might term a "Leftist culture of failure," many activists are content to rush into campaigns without attempting to assess whether it will be possible to achieve their goals or what those goals even are, resulting in a repeating cycle of defeat and demoralization.

One of SeaSol's key features is its focus on realistic goals. Over the past few years, we have developed a reliable system to win limited campaigns against bosses and landlords, by framing things in terms of "winnability" and escalating tactics. From a strategic point of view, this means engaging in "small winnable fights, snowballing into a wider movement," as one SolFed member put it.

This of course has its disadvantages—with too much of a focus on winning in the short term, and procedures that become so established they are unquestioned, you can end up with an overly quantitative way of looking at things and an unwillingness to take risks, missing opportunities to expand and try out new ways of doing things.

The danger of turning a temporary tactic into an eternal principle is a risk for SeaSol. We could get bogged down in doing the same thing over and over again. Despite several attempts, and despite IWW and other union organizing experience, we have not developed a workable strategy for moving towards organizing entire workplaces or apartment buildings. To remedy this, we hosted a series of "strategy sessions" to think about future direction, and various members have launched C-TWO, the Committee for Tenant and Worker Outreach, to move further in the direction of larger-scale, more collectivized fights. The initial step for C-TWO is extensive door knocking to gather data about major problems people face at home or at work, and which jobs and apartments are ripe for organizing.

Reproducibility and Longevity

A well-established training program counters the problem of key organizers disappearing, which has plagued many movements in the past. Together with a constant source of landlords and bosses to take on, SeaSol has survived for five-and-a-half years and is showing no signs of disappearing. Intermittent participation in SeaSol has been one of the ways in which activists scattered by Occupy's disintegration have maintained contact. Longer lasting groups act as anchors during periods of low activity, so establishing them is important in the long term.

Some organizations seem to put the cart before the horse, in terms of heavy organizational structure without any substantial activity to justify it. With much structure, merely maintaining the organization uses up all the energy of a small group. Solidarity networks are organizationally lightweight, having only the structures that are needed to keep their activity going, adding or discarding elements as needed. A phone number, a meeting space, money for posters, and a contact list are the bare minimum to get a solidarity network going.

Danger of Providing Social Services Instead of the State

As cuts increase, social movements may relieve the pressure on the state by doing its job for it. This is something SeaSol avoids, thanks to its requirements of participation and reciprocity. It's a greater problem in service-providing groups where the aid is more one-directional, such as (free food distribution group) Food Not Bombs.

TOWARDS A CRITICAL MASS OF CRISIS RESISTANCE

To HAVE ANY hope of building viable mass movements for resisting austerity and the effects of crisis, we need to start by taking on problems of manageable size given our current weakness. Starting from almost nothing, the small-victories approach of solidarity networks creates the social power needed to move on to the somewhat more ambitious projects of workfare and foreclosure resistance illustrated by SolFed and East Bay Sol's projects. Progress in larger scale organizing will be slow and fraught with obstacles, but over the years, as we build our numbers and expertise, the pace will quicken.

We should be taking an experimental, iterative approach, analyzing the weaknesses and opportunities in the social structure, finding out what works through experiment and participation, modifying our strategy based on our observations, then repeating the process.

Action, reflection, adjustment, expansion. Trying new approaches reveals new possibilities and limitations in a way that an impartial, detached observer of social processes cannot. New theory emerges from practice, new possibilities spring from the increased awareness of our collective power.

With a victory, or series of victories, achieved by members of a certain community—a particular social network of immigrants, or restaurant workers— confidence spreads and the possibilities open up for more extensive struggle in that area.

By increasing the concentration of people experienced in taking direct action within a given locale, the rate and extent of acts of resistance, building links of solidarity between different sectors and communities, and thus breaking out of the isolation and atomization of modern day life, we move towards a critical mass—a point at which acts of resistance reinforce each other, a qualitative change in the class struggle leading to a chain reaction of ever-increasing size, moderated only by repression, co-optation, or drastic changes in the economy.

Supplemented by a "culture of resistance" of shared experiences, and a vision of that future, which is a logical extension of collective power and mutual aid—a future without bosses, landlords or politicians—that emerges from this increased activity, future eruptions like those of Madison and Occupy will be vastly more powerful, less hampered by inexperience, and able to defend themselves from co-optation. Not only will they have the power to defeat austerity measures, but they will be on their way to making a total break with this corrupt, unequal, utterly limiting society.

ENDNOTES

1   "Return of the crisis: Part 1," *Aufheben* #18 (2010), http://libcom.org/library/return-crisis-part-1 (accessed July 8, 2013).

2   John Jacobsen, "Wisconsin—Next Stop, the General Strike!," 2011, http://seattlefreepress.org/2011/02/28/new-article-on-situation-in-wisconsin/ (accessed July 8, 2013).

3   Walter Winslow, "The Seattle Solidarity Network: a new kind of working class social movement" (2011), http://libcom.org/files/the-seattle-solidarity-network.pdf (accessed July 8, 2013).

4   Juan Conatz, "Wisconsin: Why a general strike hasn't happened yet" (2011), http://libcom.org/blog/some-limitations-movement-wisconsin-04042011 (accessed July 8, 2013).

5   John Jacobsen, "Recall in Wisconsin—the Alternative Was Worse" (2012), http://seattlefreepress.org/2012/06/11/recall-in-wisconsin-the-alternative-was-worse/ (accessed July 8, 2013).

6   "Wobbly Fred Thompson on the 30s depression," http://libcom.org/history/wobbly-fred-thompson-30s-depression-studs-terkel (accessed July 8, 2013).

7   ACORN is the Association of Community Organizations for Reform Now, a famous and very top-down NGO. Rather than accept unionized employees, the Seattle branch of ACORN shut down.

8   OCAP, "Direct Action Casework Manual," http://ocap.ca/node/322 (accessed July 8, 2013).

9   Jeff Shantz, "Developing Workers Autonomy: An Anarchist Look At Flying Squads" (2006), http://www.iww.org/en/node/2246 (accessed July 8, 2013).

10   Winslow, "The Seattle Solidarity Network."

11   Steel City Sol facebook page, https://www.facebook.com/pages/Steel-City-Solidarity/505161452856830 (accessed July 8, 2013).

12   Interview with David Graeber, *Washington Post*, October 3 2011.

13   Black Orchid Collective, "Occupy, to end Capitalism!" (2011), http://blackorchidcollective.wordpress.com/2011/10/16/occupy-to-end-capitalism/ (accessed July 8, 2013).

14   John Jacobsen, "Occupy Wall Street's Next Steps—Part 1" (2011), http://anarchism.pageabode.com/john-jacobsen/occupy-wall-street-s-next-steps-part-1 (accessed July 8, 2013).

15   SAFE website: http://safeinseattle.org/ (accessed July 8, 2013).

16   East Bay Sol member "R," quoted from personal correspondence.

17   Ibid.

18   Ibid.

19   *Abolish Workfare*, Solidarity Federation pamphlet.

20   Ibid.

21 SolFed, "Denied deposits? Refused repairs? Harassed by your land-lord?" http://www.solfed.org.uk/south-london/denied-deposits-re-fused-repairs-harassed-by-your-landlord (accessed July 8, 2013).

22 SolFed, "SF-IWA calls for national week of action against Office Angels" (2012) http://www.solfed.org.uk/solfed/sf-iwa-calls-for-national-week-of-action-against-office-angels-9-15-may (accessed July 8, 2013).

23 SolFed member "JP," quoted from personal correspondence.

24 SolFed, "A domino falls" (2012), http://www.solfed.org.uk/brighton/a-domino-falls-holland-barrett-quit-workfare-after-direct-action (accessed July 8, 2013).

25 SolFed member "JP," quoted from personal correspondence.

26 Shiv Malik, "Graduate's Poundland victory leaves government work schemes in tatters," *The Guardian*, 12 February, 2013, http://www.guardian.co.uk/society/2013/feb/12/graduate-poundland-government-work-schemes (accessed July 8, 2013).

27 Andrew X, "Give Up Activism" (1999), http://libcom.org/library/give-up-activism (accessed July 8, 2013).

28 Comments on article "Give Up Classtivism" at http://libcom.org/library/give-classtivism-why-class-struggle-long-boring-hard-work (accessed July 8, 2013); "Do something! A critique of activism," http://libcom.org/blog/do-something-critique-activism-28052012 (accessed July 8, 2013).

29 "no1" in forum discussion at http://libcom.org/forums/theory/what-do-anarchistlibertarian-communist-movements-need-order-grow-03072010 (accessed July 8, 2013).

30 Some of the tensions in opposition to activism are summed up pretty well by Kellstadt, http://libcom.org/library/anti-activism (accessed July 8, 2013).

31 Costas Douzinas, "Europe's south rises up against those who act as sadistic colonial masters," *The Guardian,* 28 March, 2013, http://www.guardian.co.uk/commentisfree/2013/mar/28/europe-south-rising-up (accessed July 8, 2013).

PART 4

THE RULING CLASS RESPONSE

"When the prison, stake or scaffold can no longer silence the voice of the protesting minority, progress moves on a step, but not until then."
—Lucy Parsons

MILITANT REFORMISM AND THE PROSPECTS FOR REFORMING CAPITALISM

NATE HAWTHORNE

ANYONE WHO HAS SPENT MUCH TIME AROUND THE RADICAL LEFT WILL know that there is an important historical law: the tendency of the rate of prophet to rise. The radical left has predicted at least nine out of the last four economic crises, and predicted a wide range of outcomes for the crises that actually happened: "Communism will descend from heaven and land on earth!" "The earth will open up and fascism will pour out!" And so forth. Each time the economy bottoms out, there are people who invoke bearded old demigods and intone magic words, *"hocus crisis! abra-ca-dialectic!"* in order to predict that this time—finally, at long last—capitalism is just so completely fucked that the system simply cannot recover, and thus, now, at long last, we're in a new kind of historical moment, a special emergency situation unlike other moments, which requires one last final push.[1]

Having just mocked predictions about the future of capitalism, in what follows, I'm going to make some predictions of my own. (You see, I have a particularly clear crystal ball...*accio hypocrisy!*). I think that currently capitalism probably does have the capacity to recover and to grant concessions that demobilize or prevent serious challenges to the system. My main point here, though, is about reformism. By reformism, in this chapter, I mean a social vision that limits itself only to achieving a better capitalism. And by "reforms,"

I mean deep alterations to capitalism-as-it-exists on a structural level that could rescue it from (the current) crisis and instability. I think, for the foreseeable future, reformism will very likely be the center of gravity among diverse social movements acting in response to capitalism. More importantly, I think we may see the emergence of reformist politics tied to militant tactics: fight like hell for a better capitalism.

If I'm right, this militant reformism will pose some questions for radicals. How should radicals intervene in reform-oriented movements? What's at stake in the ways we might choose to engage with reformism in our organizing? How do repression, austerity, and reform shape our movements, and how can we shape the possibilities for each? I should add that I'm aware that there's a long history of answers to these and similar questions. Other people have confronted crises in the past. Other radicals have responded to reformism in a variety of ways. This chapter is not a history of those moments or of radical responses to reform efforts, though such histories would probably be sources of important insights for us today. What this chapter is instead is a sketch or a hypothesis of militant reformism as it may be emerging in the present, and what that may mean for those of us from a communist persuasion.[2]

I, like most of my closest political friends and comrades, am young enough to have lived most or all of my life in periods of relative working-class defeat and retreat—periods of low levels and intensities of struggle. We have more experience with workplace struggles that are very small to moderate in size relative to the size of the working class as a whole. Truly massive struggles are much larger than anything that many of us have experienced. In the current period, we may see struggles of that size. If that happens, a lot of it will be, at least initially, reformist in character. We will see a rise in demands for reform—we're going to see more reformism. We already are seeing this. Whether or not reform is possible will shape how we respond to reformists.

The idea that reform is impossible is appealing.[3] If reform is impossible, then the capitalist system has fewer options for responding to massive working-class movements. We don't have to argue in favor of communism over a reformed capitalism, and we're closer to a communist society. Reformist forces can never really win out. If reformists gain (or keep) dominant positions in social movements and in ideas, the worst they can do is temporarily distract the working class away from revolutionary tasks, but they can't actually win reforms. And we, the communists, will still be here when the reforms don't actually materialize.

Unfortunately, we don't actually know that reform is impossible. To be fair, we also don't know if they're possible. Only the actual creation of reforms would demonstrate their possibility in a conclusive way. I think we can say, though, that reform is plausible. I think this is important because if reforms do happen, and radicals have been operating under the assumption that reforms are impossible, we will be unprepared.

PART ONE: THE STATE

UNDERSTANDING REFORM REQUIRES talking about the state. Capitalists tend to have a good sense of their interests as employers. These terms aren't ideal but employer-consciousness arises organically from the social relationship of employment under capitalism. Capitalist employers have a sense that their employees produce surplus value and they act accordingly. If they don't, they face threats from the rest of the economy—a capitalist who pays higher wages than other capitalists who sell similar goods and services will, all things being equal, fall behind. If they don't become more competitive, they will go out of business. If capitalist employers don't get enough surplus value from employees, they face penalties. These penalties help make employers relatively aware of their position as employers.

Awareness of the dynamics of being an employer is not the same thing as being a class-conscious capitalist, however. Every capitalist is a capitalist in relation to his or her employees, but not every capitalist acts in ways that are favorable to the capitalist class as a whole or the long-term life of the capitalist system (particularly because capitalists are usually competing with one another). As an analogy, anyone who works for a living is in some way aware of the power relationships involved in being an employee but not all employees are class-conscious workers. Workers sometimes act in ways that are bad for other workers or the working class as a whole. Similar things can happen with capitalists. Being a worker doesn't automatically provide working-class consciousness. Likewise, being a capitalist doesn't automatically make someone a class-conscious capitalist.

One of the roles of the state is to help identify needs of the current capitalist system and its long-term health, and to try to get capitalists to act in line with those perceived systemic needs. This can serve to create capitalist-class consciousness, or at least to discipline capitalists to act in ways that planners believe are good for capitalism. In some cases, this can result in long-term benefits to existing capitalists, but in other cases it involves some businesses being put out of business and, eventually, some of them or their descendants being ejected out of the capitalist class. This is part of why capitalists hesitate in the face of changes introduced by the state—no capitalist wants to lose. If they do so often enough, they or their children might have to actually work for a living. In the words of the historian of slavery, Eugene Genovese, in his book *Roll, Jordan, Roll,* "The great object of social reform is to prevent a fundamental change in class relations." This means that reformers "must fight against those reactionaries who cannot understand the need for secondary, although not necessarily trivial, change in order to prevent deeper change (…) reactionaries will insist that any change, no matter how slight, will set in motion forces of dissolution."[4]

Sometimes capitalists oppose reform because they are ideologically reactionary; sometimes they do so because they believe that they will find themselves at a competitive disadvantage in the new version of capitalism that will exist after the reform.

The state is in part a mechanism for helping identify problems that are systemic—tied to the interests of the capitalist class as a whole— and for working out how to politically respond to the capitalists' class interests. That is, visionary capitalists and their functionaries in foundations and think tanks can use the state to put forward proposals and communicate them to others to try to win them to this view. If that fails, with enough political support from other capitalists (and some workers, in many cases), particular parts of the capitalist class can get the state to do certain things, to discipline individual capitalists who aren't acting in line with what is believed to be the capitalist class' overall interests.

Individual capitalists, or fractions of the capitalist class, don't necessarily pursue the interests of the capitalist class as a whole. Often there is disagreement among the fractions of the capitalist class about which course of action is best. That a given fraction is dominant does not mean it necessarily does what is best for the capitalist class, but usually the dominant fractions, and those who the state acts in service of, believe they are doing what's best for capitalism over all. The dominant fraction can be wrong, though. One example of this is health insurance in the US. The only measure according to which "our" healthcare/health insurance (non-) system makes sense is that of the profits of insurers. The current nonsystem poses public health risks (which can become political and economic problems)—for many people, it results in less preventive care, which is cheaper to provide than other forms of healthcare. So, it causes worse health outcomes, which cause loss of economic productivity and more expensive healthcare. This arrangement also raises the costs of the same procedure in the US. By maintaining a very minimal floor—you can always get treatment in a hospital emergency room if you have an immediate healthcare problem—the system channels a very large amount of public dollars into healthcare, in addition to excessively high private healthcare and health insurance costs. Even according capitalist logic, these expenditures are, however, inefficient from an overall social perspective because high expenditures purchase lower quality healthcare. This is not good for anyone except the insurers. Some of the costs are passed on to employers, as well as causing conflicts with employees that could be avoided. This is a form of highly mediated, intercapitalist conflict about who gets what share of the total surplus wealth extracted from workers (some companies have to pay what would otherwise be profits). That this arrangement continues demonstrates that changes in these arrangements are not natural, predetermined, or built in to capitalism—they're political. Those politics include the class struggle above all, but also political conflict among the capitalists.

Sometimes an individual capitalist, or group of capitalists, pursue things that are believed by the dominant capitalists to be detrimental to the capitalist class as a whole, and so they need to be brought in line. To quote Genovese again,

> The most advanced fraction of the slaveholders—those who most clearly perceived the interests and needs of the class as a whole—steadily worked to make their class more conscious of its nature, spirit, and destiny. (...) For any such political center, the class as a whole must be brought to a higher understanding of itself—transformed from a class-in-itself, reacting to pressures on its objective position, into a class-for-itself, consciously striving to shape the world in its own image.

> Only possession of public power can discipline a class
> as a whole, and through it, the other classes of society.
> The juridical system may become, then, not merely an
> expression of class interest, nor even merely an expres-
> sion of the willingness of the rulers to mediate with the
> ruled; it may become an instrument by which the ad-
> vanced section of the ruling class imposes its viewpoint
> upon the class as a whole and the wider society. The
> law must discipline the ruling class.[5]

Genovese is overly statist when he writes that "possession of public power" is a requirement, but he is right in saying that state power plays this role in capitalism, helping the capitalist class guide and discipline itself. He continues:

> The slaveholders fell back on a kind of dual power: that
> which they collectively exercised as a class, even against
> their own individual impulses, through their effective
> control of state power; and that which they reserved to
> themselves as individuals who commanded other hu-
> man beings in bondage. In general, this duality appears
> in all systems of class rule, for the collective judgment
> of the ruling class, coherently organized in the com-
> mon interest, cannot be expected to coincide with the
> sum total of the individual interests and judgments of
> its members; first because the law tends to reflect the
> will of the most politically coherent and determined
> fraction, and second, because the sum total of the in-
> dividual interests and judgments of the members of
> the ruling class generally, rather than occasionally, pulls
> against the collective needs of a class that must appeal
> to other classes for support at critical junctures.[6]

None of this is to say that these sorts of struggles always reinforce capitalism. My point is that there is a connection between the struggle over immediate conditions and the struggle to end capitalism, but not all victories in particular struggles over the terms of life and work under capitalism bring us closer to the end of capitalism. Indeed, in certain historical circumstances, capitalists and their states or parts of their states will work to improve the lives of workers in order to make sure capitalism remains intact. Workers' struggles can sometimes temporarily serve as a tool that some capitalists use to get an advantage over others and can sometimes be a source of innovation within capitalist institutions, strengthening the system and boosting profits. Struggles and efforts can play this role even when strongly opposed by actually existing capitalists because capitalists, like workers, don't always believe in or act in accord with the interests of their class as a whole. That capitalists fight or fought hard in opposing a reform can sometimes make it seem like a given struggle or victory is more radical than it is.

PART TWO: HISTORICAL BACKGROUND

THE CHANGES THAT happened in the US in the 1930s, in response to the economic crisis, had two basic sources, which related to each other in mutually reinforcing ways: a changed view on the part of the state regarding working-class organization *and* working-class militancy. Nelson Lichtenstein has written that the labor law reforms of the 1930s involved the extension into workplaces of rights that were "thoroughly bourgeois" and yet "their achievement required something close to revolutionary action, or so it seemed during the summer and fall of 1934."[7] While there were important policy changes, as Lichtenstein writes, "a law is not a social movement." For the new policies to have "real social and political meaning, the United States required a working-class mobilization of explosive power."[8]

The government reforms and working class militancy of the 1930s changed the institutions that create the costs and benefits of unionization. And radicals played a crucial role in that. To quote Lichtenstein again, "Because of their exceptional ability as mass organizers, [Congress of Industrial Organizations (CIO) leader John L.] Lewis hired scores of communists and socialists (…) When a reporter probed his decision to hire so many Communists, Lewis replied, 'Who gets the bird, the hunter or the dog?'" That is to say, Lewis expected to make use of radicals to build the CIO, and expected to stay in control of the process and the results. Lichtenstein continues, "Such radicals were and are essential to the organization of a trade union movement, in the United States even more so than in other countries with an established socialist tradition. Indeed, if it were left to those whose aspirations were shaped merely by the trade union idea, most labor drives would have died at birth. This is because the founding of a trade union is a personally risky business whose costs and dangers are disproportionately born by those who take the early initiative." Workers who took on early militant action

> gambled with their jobs, and sometimes their lives. Most workers therefore remained passive, not because they endorsed the industrial status quo, but because defeat might well threaten what little security they had managed to achieve. (...) Only those individuals with an intense political or religious vision, only those radicals who saw the organizing project as part of a collective enterprise, and only those who understood the unions as a lever with which to build a new society could hope to calculate that the hardships they endured might reap such a magnificent political and social reward.[9]

That is to say, commitment to a vision beyond a short-term cost/benefit calculation helped create the militant minority of the working class that was one ingredient key to the restructuring of the 1930s. The other significant ingredient was the new disposition toward reform on the part of state planners. Working-class militancy played a key role in creating that new disposition as well. Rhonda Levine writes that the militant "extra-parliamentary struggles of the industrial working class forced Democratic congressmen and senators to take a more liberal position within congressional debates, thereby moving the Democratic party to the left on the political spectrum."[10] Levine also argues that the Democrats only backed the new labor relations legislation at first, in an attempt to offer a legislative alternative to American Federation of Labor-supported legislation calling for limits on work hours. The Roosevelt administration and Congress initially did not support the proposals that Senator Robert Wagner put out for dealing with industrial relations but the strike wave of 1934 brought politicians around.[11]

The combination of working class militancy and reform-minded politicians helped create the conditions where US unions gained five million members between 1933 and 1937. Lichtenstein makes the point that the US labor movement has tended to grow in bursts like this. Big upheavals happen—initially involving militant minorities of the working class and then larger numbers—and union membership grows. Between upheavals, membership tends to level out and begin to decline.

Since Ronald Reagan's attack on the air traffic controllers' union over thirty years ago, employers have been on the offensive against unions and the US government has done very little about this, in some cases aiding it. This is different from an earlier era. In the 1930s, the US capitalist state made collective bargaining a key part of economic policy and of the governance of the working people. That is, collective bargaining formed a key part of the capitalist system in the United States for a while, acting as a system of governance that channeled and shaped workers' activities and struggles, as well as helping promote economic activity by putting more money in workers' hands. The attack on unions in more recent times represents, in part, a move away from the use of unions as a tool for capitalists and the capitalist state to try to govern the working class, and a move away from the use of unions as a tool for the capitalist state to try to govern capitalists.

But militancy can re-enliven existing institutions of dispute resolution. That is, militancy can help reinvigorate older forms of institutionalizing truces in the class struggle. I think the foreseeable future might proceed in terms of tactical breaks from existing institutions. The response from the official powers will be repression, or a combination of repression and the re-enlivening of those institutions.

It can be hard to imagine existing institutions working again. Many of us have grown up politically in a time when the institutions of capitalist society have disaffected people. We are cynical about the ballot box, the court system, and so on. We are used to these institutions being of little use in helping people resolve disputes and meet needs in the short term. This cynicism about institutions is partly because the capitalists and the capitalist state have moved away from using these institutions as effective means of governing us and organizing capitalism. The 1930s crisis and eventual recovery should teach us, however: existing institutions can change.

Capitalism is made of up conflicts between capitalists and working-class people. There's tremendous conflict among some working-class people, including over how to best navigate the workers vs. capitalist conflict. Another important dynamic within capitalism is

conflict between capitalists. Capitalists get their wealth from exploit-
ing workers, but the capitalists also clash with each other over who
will get how much of a share of that wealth. That conflict between
capitalists has to be governed or it will cause larger problems. Some of
the time, the capitalist state tries to make use of the working class as a
source of power to govern capitalists.

Some of the time class struggle helps create, in the words of Michel
Aglietta, "major transformations in the social organization of labor
which alone can provide the basis for the conditions of a new and
lasting accumulation."[12] That is, sometimes class struggle helps to re-
enliven the institutions of capitalist society, or to create new institutions, and these institutions help prop up capital accumulation. This
can happen even when struggles involve tactical violations of capitalist
property rights, as in the case of the sit-down strikes that helped build
the CIO.

Currently, institutions of capitalist society are not likely to negotiate or concede. That can lead to rising working-class militancy
and more room for radical ideas to spread. Radicals, as specialists in
militancy (or at least advocates of militancy), might gain more legitimacy as a result. Then, militancy practiced in larger numbers might
re-enliven capitalist institutions. It's important to note that those institutions are tools for capitalist rule, even though they are different
sorts of tools than the guns and clubs of the police.

PART THREE:
PROSPECTS FOR REFORM TODAY

IT SEEMS TO me that the core question about the possibilities of reform
is whether or not we're currently touching objective, systemic limits
that dictate capitalist responses. In my view, the current moment is
political, about priorities and decisions, and is not dictated straightforwardly by economic possibility. Overall, arguments like "economic
conditions mean that global elites are unable to do XYZ" strike me
as wrongheaded, in part because of an overemphasis on structural
imperatives and an underemphasis on ideology and the politics of
elites. To offer an analogy, I once heard about a union organizing
drive at a facility for the developmentally disabled in the early 2000s.
This was a privatized facility that was still dependent on state subsidy
rates (Medicaid reimbursements), which had been cut or stagnant. In

contract negotiations, according to the financial data supplied by the bosses, the institution honestly couldn't afford to give the raises that the union was negotiating for. So the union lobbied like crazy to get Medicaid reimbursements raised for group homes in that state. They succeeded, and then fought to make sure the bosses actually handed over the raises. That was a case where the employer ran up against real limits in terms of profitability and simply couldn't give a meaningful concession. I don't think we're in a moment where the capitalist system as a whole has run up against a limit like that, making meaningful reforms impossible.

Before I go on, I should say that by "reform," I mean two things, which are only partly related. What really matters about reforms, from a communist perspective, is whether or not the reforms shore up capitalism in some way, making capitalism more stable or profitable, or blunting or preventing working-class struggle. Economically, it costs to implement reforms. Other than nature and expropriation, all wealth comes from workers, but the capitalists claim that wealth. So the costs of reform have to come from somewhere and often require capitalists to give up a bit of the wealth they claim belongs to them. At the same time, reforms can prove profitable despite initial costs. And reforms don't have to be economic in a narrow sense. Reforms can also include the extension of rights or the end to repression. Amnesty International lists many human rights abuses in the United States that could be eliminated, including police brutality and the death penalty. Between 2003 and 2006, the most recent years about which I can find information, police in the US killed 1553 people. These types of killings could be eliminated or reduced by reform. Doing so would also reduce the sparks that give rise to riots; while police brutality alone rarely causes riots, it is often an important catalyst.

I do think that reforms are unlikely in the near future. The current capitalist class and the government (at least in the US) seem to me more in the mood to bust heads and throw people into the street than they are in the mood to issue concessions. They have been for a while. If the working class goes on the offensive, though, this might change. And there are some voices among the capitalists and their ideologists who have called for reform. Billionaire Warren Buffett, for example, has called for more taxes on the rich, and Nobel Prize winner Paul Krugman, no radical, has been writing in the *New York Times* for a while about reforms that would help capitalism. These voices seem to be drowned out by the majority of capitalists and pro-capitalist voices, but that doesn't mean that reform is systematically impossible in the present.

At one point, most capitalists—certainly most US capitalists, and most high level US government personnel—were ideologically quite close to Klansmen. This changed. Capitalists can change their minds and decide to do capitalism differently. They don't do so in a vacuum, of course; this happens when forces within the capitalist class convince other capitalists that it's in their interests to change. Mass struggles are a hugely important factor in shaping how capitalists see their interests and in how intracapitalist class politics play out. In any case, I think that under the disposition of the current capitalists, reform is unlikely, but that doesn't mean reform is structurally impossible. We're in a volatile moment and the disposition of the capitalists may change if we see large working-class offensives.

Now I want to address two arguments I've heard, that say reform is impossible. At one point, a good friend of mine suggested that currently we are in a downturn in the global economy that is so severe that there aren't resources available for the capitalists and governments to pay for reforms. That sounds good but, historically speaking, if anything, being at a low point seems to make reforms *more* likely, not less likely.

The UK was in a major economic downturn in the 1840s. That decade saw big changes to workplace health and safety law of a kind that Karl Marx argued helped English capitalists.[13] The US was at a major low point around 1890 or 1900, an era of increasing social reform, including the regulation of food safety, "protective" legislation concerning women workers, and workers' compensation. The UK was at a low point again in the 1890s and, in 1897, the UK introduced workmen's compensation (keep in mind that reforms during this era usually involved a few years study by commissions and so on; so the impulse to reform dates from close or prior to the low economic point). The 1930s were a decade of massive global economic crisis. In the United States, the 1930s saw the creation of the National Labor Relations Act, the Fair Labor Standards Act, and the Social Security Act. So, I don't see evidence that being in a major downturn equals limited social reform possibilities. The policy planners of the 1930s certainly thought that active state engagement via social reform was a way to aid the upward swing out of the valley.

A second argument I've heard about the impossibility of reform concerns the falling rate of profit. The claim that there is a trend for the rate of profit to fall means that, over time, capitalists will get a lower percentage on their investments. That doesn't mean they will amass less wealth. It means their wealth will increase by a smaller percentage. The rate of profit would have to decline to zero, in order for the "it will all collapse under its own weight" sort of arguments to be true. And even then, it would still be possible to destroy a lot of capital, in order to create new room for growth. Given the frequency of wars, political and economic elites seem to be relatively okay with that as a fix.

Imagine a small business without much machinery. The company spends $300,000 a year and generates a profit of $100,000 a year. That's an annual rate of profit of 33 percent. Now imagine a bigger company that spends $300,000,000 and generates a profit of $3,000,000. That's an annual rate of profit of only 1 percent. But it's still a much larger real quantity of wealth—the larger business made ten times the absolute profits. Whatever else there is to say, a tendency for the rate of profit to fall is not the same thing as a tendency for capitalists to actually run out of wealth. If there are profits being made, then there is surplus value being extracted from workers and some of that surplus value could be directed toward workers as a type of reform. To put it another way—repression is expensive. If they can afford repression, they can afford reform. The low estimates say the city of Oakland spent $2.5 million cracking down on Occupy Oakland. At least some of that could have been spent differently, on reforms. At the national level, the defense budget recently got another fifty billion dollars. This too is money that could be spent differently.

There has been a massive speedup in the US, so that "Americans now put in an average of 122 more hours per year than Brits, and 378 hours (nearly 10 weeks!) more than Germans," accompanied by rising incomes for the very wealthy and high profits for capitalists.[14] It seems to me that the money is there for reform. I'm not the only one who thinks this. Billionaire Warren Buffett has made news repeatedly by saying that he pays too little in taxes.[15]

Matías Vernengo argues that current policies in the US are about where wealth is distributed among the capitalists. That is, the current moment is one in which social inequality and wealth polarization has increased rapidly, in ways that are the result of economic policy and the disposition of the capitalists. The left wing of capital has begun to argue that this has reached destabilizing proportions. For Vernengo, as for Buffett, tax policy should change to fund redistribution. [16]

Some pro-capitalist commentators have argued not only that reform is possible but that it's needed to help capitalism recover. Here's *The Economist*:

> America is currently on course for the most stringent fiscal tightening of any big economy in 2012, as temporary tax cuts and unemployment insurance expire at the end of this year. (...) For all the tirades against the Europeans, America's economy risks being pushed into recession by its own fiscal policy—and by the fact that both parties are more interested in positioning themselves for the 2012 elections than in reaching the compromises needed to steer away from that hazardous course. [17]

Similarly, Dean Baker recently argued that:

> Corporate profits were revised sharply higher for both 2009 and 2010. The share of profits in corporate sector output hit a new record high, more than a full percentage point above its previous peak. Finance was the biggest winner within the corporate sector, accounting for 31.7% of corporate profits, also a record high. (...) the economy was plunging even more rapidly than we had previously recognised in the two quarters following the collapse of Lehman. Yet, the plunge stopped in the second quarter of 2009—just as the stimulus came on line. This was followed by respectable growth over the next four quarters. Growth then weakened again as the impact of the stimulus began to fade at the end of 2010 and the start of this year. In other words, the growth pattern shown by the revised data sure makes it appear that the stimulus worked. The main problem would seem to be that the stimulus was not big enough and it wasn't left in place long enough to lift the economy to anywhere near potential output. [18]

Writing about the debt ceiling deal and rumbling about the US deficit, economist James Galbraith writes that *austerity measures* are the redistribution of wealth—in an upward direction:

> The right steps would be to lower—not raise—the Social Security early retirement age, permitting for a few years older workers to exit the labor force permanently on better terms than are available to them today. This together with a lower age of access to Medicare would work quickly to rebalance the labor force, reducing unemployment and futile job search among older workers while increasing job openings for the young. It is the application of plain common sense. And unlike all the pressures to enact long-term cuts in these programs, it would help solve one of today's important problems right away.

Galbraith writes about Social Security that:

> the financial crisis has left the country with 11 million fewer jobs than Americans need now. No matter how aggressive the policy, we are not going to find 11 million new jobs soon. So common sense suggests we should make some decisions about who should have the first crack: older people, who have already worked three or four decades at hard jobs? Or younger people, many just out of school, with fresh skills and ambitions? The answer is obvious. Older people who would like to retire and would do so if they could afford it should get some help. The right step is to reduce, not increase, the full-benefits retirement age. As a rough cut, why not enact a three-year window during which the age for receiving full Social Security benefits would drop to 62—providing a voluntary, one-time, grab-it-now bonus for leaving work? Let them go home! With a secure pension and medical care, they will be happier. Young people who need work will be happier. And there will also be more jobs. With pension security, older people will consume services until the end of their lives.[19]

Nobel Prize-winning Economist Paul Krugman says:

> We currently have a deeply depressed economy. We will
> almost certainly continue to have a depressed economy
> all through next year. And we will probably have a de-
> pressed economy through 2013 as well, if not beyond.
> The worst thing you can do in these circumstances is
> slash government spending, since that will depress the
> economy even further. Pay no attention to those who
> invoke the confidence fairy, claiming that tough action
> on the budget will reassure businesses and consumers,
> leading them to spend more. It doesn't work that way,
> a fact confirmed by many studies of the historical re-
> cord. Indeed, slashing spending while the economy is
> depressed won't even help the budget situation much,
> and might well make it worse. On one side, interest
> rates on federal borrowing are currently very low, so
> spending cuts now will do little to reduce future in-
> terest costs. On the other side, making the economy
> weaker now will also hurt its long-run prospects, which
> will in turn reduce future revenue. So those demand-
> ing spending cuts now are like medieval doctors who
> treated the sick by bleeding them, and thereby made
> them even sicker.[20]

So far, arguments like these are in the minority among the capitalists, their governments, and their intellectual lackeys, but there is
a conversation happening about them. If reform is impossible, we
don't need to think much about any of this. If reform is possible,
then arguments like these will compete with arguments about why
reform shouldn't happen. If social movements continue to rise, we'll
also see arguments that the answer is repression, not reform. I think
the outcome of those arguments among capitalists will be political.
The answer won't be inevitable and it won't be determined by the
economy in a narrow or mechanical way, which is to say, I don't think
that we've yet run into objective limits to capitalism, such that the
capitalists have no options other than keep doing what they're doing
now or get more repressive. They may well opt for either of those
choices, but none of this is inevitable or a matter of simple economic

requirements. Whatever happens will be, in part, the result of how the capitalists respond to the struggles of the working class. That capitalist response will be shaped by the changing disposition of the capitalist class—how it sees itself, how it sees the world, what it believes in, who is hegemonic within it. This is politics, not objective necessity. Austerity is the current big push. In opposition to this, we see and will see more large social movements. If social conflict gets really intense, though, ruling class priorities can change with regard to the allocation of surplus value. Reforms will be a way for the system to try to compensate, to temporarily relieve pressures from below, and to stratify the class in some way and break up the class composition that drove the uprisings.

Reforms have at least three functions. One is to oil the hinges of capitalists' actions, extending credit to companies so they can buy stuff to make stuff to sell stuff etc., in order to avoid problems that capitalists run into, which aren't an immediate/short-term product of workers' struggles. Another is to prevent or defuse social unrest on the part of some constituencies—not everyone, just enough people to keep too large a swath from boiling over too far. (One of the most interesting things I think came out of the analyses of *Race Traitor* was that white skin privilege was analogous to social democracy in this way.[21]) We saw glimmers of this possibility in the 2011–2012 struggles in Wisconsin, as the Democrats broke legislative quorum and temporarily became kind of folk heroes to many, and in the degree to which the mobilizations didn't find a way to really move beyond the interests of unionized public sector workers. The legislative recall played a similar role.

A third function of reform is to govern the capitalist class in the interests of systemic stability. That is, reforms are partly a way to spread and enforce capitalist class consciousness. While every capitalist is likely to have a clear boss-consciousness, in relation to their subordinates within their enterprise, there's no guarantee they'll be class-conscious. In some ways various laments in the mainstream press about CEOs taking the money and running, or industries that pollute, or the way insurance companies raise costs for other companies and create systemic pressures, or the problems with finance capitalists—these are all about individual capitalists or subgroups of capitalists who are not primarily thinking or acting in the long-term interests and stability of the capitalist class and system.

Reforms involve revision to institutional arrangements that direct the flow of wealth in capitalist society (wealth originating from the exploitation of the working class). We tend to call "reforms" those institutional revisions that redistribute wealth to the working class directly—wage rises, for instance—or indirectly, via "the social wage." Over the past thirty to forty years in the US, we've seen substantial institutional revisions that redirect wealth in an upward direction, and we've seen institutional revisions in the form of greater amounts of money spent on repression. In my view, if these institutional changes are possible—if there is additional wealth available for capitalists and for paying for repression—then other institutional revisions are possible. This wealth could be redirected differently; the wealth could go to reforms that improve the lives of the working class.

Setting aside the large-scale possibilities for reform, I think there is also a rising current of reformist forces within social movements today. Some reformists in social movements will encourage working within existing institutions, using measures like elections, lobbying, lawsuits, referenda and recalls, and so on. These reformists will fail as much or more than they succeed, at least for the short term. Other reformists will get more militant, and these militant reformists will play increasingly important roles, providing funding and personnel to movements. Their militancy will minimize differences between themselves and radicals. The militant reformists will quietly work together behind the scenes, on some occasions with less militant reformists. For example, the militant reformists will agree with other reformists that electoral reforms are needed, but will place less priority on pursuing that goal in the near future, perhaps based on a different analysis of where institutions are currently at. The militancy of some reformists, and often their sincerity, will confuse good-hearted radicals, who will not understand (or be able to act against) the militant reformist forces.

Part of what's going on right now for a lot of people is a collapsing future. A lot of people will have worse lives than they would have had under prior versions of capitalism. One piece of that is due to the restructuring of private and public institutions of social reproduction and the people who work in them. This will lead to serious conflict, as we saw in the struggles in Madison, Wisconsin. Antiausterity struggles are prone to militancy, defensiveness, and a type of pro-system conservatism, because they're based on defending rights and legal or property claims that capitalists and their governments are trying to eliminate.

PART FOUR: RADICALS SHOULD...

A RISE IN militant reformism would pose questions for radicals—namely, how radicals can and should relate to militant reformist groupings. I'm skeptical about what militant reformist struggles are going to accomplish. I would say radicals should avoid militant reformist struggles, unless we have nothing better to do. Then again, a lot of radicals really don't have anything better to do, and in those cases could do a lot worse than to participate in militant reformist struggles. If we do participate, then we should do so with a plan to eventually have something better to do, and be honest with ourselves about whether or not, and how, we are actually accomplishing that plan.

When we do participate in militant reformist projects, I think a lot of us on the left tend to think of ourselves as standing for things like militancy, and democracy, and a lot of us, definitely myself included, have spent recent times focusing more on how to fight effectively. We engage with current events from that place: let's learn as much as we can. Let's make these fights as effective as we can. Let's try to make this struggle more democratic. Let's work to reduce racism, sexism, homophobia, and other forms of oppression and hierarchy within this struggle. All of that is good and important. But that only takes us so far. And if we're not careful, those impulses will set us up to get played by reformists in strategic roles, such that we end up accomplishing less than we hope.

It is precisely the fact that people can get some of their needs met and their disputes resolved through existing institutions that make (or rather made, and might again make) those institutions effective organs of capitalist rule. Many of the prevailing institutions of negotiation haven't worked well in recent years, and the cost of this institutional breakdown has been low for the capitalists. With rising militancy, the costs of ineffective negotiation and dispute resolution will get higher, and we may see those institutions start to work better again, or we may see new ones created. Many of us like to say, "direct action gets the goods," which is shorthand for, "existing institutions don't pay out, so to get what you want, you need to fight outside those institutions." That may not always be true. It may end up that, some of the time, following the routines of institutions of negotiation gets the goods (and it may end up that forms of direct action to get the goods become routinized). If that happens, we'll need to drop the "our way wins better" schtick, and we'll need to be able to articulate the merits of our social vision, based on the inherent limitations of our lives under capitalism, and based on our vision of human liberation. We should aim to expand people's ethical horizons, in order to foster a sense that humans deserve more out of life than school, work, retirement, and death. We need to spread the actual social vision we believe in, that we deserve decent lives of our own choosing, and that a society where people get what they deserve is genuinely possible. We also need to spread a notion of what we need to get rid of in human society, in order to meet those ethical standards—we need a revolutionary break with what exists. In my view, struggle is important to the degree that it connects with and helps advance a longer-term social vision, radicalizes more people, and prepares people to participate in the struggles of the working class against capitalism. That is to say, alongside building power, and building willingness to use that power, there has to be a building of the values that inform how and why to use that power, so that we're ready for real social ruptures that call capitalist rule into question in a real way. At some point, militant reformism has to give way to militant radicalism; which is to say, to openly politicized struggle, beyond just short-term improvements to life under capitalism. In my view, when this happens, it will exist in tension with militant reformist institutions and groups, at best, and, at times, in open conflict. We can bet that reformist forces will scheme on radicals to keep us in our role as a loyal rent-a-mob. If our participation in reformist struggles amounts to little more than "we are loyal soldiers and we talk some politics on the side," then we're never going to pose a challenge to capitalism. Eventually, people operating within militant reformist struggles will need to move into positions of conflict with reformists, either taking over and radicalizing reformist institutions (I'm skeptical about how much this can actually succeed) or breaking out of those institutions, in order to form radical alternatives. Radicals acting as loyal members of reformist projects are just that, until we start to come into conflict with other forces within those projects. Without a plan for how to move beyond that loyal role, that's where we'll stay. I think radicals should avoid militant reform struggles—instead of militant reformism, how about practicing militant radicalism? I'm an IWW member, so I believe it's possible to build a revolutionary union that both fights for gains in the short term and advocates for replacing capitalism with a good society. We in the IWW don't have a monopoly on this vision. For another example, I find particularly inspiring and illuminating, see Solidarity Federation's book, *Fighting for Ourselves*. I mean not so much to advocate for revolutionary unionism, but rather a general approach to organizing. Revolutionary unionism is just one example. The main characteristic of this organizing is that it combines fighting for gains now with fighting against capitalism. It combines things that some radicals (wrongly, in my opinion) see as separate arenas, of politics and economics or political and mass organizing.

That said, regardless of whether or not they're politically radical, our projects will remain at the level of negotiation for the foreseeable future. Negotiation is a social relationship; it's built into the relationships between employers and employees on a small scale and between the capitalist class and the working class on a large scale. Until millions and millions of people in the working class are done negotiating, class struggle will involve negotiation. One big question we should talk about is what it would look like to actually move beyond negotiation, and what we can do to start to get to that point.

We should also talk about better and worse forms of negotiation within struggles. The social relationship of negotiation between classes can be institutionalized in a variety of ways. A rise in working class militancy can re-enliven old institutions of negotiation or foster the creation of new ones. Indeed, militant reformism is basically a call for people to fight like hell until there are better institutions in place, so that we don't have to fight so hard anymore and have better lives under capitalism. For the foreseeable future, we're probably going to be dealing with forms of negotiation between classes. But all forms of negotiation are not equal. There are two basic ways to think about what makes forms of negotiation better: how useful is a form of negotiation, for us getting more of what participants want and need; and what does a form of negotiation do to participants—how do struggles change what we want and need? [22]

Radicals should talk about what it would look like for a radical practice that is not only ideologically different from reformism, and not only a matter of spreading ideas, but different in the short term, in terms of how struggle is carried out. Some people will say that this is not currently viable. In that case, we should flesh out when struggle will become viable, how we will know, and how we can reach the point where radical alternatives become genuinely viable.

I hope this chapter helps open some conversation. I definitely don't see it as the last word on anything, and I see many of my points here as hypotheses, in need of further testing through inquiry. There are a few additional areas where I think further inquiry is especially important. These are the ones that jump out at me; I'm sure others are possible. First off, there's paying attention to large-scale economic, policy, and social movement developments at various levels—globally, regionally, and nationally. Second, tracking the intellectual development of militant reformism: the people involved in these efforts are smart, sincere, and skilled, even though they have a different social vision than we do as radicals. Paying attention to what they're writing and saying will help radicals orient ourselves. Third, case studies of specific militant reformist projects will be particularly important because militant reform projects differ from each other, due to a bunch of different factors. We'll learn better how to navigate within and against them if we're talking about them. I attempted one case study, of Occupy Homes.[23] Fourth, radicals organizing in militant reformist settings should compare notes and rigorously assess our successes and failures, in order to get better at navigating within those settings. We should also think through what our goals should and shouldn't be, realistically, and how organizing in militant reform settings can or can't help advance revolution. Fifth, and finally, we should continue to develop working alternatives in both theory and practice. Often militant reformist projects suck up radicals' time and energy because there are few radical projects that are comparable.

ENDNOTES

1   If you haven't noticed, I am slightly skeptical about predictions of
     a final crisis of capitalism. The idea of a final crisis suggests that we
     shouldn't worry much about the fact that capitalism has emerged from
     past crises, because in the final crisis, things will be different. Because
     capitalism is different today, this time around, there is no chance that
     the system can recover. To be clear, I am not saying capitalism always

has the capacity to recover from crisis. I'm saying recovery or not is an open question, and I'm implying that some people are too quick to jump to the conclusion that recovery's off the table. We should tone down the level of certainty with which we make predictions. We shouldn't assume that the system will restore itself, and we shouldn't assume it wouldn't. We should instead look around and examine what elements might form the basis for potential restoration of the system and what obstacles such a restoration will face. In my view, current signs point to eventual economic recovery, and, as I try to lay out in this chapter, I think there are ways in which the left and working class struggle can make that recovery more likely.

2   I should say, I don't argue for this political perspective here; I presume it. I don't know how much of my argument actually relies on this perspective, except that reform is only inadequate if we believe it's possible and desirable to remake society in a good way through revolution.

3   For an overview of recent arguments that reform is impossible, see Juan Conatz, "Is Reform Possible?" Libcom.org, libcom.org/blog/reform-possible-22122011 (accessed July 14, 2013).

4   Eugene Genovese, *Roll, Jordan, Roll: The World the Slaves Made* (New York: Random House, 1974), 49.

5   Ibid., 27.

6   Ibid., 46–47.

7   Nelson Lichtenstein, *State of the Union: A Century of American Labor* (Princeton: Princeton University Press, 2002), 32.

8   Ibid., 39.

9   Ibid., 45.

10   Rhonda Levine, *Class Struggle and the New Deal: Industrial Labor, Industrial Capital, and the State* (Lawrence: University Press of Kansas, 1988), 149.

11   I give an overview of the origins of the system of labor law that governed labor relations in the US during the postwar period in "Just and Peaceful Labor Relations," *Recomposition*, recomposition.info/2012/08/11/just-and-peaceful-labor-relations-why-the-u-s-government-supported-collective-bargaining/ (accessed July 14, 2013). Since the late 1970s or early 1980s, US capitalists have increasingly

abandoned this system of labor regulation. Rising working-class militancy will likely create efforts to re-enliven that system or replace it with another form of state mediation of struggle.

12   Michel Aglietta, *A Theory of Capitalist Regulation: The US Experience* (London: New Left Books, 1979), 364.

13   Karl Marx, *Capital, Volume I,* Chapter ten, Section 6. Online at http://www.marxists.org/archive/marx/works/1867-c1/ch10.htm#S6 (accessed July 14, 2013).

14   Monika Bauerlein and Clara Jeffery, "All Work and No Pay: The Great Speed Up," *Mother Jones,* http://www.motherjones.com/politics/2011/06/speed-up-american-workers-long-hours (accessed July 14, 2013).

15   Warren Buffett, "A Minimum Tax for the Wealthy," *New York Times,* http://www.nytimes.com/2012/11/26/opinion/buffett-a-minimum-tax-for-the-wealthy.html?_r=0 (accessed July 14, 2013).

16   Matías Vernengo, "The Debt Ceiling: A Guide for the Bewildered," *MR Zine,* http://mrzine.monthlyreview.org/2011/vernengo260711.html (accessed July 14, 2013).

17   "The World Economy: Be Afraid," *The Economist,* www.economist.com/node/21530986 (accessed July 14, 2013).

18   Dean Baker, "US debt deal: how Washington lost the plot," *The Guardian,* www.guardian.co.uk/commentisfree/cifamerica/2011/aug/01/us-debt-deal-washington-unemployment (accessed July 14, 2013).

19   James K. Galbraith, "Unconventional Wisdom," *Foreign Policy,* www.foreignpolicy.com/articles/2011/01/02/unconventional_wisdom?page=0,7 (accessed July 14, 2013).

20   Paul Krugman, "The President Surrenders," *New York Times,* www.nytimes.com/2011/08/01/opinion/the-president-surrenders-on-debt-ceiling.html (accessed July 14, 2013).

21   Geert Dhondt, "Toward an American Revolutionary Praxis," See www.newformulation.org/4Dhondt1.htm (accessed July 14, 2013). Dhondt's essay is worth reading. Radicals in the US should take up his call to learn more about the history of abolitionist movements. I agree with him that the history of abolition and the historically grounded criticism of white supremacy in the United States make "important

contributions to the development of an American revolutionary praxis." That said, I'm skeptical of the claim, made by him and others influenced by *Race Traitor*, that race is the most structurally important facet of US capitalism, and skeptical of the characterization of the abolitionist movement as revolutionary. It seems to me equally plausible that the abolitionist movement was an incredibly important and laudable reformist movement.

22　I have addressed the issue of what struggle does to and for participants in "Struggle Changes People," Libcom.org, libcom.org/blog/struggle-changes-people-06012012 and "Mottos and Watchwords, Libcom. org, libcom.org/library/mottoes-watchwords-discussion-politics-mass-organizations (accessed July 14, 2013). The issue of particular organizational forms has been the subject of much conversation among some of us in the IWW, related to a discussion paper called "Direct Unionism." The paper is available online at libcom.org/library/direct-unionism-discussion-paper-09052011 (accessed July 14, 2013), as are various responses, which appeared in the *Industrial Worker* newspaper and elsewhere. Scott Nappalos has recently suggested that an important factor in how radicals think about methods of struggle should be the relationship between struggle and the degree of equilibrium capitalism currently has. See Nappalos, "Thrown Off Balance," *Theory & Practice*, snappalos.wordpress.com/2013/03/10/thrown-off-balance-workers-struggles-against-equilibrium/ (accessed July 14, 2013).

23　See my "Occupy vs Eviction: Radicals, Reform, and Dispossession," Libcom.org, libcom.org/blog/1578 (accessed July 14, 2013).

STATES OF EMERGENCY
GREEN CAPITALISM AND
TRANSNATIONAL RESISTANCE

YESENIA BARRAGÁN

"The tradition of the oppressed teaches us that the 'state of emergency' in which we live is not the exception but the rule."
—Walter Benjamin, *Theses on the Philosophy of History*

FLOATING BLACK BODIES AND MILES UPON MILES OF WRECKAGE: WE know those scenes from Hurricane Katrina all too well.[1] They are etched deep within the American historical imagination, rendered what Zygmunt Bauman calls "human waste," referring to "the population of human beings rendered surplus by the remorseless advance of modernity,"[2] alongside the survivors who became environmental refugees within the borders of their own nation. And more than three months after Hurricane Sandy, officially the largest hurricane ever to have formed in the Atlantic Basin, as many as 8,200 people in the Rockaways were still without power.[3] Meanwhile, seas are rising at exponential rates, as ice melts faster than scientists ever thought possible. Rivers around the world are drying up, with soil depletion ravaging populations across Africa and South Asia. Scientists have concluded that coral reefs could entirely disappear by 2100. The hottest year on record was 2010, and the 2000s were the hottest decade in known human history.[4] "We are consuming 25 percent more than the Earth can give us each year," notes

William Rees of the School of Community and Regional planning at the University of British Columbia.[5] In scenarios based on current predictions by the Intergovernmental Panel on Climate Change, 20 percent of the world's population could be made homeless due to climate change by 2100.[6] It is indeed a good time to start asking the question: is it the end of the world as we know it?

Global elites have responded to these cataclysmic environmental transformations, in the wake of ongoing crises of capital, by developing an allegedly more benign "green capitalism" to avert inevitable environmental (and social) disaster. In the following chapter, after explaining the origins and "false solutions" of green capitalism, I will show how the green capitalist project necessarily depends on both a quick violence, felt by many marginalized communities especially in the Third World, and a "slow violence"[7] to deal with the "human waste," or "the disposable people"[8] and life forms of the world that are resisting its expansion. Moreover, I will demonstrate how the discourse and impending policy implementation of "green jobs" and a "Green New Deal" fit, not only into this larger model of green capitalism, but particularly within the current logic of austerity. In the end, green capitalist projects like the "Green New Deal" distract us from the rule of the day: the fundamental crisis is capitalism itself. An antiauthoritarian, anticapitalist critique of green capitalism is necessary to, as Walter Benjamin urges, "bring about a real state of emergency."[9] And this critique might give us a head start in analyzing the next disastrous bubble in financialized capitalism—one that could very well be used to try to (temporarily) resolve the global stagnation resulting from the existing crisis.

MOTHER NATURE MEET FATHER GREED: THE EMERGENCE OF GREEN CAPITALISM

"The only way we are going to get innovations that drive energy costs down to the China price...is by mobilizing free-market capitalism. The only thing as powerful as Mother Nature is Father Greed."
—Thomas Friedman, "The Power of Green"

GREEN CAPITALISM IS an economic response by global elites to two basic realities: the crisis of global climate change and the increasing depletion of natural resources, including water, fertile land, and even carbon dioxide pools. To address these two major issues, green capitalists argue that the free market, with the occasional (if needed) assistance of the state, is the only economic tool capable of adequately and efficiently addressing these catastrophic problems. Their bottom line is that profit and environmental sustainability can go hand-in-hand; one need not be sacrificed for the other. All that's necessary to address the climate crisis are some economic innovations by political and financial experts, sometimes with the assistance of mainstream environmental NGOs, while the "rest of us" are encouraged to "lend a hand" in our own small (but always meaningful!) ways—recycle, bike (or walk) to work, or consume less: it's your choice! And, in the context of the current economic tumult, green capitalism is one means by which the elites to can try to create a new bubble, from which they can rake in profits and perhaps stall the slow death of capitalism, even while hastening ecological collapse.

Developing out of the more mainstream environmental movements of the 1970s, "green capitalism" really got off the ground in the United States in the 1980s and especially in the 1990s, with theorists and proponents like Paul Hawken, Lester Brown, and Francis Cairncross, among others, who argued that "greening" technology and infrastructure, alongside eco-friendly shopping, would not infringe upon the profit margin, and would actually be *profitable*.[10] The idea of pollution credits, a hallmark of the green capitalist model, first emerged in the 1970s.[11] The overall idea behind pollution credits is that big industries are allotted allowances to pollute, which, over time, are increasingly "capped," until, the theory goes, industries can no longer afford to run economically on fossil fuels.

Since the 1970s, an explosion of various types of carbon markets for these credits has happened in many shapes and forms. The markets range from public to private, from voluntary to regulated, from national to international. Launched in 2005, the EU Emissions Trading Scheme, for example, is the first large emissions trading system. It is a regulated, public market, where allowances for greenhouse gas emission are distributed by governments in accordance with a national emissions cap approved by the EU Commission. In the United States, the Chicago Climate Exchange (CCX) was formed in 2007, a private, voluntary carbon emissions trading market emerging as a response to the US government's failure to sign the Kyoto Protocol. The CCX is currently North America's largest and longest running gas emissions reduction program. At the global level, in 1997, the Kyoto Protocol created the world's first international carbon market, which only came into force in 2005, when 141 countries, with the glaring exception of the United States, ratified it.

"Green capitalism" is also manifested at the everyday, local level, where conscientious Americans are encouraged to shop at organic, eco-friendly supermarkets like Whole Foods (located mostly in middle-to-upper-class, white neighborhoods), recycle, and, if you really want to be a model eco-citizen, calculate your own carbon footprint. Once determined, all you have to do is to rearrange your individual or family's work and lifestyles to reduce it. It's that easy! Ted Steinberg has usefully described this modern phenomenon as "green liberalism," the idea that "unites a faith in the ability of both price mechanisms and individual (consumer and investor) initiative to rescue the earth."[12]

Interestingly, what we assume to be hard-won environmental victories are actually children of the green liberal phenomenon. Take recycling, for example. As Steinberg notes, the history behind recycling "constitutes a profoundly individuated response to the problem of waste."[13] In the United States, beer came in bottles that could be used repeatedly, up to as many as thirty times, until the 1940s. However, World War II popularized one-way, one-use beverage containers, which we have grown so accustomed to today, available in supermarkets, corner stores, or vending machines. Getting rid of the need to deal with empty bottles meant that national brewing companies could squash local breweries dependent upon this older form of packaging. The recycling industry as we know it emerged in the 1950s, when Vermont farmers came together to ban these one-way, one-use containers, after their cows began to swallow whole glass bottles thrown into the fields. Instead of addressing the fact that these one-way, throwaway containers were the real source of unnecessary waste, the American Can Company and Owens-Illinois Glass Company established an advocacy group called Keep America Beautiful, soon joined by Coca-Cola Company, PepsiCo Inc., and other major corporations. This group began a media campaign chastising the poor, environmentally unethical behavior of individual "litterbugs." "Instead of focusing on the systemic problems with the industry's packaging decisions," Steinberg argues, "the ads located responsibility at the individual level. Litter became a matter of personal responsibility while industry practices…went unexamined."[14]

The green capitalist "solution" could not be clearer: with some "pragmatic individual action,"[15] and the hard, smart work of the experts, we shall all be saved from ourselves.

Except, it doesn't quite work that way. As Paul M. Sweezy writes:

> It is this obsession with capital accumulation that distinguishes capitalism from the simple system for satisfying human needs it is portrayed as in mainstream economic theory. And a system driven by capital accumulation is one that never stands still, one that is forever changing, adopting new and discarding old methods of production and distribution, opening up new territories, subjecting to its purposes societies too weak to protect themselves. Caught up in this process of restless innovation and expansion, the system rides roughshod over even its own beneficiaries if they get in its way or fall by the roadside. As far as the natural environment is concerned, capitalism perceives it not as something to be cherished and enjoyed but as a means to the paramount ends of profit-making and still more capital accumulation.[16]

The nature of capitalism, as Sweezy notes, is to place profit above all, no exceptions. Yet, as Richard Smith points out, "Saving the world requires that the pursuit of profits be systematically subordinated to ecological concerns."[17] In a capitalist framework, this is simply impossible. A drastic reduction of fossil fuels, necessary to avert climate catastrophe, would place private and public shareholders of such multinational corporations at risk, investors who could ultimately never be sacrificed. But in the end, even those green capitalist schemes such as the carbon market, whose theoretical goal is to gradually lower carbon emissions over time until they reach zero, do not fundamentally address the core issue: that green capitalism maintains the economic, political, and social systems of power that have put us on the fast track towards destruction in the first place. As the late Neil Smith noted, green capitalism "has become nothing less than a major strategy for ecological commodification, marketization and financialization which radically intensifies and deepens the penetration of nature by capital."[18]

However, it's also important to understand that this "green capitalist" project didn't just appear out of thin air. It's a product of a particular historic moment; that is, the emergence of neoliberalism, rooted in an earlier financial crisis of the late 1970s and early 1980s. As David Harvey has laid out, the years 1978–1980 were a revolutionary social and economic turning-point, with the shift toward a global, neoliberal, economic order. In 1978, Deng Xiaoping dramatically altered China's state-communist economy through massive economic liberalization, opening up the national economy to private investment. Just a year later, in 1979, Margaret Thatcher was elected the prime minister of Britain and subsequently initiated systemic privatization measures and antilabor policies. Across the Atlantic, in the United States, Ronald Reagan rose to power in 1980 on a staunch antiunion platform and with plans to deregulate and privatize industries, agriculture, and other bodies in the public domain.[19] "Reaganomics" is the infamous term referring to Reagan's economic policies in the 1980s, including his notorious outlining of "trickle-down economics," based on reduced government spending, reduced federal income and capital gains tax, and overall reduced government regulation. These were also the years of a massive war on poor, predominantly African-American communities under the guise of the so-called War on Drugs, coordinated repression against national liberation struggles in Central America, and levels of economic inequality unseen since the Great Depression era.[20] But these neoliberal policies weren't simply homegrown, native phenomena. They were approved and mandated by powerful multinational institutions like the International Monetary Fund (IMF) and the World Bank (WB) based in North America. In exchange for economic relief, these institutions mandated massive structural adjustment programs known as the "Washington Consensus," which ordered severe privatization of national firms, public sector spending cuts, and general deregulation of trade.

As these neoliberal economic policies began to expand and consolidate themselves over time, and as growing climate change awareness emerged in the early 1990s, environmental neoliberalism gradually began to assert its presence globally—especially in the 1990s and continuing until the present. The following section looks at the consequences of the privatization of water in Bolivia in the late 1990s as an example of this phenomenon, and offers a panoramic view of other neoliberal environmental projects that developed in this historic period, with an eye to the forms of violence (and transnational resistance) that undergird (and disrupt) its ongoing expansion.

GREEN AND RED IN BLOOD: THE GREEN CAPITALIST EXPERIMENT IN BOLIVIA AND BEYOND

THE BOLIVIAN GOVERNMENT, like those of the majority of other countries in Latin America, was also transitioning to this neoliberal economic model during the 1980s and 1990s. In particular, Bolivia underwent its first round of neoliberal economic restructuring in 1985 when, in response to the region-wide financial crisis that had begun in 1982, then-President Víctor Paz Estenssoro instituted the country's New Economic Policy. These measures called for the overall reduction of state expenditures, closure of state-owned properties like mines, the privatization of national industries, and so forth. Over the next twenty years, successive administrations followed suit and continued to further this liberalization process, and in the mid-1990s, there was a second major wave of neoliberal reforms.[21] In September 1998, the IMF approved a loan for Bolivia, but only under the condition that the Bolivian state would privatize the remaining public state agencies, including the state water agency in the department of Cochabamba.[22]

In September of 1999, the government sold the city of Cochabamba's water system to the consortium Aguas de Tunari, composed of companies from the United States, Spain, and Bolivia, led by a company named Bechtel. Aguas de Tunari was awarded a forty-year concession contract to provide and manage the drinking water supply and sanitation services in Cochabamba.[23] In addition, just a month later, the Bolivian government passed Law 2029, which essentially made autonomous community water systems illegal. This had particularly devastating consequences for Cochabamba because only 57 percent of the city's population had access to the official water system, while the remaining 43 percent received their water supply from autonomous water systems, whether from privately made wells, tanker trunks, water associations or cooperatives.[24] The law also stated that citizens had to obtain permission from authorities if they desired to collect rainwater and that Aguas del Tunari would close any remaining private wells.[25]

But things boiled over in January 2000, when Aguas del Tunari suddenly imposed inconceivably high rates that drastically increased water bills, a classic "shock doctrine," neoliberal measure. Water bills rose anywhere from 35 to 200 percent, depending on the patron. Cochabamba's residents soon found themselves spending 20 percent or more of their monthly salary on water, in the poorest country in South America, where 70 percent of citizens lived in poverty, and where the average income of a working-class family in Cochabamba was sixty dollars.[26] Fortunately, Bolivia, like many other Latin American countries, has a long, dynamic legacy of militant social movements that respond immediately to potential attacks. With an outraged population ready to mobilize, the Coordinadora, an organization formed by a group of union leaders, social activists, and concerned citizens, called for a refusal to pay the water bills. In response, Aguas del Tunari stated that, in the event of nonpayment, they would shut off the water supply. In mid-January 2000, protesters shut down the city for four long days. The infamous Bolivian Water Wars had begun.[27]

From February to March 2000, thousands took to the streets of Cochabamba to protest this neoliberal environmental assault. The protestors and organizers also faced the heavy hand of the state, when more than a thousand police were summoned to the city, where they assaulted demonstrators with tear gas and rubber bullets, leaving hundreds injured and five dead, including a seventeen-year-old boy.[28] Because of the continued resistance and resilience of the Water Wars organizers and demonstrators, the prefect of Cochabamba announced in April of 2000 that it would cancel the contract with Aguas del Tunari, in addition to withdrawing privatization measures from Law 2029 and reinstating the autonomous water system.[29] After a long and bloody war against the many authorities in power, the people of Cochabamba had won their fight. One should bear in mind that this story of violent repression and resistance is not unique to Bolivia. In Huila, Colombia, a wide coalition of *campesinos*, fishers, poor families, and activists came together in 2010 and 2011 to peacefully occupy and resist a "clean energy" hydroelectric dam that was set to displace hundreds of poor families and cause environmental devastation. In February of 2011, they faced the violent attacks of riot police, who shot into crowds that included pregnant women and children, and shot a demonstrator in the eye, blinding him.[30] In the Lower Aguan, Honduras, a UN-approved Clean Development Mechanism project focusing on palm oil cultivation gave rise to intense land conflicts between *campesino* groups and large landholders, numerous executions, and illegal arrests and torture for those resisting the huge land grabs.[31] In Espírito Santo, Brazil, the Aracruz company used stolen lands to create "Green Deserts," monocultural environmental nightmares of rows of neatly arranged eucalyptus trees that survive on toxic chemicals and enormous amounts of water, leaving the dirt as dry as a desert.[32] In 2009, more than six thousand women from Vía Campesina and the famous Landless Workers' Movement (Movimento dos Trabalhadores, MST) demonstrated across Brazil, protesting their government's support of the multinational agro-fuel industries, including Aracruz.[33] Similar stories of inconceivable violence can be found in Sumatra, Indonesia, where security forces for major, European-based palm oil companies burned and destroyed the homes of villagers who were resisting their projects, using live ammunition during the raids.[34] In spite of this immense repression, the villagers and farmers of Sumatra continue to resist and organize themselves against these corporations.

It is absolutely clear that these green capitalist projects, and capitalism in general, rely on an immediate, quick violence in order to pursue their economic objectives. The capitalist calculation is pretty simple: if anything or anyone remotely threatens or gets in the way of capital accumulation, expect nothing less than tear gas and bullets, nothing less than instantaneous repression. Shareholders' portfolios and the greater objective of environmental modernity simply cannot be risked. In fact, a new generation of young Americans got a small, albeit brief and different window into this quick-violence logic, when they faced the brutality of police forces threatened by the Occupy Wall Street encampments, in cities from New York City to Oakland in 2011–2012, while hundreds of working-class families face this violence every day, when they are brutally evicted from their homes because of the crimes of banks who are deemed "too big to fail."

But it's important to understand that green capitalism also operates on what Rob Dixon calls "slow violence," referring to "a violence that occurs gradually and out of sight, a violence of delayed destruction that is dispersed across time and space, an attritional violence that is typically not viewed as violence at all."[35] Whether poor communities located near toxic waste dumps in Detroit, Michigan, unable to see the long-term effects until it is too late, or gradual species loss over long swaths of time in the Sahara, "slow violence" produces "long dyings—the staggered and staggeringly discounted casualties, both human and ecological that result from war's toxic aftermath or climate change."[36] Green capitalism therefore flexibly adopts a quick or slow violence approach, depending on the circumstances threatening its livelihood.

Do not fear!, they say. Yes, occasionally (and necessarily), there will be some "collateral damage," but this is merely the preface to the ultimate green capitalist future, that will assuredly put us on the path towards environmental modernity. Moreover, more and more liberal and progressive elites are organizing themselves within the green capitalist model, calling for a "Green New Deal" and harkening back to Roosevelt's social welfare program in the 1930s to save us from this mess. And perhaps the most ironic part of it all is that this Green New Deal fits within the current logic of austerity.

BEYOND A GREEN NEW DEAL

"So just as social democrats in the 20th century forged a cross-class, cross-industry coalition in favour of the welfare state, so social democrats today need to forge a comparable alliance in favour of the environmentally-based economy. Green politics is no longer simply about a middle class environmental movement: it is now joined by powerful economic interests. Social democrats have to learn from how they built the welfare state economy in the 20th century in order to do it again for the green economy of the 21st."
—Michael Jacobs, "Green social democracy can rescue capitalism from itself"

"*Si no nos dejan soñar, no los dejaremos dormir.*" ("If you don't let us dream, we will not let you sleep.")
—Graffiti written on the walls during the Chilean student rebellion (2011–2012)

2008 WAS A year of economic crisis and political Hope. Voters in the United States elected Barack Obama, the nation's first African American president, who many hoped would also be the first "Green President." Speaking at George Mason University in 2009, Obama laid out the details for a green stimulus plan, which included investments in alternative energy, whether in solar or wind power, fuel-efficient cars, and ultimately "new jobs that pay well and can't be outsourced...[leading to a] cleaner, safer planet in the bargain."[37] Many hoped this green shift would signal the dawning of a "Green New Deal," a massive, government-backed, green jobs plan and environmental initiative; in short, a "green" version of FDR's New Deal project of the 1930s that put laborers back to work after the Great Depression of 1929.

Although the name "Green New Deal" may evoke images of full employment and environmental protection, any "Green New Deal" in our age of austerity would necessarily mean low-paying, unprotected, non-public-sector, green jobs. In fact, Obama himself pointed out that the majority of these jobs would be created in the private sector, and a recent report noted that low-paying, antiunion jobs were the norm in the current green economy.[38] The reality is that we are living in an age where we do not have the mass backing of powerful social movements that made the original New Deal a relatively bearable temporary economic model. Of course, one could argue that a "green job" is better than no job, and this is especially true for working-class communities who are suffering tremendously under the current economic crisis and system.[39] Yet, if we really want to build a sustainable, nonprecarious economic and environmental future for future generations, we need to take a long, hard look at the system that creates these endless cycles of precarity.

Moreover, the "green jobs" plan rests on a fundamentally jingoistic, capitalist, race-to-the-top competition against the supposed boogeyman, China. Thomas Friedman, the *New York Times* beloved liberal poster child and a chief intellectual architect of green capitalism, makes it his life's mission to sound the alarm bells of the creeping menace of a Chinese "Green Leap forward."[40] Even the progressive Green for All organization founded by Van Jones, who was appointed the "Special Advisor for Green Jobs" by Obama in 2009 before he was run out of the White House by a coalition of conservatives, is founded upon this chauvinistic, nationalist logic. As Jones notes, "'You can't take a building you want to weatherize, put it on a ship to China and then have them do it and send it back...we are going to have to put people to work in this country.'"[41] Ultimately these jingoist calls distract us from the real problem of capitalism.

Nevertheless, these calls weren't only heard in the United States. In 2008, UN Secretary General Ban Ki-moon called for a worldwide "Green New Deal" that would "revive the global economy while dealing simultaneously with the defining challenge of our era—climate change,"[42] while organizations like the Green Economy Coalition were formed to advance the expansion of a green (capitalist) economic model at the global level.[43] Ban Ki-moon was rather explicit about the class dynamics involved in a Green New Deal: "Again, a solution to poverty is also a solution for climate change: green growth. *For the world's poor, it is a key to development. For the rich, it is the way of the future.*"[44] The capitalists are eager and ready for this project, and they know big money will be involved. Pavan Sukhdev, the chair of the Global Market Center of Deutsche Bank, the same bank that is leading the European march to austerity and famously ordered the eviction of a 103-year-old woman and her 83-year-old daughter in Atlanta, Georgia, in 2011,[45]among other horror stories, claimed, "Hundreds of millions of jobs can be created, and there is no question that traditional industries like steel and cars cannot provide them... *this is a really huge business opportunity.*"[46]

Above all, even if we were to have a truly FDR-style Green New Deal, it is critical to understand that this does not fundamentally challenge the capitalist economic system that is the central problem. We should recall the late Howard Zinn's assessment of the 1930s New Deal:

> When the New Deal was over, capitalism remained intact. The rich still controlled the nation's wealth, as well as its laws, courts, police, newspapers, churches, colleges. Enough help had been given to enough people to make Roosevelt a hero to millions, but the same system that had brought depression and crisis—the system of waste, of inequality, of concern for profit over human need—remained.[47]

Fundamentally, the Green New Deal proposed by the green capitalists of the twenty-first century is a watered-down, Keynesian-flavored attempt to build the foundations for a neoliberal green economy. In so doing, it follows the privatization logic of austerity.

Only when we begin to recognize that the fundamental crisis is capitalism itself—that, as Benjamin warns, the "states of (economic) emergency" of 1929, 1982, and 2008 are "not the exception but the rule"—will we be able to address the heart of the environmental crisis. But this also means that, as Neil Smith writes, we need to think seriously about "what kind of social power it will take to democratize that production of nature."[48] We need to, as Vandana Shiva notes, "Abandon the centralized, fossilized, sclerotic model adopted (throughout) the industrial era and build a new model—a decentralized, democratic, horizontal model, where all ecosystems are respected and in which diversity is a value."[49] And as the indigenous peoples' Kari-Oca 2 Declaration states, "We need to fundamentally reorient production and consumption based on human needs rather than for the boundless accumulation of profit for a few."[50] We will only be able to achieve this when we build a unified, militant, worker, environmental, and social movement from below, one that includes self-management, direct and participatory democracy, and holistic social justice in its understanding of "green." This movement is certainly on the horizon. On February 12, 2013, Greek workers in the factory of Viomichaniki Metalleutiki in Thessaloniki, northern Greece, officially began to run their factory under control of the workers, meaning without bosses or hierarchy, functioning under directly democratic assemblies, and inspired by workers' occupations in Argentina and Chicago. Importantly, the workers have declared "they plan to move towards a production of these goods that is not harmful for the environment, and in a way that is not toxic or damaging."[51] Resisting in the European capital of the regime of austerity, these Greek workers realize that militant self-management and environmental and social justice are the only way forward.

As a Greek comrade and anarchist labor organizer once said, "We must destroy capitalism or it will destroy us." The task is clearer than ever: a revolutionary, antiauthoritarian, anticapitalist transnational movement is necessary to create "a real state of emergency" for (green) capitalism.[52]

ENDNOTES

1 For more, see Scott Crow, *Black Flags and Windmills: Hope, Anarchy and the Common Ground Collective* (Oakland, California: PM Press, 2011).

2   This is Ashley Dawson's summary of Bauman. See Ashley Dawson, "Climate Justice: The Emerging Movement against Green Capitalism," *South Atlantic Quarterly* 109, no. 2 (2010): 315. For more, see Zygmunt Bauman, *Wasted Lives: Modernity and Its Outcasts* (Cambridge, UK: Polity, 2004).

3   Stephen Nessen, "As Cold Snap Hits, Some Sandy Victims Still Lack Heat." *WNYC* online, Jan. 23, 2013.

4   Richard Smith, "Green Capitalism: The God that Failed," *Real-World Economics Review* 56, March 11, 2011: 115.

5   Stephen Leahy, "Can Capitalism Be Green?" *Common Dreams*, http://www.commondreams.org/archive/2007/05/12/1153 (accessed February 8, 2013).

6   Ashley Dawson, "Climate Justice," 315.

7   Rob Dixon, *Slow Violence and the Environmentalism of the Poor* (Cambridge, Mass.: Harvard University Press, 2011), 2.

8   Ibid., 4. See also Kevin Bale, *Disposable People: New Slavery in the Global Economy* (Berkeley: University of California Press, 1999).

9   Walter Benjamin, "Theses on the Philosophy of History" in *Selected Writings: 1938–1940, Volume 4* (Cambridge, Mass.: Harvard University Press, 2003), 392.

10   Richard Smith, "Green Capitalism," 112.

11   Neil Smith, "Nature as Accumulation Strategy," in *Socialist Register* 2006, 3.

12   Ted Steinberg. "Can Capitalism Save the Planet? On the Origins of Green Liberalism." *Radical History Review* 107 (Spring 2010): 8.

13   Ibid., 13.

14   Ibid., 14.

15   Ibid., 8.

16   Paul Sweezy, as quoted by Fred Magdoff and John Bellamy Foster, *What Every Environmentalist Needs to Know about Capitalism: A Citizen's Guide to Capitalism and the Environment* (New York: Monthly Review Press, 2011), 37.

17   Richard Smith, "Green Capitalism," 112.

18   Neil Smith, "Nature as Accumulation Strategy," 2.

19   For a good overview, see David Harvey, *A Brief History of Neoliberalism* (Oxford: Oxford University Press, 2005).

20   John Miller, "Ronald Reagan's Legacy," *Dollars & Sense: Real World Economics*, http://www.dollarsandsense.org/archives/2004/0704miller. html (accessed February 8, 2013).

21   For more on this overall process, see Benjamin Kohl and Linda C. Farthing, *Impasse in Bolivia: Neoliberal Hegemony and Popular Resistance* (London: Zed Books, 2008).

22   Robert Albro, "The Water is Ours, *Carajo*! Deep Citizenship in Bolivia's Water War," in *Social Movements: An Anthropological Reader*, (ed.) June C. Nash (Malden, MA: Blackwell Publishers, 2005), 249.

23   William Assies, "David versus Goliath in Cochabamba: Water Rights, Neoliberalism, and the Revival of Social Protest in Bolivia," *Latin American Perspectives* 30, no. 3 (May 2003): 15–17.

24   Ibid., 19.

25   Oscar Olivera, Tom Lewis, *Cochabamba!: Water War in Bolivia* (Cambridge, Mass.: South End, 2004), 9.

26   Jim Shultz, "Bolivia's Water Over War," *The Democracy Center*, http:// democracyctr.org/bolivia/investigations/bolivia-investigations-the-water-revolt/bolivias-war-over-water/bolivias-war-over-water-2/ (accessed February 8, 2013).

27   William Assies, "David versus Goliath in Cochabamba," 24.

28   Pratap Chatterjee, "Bechtel's Water Wars," *CorpWatch*, http://www. corpwatch.org/article.php?id=6670 (accessesd February 8, 2013).

29   William Assies, "David versus Goliath in Cochabamba," 30.

30   Polinizaciones, "Action Alert! Colombian Police Violently Remove Anti-dam Protesters," *Upside Down World*, http://upsidedownworld. org/main/news-briefs-archives-68/3460-action-alert-colombian-police-violently-remove-anti-dam-protestors- (accessed February 8, 2013).

31   Mary Durran, "Carbon Offsets Worsening a Human Rights Crisis in Lower Aguan, Honduras," *Canadian Catholic Organization for Development and Peace*, http://www.devp.org/en/blog/carbon-offsets-worsening-human-rights-crisis-lower-aguan-honduras (accessed February 8, 2013).

32 "Brazil: Local peoples defend biodiversity in Espíritu Santo," *World Rainforest Movement*, Bulletin No. 56, March 2002, http://www.wrm. org.uy/bulletin/56/Brazil.html (accessed February 8, 2013).

33 Michael Fox, "Landless Women Launch Protests Across Brazil," *North American Congress on Latin America*, http://nacla.org/node/5611 (accessed February 8, 2013).

34 "Cargill tied to violence in Sumatra?" *United Press International*, http:// www.upi.com/Business_News/Energy-Resources/2011/08/30/Cargill-tied-to-violence-in-Sumatra/UPI-61171314711081/ (accessed February 8, 2013).

35 Rob Dixon, *Slow Violence*, 2.

36 Ibid., 2–3.

37 Transcript of Obama's speech, http://edition.cnn.com/2009/POLITICS/01/08/obama.conference.transcript/index.html (accessed February 8, 2013).

38 "Obama releases more details about green stimulus plan," *Mother Nature Network*, http://www.mnn.com/earth-matters/politics/stories/obama-releases-more-details-about-green-stimulus-plan (accessed February 8, 2013). For a an overview on the current quality of green jobs, see "High or Low Road? Job Quality in the New Green Economy," http:// www.goodjobsfirst.org/sites/default/files/docs/pdf/gjfgreenjobsrpt.pdf (accessed February 8, 2013).

39 For an overview on the green jobs/good jobs argument, see Jeremy Brecher, "Can Green Jobs Be Good Jobs?" *The Nation*, http://www. thenation.com/article/can-green-jobs-be-good-jobs# (accessed February 8, 2013).

40 Thomas Friedman, "Who's Sleeping Now?" *New York Times*, http:// www.nytimes.com/2010/01/10/opinion/10friedman.html (accessed February 8, 2013).

41 As quoted by Thomas Friedman, "The Green-Collar Solution," *New York Times*, http://www.nytimes.com/2007/10/17/ opinion/17friedman.html?_r=2&ref=opinion&oref=slogin& (accessed February 8, 2013).

42 Ban Ki-moon, "Big Green Jobs Machine," *Project Syndicate*, http://www.project-syndicate.org/commentary/

big-green-jobs-machine#qSqD7PcRtURPxZJT.99 (accessed February 8, 2013).

43 For more, see www.greeneconomycoalition.org.

44 Ban Ki-moon, "Big Green Jobs Machine," my emphasis.

45 Fortunately, and in a rare move, police and movers refused to evict the elderly woman. See Candace Smith, "Police, Movers Refuse to Evict 103-Year-Old Woman," *ABC News*, http://abcnews.go.com/blogs/ headlines/2011/11/police-movers-refuse-to-evict-103-year-old-woman/ (accessed February 8, 2013).

46 Geoffrey Lean, "A 'Green New Deal' can save the world's economy," *The Independent (UK)*, http://www.independent.co.uk/environment/ green-living/a-green-new-deal-can-save-the-worlds-economy-says-un-958696.html (accessed February 8, 2013), my emphasis.

47 Howard Zinn, *A People's History of the United States* (New York: HarperCollins, 2005), 403.

48 Neil Smith, "Nature as Accumulation Strategy," 19.

49 Giuliano Battison, "'Green Economy': New Disguise for Global Capitalism's Old Tricks?" *Common Dreams*, https://www.commondreams. org/headline/2012/05/29-7 (accessed February 8, 2013).

50 Kari-Oca 2 Declaration, http://indigenous4motherearthrioplus20.org/ category/green-capitalism/ (accessed February 8, 2013).

51 "Occupied Greek Factory Beings Production Under Workers' Control," *Occupied London Blog*, http://blog.occupiedlondon. org/2013/02/11/occupied-greek-factory-begins-production-under-workers-control/ (accessed February 8, 2013).

52 Walter Benjamin, "Theses on the Philosophy of History," 392.

POLICING DISSENT AND COPPING A PROFIT

POLICE AND AUSTERITY IN THE UNITED STATES

ADAM QUINN

"As the fiscal conditions worsen and costs continue to escalate, many have articulated that America must learn how to
'do more with less.' However, when it comes to public safety...
this motto is simply not a viable option. Instead, law enforcement agencies must develop ways to do things *differently*."
—Department of Justice, *The Impact of the Economic Downturn on American Police Agencies*[1]

THIS CHAPTER WILL EXPLORE THE RELATIONSHIP BETWEEN POLICE
militarization, austerity during crisis, and the role of the police in
fighting "the movements against," specifically in the United States.
This militarization is best understood not just as a means to protect
austerity programs, but also as part of an austerity program itself.
The police protect revenue by containing dissent and generate revenue at the expense of those who are targeted as criminals. Though
recent trends in police militarization and repression show a unique
function of austerity during crisis, these same trends can also highlight the more general function of the police as institutionalized

guardians of capital rather than protectors of the public. Rather than using military-style units only in response to violent threats, militarized police forces have been used mostly against nonviolent crime, for acts as wide-ranging as serving warrants and suppressing peaceful protest. Police forces aren't just expanding in order to target a rise in crime rates which come with the rise of poverty rates; instead they play a critical role in criminalizing poverty and dissidence, which is necessary to supply revenue-generating prison labor, and legitimize themselves and the state.

Often, responses to police militarization limit themselves by only reacting to individual acts of police abuse of power, rather than targeting the unprecedented amount of power these abuses are founded upon. This chapter seeks to both contextualize these individual acts in a wider context of police as a political institution central to contemporary capitalism and to explain why these abuses seem to be on the rise. Finally, it will address how we might struggle against police power in a way that seeks to address and resolve institutional problems.

CONTEXTUALIZING
THE MILITARIZATION OF POLICE

SINCE THE BEGINNING of the global financial crisis, police forces throughout the world have become increasingly militarized, utilizing more military equipment, weapons, and tactics. This extreme militarization is only possible decades into the development of Special Weapons And Tactics (SWAT) teams, counterterrorism units, and the blurring of the lines between military and police. Take the history of the SWAT team, for example. Beginning in the 1960s in Los Angeles, in response to domestic terrorism and paramilitary threats, the SWAT team of old did serve a purpose in responding to violent crimes that patrol officers couldn't safely handle. Though still an example of the state's monopolization over the legitimate use of violence (e.g., the SWAT team was legitimate, while the Black Panthers they fought were not), this early SWAT team was only deployed for violent and life-threatening tasks. Over the next decade or so, there would be five hundred SWAT teams in the United States, and by the 1980s, 60 percent of US cities had a SWAT team. By 2000, nearly every US city had at least one SWAT team, and even 75 percent of small towns had one.[2]

Today, nearly all reaches of the US, and the globe, have highly armed, highly expensive police forces, many of which aren't located in areas with histories of violence. Now, in the midst of a global financial crisis where almost all public services are at risk of being cut, security remains one of the only expanding programs. Why is this militarization so unquestionably critical to the goals of the state and ruling class, and what relevance does it have to the current crisis?

In most public statements concerning this militarization, it is typically justified as a program of counterterrorism and domestic security. This chapter doesn't aim to disprove that these police forces are used for such purposes, but rather to highlight that the counterterrorism aspect of a militarized police force is not its only utility, and that militarization, crisis, and austerity are all inextricably linked. Security programs aimed at fighting terrorism and fighting crime, both violent and nonviolent, act as both national and global austerity programs and as defenses of austerity measures.

The current wars of the US and allies generate revenue for the richer nations and maintain economic and political dominance over poorer nations (while, like police, citing counterterrorism and security or peace concerns to justify their actions). Similarly, national and domestic security programs generate revenue for the state and the ruling class, while maintaining economic and political dominance over poorer people. That security generates revenue for the state is most infamously seen in the War on Drugs and the prison-industrial complex.

The analogy between the War on Terror and the War on Drugs is especially useful because of some ways in which both "wars" operate. Very specific marginalized groups are criminalized in these two wars (i.e., Muslims and young lower class black men, respectively). Localities where these groups are centered (e.g., the Middle East, and poor urban areas in the US) are where security, and, consequentially, repression are centered as well. This repression results in more political instability and violence, further justifying heightened, more militarized security, and in the securing of more revenue-generating forces of production (oil reserves or prison labor). Austerity-like programs that siphon resources from the poor go hand-in-hand with preventing resistance—each constantly giving way to more of the other.

FROM DOMINATION TO REPRESSION:
THE RECENT BEHAVIOR OF POLICE

THE RECENT BEHAVIOR of police has taken on some revealing forms, distinct from the business of usual behavior in the War on Drugs. Recent police repression of dissent and of movements against austerity highlights the police's function as guardians of capital and austerity, rather than protectors of the public. Rather than using military-style units only in response to violent threats, militarized police forces have been used mostly against nonviolent crime, including the suppression of peaceful protest. This is most noticeable at the sight of riot police, who, with helmets, shields, full body armor, gas masks, shotguns, armored vehicles, and state-of-the-art sound cannons and drones, often have more equipment than actual military infantry, purely for the task of repressing civil disobedience. This is not merely an example of a post-9/11 police force being more militarized in general, but rather is indicative of how the government views dissidence as a threat. In a recent Department of Defense training examination, for example, the answer to the question "Which of the following is an example of low-level terrorism?" was "Protests."[3] There is a revealing intentionality to every deployment of armed and armored units used to control street protests.

This distorted view of dissidence as terrorism is used to further justify the militarization of police forces. As one National Lawyer's Guild (NLG) report expressed, "In the lead-up to…conventions, the FBI, DHS, and local police departments frequently conflated anarchists with terrorists in an attempt to criminalize political ideology and create an atmosphere of fear around protests."[4] This criminalization of vague, amorphous categories like anarchism allows police to escalate their level of repression by escalating the imagined threat. As the NLG concludes, "The vilification of anarchists serves the dual purpose of justifying the government's strategies of police and state repression of protesters as well as the further militarization of police departments."[5] At once, police both target protests for repression and use them as a justification for further, more general militarization and repression.

These militarized police forces and their most well-armed units, however, do not limit themselves to responding to violent situations or controlling large protests. They conduct raids for all sorts of nonviolent suspicions to execute searches and arrests. Some recent cases have even cited search warrants for political books and pamphlets being served by fully armed FBI or SWAT teams.[6] Raids on activists and increased militarization and general police activity have taken police forces from street battles into our homes and minds.

Along with this institution-wide escalation in armament and force, rank-and-file police violence has been on the rise. Most notably, police have recently been responsible for countless shootings and killings, especially of unarmed people of color. Additionally, recent cases have shown police beating or tasing people who are already in their custody, in handcuffs or in the back of police vehicles. In locations with rising far-right movements, particularly outside the United States, on- and off-duty police often align themselves with fascist parties and groups, passionately engaging in combat with antiausterity protesters, leftists, and immigrants.[7] On the surface, these acts don't seem like they are fulfilling the police's institutional role of repressing dissent or protecting capital. Instead, they seem like acts of violence and coercion, often not ordered by higher-ups. How might we explain this rise of individual police violence?

The more overt purpose of such overuse of highly armed police units and their militaristic violence is that police are more desperately and more firmly enforcing the criminal justice system and the institutions it protects. In recent years, this means protecting austerity in moments of more intense poverty, threatening movements against, and safeguarding unstable political and economic systems. In order to enforce and protect these institutions and the people, summits, and organizations that represent them, police must make shows of force whenever there's any sort of threat. These shows of force also make further force seem more necessary—if danger is so apparently ever-present as to provoke these responses, then more armored police in more situations must be called for. This force becomes ever more apparently necessary to the individual police officers themselves, who expect to have to use their weapons and are therefore more inclined to, even in non-life-threatening circumstances.

Additionally, with police departments making cuts to some programs and ramping up others, in a time of economic instability and the changing face of policing, it's more efficient to employ undertrained police who might be more prone to mistakes and violence in the field. One study found two-thirds of police departments "reduced or discontinued training programs because of their limited budgets," while 22 percent of police departments shifted duties from sworn police officers to more affordable, less trained civilians, people who even respond to calls in the field on their own.[8] In a period of crisis, police are becoming both more necessary and more costly to the state, causing a decline in the professionalization of individual police forces in order to save costs, and a rise in the collective utilization of militarized equipment and actions to maintain order.

POLICING AS AUSTERITY

In an age of austerity, a militarized police force serves another purpose: being an austerity program itself. As already briefly discussed, after using police to identify and capture criminals, the state uses prison labor to generate revenue for both the state and the corporations that utilize such cheap, usually sub-minimum wage labor. From the 1980s until 2000, while SWAT teams went from few and far between to being a town necessity, the prison population quadrupled and the amount of people in prison on drug charges increased twelvefold.[9] The creation of an efficient and difficult to evade or resist militarized police state is paramount to the development and maintenance of such a large productive prison population. By fueling the prison population and using tax dollars to further militarize police forces, the police system is a double-edged sword of austerity.

The United States has the largest prison system in the world—despite only having 5 percent of the global population, it contains nearly a fourth of all prisoners in the world. This bloated system, which costs tens of billions to uphold, could be a top priority for government budget-slashers looking to reduce public spending. But it's not. With many state and federal prisons exceeding capacity, many states are trying to move prisoners out of state and federal prisons, for the benefit of private prison corporations and at the cost of county prisons. However, budget cuts are marginal when they occur. Instead of being a victim of austerity itself, what we see is the prison system adapting to facilitate further suction of wealth from the criminalized.

The statistical link between prison and austerity has, on the surface, become questionable or somewhat invisible during our current crisis, but upon further investigation, becomes clearer than ever. There have actually been nearly negligible decreases in correctional populations in state and federal prisons since the beginning of the crisis (a

1 to 2 percent decrease each year since 2008). However, this decrease has overwhelmingly been in the probational population (75 to 85 percent each year), with many state prison populations still on the rise.[10] While the correctional population is declining incredibly slowly, after decades of ever-increasing prison populations (from 1972 to 2008, there was an over 700 percent increase in the prison population), the ratio of prisoners to probationers is actually increasing.[11] Though there are several factors in the slight drop in the prison population, most of it is attributable to the fact that these statistics, though the most commonly referred to and most accessible, don't include county and private prison systems, which are taking over for the massively bloated state and federal prisons. In fact, most of the prison population decrease is actually attributable to a decline in California prisons, which, following a 2011 Supreme Court ruling that they had to reach 137 percent prison capacity by 2013, moved most of the state prison population to county facilities.[12]

These statistics leave out a critical piece of information: the number of inmates in for-profit prisons. This increase in prisoners over parolees is intentionally driven by for-profit prisons, as the Corrections Corporation of America said in 2010 to the Securities and Exchange Commission: "The demand for our facilities and services could be adversely affected by... leniency in conviction or parole standards and sentencing practices."[13] These private prison corporations pour tens of millions of dollars into lobbying. The result is that, while the amount of people in correctional facilities hasn't changed much since the start of the crisis, the amount of people in for-profit prisons has.

Prison austerity hasn't led to millions more in the correctional system, but it has led to millions more in prison for profit. Take Indiana, for example, a state with for-profit correctional facilities. From 2000 to 2010, Indiana's prison population skyrocketed by 47 percent. But in that same time period, its crime rate only dropped by 8 percent.[14] This increase is hardly unique to Indiana and is very attributable to privatization. As a 2008 article explains, despite private prisons being in only a few states, "Ten years ago there were only five private prisons in the country, with a population of 2,000 inmates; now, there are 100, with 62,000 inmates. It is expected that by the coming decade, the number will hit 360,000."[15] Between 2010 and 2011, as federal and state prison populations dropped slightly, there was a 14 percent increase in the private prison population.[16]

Though austerity programs within the prison system are most dramatically visible in for-profit prisons and are driven by privatization, publicly operated prisons still play an important role in generating revenue and reducing deficit. Prison labor is increasingly being used to replace work that would otherwise be done by public workers or contractors. Inmate labor reduces prison costs by, for example, having maintenance work done in their own prison, and it can also allow for the cutting of government jobs, as these workers work on public highways and water systems, in parks and graveyards, and so on. Many jails even have Inmate Labor Assistance Programs, where nonviolent offenders can pay to do work for nonprofits instead of staying in jail (which might account for much of the small, recent decrease in the prison population). It is important to note, as we examine the relationship between police, prison, and austerity, that prison labor doesn't just extract profit from the imprisoned, but it also replaces work that would otherwise be done by public employees.

In addition to supplying the prison-industrial complex, a militarized police force also generates revenue at the expense of taxpayers by consuming from the military-industrial complex, which has a close relationship with the research and development of federal police and armed forces. Though many local police departments have strained (though usually still increasing) budgets that don't leave much room for acquiring new equipment, this industry has been kept alive by federal programs. First, the Department of Homeland Security provides large grants to departments for the purchase of military grade equipment and vehicles, often providing hundreds of thousands of dollars for small towns to purchase armored vehicles. Also, since early on in the financial crisis, federal stimulus programs have provided grants ranging from hundreds of thousands to millions of dollars for SWAT weapons, armor, and vehicles for local police departments.[17]

CRIMINALIZATION AND RECESSION

Interestingly, and almost paradoxically, there is a correlation between police funding, prison funding, and prison populations, but not between these and the crime rate. Police aren't expanding in order to target a rise in crime rate accompanying the recession's rise in poverty rates; instead they play a critical role in criminalizing poverty and dissidence, in order to protect the revenue of the ruling class and generate revenue themselves, at the expense of the inmates.

To understand this process of criminalization, it must be stressed that prison inmates are not simply just anyone who broke the law. Police play a critical role in the criminalization of the marginalized and vulnerable, in order to feed the prison system. The poor, non-white, and mentally ill are all far more likely than anyone else to end up in prison, and not because they are so much more likely to be deserving of prison. These groups, who don't have much social or economic power, can be dehumanized through class elitism, racism, or ableism, seen to be parasitic or violent, or are simply unheard. Of course, targeting these groups both requires and contributes to their further marginalization, and has the clear purpose of making the status of prisoners more invisible or legitimated.

Race is probably the most visible disparity within the prison-industrial complex. Looking at state and federal prison populations, 3 percent of black men in the United States are imprisoned, and 1.2 percent of Hispanic men are imprisoned, while only 0.5 percent of white men are in jail or prison.[18] In private prisons, the racial disparity tends to be even greater. Simply put, far more black and Hispanic men are in prison in relation to their population than white men. As evidenced in racial profiling, which leads to increased searches, more stop-and-frisks, and a higher conviction rate of blacks and Hispanics, this racialized ratio is not the result of blacks or Hispanics being involved in more crime, but the result of these groups being targeted by police and by the criminal justice system. In an era of austerity, the black and Hispanic populations hold more public sector jobs, rely more on social welfare programs, and face far higher unemployment rates than the white population. This makes these groups especially vulnerable to police violence and criminalization. In 2013, the rate of police shootings of people of color is even now on the rise, compared with the already bloody 2012. While facing the worst of austerity, people of color face the greatest threat from police.

Likewise, the mentally ill are increasingly targeted and criminalized. A 2006 study by the Bureau of Justice Statistics found that more than half of all prison and jail inmates had mental health issues, a number which had quadrupled since 1998.[19] Meanwhile, under a third of the prisoners in the 2006 study with mental health issues had received treatment since their admission, ensuring a lack of rehabilitation that creates repeat offenders. The issue of mental health and prison has exploded recently, as state-funded hospitals for the mentally ill have been shut down. Today, the three largest mental facilities in the country aren't hospitals, but jails (specifically, Los Angeles County, Rikers, and Cook County Jail).[20] As cuts and austerity measures are implemented in mental health services, more people end up in prison. This is likely similar for other public institutions: as safety nets and social welfare programs are cut, more people can be funneled into prisons.

Though prisons are clearly a means of austerity themselves, the issue of prisons is incredibly far-reaching and interconnected with issues of political repression, white supremacy, corporate welfare, and public health. It would be difficult to address austerity, contemporary capitalism, and the politics of domination, marginalization, and oppression, without also addressing police and prisons.

HOW WE MIGHT RESPOND

OFTEN, RESPONSES TO police militarization take place only in relation to individual acts of police abuse of power. This approach is limited for a number of reasons. First, they typically can't sustain a movement. Though a small number of organizers might remain active in anti-mass-incarceration campaigns, typically such campaigns only experience small bursts when a particularly dramatic unjust beating, arrest, or sentence is carried out by the state. Both the everyday violence of police and the unprecedented amount of power these abuses are founded upon gets ignored, and for good reason: most people are aware of a lot of everyday police violence; they just don't see it as so problematic as to discredit police in general, and consider some of it to be a necessary and legitimate police activity.

This ties into one of the greatest challenges around organizing against police as an institution. Critiquing police is tricky when it's not about specific acts. While police enforce violent institutions like capitalism, and often commit acts of violence themselves, they also protect individuals from violence, defending people from physical and sexual assault, arson, and murder. Police enforce private property, which keeps workers separate from the means and products of their production, and keeps the rich and the poor. But they also enforce *personal* property, defending your home and person from theft. And, while police enforce many unjust or repressive laws and orders of the state, they also facilitate some beneficial public services (like emergency services, assisting in road work, and so on). Many of us have been harassed, beaten, arrested, and jailed by police, but many of us have also been assisted or even rescued by police.

So, in the face of critiques of police as an institution, many will just claim police officers as individuals are well intentioned or doing their best in a dangerous public service job that is necessary for our safety. Some critics of police would respond by saying that most police officers are authoritarian, racist, or violent individuals; "All Cops Are Bastards," as the saying goes. Whether or not there's truth to such claims doesn't really matter; going back and forth about the morality of individual police officers won't push us very far toward institutional justice for all. There's a more revealing question to ask besides that of whether or not police are bad people: do police have to enforce violent systems, in order to protect individuals from violence, enforce private property to protect personal property, and repress the public to provide public services?

The answer may depend on how you define police but, either way, the answer should suggest we don't need to live in a world where people with weapons, legal authority, and social power enforce systems of violence, inequality, and unfreedom. We can imagine a world where there are trained and committed people to call when you witness a fire or a car accident, but the performance of these activities doesn't legitimate an otherwise repressive institution. But how do we create this world?

We should be actively fighting against police violence and repression, and along with our anger, we should be asking ourselves what sorts of actions we can take to fill certain socially desirable aspects of police work. There are a number of actions people currently take to try to accomplish this goal, but clearly, as they have not yet succeeded, it's worth evaluating their effectiveness.

Many programs like Neighborhood Watch are limited for a number of reasons. First, such volunteer-run organizations lack accountability and can share so many of the same problems of police violence, as seen with the killing of unarmed seventeen-year old Trayvon Martin by neighborhood watch coordinator George Zimmerman. Neighborhood watch programs are limited by their adoption of many police attitudes and tactics, and they don't engage in radically alternative methods of dealing with conflict. Also, any reappropriation of current public service and defense roles can't be accomplished on a volunteer basis without extensive community support and funding, so organizations like Neighborhood Watch tend to be supported mostly by police. They tend to organize with and for the police, and are trained to watch for and report crime, rather than to deal with it within communities in a grassroots, nonviolent manner.

There are programs like Copwatch, through which people watch and film police to either ensure abuses don't happen or to provide accountability for such abuses. While the importance of such initiatives cannot be understated, they won't be the end-all to policing as an institution, considering they don't replace the provision of public services and safety. Some local Copwatch programs have extended their goals and actions to address issues of police and police violence through web media, discussions, and events. While this is no doubt effective and worthwhile, it may still lack the collective push necessary to create lasting change. Even after awareness is raised and we meet some public needs of safety and service with horizontal, grassroots organizations, collective direct action will need to be sparked, in order to bring our efforts from building solidarity within our communities to replacing the oppressive institutions of our society more broadly.

With enough organizing to raise awareness of police issues and build solidarity, and with enough of our communities ready to offer an alternative to policing when moments of opportunity arise, we might be prepared to respond effectively to such rifts when they come up. A prefigurative political praxis of security, safety, and public service will need to be executed on a smaller scale, ready for when further spaces open up for resistance. Through this process, we will learn more about what we can do and how we can live.

CONCLUSION

In many ways, which might not be clear until we look back years from now, police repression is changing during our era of crisis and austerity. However, we can see several ways in which police protect and create austerity and capital, which is related to so many of our contemporary problems. This chapter was unable to cover many of these issues, including, for example, immigration and austerity. Though it also funds militarized police departments, Homeland Security's greatest budget increase in 2013 is for a globally unprecedented expenditure on border control. The border is becoming militarized by federal and state police, who utilize everything from drones to armored vehicles. Thousands of immigrants are being thrown into detention centers, and immigration reform is coming to the forefront of mainstream American political discourse. This militarization plays an important role in shaping the daily lives of millions in border regions and the futures of millions of undocumented immigrants.

In order to effectively combat police repression, we need to raise awareness of how it is connected to issues we face in our daily lives, like race, class, and, in our era of crisis, austerity. We need to link up our broader movements against racism, imperialism, globalization, borders, austerity, and so on, with movements against policing, because police enforce and reinforce these systems of domination and control. We can make all of our movements stronger by providing mutual aid networks of protection, safety, and conflict resolution. Such networks can make our own communities of resistance safer and more inclusive, alleviate the problems faced by millions of victims of the criminal justice system, and allow the state to repress dissent less effectively.

ENDNOTES

1   United States Department of Justice, "The Impact of the Economic Downturn on American Police Agencies," *United States Department of Justice*, www.cops.usdoj.gov/files/RIC/Publications/e101113406_Economic%20Impact.pdf (accessed April 30, 2013).

2   Radley Balko, "ACLU Launches Nationwide Police Militarization Investigation," *The Huffington Post*, http://www.huffingtonpost.com/2013/03/06/aclu-police-militarization-swat_n_2813334.html (accessed May 3, 2013).

3   "Pentagon Exam Calls Protests 'Low-Level Terrorism,' Angering Activists," *Fox News*, http://www.foxnews.com/story/0,2933,526972,00.html (accessed May 3, 2013).

4   National Lawyers Guild, "Developments in the Policing of National Special Security Events: An Analysis of the 2012 RNC and DNC," *National Lawyers Guild*, http://www.nlg.org/developments-policing-national-special-security-events-analysis-2012-rnc-and-dnc (accessed May 3, 2013).

5   Ibid.

6   Will Potter, "FBI Agents Raid Homes in Search of 'Anarchist Litera-
     ture,'" *Green is the New Red*, http://www.greenisthenewred.com/blog/
     fbi-raid-anarchist-literature-portland-seattle/6267/ (accessed May 3,
     2013).

7   For one particularly chilling example, see this report on fascist-affili-
     ated Greek police torturing antifascist protesters: Maria Margaronis,
     "Greek Anti-fascist Protesters 'Tortured by Police' after Golden Dawn
     Clash," *The Guardian*, http://www.guardian.co.uk/world/2012/oct/09/
     greek-antifascist-protesters-torture-police (accessed June 22, 2013).

8   United States Department of Justice. "The Impact of the Economic
     Downturn on American Police Agencies," 20.

9   Human Rights Watch, "Incarcerated America," *Human Rights Watch*,
     www.hrw.org/legacy/backgrounder/usa/incarceration/us042903.pdf
     (accessed May 1, 2013).

10   US Bureau of Justice Statistics, "Bureau of Justice Statistics (BJS)—
     National Prisoner Statistics (NPS)," *Bureau of Justice Statistics* (BJS),
     http://bjs.gov/index.cfm?ty=dcdetail&iid=269 (accessed May 3, 2013).

11   "Prison Count 2010," *PEW Center*, www.pewtrusts.org/uploadedFiles/
     wwwpewtrustsorg/Reports/sentencing_and_corrections/Prison_
     Count_2010.pdf (accessed April 30, 2013).

12   E. Ann Carson and William Sabol, "Prisoners in 2011," *United States
     Department of Justice*, bjs.gov/content/pub/pdf/p11.pdf (accessed May
     1, 2013).

13   American Civil Liberties Union, "Private Prisons," *American Civil
     Liberties Union* (ACLU), http://www.aclu.org/prisoners-rights/private-
     prisons (accessed May 3, 2013).

14   "Indiana Overview," *Justice Reinvestment*, http://justicereinvestment.
     org/states/indiana (accessed May 3, 2013).

15   Vicky Pelaez, "The Prison Industry in the United States: Big Busi-
     ness or a New Form of Slavery?" *Global Research*, http://www.global-
     research.ca/the-prison-industry-in-the-united-states-big-business-or-a-
     new-form-of-slavery/8289 (accessed May 3, 2013).

16   Carson and Sabol, "Prisoners in 2011."

17 Radley Balko, "A Decade After 9/11, Police Departments Are Increasingly Militarized," *The Huffington Post*, http://www.huffingtonpost.com/2011/09/12/police-militarization-9-11-september-11_n_955508.html (accessed May 3, 2013).

18 Carson and Sabol, "Prisoners in 2011."

19 Doris James and Lauren Glaze, "Mental Health Problems of Prison and Jail Inmates," *Bureau of Justice Statistics*, bjs.gov/content/pub/pdf/mhppji.pdf (accessed May 12, 2013).

20 United Press International, "Jails Are Top Mental Health Institutions." *UPI*, http://www.upi.com/Health_News/2010/07/12/Jails-are-top-mental-health-institutions/UPI-27621278982109/ (accessed May 13, 2013).

DIMENSIONS OF CRISIS IN GREECE

CHRIS SPANNOS

AN INTRODUCTION TO THE MULTIDIMENSIONS OF CRISIS

EVERY *CRISIS OF CAPITALISM* IS BORN FROM *CAPITALISM THE CRISIS*. BUT this hereditary relationship is often assumed to be separate rather than inherent. Questioning capitalism's continued existence is overwhelmingly beyond the pale and so—for many—unthinkable. Capitalism is assumed, not perceived. It is assumed to be from some origin outside ourselves. Its origins do not require proof, like Immaculate Conception—*it just is*. For others, it may be understood as a natural law of history or the highest expression of human nature and evolution. Out of such conceptions of capitalism grow a one-dimensional understanding of our present period as a period of capitalism in crisis: crises are part of the natural order of things; capitalism suffers crises just as we may suffer floods or earthquakes. Rather than exposing the patterns and organization of capitalism, such a conception hides its structure from systemic interrogation.

A multidimensional understanding sees that capitalism *is itself a crisis*. Capitalism—as a system of institutional components facilitating production, consumption and allocation, that together comprises the type of economy we have—is itself part of a larger societal apparatus and *is the problem*. This view holds that—rather than being the product of divine intervention or some other external force—capitalism, and in fact all society, is a human-made, social-historical creation. And so it follows from this that capitalism is just one way to organize an economy. This view accepts the possibility that society and its institutions can be self-consciously reorganized for different—better—outcomes. Rather than seeing crisis only when "growth," profits, and power are negatively affected, this view knows that people experience crisis in every moment of their daily lives. There is an understanding that too many of us have no control over where we live, how well we live, over what we create and produce, or the decisions that overwhelmingly affect our lives; and, unless collective action is taken, are condemned to live an existence of alienation in service to the interests of others; interests different and often antithetical or contradictory to our own.

By counterpoising the above two views, between one- and multi-dimensional analysis, I have provided an oversimplification of a complex society. Society does not only consist of institutions that govern how we make, use, and distribute the material means of life. We are cultural beings who live in community with others, and mark and celebrate life in diversely colorful ways together. We form intimate relationships, are raised in families, and some of us choose to create our own sorts of families too. We learn, create, imagine. We do all this on a planet with finite material resources, which we exploit irrationally and unfairly. We are born into countries with already established political systems and roles for elites who make decisions in our name, feeding lies to obliging corporate media, alienating us from meaningful political engagement, while giving us the "opportunity" to vote for one or the same party or representative once every few years. Those of us who are not consigned to the economic periphery enjoy lifestyles unfathomable to the families of those who may have been buried alive working in exploitative conditions while sewing the fabric we are comfortably wearing now.

Focusing on the economy, the one-dimensional versus multidimensional simplification is made to illustrate how different takes on capitalism can help us understand an aspect of our world and time. The one-dimensional view narrowly defines economic and financial crisis as negatively affecting profits and power. The multidimensional view shows us that crisis is embedded into the "genetic" structure of capitalism's defining institutions: private ownership of productive assets, hierarchical divisions of labor, markets, and remuneration based on luck and bargaining power. This view allows us to measure our present society against past and future possible alternatives. Because of this, we can imagine that other building blocks for other types of economy are not only desirable, but also possible; even, as the title of this book suggests, necessary for the future of our survival; and that the self-conscious creation of these structures could be not only vastly better than today, but under peoples' direct self-governing control.

Continuing this line of thought opens many other doors to understanding social and material crisis. Yet the one-dimensional understanding dominates as the established worldview, putting a multidimensional understanding beyond the boundary of acceptable thought and action. This one-dimensional view takes the form and content of world events for the purpose of reproducing ruling relations. Acceptable boundaries are partly formed through socialization and education. But on leaving school classrooms, the apparatus of mass media supplies knowledge, information, news, and publicizes as *ordinary* very specific beliefs, values, and attitudes. In this way, media is one of the primary forms through which the process of ideological legitimization of established society occurs.[1] The media play the role of mediators between powerful entities such as governments and corporations and, through public discourse, the rest of us. The media provides the everyday platform from which the discourse over the unperceived global crisis of capitalism takes place, and through which movements against social and material crisis are mediated.

Events in Greece have received special attention from the media over the last few years, as the global financial crisis has unfolded. Greece occupies a special position among a bloc of countries interlocked in the European Union, and a smaller group of countries within them (Spain, Portugal, Ireland, Italy) that together threaten the stability of the Eurozone. Greece is struggling today against becoming a failed state and accepting "handouts" from other European countries; but for years, Greece accepted its role within the Eurozone, running trade deficits as Germany ran trade surpluses. At the same time, the Greek state's monopoly on violence is faltering. Its public legitimacy is in deep doubt.

Even prior to the sovereign debt crisis reaching Greece, in December 2008, the media made a clear effort to limit the social and historical consequences of the Greek uprising, which was sparked by the police murder of the young student Alexandros Grigoropoulos. The rebellion was a radical moment and was one of the first among many important uprisings that have happened since and have characterized the early twenty-first century. What makes Greece interesting—aside from its position in the global economy—is that the Greek rebellion contained an explicitly revolutionary content and character that reverberates today.[2] In addition to its role in the global financial crisis, Greece offers an example of how the forces of power and control sought to socially regulate this historic uprising's impact.

ONE-DIMENSIONAL GREECE

In its search for explanations of the global capitalist crisis, the one-dimensional view falls short of considering how patterns and structures of global power may be the source of the problem. Instead, a scapegoat must be found. The media have created and refined negative perceptions of Greece to fit established explanations. Greece has been transformed in the global imagination from its old static position as a "cradle of western civilization" into a new negative signifier.

In his 2009–2010 study, "At the Eye of the Cyclone: The Greek Crisis in Global Media," Andreas Antoniades found that Greece evolved from being the focus of criticism to being a negative reference point.[3] Greece, he wrote, was portrayed as the corrupted Other of the rational western society. As the corrupted Other, western media portrayed Greeks as lazy and morally offside—contributing to Greece's sovereign debt crisis. Despite the Organization for Economic Cooperation and Development's (OECD) report stating that Greeks are some of the hardest-working people in Europe and the world, the media produced a seemingly endless fountain of negative tropes to reinforce this view.[4] Greeks were described as having a "lack of credibility" and embodying "irresponsibility."[5] News media repeated allegations that hard working northern Europeans were made to pay for the laziness of those who take siestas in the South. Yet, statistics from the OECD also tell us that, taking into consideration hours worked, the real retirement age of workers in Greece is later than in Germany.[6]

While continental European media reported negatively about Greece in 40 percent of its coverage during the period in question, Antoniades's found that Anglo-Saxon press, such as the *Times of London* and the *New York Times*, were the most negative, with the latter far out weighing the former. Almost 70 percent of *New York*

Times coverage was excessively negative. The *New York Times* applied negative references to Greece by using words and descriptions that included "Greek style financial crisis," "profligacy," "precarious economy," "Greece of the North," "Athenian affinity for deficits and debt," "Greece as the world's worst performer," "Tax evasion as a national pastime," "The transit system in New York has turned into Greece: dead broke," "we are not Greece," and so on.[7]

US media juxtaposes itself with European media by covering Greece as a European problem and by criticizing the inability of the European Union, its institutions, and its member states to take effective action to resolve the crisis. Their representation of the Greek crisis has centered on the notion of "containment," so that Greece's "disease," if it can't be cured, does not spread to the rest of the highly indebted and fiscally unstable peripheral Eurozone countries of Portugal, Italy, Ireland, and Spain (PIIGS). Therefore, as the derogatory comments go, Greece is the *new* "sick man of Europe."[8]

We should ask: but what is this "disease" exactly? Is the disease what prompted the widely reported 2009 admission by former Greek minister George Papandreou that the "Greek economy is in intensive care?" Since Papandreou made this statement, Greece's jobless rate has almost tripled, to 27.2 percent (January 2013). At the time of this writing in May 2013, youth unemployment has skyrocketed to 59.3 percent among youth aged between 15 and 24. Yet the Greek government continues to force austerity on its people as the drug to cure the illusive "illness." By instituting policies that force people to pay in this way, Papandreou thus revealed a one-dimensional belief in the role of people to fulfill "our" objectives to work towards continued growth of power and privilege for elites. This is the meaning of the "disease" that the ruling media say must be "contained," so that it does not affect the wealth and power of other Eurozone elites, and likewise so that protests and rebellions do not spread. And this is why austerity as a solution to the crisis of capitalism is focused not on raising revenues from those profiteering, but on cutting jobs, wages, and social benefits—and with disastrous human consequences.

But does the proposal of economic austerity, as the established solution to the global crisis of capitalism and the spectacular pauperization of people and whole countries, not also serve to reproduce the very forces that perpetuate and make this problem worse? Austerity accelerates privatization of society and individuals, which in turn tears apart the social and material fabric of everyday life. In his seminal text, *Modern Capitalism and Revolution*, the Greek French philosopher, Cornelius Castoriadis, wrote that *privatization is one of the most striking features of modern capitalism* because it destroys the collective social relations that are the basis for people coming together to solve the important problems of the day. It depoliticizes. It drives society to provide private rather than public solutions, and pressures people to act alone in a spiral away from others.[9]

Were Castoriadis writing today, we would no doubt interpret his words as insightful commentary on our present period. But he is not writing today. He was writing in 1959, during the postwar economic boom that is widely accepted as the "Golden Age of Capitalism," a period of economic prosperity lasting into the 1970s. This implies that *even at the best of times*, capitalism is a system of barbarism. But times have changed since Castoriadis made his prescient observation: we now live in the worst social and material crisis since the Great Depression and, at the time of this writing, with no end in sight.

If austerity were featured in a movie, it might darken the sky like the crows before they swooped down to terrorize people in Alfred Hitchcock's *The Birds*. By legitimizing austerity, the media help eclipse the search for the true structural causes of crisis. They tell the European economic austerity story from the point of view of markets, investors, lenders (who are often also the main sources for news), and the governments who, we are told, have to make "difficult decisions." The populations of these countries and their austerity-induced pain are buried.[10] Media reports obscure their underlying partiality toward markets that "shuddered" in response to protests or the political instability that "startled" investors, never mind that austerity on top of economic crisis is like "bleeding a patient to death."[11]

Exceptions in one-dimensional media reporting provide the illusion of objectivity and balance. While editors and institutional pressures set established boundaries on what is covered and how it is covered, multidimensional exceptions take different forms. Sometimes the conditions of social and material crisis can deteriorate so far for people that the dominant narrative opens windows for critical perspectives to pass through. But these windows are not always guaranteed to open. They are usually momentary and close quickly—unless events force them to open wider and for longer periods of time.

During Occupy Wall Street (OWS), both national and local media in the US seemed to have placed a de facto embargo on their coverage of the movement, including the *New York Times*, even though OWS was occurring right in its backyard.[12] The embargo persisted until police teargassed and arrested protestors en masse on the Brooklyn Bridge. This ended the blackout, as the movement, and police conduct relating to it, forced its way into the international spotlight. In this moment, mass apathy was shaking off its big sleep and OWS finally caught up with the European squares movement and "Arab Spring" uprisings in North Africa and the Middle East—even if ruling media flipped the script to tell the story the other way around, with headlines declaring "Occupy Wall Street Goes Global."[13]

OWS momentum spread across the US and pushed the boundaries of acceptable thought and action. For the first time in decades, capitalism was suddenly no longer assumed but perceived; and in that recognition of capitalism as a form, as a distinctive system, our economic system could be called by its name, "capitalism." Names are labels for things. Capitalism became a tangible thing, rather than an assumption used to rationalize how unjust life has been, currently is, and always will be. Things can be replaced, improved, discarded. Suddenly room for new conversation and organization seemed to have broadened. Yet, the genie was eventually violently put back into the bottle, though not securely and not for good. Repressive forces evicted the occupations, but their ideas still live on; as does the possibility for deepening our understanding of systemic problems.

Since global economic turmoil still persists, there continue to be windows of opportunity for critical perspectives. Even during times of "business as usual," exceptions are occasionally built into the structure of dominant media institutions to add to their "credibility" as "balanced" and "objective" providers of "information" and analysis. The world's most powerful newspaper, the *New York Times*, can portray itself as "balanced" by surrounding their Nobel Prize-winning neo-Keynesian economist Paul Krugman with pundits and journalists who know very little about economics, yet praise the authority of capitalists, managers, and markets over people. By hosting minority voices critical of austerity, one-dimensional media institutions are able to maintain the acceptable boundaries of thought.

In times of steady, profitable growth for capitalists, the acceptable boundaries for what is newsworthy, and how events deemed newsworthy are reported, are narrower. This occurs not through some conspiracy of our news media or surreptitious policing of news desks, but because of institutional boundaries that protect the interests of those in profit and power within our society. Boundaries are learned through the internalization of values reinforced by society's dominant institutions and their outcomes. Our education system, for example, breeds obedience and conformity; individualism, competition, and careerism help delimit boundaries of acceptable modes of questioning and options for behavior. Such values naturally oblige and are profusely expressed by those who travel on the assembly line of our higher education system and attain the few available jobs in news media.

MEDIATING THE SOCIAL-HISTORICAL MOMENT OF THE 2008 GREEK REBELLION

IF THE ONE-DIMENSIONAL view of economic crisis looks at Greece from the top down and is overwhelmingly concerned with reproducing ruling relations, then the multidimensional view sees the crisis from the bottom up and is concerned with the structural transformation of those relations. The problem is that the ruling relations that dominate existing society are capable of containing the forces that have the capacity to break containment. These tendencies are in opposition. As Herbert Marcuse observed in his classic text, *One-Dimensional Man*, ruling relations dominate by using whatever preconditions exist to prevent a reversal.[14] But occasionally the forces, as the Greek uprising did in December 2008, break through containment to explode society.

By using critical discourse analysis, linking language and power, researchers have shown how the media "managed" the December events. The media practiced the art of "mediation," selecting and moving the meaning of events or texts to another signification so that over time the original sense is lost or transformed, and replaced with an altogether new meaning and purpose that serves ruling interests. In his study, "'Greek December' In Political and Media Discourse," George Polymeneas examines the linguistic features of political and media representation of the December events by analyzing three parliamentary addresses delivered by then-Prime Minister Kostas Karamanlis and how newspapers reported on his speeches.[15] Polymeneas argues that the media deliberately attempted to limit the social-historical consequences of the uprising, despite—or perhaps because of—its radical character.

The process through which we represent any events or information—whether as individuals casually conversing, authors writing carefully crafted book chapters, or mass media producing news and information—generally include the three methods of (1) direct quotation, (2) summarizing, and (3) interpretation. Polymeneas explores how Greek newspapers applied these methods of representation to Karamanlis's speeches and how the uprising was subsequently mediated. Through linguistic analysis, Polymeneas found a correlation between the language Karamanlis used and, perhaps unsurprisingly, his ideological interest in serving his political party's goals. The data showed that the Prime Minister's dual intention was to focus on the "riots" and property destruction, while also downplaying the police murder of the young Alexandros Grigoropoulos, and the massive street mobilizations and occupations that followed in its wake. Karamanlis did this by equating mobilizations in the streets with "riots," and juxtaposing those "extremists," whose motive is "violence" and destruction, with "citizens" and their "property." This can be seen in three samples from one of Prime Minister's speeches:

1. "Their acts were against innocent citizens and their properties. And, hence, they were against the entire society."

2. "The duty of the government—of any government—is the protection of society as a whole."

3. "In these critical hours the challenge is clear-cut: We have to shield democracy against the violence of the extremists. This is why the duty of each one of us at the moment is national unity."[16]

Depending on their political orientation, the press represented Karamanlis's views by using the three methods of direct quotation of the Prime Minister's speech, summarizing of his views, or interpretation—each for their own political interests to agree, disagree, or manipulate. But the overall outcome, as Polymeneas observes, was an "ideological 'narrowing' of 'December's' potential impact and implications…" This was achieved first by filtering events through a broad generic frame, and then using a narrower frame, limited to government policy and efficiency. The final stage of extracting the uprising's radical content came when the press and Prime Minister reached a consensus that the problem was "government vs. the other political parties," which, as Polymeneas explains, was first proposed by the press and then adopted by Karamanlis in his third speech.

By examining the process of how one-dimensional media mediate events in the process of setting acceptable boundaries of thought and action, we have moved away from looking at the subjects rising up. This is because most news is one-dimensional; it is not about actual events, but about what powerful institutions and people have to say about how other powerful people and institutions are affected.

BEYOND THE BOUNDARY: TRAVERSING THE PASSAGE TO AUTONOMOUS THOUGHT AND ACTION

DISCUSSING THE MEDIA's interpretation of the so-called *crisis of capitalism* versus *capitalism the crisis*—one-dimensional versus multidimensional representation respectively—is important, as I have argued above, because the media is one of the primary filters through which we learn about and come to perceive local, national, and global events and, so, our reality. It is mostly through the media that the public learns about the global governance and economics deemed fit to report. For most of us, our relation to the media is similar to our relation to any other means of production—dispossessed, and without control over its form, content, or whose interest it serves. As the media itself is also a means of production, some of the things it produces—aside from material objects (such as all its mediums of delivery: computers, mobile devices, newspapers, TVs, radios, magazines, and offices, which imply mining, construction, deforestation, transportation, etc.)—are *significations as the representation and meaning of reality*. This applies even—and especially—to the media's omissions of events (as though they never occurred) and interpretations of the events it does report on.

Significations provide meaning. However, after being filtered and refined, through a process of mediation, they encompass a new *totality* of social and material relations reflected back to us, which help define our role as participants in society. What is reflected back to us is not the world as it is, but the world as those in positions of profit and power want it perceived; the media is part of an apparatus of meaning shaped to serve interests other than our own; and this compels us to embrace its meaning *for the reproduction of itself.*

It is important to note the blurry distinction; namely, that what is reflected back to us *is and is not* reality. What we do in every moment of our lives (at home, at school, at work, in our community, in our personal relationships) is arguably more our "reality" than any data about our lives reflected back to us in advertising, music, movies, newspapers, or on social networking sites, TV, or radio—even if media now penetrate more deeply than ever into the private sphere. But it is not enough to say that we both shape and are shaped by our media; or, put another way, *that we shape and are shaped by our social and material world.* We are also *self-conscious beings*, who shape and are shaped by other self-conscious beings and, beyond that, because of our self-consciousness, have the capacity to *shape ourselves.* The media, as a central processor of reality, is only one component of how our world is actually shaped. But those who own and control this *means of meaning production* are far more powerful than us at disseminating their messages and shaping context.

Despite the Greek government and media's power to delimit the historical impact of the Greek December, it burst asunder the established boundaries of thought and action. It is undeniable that the spectacular images of Athens on fire, with banks burning intensely, engulfed in flames and billowing black clouds of smoke, were characteristic of these events and caught the media's attention. The Greek government and media, as we analyzed in the previous section, deliberately sought to downplay other more important features: the murder of Grigoropoulos, mass demonstrations in the streets, numerous occupations, and reasons that people gave for their actions. Greek Prime Minister Kostas Karamanlis, along with the press, sought to depoliticize the events and appeal to "citizens" by striking chords of concern about destruction of private property.

Even though the government and media sought to recuperate the December events, placing them back into the established narrative, there are facts of everyday life that we all know. Everybody knows that our lives are becoming more precarious. We all understand that, if we are not already surviving at subsistence level, we are only one or two paychecks away from falling short of meeting our basic needs; that it is hard, and getting ever harder, to endure this existence. We must have debt to survive, but those who are unable to obtain debt are excluded from living under decent material conditions; those who are able to obtain debt must then shovel themselves out—through years of labor—from their own debt graves. Everybody knows that it hurts to be in a position of need and also that it is humiliating to ask for help. Everybody knows that things are getting worse.

Government and the media are blind to how capitalism destroys people's lives. In Greece, they use destruction of private property to cover over the underlying reality that no amount of banks burned to the ground or property destroyed during the 2008 uprising—or since—can compare to the amount of private property capitalism has cannibalistically destroyed. In 2011, the Greek paper *Kathimerini* reported that more than 68,000 small businesses had shut down by September of that year.[17] By September 2012, *Reuters* reported that a third of the shops in Athens's city center had been shut down.[18] As of April 2013, the National Confederation of Greek Commerce reported "an unprecedented 150,000 small and medium-sized businesses have closed."[19]

Just as the media's one-dimensional view of crisis is unable to reveal the ravishing forces of capitalism as a system, so too is it unable to see the superlative forces of collective action, *when those taking action are contestants in the struggle against established boundaries.* This is because these movements are attempting to institute their own actions, ideas, and meaning. Viewed this way, *they are agents of signification*—themselves constituents, antagonists, bystanders, or observers—actively engaged in the production and maintenance of meaning for themselves and others.[20]

While mass media regulation of these movements aims to portray it as irrational or without purpose, collective action can sometimes break free from society's dominant logic and institutions by putting into motion its own self-conscious actions, relations, and behaviors. To outside observers, these motions may not make much sense. But when these acts of self-creation do occur, they are acts of autonomy: *the self-conscious creation of new social relations and institutions.*

By the third week of the 2008 December revolt, reports claimed that students were occupying approximately eight hundred high schools and two hundred university departments across Greece. It was not possible for the media to understand the radical content of the events because the participants' own frame, as frame analysis applied to collective action suggests, included their own meaning and objectives, which were radically different.[21] The "Liberated City Hall of Aghios Dimitrios" serves as a good example. The communiqué declared:

> Within the frame of this insurrection, the City Hall of Aghios Dimitrios has been occupied since the morning of Thursday Dec. 11, so that it may become a place of counter-information, meeting, and self-organizing of the residents of the wider region and for the collective formation and implementation of actions. A main component of this occupation is the daily popular assembly with participation of up to 300 people, a process that functions in contrast to the entrusting of the management of our demands as well as of our struggles to whichever "representatives," elected or not. A process that tends to be implanted deeply into the consciousness of its participants [in] their role as political beings.

This communiqué provides a window through which we can view the radical character of the Greek uprising, one that media had to shut out because it was part of a deep and wide struggle against the established order that carried with it, however disjointed, demands for a new society. This struggle continues today—ebbing and flowing—and has created more than five hundred experiments in autonomous social institutions since 2008. These experiments include social centers; social clinics and kitchens; pirate radio; and efforts at workers' self-management, like Vio.Me., the mineral factory now under direct-democratic workers' control in Thessaloniki, Greece's second largest city. The established order is attempting to repressively contain many of these efforts by evicting squats and shutting down radical media. Mass media continue to mediate the movement on and off the street. But this contestation is far from over.

CONCLUSION

THOSE WHO VIEW capitalism in crisis through a one-dimensional framework see only how crisis negatively affects power and privilege.

Even while profits for large corporations increase during the "crisis," austerity is imposed to squeeze ever more from the disenfranchised. Those with a multidimensional view of crisis see that the very structure of capitalism *is the crisis* and that it negatively impacts upon every moment of our lives. By assessing the *multidimensional totality of crisis*, we can see that society as a whole—its very fabric and organization, that which binds it all together, its meanings, objectives, social roles and relationships, and the process of socialization—is being destroyed.[22] This view calls for radical imagination and the self-conscious creation of new, established boundaries for thought and action.

ENDNOTES

1   Norman Fairclough, *Language and Globalization* (New York: Routledge, 2006).

2   Chris Spannos, "Greek Uprising, Echoes of Castoriadis: 1968, Autonomy & the Self-Managed Society," *ZNet*, http://www.zcommunications. org/greek-uprising-echoes-of-castoriadis-1968-autonomy-and-the-self-managed-society-by-chris-spannos (accessed May 9, 2013).

3   Andreas Antoniades, "At the Eye of the Cyclone: The Greek Crisis in Global Media," Working Paper (Athens: ACIPE, 2012).

4   OECD data shows that this has been true for more than a decade. See OECD.StatExtracts, "Average annual hours actually worked per worker," OECD website, http://stats.oecd.org/Index.aspx?QueryId=10162 (accessed May 9, 2013).

5   Antoniades, "At the Eye," 2012.

6   Alex Andreou, "Exploding the myth of the feckless, lazy Greeks," *NewStatesman*, http://www.newstatesman.com/blogs/world-affairs/2012/05/exploding-myth-feckless-lazy-greeks (accessed May 9, 2013).

7   Antoniades, "At the Eye," 2012.

8   Steven Panageotou, "A Critical Literature Review of the Greek Financial Crisis" (Globalization and Social Theory, 2011) Academia.edu website, http://www.academia.edu/1048480/A_Critical_Literature_Review_of_the_Greek_Financial_Crisis (accessed May 9, 2013).

9   Cornelius Castoriadis, under the pseudonym "Paul Cardan," *Modern Capitalism and Revolution* (Socialisme ou Barbarie, 1960–61) Translated into English by Christopher Agamemnon Pallis, under the pseudonym "Maurice Brinton" (London Solidarity, 1965).

10 Chris Spannos, "Europe's Protests: The Times' False Impartiality Toward Markets & Austerity," *NYT eXaminer*, http://www.nytexaminer. com/2012/09/europes-protests-the-times-false-impartiality-toward-markets-austerity (accessed May 9, 2013).

11 This analogy of "bleeding the patient to death" has been made by the economist William Black.

12 Chris Spannos and Kalle Lasn, "Mainstream Media & the Magic of Occupy Wall Street," *NYT eXaminer*, http://www.nytexaminer. com/2011/12/mainstream-media-the-magic-of-occupy-wall-street-kalle-lasn-interview (accessed May 9, 2013).

13 This headline appeared on October 15, 2011, when OWS occupied Times Square. Actions that day occurred as part of an International Day of Action that European movements had called and had been organizing for months prior. I had interviewed Spanish activists and organizers while visiting Madrid in September of that year. They spoke at length about organizing and promoting the International Day of Action. While participating in the occupation of Times Square, I and others were shocked to see the headline "Occupy Wall Street Goes Global." As exhilarating as it was to see our action pass overhead in Times Square headlines as we looked up from our assemblies, it was disappointing that the headline reversed reality, to make it seem like we were suddenly leading a global movement with which we had only just begun to catch up.

14 Herbert Marcuse, *One-Dimensional Man* (Boston: Beacon Press, 1991, original 1964).

15 George Polymeneas, "'Greek December' In Political and Media Discourse," Academia.edu website, http://www.academia.edu/2123823/_ Greek_December_in_Political_and_Media_Discourse_Analysing_the_ PMs_Addresses_and_Newspaper_Reports (accessed May 9, 2013).

16 Ibid.

17 Karolina Tagaris, "Shopkeepers Shutter Shops as Crisis Bites," Ekathimerini.com website, http://www.ekathimerini.

com/4dcgi/_w_articles_wsite1_1_25/09/2011_407902%20 (accessed May 9, 2013).

18 Karolina Tagaris, "Crisis Shuts a Third of Shops in Athens City Centre," *Reuters*, http://www.reuters.com/article/2012/09/24/us-greece-business-idUSBRE88N0NW20120924 (accessed May 9, 2013).

19 Helena Smith, "Greece Suffers More Misery as Retails Sales Slump by Nearly a Third," *The Guardian*, http://www.guardian.co.uk/world/2013/apr/30/greece-misery-retail-sales-fall (accessed May 9, 2013).

20 Robert D. Benford and David A. Snow, "Framing Processes And Social Movements: An Overview and Assessment," *Annual Review of Sociology* 26 (2000).

21 Ibid.

22 Castoriadis, *Modern Capitalism*, 1960–1961.

INSURGENCY CONTROL
TOOLS OF REPRESSION IN THE AGE OF AUSTERITY[1]

SEAN PARSON AND LUIS A. FERNANDEZ

INTRODUCTION

ON JULY 25, 2012, THE FEDERAL BUREAU OF INVESTIGATION (FBI), IN conjunction with local agents from the Joint Terrorist Task Force (JTTF) and Portland Police Bureau, raided three activists' homes in Portland, Oregon. Heavily armed and dressed in military-style gear that included army helmets and goggles, the agents entered the homes in search of antigovernment or anarchist literature. While the agents made no arrests, they did confiscate several hard drives, anarchist flags, cell phones, address books, and black clothing. On the same day, law enforcement in Olympia and Seattle delivered grand jury subpoenas to activists in those cities, making this a coordinated, multistate effort. The day of the raids, the agents refused to explain their actions, stating only that it was part of an ongoing "violent crime investigation."[2]

A few days after the raids, law enforcement released more information. They argued that the raids were linked to the 2012 May Day protest in Seattle, Washington, where individuals broke the windows of several corporate buildings and a federal courthouse. This protest involved individuals who had been part of the Occupy Wall Street movement prior to the May Day demonstration. In hindsight, it appears that law enforcement conducted intelligence investigations before the May

Day protest, and continued the surveillance in the following months. In addition to surveillance, law enforcement opened a grand jury investigation to "collect" additional evidence, dragging several activists through the criminal justice system for not turning state's evidence. In all, four activists served jail time, even though none were named in any criminal activity, other than refusing to speak to a grand jury.

Unfortunately, this type of action is part of a disturbing trend: the use of police "raids," grand juries, surveillance, and investigations to repress radical movements. Police raids of anarchists prior to large protest are now almost a cliché, both in the United States and Europe.[3] For instance, police raided homes prior to the 2009 G8 protests in London, before the 2010 G8 protests in Toronto, and again for the 2012 NATO protest in Chicago. While raids are commonplace before protests, this chapter argues that the recent economic collapse, along with the ensuing austerity measures, has intensified what was already a troubling development: the use of legal, informational, and physical maneuvers to decrease radicalization by increasing the cost of being a radical activist. In sum, this chapter argues that we are witnessing the intensification of what we term *insurgency control*, aimed at pacifying a potential rebellion. However, the difference this time (as opposed to the 1960s and 1970s, as we discuss below) is the existence of a more robust and wider network of law enforcement coordination, a hardy technical system of information gathering, and the use of legal tactics aimed to suppress dissent.

This chapter starts with a brief historical description of insurgency and counterinsurgency, examining COINTELPRO (the Counter Intelligence Program in the FBI) as a modern example. We then discuss how policing of movements took a momentary shift toward the policing of protest, or what looked like a more gentle type of control. We conclude with an outline of what *insurgency control* looks like, suggesting that it is a hybrid form of control involving a mixture of protest policing and counterinsurgency tactics. Insurgency control, then, is the way that the state is responding to mobilizations after the economic crisis.

DEFINITION AND HISTORY OF COUNTERINSURGENCY

Generally speaking, an insurgent refers to an individual who is rebelling against a recognized authority, such as an established government. This rebellion can include armed or passive resistance, since it is the act of rebellion itself that matters. In turn, insurgencies involve groups of individuals with similar goals, attempting to destabilize a recognized power. The emphasis here again is on destabilization. Thus, insurgency focuses on acts that directly challenge the status quo, seeking to fundamentally change it, not simply reform it.

Counterinsurgency, then, refers to the actions that a government takes to suppress a potential or ongoing rebellion.[4] There is a current debate about the precise way to think about counterinsurgency, with some arguing that the concept is neither a concept nor a full strategy.[5] Rather than enter into this debate, we place counterinsurgency as part of the 2,000-year history of statecraft. That is, counterinsurgency is another way that the state goes about countering resistance to its own authority. Thus, counterinsurgency can be a framework, a tactic, and a strategy, depending on what the state needs for its own defense. It can take many forms, ranging from passive information campaigns to aggressive divide-and-conquer strategies designed to split the general population from the insurgents. Here it is important to see that counterinsurgency exists within a continuum of practices that can swing from media work to full-blown military attacks on insurgents. In short, counterinsurgent campaigns seek to protect the official power of authorities and undermine the claims for authority and legitimacy by insurgents.

The use of statecraft that looks like counterinsurgency has, as mentioned above, a long history, one directly linked to colonialism. For instance, the British authorities deployed counterinsurgency tactics in the 1950s, when they "relocated" 400,000 Chinese Malayans from their territory.[6] They aimed to reduce the chances of the Malayan Communist Party gaining support from the general population. In another example, French authorities detained 24,000 Algerians and killed 3,000, using counterinsurgency actions during the Battle of Algiers.[7] Perhaps the best-known example comes from the United States war in Vietnam, during which the US military sought to "pacify" the Vietnam insurgents by winning the hearts and minds of the people.[8]

The US also has a domestic tradition of deploying counterinsurgency. Throughout much of the twentieth century, the US government engaged in political repression of "subversives." Shortly after the Haymarket Square bombings in Chicago, many cities, such as New York and Chicago, created their own "red squads," in order to conduct surveillance and investigate supposed communist and anarchist activists. After World War I, Attorney General A. Mitchell Palmer formed the General Intelligence Division of the FBI as a measure to target national insurgents. In time, this division of the FBI produced a list of 200,000 potential radicals and subversives who posed a "threat" to national security. Many of these individuals were eventually arrested and deported during the Palmer Raids.[9]

While the government moved away from domestic surveillance during the late 1920s and early 1930s, in 1936, Franklin Roosevelt ordered J. Edgar Hoover to once again use the FBI to investigate the political activities of domestic radical groups.[10] This planted the seeds for what came to be known as the Counterintelligence Program (or COINTELPRO).

COINTELPRO officially started in 1956 and ended in 1971. The program used counterinsurgency tactics to "disrupt, discredit, and neutralize" political organizations that J. Edgar Hoover deemed threatening to the security of the United States. Looking at the history of this program, we see that COINTELPRO was used both against leftist groups *and* racist white power groups (like the KKK) but in differing ways. David Cunningham, in *There's Something Happening Here: The New Left, the Klan, and FBI Counterintelligence,* argues that the FBI attempted to steer the racist right away from public acts of violence, while the FBI encouraged the New Left toward aggressive insurgent acts, in an attempt to undermine their legitimacy.[11] This allowed the FBI to down come harder on left activists.

COINTELPRO, like counterinsurgent strategies of the colonial period, used a wide range of tactics, from infiltration and agent provocateurs to legal harassment (use of grand juries, false arrests, etc.), even using targeted killings, all aiming to disrupt various social movements throughout the United States and its colonies. For instance, counterinsurgency tactics were used to undermine the civil right movement (including the NAACP, Martin Luther King Jr., and the Student Nonviolent Coordinating Committee), the Black Power movement (including the Black Panthers and Nation of Islam), the American Indian Movement, the Puerto Rican independence movement, the Chicano movement, the New Left, the antiwar movement, and others.

In Puerto Rico, COINTELPRO worked in conjunction with the *carpetas* program, a counterinsurgency campaign in Puerto Rico in the

1930s used to stifle the independence movement in the small island colony. During the 1960s, the FBI, working with the Puerto Rican government, ran a campaign against the student pro-independence groups through:

> (1) A disinformation drive through op-eds and articles in "friendly" newspapers and media outlets; (2) the use of intimidation tactics against media that might support independence; and (3) efforts to discredit and divide the leadership of the independence movement, such as making up false stories of infidelity.[12]

While these tactics were used against other groups, such as the Black Panther Party, in Puerto Rico, the COINTELPRO tactics of the *carpetas* program continued unabated until the 1980s. During that fifty-year period of counterinsurgency, the Puerto Rican government collected information on more than 75,000 individuals involved in independence, socialist, feminist, peace, and other left-wing movements. While the political impact of this surveillance is unknown, in 1999 the Puerto Rican government officially apologized for their *listas de subversivos*.

COINTELPRO eventually made black nationalist groups the center of its domestic campaign. This was especially true of the Black Panther Party for Self Defense, which by 1969 had been the target of 233 different operations, accounting for nearly 80 percent of all COINTELPRO operations against black nationalist organizations. The goal of the FBI in targeting the black nationalist movement was, according to J. Edgar Hoover, to "prevent the coalition of militant black nationalist groups" because "an effective coalition of black nationalist groups might be the first step toward a real Mau Mau in America."[13] In the eyes of the FBI, comparing civil rights leaders and black nationalists to the Mau Mau uprising in Kenya during the 1950s connected Martin Luther King Jr., the Black Panther Party, and the Student Nonviolent Coordinating Committee with anticolonial, armed resistance in Africa. In order to ensure that there was no "Battle for Algiers" in the United States, their main concern was to stop the movement from gaining political traction and thus "preventing militant black nationalist groups and leaders from gaining respectability." The FBI described preventing this coalition thusly:

> You must discredit these groups and individuals to, first, the responsible Negro community. Second, they must be discredited to the white community, both the responsible white community and to the "liberals": political, religious, and civil groups and individuals who have vestiges of sympathy for militant Black Nationalist groups simply because they are Negroes. Third, these groups are to be discredited in the eyes of the Negro radicals, the followers of the movement.[14]

The FBI viewed black insurgency in the US not as a form of political protest or claim for rights, but as a threat to the very order of American authority and liberal democracy. In the US, this threat of black insurgency highlights the link that Joel Olson describes between liberal democracies and white supremacy.[15]

The program was officially stopped in 1971, after activists with the Citizens Commission to Investigate the FBI uncovered incriminating evidence about federal misconduct during the "burglary" of an FBI office in Media, Pennsylvania. While officially ending in 1971, serious questions remain about whether COINTELPRO-like operations continued, especially against the American Indian Movement. At the center of these questions is the role of the FBI in the Wounded Knee shootout in 1975, in which two FBI agents were shot, and Leonard Peltier and two other AIM activists were arrested and imprisoned for their murders. Likewise, journalist Will Potter has investigated the ways in which COINTELPRO-like operations have continued against Animal and Earth Liberation activists in his book, *Green Is the New Red*. This can be seen in the expanded usage of grand juries, infiltrators, and surveillance associated with the government's "Operation Backfire" campaign against environmental activists in the post-9/11 era. In this new era of response, activists from Rod Coronado and Daniel McGowan to the SHAC 7 have been convicted of "eco-" and "animal-industry" terrorism, and ultimately silenced in Communication Management Units (also known as "little Guantanamos").

In the view of the state, the actions of New Left and ethnic power movements in the 1960s and 1970s were not forms of protest, but insurgencies that sought to undermine the state and capitalism. This is an essential point, since the justification and legitimacy of counterinsurgency tactics requires the portrayal of activists as deeply threatening to the social and political order. During the 1960s, the Cold War against the Soviet Union highlighted the deep inequality in American society—especially along lines of race and gender—as Soviet forces often sided with anticolonial movements in Asia and Africa. Hoover saw a potential crisis developing that could, if left unattended, be a threat to the state and the rule of capital. As such, these movements had to be stopped, before a full insurgency unfolded in Black, Puerto Rican, Indigenous, and Chicano populations, as well as in leftist student communities. As a result, the FBI used counterinsurgency tactics to attack these movements, aiming to reduce any potential for a homegrown insurgency.

POLICING VS. COUNTERINSURGENCY

THIS SECTION INVESTIGATES how the state responds to *contemporary* protest. We argue that the economic crisis of 2008 once again (like in the 1960s and 1970s) left the state particularly vulnerable, not only to mass protest movements, but also to possible insurgencies. Before we describe how law enforcement responded to the movement in 2008 and how police use an insurgency control model, we will first describe the difference between protest and insurgency, to allow the reader to follow the shift more clearly.

The word "protest" evokes images of a political minority taking a public stand against some injustice, such as the civil rights or women's movements of the 1960s and 1970s. More specifically, the term refers to actions taken against authority (government or corporations), seeking a change in a policy, a law, or towards the reformation of an institution or system. The key word here is reformation, as protest is often conceptualized as pushing for reforms and not wholesale revolution. As such, groups can adopt a variety of tactics, including marches, pickets, civil disobedience, and even direct action, in order to challenge power. Theoretically speaking, the US Constitution protects the civil liberties of individuals engaged in dissent. However, in reality, the situation is more complicated.

In the 1980s, as social movements became more institutionalized, law enforcement developed a set of practices to police protest, aiming to minimize their impact. These tactics moved away from the more aggressive tactics deployed in the 1960s and more toward a subtle mode of control that used regulations and negotiations to pacify an already relatively passive type of dissent. Again, it is worth noting that both of these forms of policing fall within the counterinsurgency continuum, ranging from brutal practices to softer modes. Scholars describe the less aggressive tactics as the "negotiated management" model.[16] Most popular in North America and Europe, this model shifts away from the indiscriminate use of force, a tactic practiced in the 1960s and 1970s, as described in the previous section. According to McCarthy and McPhail, the key to the "negotiated management" approach is to respect protesters' claim to the First Amendment.[17] Thus, it involves police offering movement leaders concessions in exchange for an agreement to self-police, often working closely with "peacekeepers," activists who self-regulate the behavior of people involved in a demonstration. With the advent of permits, the police negotiations began when activists requested marching permits to gather in public areas. In sum, this approach worked with a liberal democratic understanding that protest is necessary, but must be regulated to protect both the rights of the protesters and ensure the general security of the public. In practice, this approach disciplined some activists into behaving in a nonthreatening way, thus fulfilling some of the goals of a counterinsurgent strategy.

By now, most activists should be well aware of the protest policing tactics that law enforcement use to control large protests. These, of course, include the use of tear gas, pepper spray, fencing, and "protest zones." If you were on the streets in the last decade, then you are likely familiar with these forms of repression. Less clearly visible were the forms of repression that involved surveillance and monitoring of protesters. It is these less visible tactics that intensified after the 2008 economic crash, as we will see in the next section.

Insurgencies are significantly different from protests. While protests are, in theory, constitutionally protected behavior, insurgencies are not. In the United States, this very distinction is embedded in First Amendment case law. The legal system makes the distinction between peaceful assembly and fomenting rebellion. The latter constitutes criminalized behavior. For instance, in *Schenck v. United States* (1919), a case dealing with socialist leafleting, the Supreme Court ruled that you cannot "yell fire in a crowded theatre," limiting political free speech. This became known as the "clear and present danger" test. This was radically expanded in *Dennis v. United States* (1951), when the court ruling supported the arrest of eleven Communist activists for "advocating the violent overthrow of the US," for simply forming a Communist organization dedicated to educational activity. No one ever asserted that the activists planned or coordinated such actions, but the court ruled that their ideology promoted it. By the late 1960s, the "clear and present danger" test was replaced in *Brandenburg v. Ohio* (1969). This new approach allowed for "theoretical" discussion regarding revolution, but specifically allowed for the criminalization of any revolutionary organizing action.

Given that these are legal distinctions, they also come into play around issues of political work. Generally speaking, insurgencies involve an "organized, protracted political-military struggle designed to weaken the control and legitimacy of the established government, occupying power, or other political authority while increasing insurgency control."[18] An insurgency is directly threatening to the existing order.

To quash ongoing or potential insurgencies, the state uses counterinsurgency tactics. These include military, paramilitary, political, economic, psychological, and civic actions, targeting the hearts and minds of the local population to isolate and reduce the legitimacy of insurgents. According to the *US Army and US Marine Corps Counterinsurgency Field Manual*, counterinsurgency campaigns should have integration, unity of command, and unity of effort.[19] Integration refers to having a "comprehensive strategy employing all instruments of national power," mixing different governmental and civilian actors. Unity of command and effort means that counterinsurgency strategies must unify the command structure of different types of military and police agencies, so that they are working in coordination with each other, joined by a common effort. Most important is that counterinsurgency strategies involve the integration of multiple agencies into a command structure that allows for cross-communication. It is this characteristic that is most evident in the control of the Occupy Movement in the post-crisis environment.

THE CRISIS, THE OCCUPY MOVEMENT, AND INSURGENCY POLICING

IN THE SUMMER of 2008, the United States housing bubble burst and sent the entire global economy into crisis. In the US and much of Europe, governments responded to the crisis not by reinforcing the social safety net but by embracing austerity measures. Austerity here refers to measures taken to reduce expenditure in an attempt to shrink the growth of budget deficits caused by the housing bubble. Given the prevalent neoliberal ideology, cuts in expenditures came at the expense of the working class. In Europe and the US, the cuts resembled the structural adjustment policies the IMF and World Bank imposed on Latin America, Africa, and Asia in the 1980s and 1990s. In time, these austerity measures led to the revival of social movements and popular resistance, especially in Europe. While the resistance to austerity is clear in countries like Greece and Spain, the student resistance to tuition hikes in the UK and Quebec, Canada were also expressions of dissent against the measures.

In the US, the response to the crisis emerged first from the right, i.e., from the Tea Party. The Tea Party became a media darling in 2009 and used this popularity to gain massive inroads in state and federal government in 2010. While many liberal commentators warned about the danger of the Tea Party insurgency of 2010, of the return of the militia fear of the 1990s, there was no coordinated local, state, or federal policing response to the movement.[20] In Arizona, armed individuals (sometimes with assault rifles) attended Tea Party demonstrations and rallies in the months after the financial crisis and the election of President Obama. Particularly absent from the demonstrations were the armed riot police aiming to "protect" the population from Tea Party members. In time, the Tea Party managed to push US policy on debt and public funding further to the right, as evidenced by the 2010 Republican budget (a.k.a., the Ryan budget), which included massive cuts to social services, education, and supposed "entitlements" like Social Security and Medicare. The success of austerity policies in the US, from the perspective of the right, can also be seen in the record rise of corporate profits, increasing economic inequality during the Obama administration, and further concentration of corporate control of public goods.

It is within this context that the Occupy Wall Street Movement (OWS) emerged in September 2011. The movement arose differently than the Tea Party in several important ways. First, OWS grew closer to the grassroots and lacked an equivalent of the Koch brothers to fund it. As such, it grew more spontaneously, more quickly, and was more expansive. Second, the movement was instantly networked around the world, following the lead of movements in Europe, and helping spread them to other parts of the globe. These links are important, since, for a moment, activists were in communication with organizers in Greece, Spain, and Egypt. Third, OWS was not armed and in most places did not threaten the use of political violence.²¹ Yet, at the same time, it was more confrontational than the Tea Party. Occupying parks across the US put protesters in the direct path of important social issues, such as homelessness and the disappearance of public space, which produced some confrontations with local law enforcement. Evidence of the confrontations comes in the number of arrests, which as of the writing of this chapter (May 16, 2013) totaled more than 7,000 people in the US. Finally, the movement was not linked to electoral reform, instead putting forward demands that directly engaged capitalism, colonialism, the corporate state, and empire. These differences were significant enough to trigger a more coordinated attack on the movement and toward spin-off mobilizations that followed in Oakland, Portland, Seattle, and elsewhere.

Unlike the nonexistent suppression of the Tea Party, law enforcement reaction to OWS was not only sophisticated, but also more coordinated than we could have imagined at the time. Very recently released FBI documents demonstrate the intensification of the disturbing trend we described in the opening of this chapter, so much so that we venture to classify this response to OWS as *insurgency policing*.

We propose that *insurgency policing* is what the state used to respond to left-wing mobilizations after the crisis. Insurgency policing is a hybrid between protest policing and counterinsurgency. That is, an examination of the state's response to OWS demonstrates that the movement was controlled with a set of strategies and tactics that are neither fully protest policing nor counterinsurgency. Insurgency policing appears to have the following four characteristics:

a. an intensification of coordinated efforts across public and private agencies;
b. heavy data collection through surveillance;
c. a preemptive quality that targets activists before they break the law;
d. the identification of activists as insurgents and real threats to the capitalist system, allowing for the deployment of the already-in-place terrorist fighting apparatus.

The first characteristic of insurgency policing is a significant intensification of law enforcement cooperation and coordination across agencies. However, it is important to note that these efforts were not caused by the crisis. Rather, this is only the unfolding of a system put in place after the September 11 attacks. You can see this new public and private cooperation particularly clearly in the state response to Occupy Wall Street. At the time of the crackdown, we wondered how multiple cities were able to arrest individuals at roughly the same time across the United States. We now know.

Documents recovered through the Freedom of Information Act show that in New York City, the Department of Homeland Security (DHS), the Federal Bureau of Investigation (FBI), the New York Police Department (NYPD), and other agencies coordinated their response to OWS.[22] In addition, the documents describe a partnership between public agencies and private-sector organizations, including having cops work with banks to target and arrest protestors. The coordination of arrests was extensive, with police departments in diverse cities, such as Denver, Colorado; Richmond, Virginia; Anchorage, Alaska; and Jackson, Mississippi, all having worked closely with private banks and shared intelligence with each other.

In addition to banks, the FBI and other enforcement agencies worked closely with at least six university campus police organizations. According to the Partnership for Civic Justice, "campus officials were in contact with the FBI for information on OWS. A representative of the State University of New York at Oswego contacted the FBI for information on the OWS protests and reported to the FBI on the SUNY-Oswego Occupy encampment made up of students and professors."[23] The network of agencies working in conjunction with each other is impressive.

Most disturbing is the discovery that the Domestic Security Alliance Council (DSAC) was helping facilitate information sharing between public and private agencies. According to the DSAC website, they describe themselves as:

> A strategic partnership between the FBI, the Department of Homeland Security and the private sector, [that] enhances communications and promotes the timely and bidirectional effective exchange of information keeping the nation's critical infrastructure safe, secure and resilient. DSAC advances elements of the FBI and DHS missions' in preventing, deterring, and

> investigating criminal and terrorism acts, particularly
> those effecting interstate commerce, while advancing
> the ability of the U.S. private sector to protect its em-
> ployees, assets and proprietary information[24]

What is important here is the network of public and private agencies at the local, regional, and national level. It is this network that
characterizes insurgency policing, a type of control that aims to reduce the possibility of an uprising like the Arab Spring.

Another aspect of insurgency policing is the reliance on heavy
collection, use, and transmission of surveillance. For instance, the
American Civil Liberties Union and the National Lawyers Guild issued a report describing the extensive surveillance that the Boston
Police Department, in conjunction with the regional fusion center,
gathered before, during, and after the Occupy mobilizations.[25] This
included officers monitoring demonstrations and protests, tracking
the ideology and beliefs of activists, as well as documenting the internal dynamics of activist groups, while capturing and disseminating
the information through the fusion center. Fusion centers are a key
component in this control formulation. They are information-sharing
centers created after 2003, in response to the perceived failure of government agencies to share intelligence information that could have
prevented the terrorist attacks on September 11, 2001. The centers are
run by the Department of Homeland Security and the Department
of Justice, and effectively link local law enforcement with national
and international police agencies. They are designed to promote information sharing between the Central Intelligence Agency, FBI, US
Department of Justice, US military, and various local and state agencies. As of 2012, there are over seventy-seven fusion centers across the
United States, a number that does not include private centers that
collect similar information.[26] The centers collect information on "all
crimes," seeking to uncover local, national, and international links
leading to the prevention of terrorism. However, it is worth noting
that fusion centers are under close scrutiny for shabby data gathering
and for not leading to the prevention of a single terrorist instance.[27]

Regardless of their effectiveness, the importance of the fusion
centers is the ability of the state to link data gathered in a local system, say in Portland, Oregon, and to disseminate the information to
Seattle, Washington, if needed. This puts into place a way to share

information that was not present ten years ago, which will likely be used in the future to track mobilizations like OWS. It is worth noting here a difference between insurgency policing and counterintelligence. While counterintelligence seeks a centralized command structure and data warehousing, insurgency policing is more about decentralizing the information and structure. In a way, it is a networked set of controls to target something like a networked type of insurgency.

Finally, insurgency policing involves categorizing domestic activists and protestors as a threat to state power and authority. As is the case with counterinsurgency tactics, the aim of insurgency policing is to prevent a mass mobilization. This is most evident in the FOIA report describing how the Department of Homeland Security viewed the OWS mobilizations (called Days of Rage) planned for September 17, 2011. The document reads:

> Referencing the demonstrations of the 2011 Arab Spring events, the "US Day of Rage" desires to mimic the revolutionary wave of the demonstrations and protest that have occurred in the Arab world. The overall goal of the "US Day of Rage" protest is to conduct unorganized protest in major metropolitan areas with special attention on banking and financial institutions.[28]

Here we see two important points. First, OWS is depicted as having the potential to overthrow the US government, similar to what happened in Arab nations. Second, it demonstrates the recognition by the state of a type of anticapitalist uprising aimed at the banking industry at a time of economic turmoil. These two aspects alone provide the justification, in our view, for triggering the type of crackdown that we witnessed against OWS.

In sum, when looking back at the state reaction after the crisis, we see an insurgency-policing model of control aimed at demobilizing the potential for networked, left-wing insurgencies.

CONCLUSION

ON APRIL 15, 2013, a pressure cooker bomb went off near the finish line of the Boston marathon. The bombing killed three people and injured 264. In the aftermath of the bombing, the FBI, Joint Terrorist

Task Force, Department of Homeland Security, and the local fusion center, in conjunction with the telecommunications companies, compiled over ten terabytes of data, by accessing all phone, video, and text messages sent from the surrounding area over a twenty-four-hour period. This massive collection of data was examined using facial recognition software and other statistical programs, in the hopes of identifying the bombers.[29] This massive data collection and analysis operation heralds an image of what future insurgency policing might look like.

It is important to note, however, that even with the massive technological and surveillance programs available to the federal government, and the massive amounts of money devoted to expand the surveillance-industrial-complex since September 11, there have been few "successes." Even in Boston, after that massive data mining operation, the chief of police admitted that facial recognition software and the ten terabytes of data were not useful in finding the bombing suspects. What led to their capture was the release of information to the public. This, of course, is well in line with insurgency policing practice; turning to the local population for help. Keep an eye out for this practice during public protests.

In general, this is still a reminder that even though technology is developing at a rapid speed—and the US government is eroding the few protections of civil liberties it once had—the government is far from all-powerful. This article, while detailing a new and troubling trend in activist repression, is not all gloom and doom. Even with expanded surveillance and information gathering, the grand jury witch-hunts, and the coordinated campaign to undermine and "neutralize" the movement, the grand jury resistors in Portland and Seattle have seemingly stood strong and defiant. While insurgent policing is a new development, one that further limits our political and civil rights, understanding the way it operates will allow activists to resist. This means that we too need our tactics and strategies to evolve as quickly as the state develops theirs.

ENDNOTES

1   The authors would like to thank Kristian Williams for providing a strong and useful critique of the ideas presented in this chapter.

2   Sarah Mirk, "FBI Raids Homes in Northwest: Looks Like They Might Be Targeting Anarchists," *The Portland Mercury*, July 25, 2012, http://www.portlandmercury.com/BlogtownPDX/archives/2012/07/25/fbi-raids-homes-across-northwestlooks-like-targeting-anarchists (accessed March 1, 2013).

3   See their documentation in Luis Fernandez, *Policing Dissent: Social Control and the Anti-globalization Movement* (Brunswick, N.J: Rutgers University Press, 2008); Jeffrey S. Juris, *Networking Futures: The Movement Against Corporate Globalization* (Durham, NC: Duke University Press, 2008); Amory Starr, Luis Fernandez, and Christian Scholl, *Shutting Down the Streets: Social Control and Political Violence in the Global Era* (New York: New York University Press, 2011); Christian Scholl, *Two Sides of the Barricade: (Dis)order and Summit Protest in Europe* (New York: SUNY Press, 2013).

4   Roberto J. Gonzalez, *American Counterinsurgency: Human Science and the Human Terrain* (Chicago: Prickly Paradigm Press, 2009).

5   For a full treatment of this, see Colin S. Gray, "Concept Failure? COIN, Counterinsurgency, and Strategic Theory," *Prism* 3, no.3 (June 2012): http://www.ndu.edu/press/concept-failure.html (accessed on May 14, 2013).

6   John Nagl, *Learning to Eat Soup with a Knife: Counterinsurgency Lessons from Malaya and Vietnam* (Westport: Praeger Publishers, 2002).

7   James D. Campbell, "French Algeria and British Northern Ireland: Legitimacy and the Rule of Law in Low-Intensity Conflict," *Military Review* (March–April 2005): 3–4.

8   Kurt Jacobsen, *Pacification and Its Discontents* (Chicago: Prickly Paradigm Press, 2009).

9   Ward Churchill, *In a Pig's Eye: Reflections on the Police State, Repression, and Native America* (Oakland, AK Press, 2002); Ward Churchill and Jim Vander Wall, *Agents of Repression: The FBI's Secret Wars Against the Black Panther Party and the American Indian Movement* (Cambridge, MA: South End Press, 2002).

10   Athan Theoharis, *Spying on Americans: Political Surveillance from Hoover to Huston Plan* (Philadelphia: Temple University Press, 1978).

11   David Cunningham, *There's Something Happening Here: The New Left, the Klan, and FBI Counterintelligence* (Berkeley: University of California Press, 2004).

12 Rene Francisco Poitevin, "Political Surveillance, State Repression, and Class Resistance: The Puerto Rican Experience," *Social Justice* 27, no. 3 (2000): 93.

13 Quoted in Susie Day and Laura Whitehorn, Day, Susie and Laura Whitehorn, eds, "Human Rights in the United States: The Unfinished Story of Political Prisoners and COINTELPRO," *New Political Science* 23, no. 2 (2001): 286.

14 Day and Whitehorn, "Human Rights in the US," 286.

15 Joel Olson, *Abolition of White Democracy* (Minneapolis: University of Minnesota Press, 2004).

16 Clark McPhail, David Schweingruber, and John McCarthy, "Policing Protest in the United States, 1960–1995," in (ed.) D. della Porta and H. Reiter, *Policing of Protest: The Control of the Mass Demonstration in Western Democracies* (Minneapolis: University of Minnesota Press, 1998).

17 John McCarthy and Clark McPhail, "The Institutionalization of Protest in the United States," in (ed.) Sidney Tarrow, *The Social Movement Society: Contentious Politics for a New Century* (Boulder: Rowman and Littlefield, 1997).

18 US Army and US Marine Corps, *Counterinsurgency,* FM 3-24, MCWP 3-33.5 of 15 December 2006, http://www.fas.org/irp/doddir/army/fm3-24.pdf (accessed on March 15, 2013).

19 Ibid.

20 Recently, it came out that the Internal Revenue Service flagged so-called Tea Party patriot groups for extra scrutiny in the application for federal tax-exemption status. Tea Party groups are now calling for investigations and feel they were unfairly treated. However, in the views of the authors, while this is government harassment, it does not rise to the level of policing that the groups we describe here experienced.

21 This statement requires a qualification. While OWS did threaten violence in some places, such as Oakland, California, in the vast majority of cities it did not. Our reference is to the majority of occupations.

22 Partnership for Civil Justice Fund, "New Documents Reveal: DHS Spying on Peaceful Demonstrations and Activists" (April 2, 2013).

23 Partnership for Civil Justice Fund, "New Documents Reveal," 2013.

24 Domestic Security Alliance Council, http://www.dsac.gov/Pages/index.
aspx (accessed March 15, 2013).

25 American Civil Liberties Union and National Lawyers Guild, "Policing Dissent: Police surveillance of Lawful Political Activity in Boston,"
October 2012, http://aclum.org/policing_dissent (accessed April 25,
2013).

26 Torin Monahan and Priscilla M. Rega, "Zones of Opacity: Data Fusion in Post-9/11 Security Organizations," *Canadian Journal of Law
and Society* 27, no. 3 (2013): 301–317.

27 American Civil Liberties Union and National Lawyers Guild, "Policing
Dissent."

28   See the FBI Situational Information Report in Partnership for Civil
Justice Fund 2013: 1.

29 Frank Konkel, "Boston Probe's Big Data Use Hints at the Future,"
FCW: The Business of Federal Communication, Online edition (accessed
April 26, 2013).

NATIONALISM'S CHILLING EFFECT ON ANTI-AUSTERITY MOVEMENTS

THE CASE OF ISRAEL'S "TENT PROTESTS"

URI GORDON

THE ISRAELI "TENT PROTEST" MOVEMENT CAME AND WENT OVER THE space of six weeks in the summer of 2011. It started on July 14, when Daphni Leef, a freelance video editor from Tel-Aviv, pitched a tent on Rothschild Boulevard in the city center, after she had to vacate her rented apartment due to renovations and discovered that a new flat would be beyond her means. Leef created a Facebook event for her protest and was joined by several friends. Within twenty-four hours, dozens of tents were standing on the grassy sidelines of the prom- enade, and over the next fortnight, more than sixty encampments appeared in almost every Israeli town and city—mirroring, in many ways, the use of public space by protest movements across the globe, and anticipating the Occupy movement in the United States. The protesters' agenda expanded rapidly from housing prices to include the high cost of living, the government's social and economic policies, and the high concentration of wealth in Israeli society.[1] Calls for a return to the old welfare state were widely heard.

It was doubtlessly the largest protest movement in Israel's history. Weekly Saturday night demonstrations drew increasing numbers of people, with a crowd of over 400,000 participating in the last major demonstration on September 3, 2011. Though the participants largely represented the faltering middle classes, polls indicated up to ninety percent support for the movement from the general public. On the streets, a sense of empowerment and community was palpable. The tent cities became sites of direct democratic self-management, practical cooperation, and public discussion of social affairs. They were a breath of fresh air in a society that had become increasingly atomized and consumerist. For many people, participation in this movement was their first experience of collective mobilization, and their first opportunity to educate themselves on social and economic issues.

Although the Israeli protests preceded the US Occupy movement, they followed close on the heels of the Arab Spring and the Spanish *Indignados* mobilizations—precedents that were not lost on the tent-city dwellers. Some activists situated their mobilization within the Middle Eastern context, with a placard on one street corner even renaming it "Rothschild-Tahrir," yet direct connections with protesters in Egypt, Tunisia, and Bahrain were nonexistent. The *Indignados* movement, on the other hand, had a much more direct influence in seeding the Israeli movement's practices of popular assembly. Aya Shoshan, an activist involved in the Rothschild camp from early on, had just returned from Spain and was quick to teach the protest instigators about hand signals, stack-taking, and facilitation. Though never adopting a formal consensus process (decisions were usually adopted by what protesters came to call a "clear visual majority"), its more deeply significant elements—active listening, compassion, and a sense of common purpose—were widely on display. These practices were so different from the usual Israeli mode of impatient and conflictual argument that, for many protesters, they were nothing short of a revelation. Within two weeks, advanced by media attention to "twinkling" and other curiosities, they spread throughout the country.

Yet compared to similar events around the world, one is tempted to designate the Israeli tent protests as the tamest specimen in the current global wave. Not only did calls for discrete welfare policies replace any explicit anticapitalism, but there was a widespread insistence on the movement's "apolitical" nature and an avoidance of any direct confrontation with the Netanyahu government or calls for new elections. Instead, protest leaders repeatedly expressed a desire that the current government solve the country's social problems and somehow abandon its explicitly neoliberal ideology.

One explanation for this tameness is that Israel has been largely isolated from the world financial crisis, and has experienced relatively low unemployment, steady growth, and no special austerity measures. But a more substantive explanation stems from the elephant in the room (or on the boulevard): a movement mobilizing around social justice effectively ignored the social conditions of millions of Palestinians living under Israeli military occupation with an often minimal standard of living and few, if any, political rights. This was an Occupy movement that ignored the other real occupation taking place in its own backyard. Some obvious factors determining the lack of spending on education, welfare, and social services—namely a bloated security budget and the heavy subsidizing of settlements in the West Bank—remained largely unmentioned. Instead, the Palestinians continued to be viewed as extrinsic to Israeli society, rendering the occupation irrelevant to narrower questions of social justice "inside" Israel.

This lack of discussion discloses the central factor impeding the Israeli movement: the chilling effect of the patriotic, state-loyalist discourses that have reached unprecedented prominence in Israeli society in recent years. Indeed, the movement is best understood as an all-too-brief interlude in Israel's ongoing move away from democracy, evident in the recent wave of legislation against minorities, refugees, and human rights organizations, and in the McCarthyist campaigns against academic and civil society opponents of the occupation. This might provide lessons for present and future mobilizations, if we want to avoid the recuperating effects of nationalism in our movements.

LEFT-WING PROTEST IN THE ISRAELI CONTEXT

In Israel today, any association with the term "left" is enough to brand a person as disloyal and outside the mainstream consensus. Israeli society is becoming increasingly entrenched in its siege mentality, viewing international censure of the occupation as a threat to the very existence of the Jewish people. In such a context of collective hysteria, aligning oneself explicitly with the "left" is tantamount, in the eyes of many Israelis, to consorting with the enemy.

Such an atmosphere is not created on its own. On the contrary, it is manufactured and inflamed both by the discourse of existential threat that is repeatedly used by governing politicians (most prominently by Prime Minister Netanyahu in reference to Iran's nuclear program) and by a wide array of institutional policies. The present Israeli parliament (Knesset) has approved, or is debating, a slew of antidemocratic bills directed primarily against the country's Arab minority and human rights organizations. Laws already approved include: a law allowing the imprisonment, without trial, of asylum seekers and refugees, as well as their children, who enter Israel via the border with Egypt; a law enabling civil lawsuits against individuals who call for a boycott of settlement products; a law authorizing the revoking of citizenship of persons convicted of terrorism or espionage; a law authorizing the relinquishment of state monetary support for any body or institution that marks the date of Israel's establishment as a day of mourning for the displacement of Palestinians in 1948; and a law permitting acceptance committees to villages and communities to turn down a candidate that does not fit their "social fabric," effectively barring Arabs access to Jewish communities.[2]

This legislation evinces a power trip by a completely stable right-wing coalition enjoying an unprecedented parliamentary majority. Add the fact that many of these bills have been supported, or even initiated, by members of the major opposition party, Kadima, which has recently joined the coalition, and the picture becomes one of a group-minded, right-wing parliament attempting to revise the ground rules of Israeli politics by exorcising elements it considers disloyal to the Jewish national collectivity.

Alongside these parliamentary efforts, for the past several years, a number of extraparliamentary organizations including NGO Monitor, Israel Academia Monitor, Yisrael Sheli, and Im Tirzu have been conducting a McCarthyist campaign against critics of the occupation in universities and civil society. Their efforts have included the conspicuous filming and recording of left-wing academics' lectures, "blacklist" websites stalking their publications, and public utterances, and right-wing counter demonstrations at gatherings of the small remains of Israel's peace movement. Thus, even traditional, liberal institutions known for very mild dissent are privately brought to heel through the efforts of right-wing, self-styled watchdogs.

Accusations that the tent city protests of 2011 were left wing surfaced early on. Settler leaders acted first, with Ariel mayor Ron Nachman saying, "all kinds of left-wing organizations have taken over the protests and are keeping us away," and Efrat mayor Oded Revivi stating that the only apparent goal of the protests was to topple the government.[3] More insidiously, the Prime Minister's office used its battery of paid commentary writers to bombard news websites and Facebook pages with comments, supposedly posted by unaligned readers, to the effect that the protesters were at best "spoiled shirkers" who "expect the government to fund their housing," and at worst "antisemitic," "communists," and "traitors."[4] Senior politicians from the governing Likud party soon joined in. Two weeks into the protests, the Knesset convened to debate motions of nonconfidence tabled by the opposition. Replying on behalf of the government, Minister Benny Begin accused the protesters of hiding their political agenda, and "pretending as if it is all spontaneous and that there is no assistance, no speech writers, no advisers, among them surely also people with a distinct political agenda, which first of all targets the personality and status of Prime Minister Binyamin Netanyahu."[5] In the same session, Knesset Speaker Reuven Rivlin went as far as to say that he identified "buds of anarchy" in the protests,[6] echoing culture minister Limor Livnat's statement earlier that day that the protests were instigated by "particular anarchist groups."[7]

The tiny Israeli anarchist movement, it should be clarified, hardly participated in the protests and was certainly far from being their instigator. This was in stark contrast to many of the other contestations over public space throughout the world, such as Occupy, the *Indignados*, or the later stages of the movement in Egypt, where anarchists had active roles. When activists from Anarchists Against the Wall tried to set up their own group of tents on Rothschild Boulevard a few days into the protests, they were vocally denounced by other protesters for bringing in an explicit antioccupation agenda, and soon decamped to the "Lewinsky" tent city opposite Tel Aviv's central station, which had a large presence of actual homeless people and African refugees—constituencies with which they had been in active solidarity for several years. For the most part, however, Israeli anarchists ignored the protests and remained focused on joining nonviolent Palestinian demonstrations in the West Bank.

A further assault came a month later, on the eve of the September 3 demonstrations, when right-wing *Ma'ariv* journalist Kalman Liebskind published an "expose" alleging that the leaders of the National Left (a shelf-party that mixes nostalgia for the Rabin administration with Zionist patriotism) had met with US Democratic Party strategist Stanley Greenberg in March 2011, to discuss how a political upheaval could be initiated.[8] According to Liebskind, the initiative was an effort to spawn a large protest, based on a multitude of groups and organizations, and use the mass of individuals who would rise up to decide future elections. The fact that the National Left had later donated several tents to the Rothschild protesters was considered enough to establish a causal link with the March meeting.

AVOIDING "LEFTISM," ENDORSING NATIONALISM

AGAINST THIS BACKDROP, it is not surprising that protesters did everything to remain seen as mainstream. Although Leef and her friends were indeed aligned with the left, the public atmosphere led them and the vast majority of movement participants to avoid, at all costs, being perceived as "leftists"—a term which is all but synonymous with "traitors" in Israel these days—and to foster deliberate self-censorship, which not only silenced any engagement with the Israeli–Palestinian conflict, but also defused confrontation on socio-economic grounds. Efforts to recreate a welfare state were not presented as a matter of social conflict along class lines, but instead as an appeal to social unity through an expression of "true Zionism"—rhetoric that panders to Israelis' nostalgia for the collectivism and republicanism of the early state. At the same time, the protests functioned as a kind of safety valve for social dissent about issues that had never been strongly associated with questions of national security or demographics, and thus remained part of the legitimate public discourse, rather than a challenge to it. It is worth noting that several Arab communities also established protest sites in Umm el Fahem, Tira, and Jaffa, among others. Though never said explicitly, their mobilization can be interpreted as having been enabled precisely because of the tent city protests' lack of radicalism. The widespread declaration of an apolitical stance created a safe space for Palestinian citizens of Israel to express their discontent with decades of discrimination and underdevelopment, without it being seen as a sign of disloyalty.

Perhaps the most striking example of the unholy matrimony between social justice and nationalism heard in the language of the Israeli protests came after the military escalation that took place a week into the mobilization. On Thursday, August 18, 2011, a group of Palestinian militants crossed the Egyptian border near Eilat, in southern Israel, and attacked a public bus, an Israeli army patrol, and a private vehicle, killing eight and injuring forty. The Israeli air force retaliated with attacks on multiple targets in the Gaza Strip, killing fifteen and injuring dozens, including unarmed civilians. Palestinians, in turn, fired rockets into Israel, killing a civilian and injuring close to a dozen. Exchanges of fire would continue for another week.

The military escalation did not take the protest movement by surprise. Indeed, some version of such a turn of events had been widely anticipated among tent activists. One leading Israeli security commentator even raised the possibility that the prime minister would initiate a military adventure to distract people from the social protests, although concluding that chances were slim.[9] In any event, protest organizers decided that the demonstrations planned for that Saturday would still go ahead, but as silent, candle-lit marches, without speeches or music. From this point on, statements by movement spokespeople pandered directly to sentiments of vulnerability and patriotism. In her call for the silent march, protest leader Stav Shaffir explicitly sought to assimilate the movement's goals into the hegemonic discourse of security:

> ...full of sorrow for the loss and anxious about our
> country's fate, we bear the responsibility of continuing
> to act [...] without societal security, there is no security
> at all. Without social justice, there is no security at all.
> Our security is our home, and our health, and our welfare, and our education. The unity of our society—is
> our security.[10]

The call-out for the silent march from a representative of the Jerusalem tent city went even further:

Quietly, but resolutely. Because the nation demonstrating is the same nation absorbing the blows of fire from our enemies, and its staunch demand for a deep change in economic priorities and for overall social justice does not come at the expense of the struggle against terror— on the contrary. A nation whose sons are bound by mutual guarantee, and fight together for the future and the fortitude of the State of Israel, is a strong nation who can face all its enemies.[11]

Such wording would probably shock any movement participant in New York, Barcelona. or London. But in Israel, it came quite naturally and remained unchallenged.

PROSPECTS

AFTER THE LAST large demonstration, it didn't take long for Israel to return to business as usual. A state-appointed committee made a set of recommendations on education, taxation, and welfare, which the government endorsed, but is unlikely to implement in practice (seventy percent of government decisions in Israel are never implemented.)[12] While sporadic protest events have continued to take place, Israeli society seems to have sunk comfortably back into its proverbial couch, consuming its usual cocktail of fear, consumerism, and reality TV. Shafir and student leader Itzik Shmuli cashed in on their roles in the protests to become MKs for the Labor Party. The establishment also embraced Daphni Leef, having accepted an invitation from the Israel Ministry of Public Diplomacy (Hasbara) to speak at campus counterevents during Israel Apartheid Week in the United Kingdom. "I am not here to say what a wonderful place Israel is," she told a London paper for Israeli expats, "I am here to explain that there are wonderful things happening within Israeli society and there is a very complex socio-economic reality in Israel."[13] Even more disappointing is the fact that the protests have had no effect on voting patterns. Netanyahu's Likud Party remained in power following the January 2013 elections, retaining a secure coalition with the right wing and a new secular, middle-class party. Israeli voters continue to desire a strong right-wing government that will resist international pressure to end the occupation, even if this same government continues on its path of neoliberal impoverishment of the 99%.

Radicals involved in movements responding to the economic crisis and austerity measures can learn an important lesson from the Israeli case. Although the nationalism that domesticated the protests in Israel is a uniquely powerful factor in that context, other countries are also experiencing a rightward tilt that often exhibits xenophobia and fear of the "Other." With the rise and strengthening of right-wing movements—such as the neo-Nazi Golden Dawn in Greece or the populist, anti-immigrant Tea Party in the United States—radicals can look to the experiences of the tent protests in Israel as an early warning sign. This would both put them on guard against the temptation to appease right-wing zealots through appeals to populist sentiments, and prepare them to intervene in mobilizations that *begin* without a sense of radical commitment and try to distance themselves from structural criticisms of capital and the state.

ENDNOTES

This essay was adapted from an earlier version, Uri Gordon, "Israel's Tent Protests: The Chilling Effects of Nationalism," *Social Movement Studies: Journal of Social, Cultural, and Political Protest*, 2012: 1–7.

1   OECD—Organization for Economic Co-operation and Development, "Divided We Stand: Why Inequality Keeps Rising, Country Note: Israel," OECD website, http://www.oecd.org/dataoecd/3/42/49559314. pdf (accessed March 4, 2013).

2   ACRI—The Association for Civil Rights in Israel, "Update: Anti-democratic Legislation Initiatives," ACRI Website, http://www.acri. org.il/en/2012/08/02/update-anti-democratic-legislation-initiatives/ (accessed March 4, 2013).

3   Y. Breiner, "Settlers: 'We Also Suffer from a Housing Shortage, but the Protests are Leftist'" (Hebrew), *Walla News*, http://news.walla. co.il/?w=/22/1844729 (accessed March 9, 2013).

4   M. Avrahami, "Tent Protests aren't breaking through in social networks: 48% of comments are negative" (Hebrew), ICE, http://www. ice.co.il/article/view/278925 (accessed March 9, 2013) and S. Genosar, (Talk Show in Hebrew), Yediot Aharonot, http://www.scribd.com/ doc/64478542/סינוממה-מיקבבקוטה-ריקחת-מעה-דגנ-ע-שי-תצעומי- יביב (accessed March 9, 2013).

5   The Knesset, "Session 268 of the 18th Knesset," *Knesset Annals*, 39 (Hebrew), www.knesset.gov.il/plenum/data/03529811.doc (accessed March 9, 2013).

6   Ibid., 94.

7   P. Wolff, "Knesset speaker on the protests: I identify buds of anarchy" (Hebrew), *Walla News*, http://news.walla.co.il/?w=/1/1846374 (accessed March 9, 2013).

8   K. Liebskind, "This is the Best Planned Spontaneous Protest You've Ever Seen" (Hebrew), NRG Maariv, http://www.nrg.co.il/app/index.php?do=blog&encr_id=79974780b5e0d394fddbd1a00f4f21d3& id=2804 (accessed March 9, 2013).

9   Y. Melman, "Methods of Diversion," *Ha'aretz*, http://www.haaretz.com/weekend/week-s-end/methods-of-diversion-1.377120 (accessed March 9, 2013).

10   S. Shaffir, "The Silent March—A letter to the tent cities," (Hebrew) Facebook note.

11   Anon., "Dialogue circles: Between social justice and national fortitude" (Hebrew), Facebook event, http://www.facebook.com/events/221411751239242/ (accessed March 9, 2013).

12   The Knesset, "Protocol 152 of the Committee on State Comptroller Affairs" (Hebrew- P. 19), http://www.knesset.gov.il/protocols/data/rtf/bikoret/2011-01-18.rtf (accessed March 9, 2013).

13   U. Glasser, "Face of a Nation," *Alondon*, http://www.alondon.net/index.php?action=art&id=5677 (accessed March 9, 2013).

MARIKANA
A POINT OF RUPTURE?

BENJAMIN FOGEL

AUGUST 16, 2012 WILL SURELY JOIN JUNE 16 AND MARCH 23 AS A DAY of infamy in South African history; the police force of a democratically elected government shot 102 black working-class miners—killing 34 and wounding 78—and arrested an additional 270 men at the Lonmin (London Mining) mine in Marikana. This followed the deaths of ten other men in the week building up to the massacre, beginning with the murder of two miners, allegedly by NUM (National Union of Mineworkers) officials. The initial coverage of the massacre in the print media and the TV footage that played out to the world appeared to indicate that the miners, carrying traditional weapons, were shot in a suicidal charge at the police lines. The blame for the deaths was largely placed at the feet of the "violent miners" or the perceived opportunism of the independent union AMCU (Association of Mining and Construction Workers Union), which supposedly "led" workers along with false promises to deliver successfully on the workers' basic demand of an R 12,500 (around USD 1,300) monthly wage.

> An economic crisis occurs, sometimes lasting for decades. This exceptional duration means that incurable structural contradictions have revealed themselves (reached maturity) and that, despite this, the political forces that are struggling to conserve and defend the existing structure itself are making every effort to cure

> these contradictions, within certain limits, and to over-
> come them. These incessant and persistent efforts form
> the terrain of the "conjunctural" and it is upon this ter-
> rain that the forces of opposition organize.[1]

Gramsci's oft-cited formulation offers an entry point for an understanding of South Africa—the "miracle" country as of 2012. South
Africa, despite eighteen years of majority rule, continues to be one of
the most unequal societies on an increasingly unequal planet, and is in
crisis. Around half the population, mostly black Africans, live below
the poverty line.[2] Almost half of all black African households earned
below R 1,670 a month in 2005–2006, while only 2 percent of white
households fell into that income bracket.[3] South Africa ranked as the
second most unequal country in the world after Namibia, according
to the 2011 World Bank measure, using the Gini coefficient. Unemployment consistently hovers unofficially at around 40 percent, and
among eighteen- to twenty-five-year-olds, it is now over 60 percent.[4]
Despite some improvements in recent years, millions of households
still lack access to basic services and the education system still equips
most blacks for little other than a future as unskilled labor. This is
despite the existence of the much-lauded "progressive constitution,"
with a Bill of Rights that supposedly insures access to basic socio-
economic rights. To put this in simpler terms, South Africa is fucking
unequal and the black African working class and unemployed Africans continue to be the worst off.

This is normality. What the Marikana massacre marks is the most
visible display of the failure of the ruling ANC's hegemonic project,
and the inability of the forces struggling to conserve the "existing
structure" to contain multiple forces emerging from the ongoing crisis in South Africa. The ANC, despite its seemingly unchallengeable
political supremacy, and its faltering political alliance with the 2.2
million-strong trade union federation COSATU (Congress of South
African Trade Unions) and the politically, spiritually, and morally (but
not financially) bankrupt SACP (South African Communist Party),
has been unable to forge a viable social compact with local capital
capable of benefiting the majority of South Africa. They've been unable to either create sufficient jobs to combat mass unemployment or
bring down levels of inequality—which have increased since the end
of the bitter struggle that brought about the demise of apartheid.

The ANC adopted a twofold economic strategy, by which policies would be introduced to create a black "national bourgeoisie," to counter the hegemony of white capital both in South Africa and worldwide.[5] To achieve this, they followed a "development" program, based on attracting foreign capital investment through capital-intensive projects, intended to create favorable business conditions and unleash domestic capital from the chains of apartheid-era sanctions and regulations. What in fact happened was that the still-fetishized foreign investors failed to materialize, and domestic capital was free to relocate to the more temperate financial climates of the North. Many of South Africa's largest firms, such as Anglo American, relocated to the UK, while South African capital was free to pillage the rest of the continent, which it had previously been unable to access. On the local front, South Africa effectively introduced a self-imposed structural adjustment package, under the auspices of the ironically named "GEAR" (Growth Employment and Redistribution) policy introduced in 1996, which saw the privatization of basic services (that the government is constitutionally obliged to provide), rapid cuts in the public sector, and the privatization of state-owned entities.

Over a million jobs were lost. Meanwhile, the South African manufacturing sector declined dramatically due to the relaxation of trade tariffs, forcing local industries to compete with India, China, and Indonesia, etc., and leading to further job losses. The rise of the financial sector and the traditional economic base of "extraction" have largely overshadowed production in South Africa.[6] Formalized work is also on the decline. Instead, government policy and capital is increasingly forwarding precarious labor as the solution to the unemployment crisis, through the promotion of labor brokering and the so-called "youth wage subsidy," which aims to alleviate youth unemployment through subsidizing businesses that employ young people for low wage work to earn "experience" (i.e., to be superexploited).

The mining industry is at the root of both South Africa's wealth and its tragedy, and still forms one of the key sectors of the economy, as part of the so-called MEC (Minerals-Energy Complex). However, since 1994, the MEC has shrunk due to the increased financialization of the South African economy in line with global trends. Employment in the MEC core has been in decline since the late 1980s, dropping from 1.4 million in 1987 to 1.1 million in 2010. In 2010, the share of

MEC sector output to GDP continued to be significant, fluctuating between 21 percent and 23 percent, even if shifting in composition. [7]

Furthermore, the platinum sector has outpaced the gold sector as the most profitable mining industry, in light of declining gold reserves and the rise of a global demand for platinum in recent years, which has seen the price of platinum rise significantly. South Africa accounts for 70 percent of global platinum production. Platinum mining now employs 24,000 more workers than the gold sector. Appalling pay and dangerous work conditions persist in the mines to this day. In the Lonmin Marikana mines, rock drillers are each asked to perform a job usually meant for three people. The miners' pay is linked to performance bonuses based, in part, on the quantity of work performed, as miners are asked to compete against each other. This is a classic example of the neoliberal restructuring of the workplace, where miners work twelve-hour days for the mere possibility of a bonus.

The rock drillers at Marikana were earning around R4,500 a month after deductions and, on average, each rock driller had around eight people to support on that meager sum. The appalling living conditions in mining communities, where the majority of black workers live, exist side-by-side with skilled workers' compounds (almost entirely white), which resemble the gated communities of rich, suburban South Africa, complete with shopping malls and golf courses.

The structural crisis, which reached its height in the 1980s, forced white capital to abandon apartheid, as it was perceived to no longer be the most efficient vehicle for capital accumulation.[8] This process began with covert meetings between the captains of South African industry and the ANC leadership-in-exile and ended in the high drama of CODESA (Convention for a Democratic South Africa).

Those who have benefited most from this transition were white South Africans and white capitalists, who saw their international pariah status revoked and the new system slanted to their benefit. A new black middle class and a small black bourgeoisie have also benefited. While the media is flush with lewd reports of their perceived lavish lifestyles, many of those dubbed "black diamonds" by the media rely primarily on their access to credit, while satisfying white capital's need to display a black superstructure, in order to disguise the continued base of white ownership. Much of this emergent black bourgeoisie has relied on political connections and access to the state as a vehicle for accumulation. A select few, the likes of Patrice Motsepe, have amassed vast fortunes, and others, such as the once-militant ex-chairperson of NUM turned McDonald's franchise owner, Cyril Ramaphosa, have made the seamless transition to billionaire status through amassing shares and board positions in London Mining (Lonmin). Members of both the Zuma and Mandela families have seen a similar change in fortune over the last few years as well.[9]

As structural unemployment persists, those who are lucky enough to find work find their income insufficient for keeping up with the steep increases in cost of living, large swathes of the country lack access to basic services, and a recipe for militant protest arises. South Africa has been described as the protest capital of the world. In the last three years, there have been an average of 2.9 "gatherings" per day, resulting in 12,654 "gathering" incidents in 2010–2011.[10] Such statistics say little about the actual political character of these protests and they shouldn't necessarily be taken as a sign of the rise of a new counterhegemonic bloc in the country. Indeed, to refer to Gramsci's formulation, these protests indicate the forces emerging in relation to the continuing crisis, which those political forces seeking to preserve the existing structure are unable to overcome. What, in effect, these political forces stand for, as a whole, remains an open question and the crisis is expressed in the "vocabularies of the local."

What is clear though is that there is a deep social unrest, which has been escalating over the last few years. Meanwhile, the government has been either unwilling or unable to craft a program capable of reducing poverty and inequality, or to cajole white capital into some sort of sustainable social compact à la the East Asian developmental state often promoted as a model for South Africa to emulate. Less has been said about the nature of proletarian insurgency at the workplace—violent and militant strikes are a regular feature of South African labor relations, due to a high level of militant consciousness and unionization among the black South African working class. With union leadership increasingly being co-opted into ANC politicking and forming "working relationships" with capital, workers have been embarking on wildcat strikes to achieve their demands—particularly in the mining sector. The rise of independent unions such as AMCU (Association of Mining and Construction Workers Union) is a direct response to the inability of established trade unions within COSATU to represent workers' interests.

Independent unions such as AMCU should not necessarily be regarded as more "progressive" or "worker-centered" than the formations they split from. Indeed, AMCU, for example, describes itself as an "apolitical" union, and aspires to win majority recognition at NUM's former citadels in the Platinum Belt, and settle down to normalize relations between labor and capital in the sector. Furthermore, if the "left" or COSATU don't manage to intervene in support or take advantage of intensified class struggles, such as the recent farmworkers' uprising in the Western Cape, the space that opens up could be seized by reactionary and opportunistic forces employing a populist political methodology. For example, the rise of a new union, BAWUSA (Bawsi Agriculture Workers Union of South Africa), in the town of De Doorns (the epicenter of the farmworkers strike), whose leadership consists of black agricultural capitalists and labor brokers with links to the ANC, became the leading force in the area when COSATU went AWOL and the left was not able to extend solidarity to the uprising in the town.

The existing set of labor relations in South Africa has seen the continuation of the apartheid-era, two-tier model of skilled, mostly white, middle- and upper-income work for a select few, while the majority of blacks find themselves competing over the few jobs available to "low wage" and "unskilled labor," such as those at Marikana. The persistence of these labor structures and high unemployment has meant that those with work often have to support large and extended families on their low wages, restricting both the growth of an internal market in South Africa and ensuring that most employed black South Africans still live in appalling conditions. This is not a "challenge," as described by ANC Secretary-General Gwede Mantashe at a recent COSATU conference—this is a crisis, one that has been building for decades.

In the first major industrial action of last year, platinum miners at the Implats (Impala Platinum) mine won an R 5,000 increase in the face of state repression and violence. But the last few months have seen the most sustained and militant victorious proletarian struggle since the fragile birth of "liberal democracy" in 1994, following the brutal massacre of thirty-four workers on August 16, 2012, by police at the Marikana mine, which is owned by the British company Lonmin. The massacre of these workers occurred in the midst of a wildcat strike brought about by the perceived failure of the dominant mining union NUM (National Union of Mineworkers) to protect the interests of workers. Miners still operate in the same hyperexploitative extractive sector and within the two-tier labor market that has been both the primary source of South Africa's riches and its tragedy for over a hundred years. Men plucked from the former bantustans go up north, far removed from their friends and family, to work for as long as twelve hours a day, for an average wage, after deductions, of around R 4,500 a month (around USD 550). To put this into perspective, Frans Baleni, the chairperson of NUM, earns around R 1.4 million (USD 165,000) a year. This is what drove the miners to strike, demanding R 12,500 a month (USD 1,512). They downed their tools and embarked on a six-week strike, during which they faced down the power of state and capital.

Reports on September 18 suggested a deal had been reached between the miners and Lonmin for a 22 percent salary increase across the board and an R 2,000 bonus for returning to work. Despite the fact that the miners didn't win their R 12,500, this is still a historic victory. The miners, with little or no support from "civil society" or the "left," and facing a hostile media, managed to face down a state prepared to kill to defend the interests of capital, and wrangle a demand still deemed "irrational" by a morally decrepit bunch of hacks and economists (still mostly lily-white) who style themselves as the voices of reason in this country. Rock drillers working at platinum mines in Canada, performing exactly the same job, get paid around $130,000 a year—earning more in a month than South African miners earn in a year. Reports from miners have suggested the company has been lying about the nature of the increase, is still skiving off money from the workers, and, despite the increase, miners on the ground are still dissatisfied with their pay, indicating that the saga of Marikana is far from over.[11]

The miners were forced to negotiate, as the police had imposed an unofficial state of emergency in the area, with the near-full support of the red-baiting, panicked corporate media. Another three people were murdered, however, bringing the total death toll to forty-seven. Workers reported that any man on the streets at night in the area was a target for the police, and police forcibly dispersed and attacked any attempted gathering, while patrolling the streets with armored cars and assault rifles (the same rifles used to shoot down the miners on August 16).[12] Police also raided the hostels and homes of the miners, in an attempt to intimidate them the weekend before the deal was reached. Reports indicated that they shot several people, including the local ANC councilor, who later died from her injuries.[13]

The deal reached at Marikana did not mark the end of the industrial unrest that spread across South Africa's platinum belt with two months of wildcat strike action; rather it marks the beginning of what is surely an intensification of proletarian struggle in the mining sector. I say this for reasons other than the continued existence of appalling living conditions and low remuneration for miners.[14] What Marikana illustrated is the violence that the state is willing to unleash in defense of capital and its allies, in this case in the form of NUM. This, as I will discuss later, is part of a pattern of increasing violence that has been deployed to break up community and social movement protests. Furthermore, it shows that it is possible to take on the full force of the state and capital and win. It inspired miners across the platinum belt to fight for an R 12,500 minimum wage across the sector. Finally, it has shown that the established "representatives" of the working class, in the form of NUM and COSATU, are incapable and unwilling to take up the demands of the workers, and unable to provide either a straight condemnation of the massacre or any material aid to the workers. If anything, NUM has been shown to be an agent of both the interests of the ruling Zuma faction within the ANC and the mining industry.

The situation brings to mind Rosa Luxemburg's remarks on the German printers' union, written in the heady days of 1907:

> The classical embodiment of that trade-union policy which prefers peace to struggle, settlement with capitalism to conflict, political neutrality to open support for the Social-Democratic Party, and which, filled with scorn for revolutionary "fanaticism," sees its ideal in the English type of trade union. It has taken a long time, but now the fruits of such a policy have become obvious to even the most shortsighted of persons.[15]

Gramsci suggests that as "hegemony," or rule by consent, breaks down, direct violence will increasingly be relied on to preserve the established order. The South African government has increased its use of repressive force and tactics over the last few years,[16] as the police were militarized for the World Cup. Military ranks have been reintroduced and the number of police shootings rises every year. Police "generals" have taken up slogans like "shoot-to-kill." Force has been used on a consistent basis to break up community protests and target social movement activists. Police Commissioner Riah Phiyanga described the action of the police after the massacre, saying, "All we did was our job, and . . . in the manner we were trained."[17] To further illustrate how the police accomplished their job so well, Phiyana states, "Whatever happened represents the best of responsible policing. You did what you did because you were being responsible. You were making sure that you continue to live your oath."[18]

This began not in Marikana but with the torture of activists from the Landless People's Movement (LPM), and became more visible with the pogrom against the shack-dwellers' movement, Abhali Basemjondolo (ABM), at the Kennedy Road settlement in Durban in 2010, and last year's televised murder of Andreas Tatane by the police in Ficksburg.[19] This suggests that the violence that occurred in Marikana was not an isolated incident; rather it fits in with the character of "political violence" which has become an increasingly visible presence in South Africa. The ANC under President Zuma has thrown off much of its socialist and "progressive" trappings, despite the craven unconditional backing of this faction by the SACP and aligned elements of COSATU, particularly in NUM. A masculinist discourse of patriarchal tradition has become the dominant feature of Zuma's attempt to anchor the ANC in something resembling a coherent ideology.[20] While the ANC attempts to make up for its failures through the employment of outright repression, this repression is partially condoned by the anti-working-class and reactionary media, as well as fully condoned by the center-right opposition party, the Democratic Alliance (DA)—whose support base and political character is largely formed by ex-National Party (NP) voters, despite the DA's liberal pretensions.

Where does that leave the independent South African left? Mostly in a position of increased isolation from working-class struggles. The South African left has, to an extent, been pursuing what I consider to be a contradictory strategy in relation to COSATU and the SACP, which, I suggest, are organs of the state, subordinate to the ruling party. The independent left has been very careful to not sever its ties with COSATU and elements of the SACP. This strategy is based on the assumption that these organizations form the potential for a revolutionary base that will eventually abandon the ANC, due to the ANC's continued support of anti-working-class, neoliberal policies. This is apparent in the new policy gospel of the party, the NDP (National Democratic Plan), which can be described as GEAR 2.0; in essence, a repeat of the same disastrous neoliberal economic policies implemented in 1996. In particular, a call for a social compact based on "wage suppression," in return for not retrenching workers, while waiting for the arrival of foreign investors. These organizations would, in theory, then turn to the independent left and a new mass workers' party would emerge, capable of challenging the hegemony of the ANC. At the same time, much of the independent left has attempted to win over social movements and communities to a socialist project. The problems with this strategy are multiple and I will, in the interest of brevity, not delve into all of them. I will instead identify a few key flaws.

The first and most obvious flaw is that these goals lead to a contradiction in terms of prioritizing struggles. A key problem is that the SACP in particular, and elements of COSATU, adopt a paranoid, authoritarian stance toward protest and politics, located outside of the ruling alliance, and are often complicit (as evidenced by Marikana) in state repression directed towards movements and communities which the left is trying to "win over." This contradiction is not trivial, and has often resulted in the left being held in deep suspicion by the so-called left within the ruling alliance. Often some of the most vocal "left" critics of the ANC maintain cozy relationships with the likes of the odious South African Communist Party Secretary-General Blade Ndzimande and his eager deputy, and chief ideologue, Jeremy Cronin, and others, or they even consult for the state. This further hampers the ability of the left to build working and sustainable connections with communities in struggle, and has resulted in a tendency to attempt to channel local struggles towards the "real" enemies—neoliberalism and the World Bank—at the expense of the local contradictions which gave rise to these struggles in the first place. Elements of the left somewhat contradictorily want to maintain their relationships with COSATU officials and not risk their relationship with the federation, but at the same time support independent working-class struggles in splinter unions or the strike committees that emerged during the Marikana strike wave.

This contradictory policy has alienated much of the independent left from local struggles and has further hampered the ability of the independent left to establish zones of counterpower or powerful movements capable of challenging the hegemony of the ANC. The origins of this problematic position lie in the age-old left tradition of fetishizing the state as the source of all progressive change. The state is treated as an instrument that, if only the right people were in charge, could be capable of bringing about transformative change. The result is a general immobility of the left if the conditions are not right for "the revolution" or the seizure of state power. This leads to inertia and is one of the primary reasons for what has been an observable decline in the power and ideas of the left following 1994. This is closely linked to the demobilization of the mass movements and grassroots locales of counterpower that emerged in the 1980s for a variety of reasons, including a widespread faith in the ANC's ability to bring about transformative change in South Africa, and the ANC leadership's attempt, upon returning from exile, to monopolize their power within the wider democratic movement, at the expense of the leaders who emerged from domestic mass struggles.

The second problem with the left's position lies in the changing character of the South African black proletariat and their relation to COSATU. Marikana marks a point of departure or rupture, if you like, within these relations. It is fair to assert that most of the COSATU leadership has been incorporated into the ANC. Many have made the transition between union leadership positions and government posts. COSATU as an organization intervened directly in internal ANC politics to help Zuma unseat then-president Mbeki and bring Zuma to power. Since then, COSATU has found itself prioritizing ANC politics at the expense of the interests of workers.

This is not to say that COSATU, or even the ANC, is a homogenous bloc. As a 2.2 million strong formation, COSATU contains a multiplicity of ideological and political currents. The 300,000-member NUMSA (National Union of the Metalworkers of South Africa) is perhaps the ANC's most vocal radical critic, consistently pointing out the ANC's embrace of neoliberalism and SACP's complete dismissal of worker's struggles. COSATU General Secretary Zwenlinzima Vavi, despite his own past role in helping to bring Zuma to power, is the most prominent public figure to offer a leftist critique within the ruling alliance, something that has won him no friends among the power elite of the ANC and SACP. ANC and SACP factionalism has been imported into COSATU.

The SACP's own desire to control the worker's moment has been present since the birth of the black trade union movement in the 1970s. It has since tried to subjugate the workers' movements in the loving but iron embrace of the SACP's politburo. The SACP, it should be noted, has largely liquidated itself into the Zuma faction of the ANC. Until now, the independent political currents within COSATU have been strong enough to resist this attempt, but it seems the balance of forces at the leadership level have shifted towards the SACP and thus the Zuma faction.

This reality is combined with the precarious state of the mining industry in South Africa. The South African gold industry is in its last days, as gold reserves, historically the foundation of the South African economy, decline. And platinum prices continue to drop. This is the real reason for the intensification of extractive mining practices, with workers left uncompensated for the added risk. The wave of wildcat strikes moved into the gold sector and saw 40 percent of gold production in the country shut down,[21] as workers, inspired by Marikana, took up the R 12,500 minimum wage demand;[22] this demand might even have been taken up by workers in neighboring Namibia *and* by workers in the South African transport sector (which has seen 20,000 workers go on strike).

Unions like NUM have responded to this by forming close relationships to companies such as Lonmin and Anglo American, agreeing to keep a check on workers' demands and negotiate gradual increases, in return for favorable treatment and business links for ex-NUM leaders like Cyril Ramaphosa and Marcel Golding. Furthermore, NUM's investment wing (standing at R 2 billion) has even invested in the mining sector! This, combined with unions' continued attachment to the ANC, which has pursued, as indicated earlier, a rather orthodox neoliberal line since coming to power, has in effect resulted in an antagonism displayed most clearly at Marikana, with a union leadership increasingly removed from the shop floor, unable and unwilling to represent the interests of workers.

This antagonism has led to the wave of wildcat strikes coming to its first point of rupture at Marikana; workers have, in effect, been forced to become an autonomous force, in order to secure their interests through unsanctioned militant action.[23] As unions and the ANC continue to fail to support workers in their demands for a living wage, working-class action will continue to take on such autonomous characteristics, united in hostility both to capital and to organs of state power in the form of unions like NUM and local ANC branches.[24] As the state is unable to provide some sort of solution to the organic crisis present in South Africa, it will rely on repression to contain industrial action and community protest. Marikana indicated that, in order for workers to achieve their demands, they need to operate autonomously, independent from their union representatives. Marikana inspired a wave of wildcat strikes across the mining sector that lasted for about two months. In this, class consciousness on the shop floor appears to be emerging, despite the SACP's pathetic attempts to claim that the actions at Marikana were led by some sort of third middle class force,[25] that doped up the miners with *muti* (traditional medicine), and was aligned with the forces of imperialism and the bogeyman of expelled ANCYL (African National Congress Youth League) President Julius Malema.[26] They also absurdly charged that these strikes were the result of a "lack of class consciousness."

It is from this recognition of the increasingly autonomous nature of the South African proletariat that any sort of left strategy should emerge from Marikana. I can't claim to have all the answers, but two things stand out. First, there is a need for the left to abandon the CO-SATU leadership as working partners, particularly considering that much of it is comprised of SACP apparatchiks, and instead attempt to build working relations and provide material aid to workers on the shop floor.[27] This doesn't mean the left shouldn't engage with the leadership of progressive unions within COSATU or that we should attempt to undermine existing COSATU unions through attempting to build new formations. Rather, the focus should be on appealing directly to workers. With the unity of COSATU in doubt and the possibility of NUMSA potentially leaving COSATU, the balance of forces in South Africa could be in for a future shakeup, and a left with links to militant workers could find new spaces opening up, of which to take advantage.

The second lesson is the need to build fortresses of counterpower at a distance from the state; instead of NGOs, legalistic tactics, and insular debate, we need to create zones that show the possibility of challenging the hegemony of the ANC. We need to invest in culture, alternative radio stations, new publications, and communities, drawing on South African's history of grassroots militancy and civic organizations. An insurgent movement, capable of challenging the structure of a country in crisis, needs to abandon the politics of mediating the masses' interests, and instead focus on building zones in which a revolutionary future can be glimpsed. Furthermore, urgent solidarity is needed with intensified class struggles. The left's reaction to both the

Marikana strike wave and the farmworkers' uprising were slow. Due to a lack of resources and uncommunicative structures, it took much too long for active displays of solidarity to reach workers. Why should workers look to the left for anything, if the left doesn't earn their trust through actively supporting their struggles materially, not just in the form of press statements? Now is not the time to talk about the "armed seizure of state power," (indeed, state power seems to be part of the problem) but that does not mean we can sit back and wait.

ENDNOTES

1 Antonio Gramsci, *Selections From the Prison Notebooks* (New York: International Press, 1971), 178.

2 Hein Marais, *Pushed to the Limit: The Political Economy of Change* (Cape Town: University of Cape Town Press, 2011), 203.

3 Ibid.

4 Claire Price, "Youth unemployment: South Africa's ticking bomb," *Mail and Guardian*, http://mg.co.za/article/2012-02-21-youth-unemployment-south-africas-ticking-bomb/ (accessed May 16, 2013).

5 See the prescient condemnation and critique of the "national bourgeoisie" in Franz Fanon, *The Wretched of the Earth* (New York: Grove Press, 1963).

6 I base this account on the outstanding Hein Marais, *South Africa: Limits to Change: The Political Economy of Transition* (London: Zed Books, 2008).

7 Ben Fine and Susan Newman, "Systems of Accumulation and the Evolving Minerals-Energy Complex," in (ed.) B. Fine, J. Saraswati, and D. Tavasci, *Beyond the Developmental State: Industrial Policy into the 21st Century* (London: Pluto, in preparation).

8 See Steve Gelb, "Making Sense of the Crisis," *Transformations* 5 (1987): 5.

9 Editorial, "Aurora's Zuma must be held to account for mine debacle," *Times Live*, http://www.timeslive.co.za/opinion/editorials/2012/01/13/aurora-s-zuma-must-be-held-to-account-for-mine-debacle (accessed May 19, 2013).

10   Peter Alexander, "Protests and Police Statistics in South Africa: Some Commentary," *Amandla!*, http://www.amandla.org.za/home-page/1121-protests-and-police-statistics-some-commentary-by-prof-peter-alexander (accessed May 19, 2013).

11   Heidi Swart, "Lonmin Miners Crack Under Pressure," *Mail and Guardian*, http://mg.co.za/article/2012-09-21-00-lonmin-miners-crack-under-pressure/ (accessed May 19, 2013).

12   Ibid.

13   Mandy De Waal, "Marikana's Theatre of the Absurd Claims Another Life," *Daily Maverick*, http://www.dailymaverick.co.za/article/2012-09-20-marikanas-theatre-of-the-absurd-claims-another-life#.UZlFdb-VQHCs (accessed May 19, 2013).

14   Mandy De Waal, "Unsafe House, Unsafe Job? The Foul Truth About Living Conditions in Marikana," *Daily Maverick*, http://www.dailymaverick.co.za/article/2012-09-27-unsafe-house-unsafe-job-the-foul-truth-about-living-conditions-at-marikana#.UZlLpbVQHCs (accessed May 19, 2013).

15   Rosa Luxemburg, "The Two Methods of Trade-Union Policy," *Marxists. org*, http://www.marxists.org/archive/luxemburg/1907/10/24.htm (accessed May 19, 2013).

16   Christopher McMichael, "The South African Police Service and the Public Order War," *Think Africa Press*, http://thinkafricapress.com/south-africa/police-service-and-public-order-war-saps-marikana-lonmin (accessed May 19, 2013).

17   Sapa, "Phiyega Footage at Marikana Inquiry," *Sowetan Live*, http://www.sowetanlive.co.za/news/2013/01/22/phiyega-footage-at-marikana-inquiry (accessed May 19, 2013).

18   Ibid.

19   See Kerry Chance, "The Work of Violence: A Timeline of Armed Attacks at Kennedy Road," *School of Development Studies Research*, Report No. 83 (2010).

20   Richard Pithouse, "Facing Reality," *The South African Civil Society Information Service*, http://www.sacsis.org.za/site/article/1404# (accessed May 19, 2013).

21   David McKay, "Strike Contagion Shuts Down 40% of SA Gold," *Miningmx.com*, http://www.miningmx.com/page/news/

gold_and_silver/1405955-Strike-contagion-shuts-down-40-of-SA-gold#.UZletbVQHCs (accessed May 19, 2013).

22   Catherine Sasman, "Strikes Due to Social Inequality—Experts," *The Namibian*, http://www.namibian.com.na/index.php?id=28&tx_ttnews%5Btt_news%5D=87702&no_cache=1 (accessed May 19, 2013).

23   I take this understanding of the autonomy of the working class loosely from the Italian *autonomia* theoretical tradition, although the theoretical tendency emerged in a vastly different socio-political context, with its description of the emergence of the "mass worker" in the Keynesian planner states in the 1960s and 1970s. I find it provides a useful starting point in Negri's concept of the "self-valorization of the working-class" (see "Worker's Party Against Work," in *Books for Burning* [London: Verso, 1973, 2005], 74–77), referring to the working class's ability to define itself as a class outside of the logic of the state and capital.

24   It remains to be seen whether workers will abandon the ANC in the absence of any realistic alternatives, either in the form of the parliamentary opposition or the extraparliamentary left.

25   Hlongwane, "South Africa: Cosatu Congress."

26   Malema has perhaps been the only prominent political actor in the country to display any sort of support for the miners in the form of both his unique brand of rhetoric—think Hugo Chavez meets Kanye West—and material and legal aid. Malema has been accused rightly of using Marikana to hit back at his nemesis, President Zuma, and has faced both death threats and threats of arrest from reactionary white formations and the state. Despite his opportunism, he has shown up the cowardice of the ruling alliance's response to Marikana.

27   Leonard Gentle, "Mangaung Versus Marikana: COSATU Chooses Sides," *The South African Civil Society Information Service*, http://www.sacsis.org.za/site/article/1435 (accessed May 19, 2013).

PART 5

EDUCATION AND THE STUDENT RESPONSE

"Washing one's hands of the conflict between the powerful and the powerless means to side with the powerful, not to be neutral."
—Paulo Freire

REVOLUTIONARY TERRAINS AND HIGHER EDUCATION IN THE US

WILLIAM ARMALINE
AND ABRAHAM DELEON

INTRODUCTION

PREVIOUS WORK AND OTHER CHAPTERS IN THIS VOLUME SHOW THAT recent social movements, including the Arab spring, European antiausterity movements, Occupy movements, and labor movements, in the wake of the global "great recession," are substantially fueled by young adults facing uncertain if not dire economic, social, and ecological prospects.[1] Whether looking at student populations in Quebec, global indigenous populations in the Idle No More movement, mining populations in Asturias (Spain), or the credentialed "graduate with no future" in Barcelona or Madrid, those resisting share expectations unmet by the neoliberal capitalist project of the last half century.[2] Sustainable employment, a healthy biosphere, a living wage, and social security are growing uncertainties in much of the world, even for those privileged enough to obtain credentials at Western universities.

Given the broader political-economic context provided in this volume, how would we describe the economic conditions and outlook of those entering (students, young adults, immigrant populations) and re-entering (those forced to find more or different work) the "educated" workforce? What if the fundamental ideologies legitimating educational meritocracy and wage slavery no longer resonate with workers and stakeholders? *What opportunities emerge for teachers and public intellectuals as fundamental beliefs and expectations about school and work under capitalism break down?*

WHAT DO STUDENTS AND NEW WORKERS FACE?

AS THE OSCAR-WINNING documentary *Inside Job* (2010) and a mountain of research makes clear, the crash of 2008 should be understood instrumentally as the result of reckless criminal fraud for the sake of redistributing and concentrating wealth upward, and structurally as a manifestation of capitalism in cycles of crisis.[3] "Nonpartisan" state sources such as the US Congressional Research Office verify that the wealthiest among us were generally untouched by the crisis and that many at the top actually increased their wealth and concentration of capital.[4] Not coincidentally, as we pen this chapter, *Bloomberg News* reports, "World's Wealthiest Gain $45 Billion as Dow Reaches 15,000."[5] In other words, the claims made by the Occupy movement and their concerns for the resources held by the global "1%" seem to be quite salient. Primary US markets have doubled in value from 2008 at the bottom of the market crash and stand at record highs. The companies and banks that caused the recession have completely recovered, and US corporations in the powerful financial, tech, oil, and pharmaceutical industries enjoy record profits.[6]

As one intellectual founder of Western capitalism put it, "For one very rich man there must be at least five hundred poor, and the affluence of the few supposes the indigence of the many."[7] Wealth disparity in the US and much of the world continues to climb. By 2010 in the US, "The top 1% of households (the upper class) owned 35.4% of all privately held wealth, and the next 19% (the managerial, professional, and small business stratum) had 53.5%, *which means that just 20% of the people owned a remarkable 89%, leaving only 11% of the wealth for the bottom 80%* (wage and salary workers)."[8] Smiley and West's *The Rich and the Rest of Us* and Hedges and Sacco's *Days of Destruction, Days of Revolt* thoroughly illustrate growing poverty in the United States, and the increase in size and number of "sacrifice zones," where extreme and lasting poverty continue to strangle ex-manufacturing cities, rural and mining communities, and native reservations.[9] As Smiley and West report, the wealthiest 400 families in the US own more than one half of the population (140 million), who are now at or near poverty.[10]

For the first time since the government started measuring long-term unemployment in 1948, 6.3 million people in the US had been unemployed for six months or more in 2009.[11] Shrinking unemployment rates in the US (under 8 percent) should be seen as an *illusion* of recovery for working people. It should be understood as part of the broader trend of rising service sector and contingent work in the US since economic globalization "from above," where living-wage jobs (many in manufacturing) were replaced by service sector work and the now iconic, near-mythical "American middle class" was replaced by automation and cheaper labor pools. It should also be understood in detail: real unemployment (including those who have dropped out of the labor market entirely) remains consistently around 14 percent in the US.[12] Further, a great majority of the jobs created in the so-called "recovery" are low-paid, highly contingent positions in the service sector or temporary work force.[13] Unemployment and its effects are concentrated among the most marginalized: for youth and young adults (sixteen to twenty-four), unemployment rose to nearly 20 percent at the recession's peak in 2008[14] and African American unemployment remains twice that of the national average.[15]

Those with a college education in the US enjoy lower unemployment rates, higher average wages, and lower rates of incarceration.[16] This doesn't mean college grads in the US are faring well in the job market. Nearly half of recently employed US college graduates work a job that didn't require an undergraduate degree—including over five million working in jobs that require less than a high school diploma.[17] This trend will likely continue as graduation rates far outstrip high-skilled, living-wage job availability.[18]

The search for sustainable employment is complicated by rising student debt loads. State and local funding of education has fallen in real dollars per student by one third since 2001,[19] while tuition rose dramatically for community colleges (40%) and four-year universities (68 percent) nationwide.[20] Collective student debt in the US rose from $400 billion in 2004 to nearly a trillion dollars today. Both the number of those with debt and the amount they owed as individuals rose by 70 percent between 2004 and 2012.[21] The average balance of US student borrowers is now $25K per person, up from $15K in 2004.[22] As we submit this chapter, the rates for federally subsidized student loans are set to double (to 6.4 percent) on July 1, 2013, and a current Republican bill passed by the US House of Representatives proposes tying these rates to those in the private market.[23]

The US Congress and Obama administration promote agendas of federal deficit reduction through cuts to some of the few remaining social safety nets: Social Security, Medicare, and Medicaid, while many of the most powerful corporations continue to pay nothing in taxes, and the financial institutions and practices that led to the 2008 collapse continue virtually unabated. The now-popular term for state policies that make the poor pay for the blunders and gluttony of the rich is "austerity"—a word that also refers to ascetic discipline and simplicity. The concept actually refers to the continued privatization of public resources and assault on organized labor—practices not unfamiliar throughout economic globalization and reinvigorated by opportunities created by the global recession. Its use demonstrates the cultural expressions of capitalism through language (for more on this, see the chapter in this collection by Chris Spannos), connoting dominant neoliberal messaging and a retelling of history, where the recession of 2008 was caused by the greed and unrealistic expectations of the working class, rather than the criminal fraud of banks and private firms. The masses need to be disciplined—to be more austere in their way of life and in their expectations.

Politicians and corporate media successfully and dutifully sell austerity as the solution to our recent economic crisis in the face of abject failure. Austerity and other forms of socio-economic tyranny created and continue to exacerbate massive unemployment in Europe and regions of the Arab spring movements. Unemployment in the Eurozone rose to an all-time high of 12.1 percent in March 2013. Those under 25 years of age face the worst unemployment rates (24 percent). Unemployment for those under 25 ranges from 7.6 percent in Germany to a whopping 59 percent in Greece.[24] Young peoples' involvement in the recent overthrow of Mubarak in Egypt (only to end up with the short-lived, quasi-fundamentalist Morsi administration, pushed out by a "soft" military coup with no democratic political solution in sight) can in part be explained by a lack of economic opportunities. The young continue to make up a vast majority of the country's unemployed, like in Europe and the US, with poverty on the rise and the Egyptian economy unable to offer enough new jobs (200,000 per year) for its educated graduates (700,000 per year).[25] Notably, the business press is well aware of the growing population of *hittistes* (those who stand against the wall) in Yemen, *shabab atileen* (unemployed youths) in Egypt, NEETs (not in education, employment, or training) in England, *mileuristas* (earning less than 1000 EU per month) or *Indignados* (the indignant) in Spain, or the *freeters* (free workers) in Japan. They were dubbed a global "youth unemployment bomb" in a 2011 *Bloomberg BusinessWeek* cover story.[26] The social movements against neoliberal capitalism and state austerity detailed in this book demonstrate that the business community and their press might have real reason to worry, as the significant force behind these movements are young people with less and less to lose. Many of these young people are well educated, and their resistance is to some extent fueled by their inability to find work on par with their expectations and credentials.

PUBLIC SCHOOLING AS VALUABLE CONTESTED TERRAIN

OUR CURRENT POLITICAL economic conditions present a world of opportunity for those of us in positions to act as public intellectuals and otherwise infiltrate major social institutions. This does not assume that radical intellectuals serve as the bastion of radical hope, or that some romanticized "revolutionary vanguard" of university professors are somehow elevated subjects, nor are we suggesting that folks need to work within the system, get a job, and wear fancy shoes to organize and act effectively. Our chapter is not suggesting that we are at some manifest moment of inevitable revolution that must be seized—or else!

Instead, we argue that public universities and schools are crucially important terrains for social struggle, and current political economic conditions and social movements suggest the contemporary importance and urgency of (re)capturing this terrain.[27] Public education is increasingly occupied and controlled by owning class (largely corporate) interests at great cost to the rest of us. Public universities are one of the few public spaces where the culture of free and critical inquiry necessary for democratic societies has foundation enough to still thrive—though not without threat and exceptions.[28] Like all public space and resources under the logic of neoliberalism, the public university is increasingly privatized and reduced to market functions.

The corporatization and privatization of the university system in the US has been documented for some time.[29] However, too few people talk openly about the crucial role of universities in the science and application of domination. In the era of global economic restructuring, universities provide the ideological[30] and intellectual (research and development—"R & D")[31] capital for the most brutal policies (neoliberal "development") and industries (pharmaceuticals, private military contractors, the bio-chemical industry, fossil fuel companies) on the planet—all at public cost. For a specific example, one might look to the "Energy Biosciences Institute" formed in partnership between UC Berkeley, the University of Illinois at Urbana-Champaign, the UC Lawrence Berkeley National Labs, and British Petroleum [BP], and funded by a $500 million gift from BP, in return for rights to all research and resulting patents and significant control over the direction of the Institute. It represents the largest "industry-academia alliance"[32] and "corporate funding package"[33] in history. To be clear, the oil company that single-handedly soiled the Gulf of Mexico, while escaping any major legal or economic consequences, now controls alternative fuel research at one of the most powerful "left-leaning" public institutions in the world. Like many multinational corporations, BP sees the university as an important and valuable institution to control in the pursuit of minds and market share. As a result, their actions march us closer to self-imposed climate disaster, while solidifying and expanding corporate rule over depleting public space and resources.[34]

Public schools are an incredible revolutionary terrain precisely *because* they are an essential tool of domination for owners and rulers. This function is largely achieved through what Aronowitz[35] calls *schooling*—the socialization process necessary to train new, disciplined[36] workers, delivered through a pedagogical model that Paulo Freire[37] called "banking education." Banking education is easy to spot in the current educational culture of standardization and free market (read: parasitic) forms of higher education à la Phoenix University. Banking education reduces pedagogy to the one-way communication of what dominant interests label as legitimate and important knowledge from teacher to student. Students are voiceless, empty objects judged and sanctioned based on their ability to bank away and regurgitate the necessary facts and responses, while displaying the appropriate self-regulating and self-policing Foucauldian discipline desired in a wage slave. Teachers are reduced to cogs in these models too, held accountable to the extent to which their students fall into line and commit material to memory, no matter how irrelevant or alienating. One could not better describe contemporary public high schools under NCLB (No Child Left Behind)/Race to the Top or state universities as public coffers shrink under privatization schemes post-2008 crash. More importantly, the process of schooling represents dominant interests' structural ties to schools as a mechanism to reproduce and reinforce their dominant positions.

In contrast, we might think of *education* as "the collective and individual reflection[38] on the totality of life experiences: what we learn from peers, parents (and the socially situated cultures of which they are a part), media, and schools."[39] Education takes place in all facets of life and is related to the free and full cultural and intellectual development of individuals and communities. Education can and should flourish in public schools, universities, and cultural centers as well, but this is not an automatic function. As already noted, these spaces are easily dominated and choked out by the powerful if such power remains unchecked. Further, the development of education as defined here arguably requires spaces of intellectual, artistic, and cultural development demonstrated in many Dewey democratic school models.[40] It also requires a pedagogical approach, in direct contrast to banking education, that facilitates mutual human enlightenment and community building, rather than creating isolated, silenced, objects of capital. Fortunately, educational theorists have been developing such "critical pedagogies" for some time. Critical pedagogy values creativity, dialogue, and a reflexive approach to knowledge that shows the political nature of what we think we know. It attempts to reveal power relationships, while developing counter hegemonic knowledge and movements through a pedagogical approach that is open to revision and critical of the status quo. Critical pedagogy is thus antiracist, antisexist, and remains heavily influenced by Marxist critiques of social class and efforts to imagine alternatives to capitalism. "Radical" scholars and educators have also since proposed anarchist and left libertarian forms of pedagogy that arguably connect with and reflect the mutual political visions reflected in this volume and the front line of contemporary anticapitalist (not to mention anticolonial, patriarchal, or racist) struggles.[41]

Public schools and universities in the US, and much of the indus-trialized world, serve as both a mechanism of domination (school-ing) and a potential space and tool for individual intellectual growth and collective empowerment (education). Those who doubt the latter would struggle to explain the Athens Polytechnic Institute as home to far left resistance in Greece since the 1973 uprising against the mili-tary junta; the student-led Canadian "CLASSE" movement (see the interview with Jamie Burnett following this chapter and Bell 2013); student organizing in Tunisia or Egypt leading up to and during re-cent revolutionary movements;[42] college student participation in the Occupy movement;[43] or high schools and universities electrified in re-sistance to banning books and ethnic/cultural studies programs in the American southwest.[44] And these are only examples from the last five years. Public schools and universities are ongoing vehicles for some of the most radical, notable, and successful forms of political activity today, and they should be treated as a significant revolutionary terrain by those of us in anticapitalist movements.

Here we mean to demonstrate the uniqueness of public schools and universities as sites of resistance and institutions worthy of working-class capture. One of the key hegemonic mechanisms of domination and the reproduction of capitalism—the school—can often become a site of counterhegemonic resistance. Global resistance to the meltdown of 2008 and the broader system of neoliberal capitalism doesn't occur in these sites coincidentally. They manifest here in part because university communities are relatively privileged, lending the time and resources necessary for effective organizing and direct action campaigns. We find resistance in universities also because capitalism runs on the hegem-onic domination of hope, want, and worldview[45]—particularly for new generations of workers and security forces (police and military). Work-ers have to be convinced that the system has something to offer them for their toil, through the justification of massive inequalities as simple results of individual success and failure (meritocracy) in a well-func-tioning system. When the state and capitalists fail in their ability to do so, schools potentially educate and empower future resistance. This was not lost on Marx or Gramsci ("war of position").[46] The fundamental ideological necessity of the capitalist system also appeared in Weberian critiques of Marx over a century ago.[47]

We might refer to the constructed expectations of university stu-dents and other workers in training as the "false promises" of higher education in the new global economy:[48] that dedicating time and money (if one has the privilege) to educational credentialing ensures entry to a professional career, a living wage, the ability to support a family, and retire before death if one so chooses. Those who sacrifice, work, and study hard will be rewarded in the free market by their ability to out-compete others in the race for the best jobs or business opportunities. Students are told to take on debt as an investment toward a sustainable career, while those pushed out of work are told to do the same, in order to regain a competitive edge in the shifting job markets with a new or improved credential. Those who already work are told to work more and harder for less in real dollars in order to collect social security, pensions, and the chance to retire later in life.

As poverty, unemployment, and debt rise for workers, public schools and universities shrink and privatize, and austerity undercuts workers' chances at retirement and other benefits (such as healthcare), traditional rewards appear as fantasy. Students are being forced to pay more and more for educational credentialing while there are fewer and smaller rewards for making the sacrifices necessary to attend and excel in school—the "youth unemployment bomb" previously mentioned. These young people significantly fuel some of the most notable anticapitalist and otherwise revolutionary movements across the globe, as the false promises of meritocratic education under capitalism are exposed at moments of crisis and rupture like those following 2008.

STRATEGIC OPPORTUNITIES FOR TEACHERS AND STUDENTS

WHAT HAPPENS AS young people and other potential labor pools are forced to live with ever-decreasing expectations in return for their work and sacrifice? The answer: any number of things. We can certainly say from the contemporary resistance movements previously mentioned and explored in this volume that working and student populations are reacting in part by organizing and taking action against neoliberal capitalism and the various structural sources of economic, social, and ecological unsustainability. However, one could just as easily say that the same conditions give rise to people's participation in more destructive and pathological types of organization, resistance, and opportunity as offered by North American drug cartels, fundamentalist militias, or fascist parties. Indeed, left-leaning Egyptians had real reason to fear a revolution betrayed by an increasingly fundamentalist and centralized Morsi administration, quickly replaced in a military coup. The same structural conditions serve as recruiting tools for both Occupy and Tea Party movements in the US or both anarchist and fascist (Golden Dawn) movements in Greece. Public education is an important terrain of struggle in part because counterhegemonic resistance must be informed and vetted by an active and open civil society.

Critical educators have done a great deal to investigate the complexity of "resistance" as it manifests in school and work. Studies of student resistance to dominant forms of schooling find that often when resistance is uninformed, it becomes self-destructive and relatively ineffective. Poor students or students of color in these studies would recognize that their schools alienated them or simply trained them for a subordinate place in society, but chose forms of (often individual) resistance (open defiance, skipping school, or dropping out altogether) that only ensured their minimal life chances, while having no effect on structure or policy.[49] Alternatively, we might turn to the forms of informed resistance demonstrated by high school students in the ongoing Chican@ studies movement, where students continue to resist the banning of books and empowering curricula through community organizing and direct action—including the storming and stopping of school board meetings that received national media attention a year ago.[50] This movement, like that of the CLASSE movement in Quebec, is successful in part because of the informed connections made between teachers, students, and the community in open democratic forums, typically in streets and schools. *In many ways, teachers, students, and community members work together, in order to transform schools from a place of hegemonic schooling to a site of counterhegemonic resistance and critical education.*

In our current political-economic context, public schools and universities are a valuable terrain that corporate owning class interests actively dominate as a point of structural necessity—to train and socialize the next generations of "educated" workers and tax payers. Their domination is made quite clear through the well-documented privatization and corporatization of public schools and universities in the US. Not coincidentally, public schools and universities are significant sites and resources for some of the most notable anticapitalist and otherwise revolutionary movements of our time. Those of us with access to public schools as teachers and students have an opportunity to help (re)capture the terrain of public education at crucial points of crisis where students and community stakeholders must confront the false promises of capitalist schooling.

PLAYING OUR (WAR OF) POSITION

The United States is the most powerful, and perhaps most brutal, military and police state the world has ever known, engaging in more wars, forms of state terror, and incarceration of its domestic population than any nation in modern history. We find Gramsci's argument for a "war of position" particularly compelling in such a context.[51] We've suggested so far that public schools and universities represent an incredibly valuable terrain in contemporary anticapitalist struggles in the US. This is not a new argument by any means, however we find ourselves now with unique opportunities to engage in important work—as the false promises of educational credentialing (and accompanying debt) are made more obvious for students, workers, and community members navigating the global recession and its lasting effects. Further, owning class interests see value and invest heavily in controlling the terrain of public education for hegemonic and instrumental purposes.[52] Our collective failure to contest these interests comes at great cost.

How should teachers and students engage in the war of position as it plays out across the terrain of public education? An extended conversation well beyond the scope of this chapter is required to address this question. However, we would like to introduce a conceptually simple (but in action somewhat difficult) set of strategies for anticapitalists with access to public schools and universities. First, capable anticapitalist teachers and scholars need to *infiltrate* powerful public schools and universities, as many already have. This should not be confused with an argument for "working within the system." Instead, it is to recognize the very real strategy of populating powerful institutions (and powerful positions within those institutions) in order to transform them, their function, and their relationships to the state and civil society. Anyone familiar with contemporary university administration, university or school district governing boards, or moneyed departments (business, engineering, biotechnology, and so forth) can speak to corporate success employing the same strategy. We find it particularly important for radical educators (teachers and professors) to infiltrate influential public schools, in part for the unique roles to be played by public, organic intellectuals in broad social movements. We do not envision infiltration as some grandiose act that will bring the agitator accolades. Instead, infiltration is a nuanced performance by educators who find opportunities to expose, explore, and rethink the many contradictions and paradoxes offered by neoliberal capitalism. These educators then have the choice to employ any number of tools, including critical pedagogy, in order to make schools more transformative, democratic places. They can accompany students and community stakeholders in very real ways to reflect on existing societal arrangements while organizing to change them.[53]

Second, successful infiltration allows for the use of one's position (as a professor or teacher for instance), in order to engage with students and community stakeholders to *sabotage* intellectual production for the purposes of coercive (military R & D), economic (neoclassical economics and neoliberal policy), and ideological ("schooling") domination via public universities. Sabotage is a long-standing successful strategy in the history of left resistance in arenas of material and ideological production. Though it faces difficult odds in the increasingly privatized university, faculty governance, faculty/teacher/student unionization, and strategic forms of direct action and disobedience can be powerful tools in concert to challenge the direction of policy and public resources in public schools and universities.

Finally, successful infiltration allows for the *reappropriation* of public resources for counterhegemonic purposes. In this sense, we have to do more than simply talk shit in classes, general assemblies, or co-op meetings and union meetings. We need to fight for tangible resources that are otherwise captured by competing state and corporate interests. This can be done in any number of ways: capturing public and private (even better) grant funds; democratizing schools in more meaningful ways; rethinking shared governance at colleges or finding alternative ways to embark on department decision-making strategies, when it comes to allocation of public funds; challenging the privatization of and lack of transparency in university research foundations and semi-private "satellite" services; and so forth. Broadly, reappropriation involves the transformation of public schools and universities as resource rich public institutions and physical spaces. Part of a war of position, it is the attempt in the public educational sphere to create "alternative institutions and alternative intellectual resources within existing society."[54] This can be done through the democratic recapture, control, and repurposing of school and university resources by community stakeholders, students, teachers/faculty, and staff. It means rethinking the purposes of education and what it means to live an "intellectual life." Public intellectuals have an important role to play by instigating and informing these sorts of conversations, in addition to participating in broader counterhegemonic, anticapitalist resistance and the imagining of life and learning after capitalism.

ENDNOTES

1   W. T. Armaline and W. D. Armaline, "Education's Diminishing Returns and Revolutionary Potential in the US and Beyond," in *Accumulation of Freedom: Writings on Anarchist Economics,* (ed.) Deric Shannon, et al. (Oakland: AK Press, 2012); Paul Mason, "Twenty Reasons Why It's Kicking Off Everywhere," *BBC News,* http://www.bbc.co.uk/ blogs/newsnight/paulmason/2011/02/twenty_reasons_why_its_kicking.html (accessed March 19, 2013).

2   Mason, "Twenty Reasons."

3   Matt Taibbi, *Griftopia* (New York: Spiegel & Grau, 2010); Greg Albo, Sam Gindin, and Leo Panitch, *In and Out of Crisis: The Global Financial Meltdown and Left Alternatives* (Oakland: PM Press, 2010); David McNally, *Global Slump* (Oakland: PM Press, 2011); Charles Ferguson, *Predator Nation: Corporate Criminals, Political Corruption, and the Hijacking of America* (New York: Crown Publishing, 2012).

4   Lina Levine, "An Analysis of the Distribution of Wealth Across Households, 1989–2010," *Congressional Research Service,* http://www.fas.org/ sgp/crs/misc/RL33433.pdf (accessed March 22, 2013).

5   Pamela Roux, "World's Wealthiest Gain $45B as Dow Reaches 15,000," *Bloomberg BusinessWeek,* http://www.businessweek.com/ news/2013-05-03/world-s-wealthiest-add-45-billion-as-dow-average-reaches-15-000 (accessed May 3, 2013).

6   Apple posted record quarterly profits of $13.1 billion in 2012, beating out Exxon-Mobile as the most valuable corporation on earth, see: Harry Wilson, "Apple is World's Most Valuable Company After iPhone Frenzy Drives Record Profits, *The Telegraph,* http://www.telegraph.

co.uk/technology/apple/9037186/Apple-is-worlds-most-valuable-company-after-iPhone-frenzy-drives-record-profits.html, (accessed March 19, 2013).

7   Adam Smith, *An Inquiry Into the Nature and Causes of the Wealth of Nations*, Book V, chapter 1, volume 2 (London: Methuen & Co., (1904 [1776]), http://www.econlib.org/library/Smith/smWN20. html#B.V,%20Ch.1,%20Of%20the%20Expences%20of%20the%20 Sovereign%20or%20Commonwealth (accessed April 1, 2013). Notably, Smith continues to say that the state ("civil magistrate") functions to keep the poor from settling the score with the rich (Smith, *The Wealth of Nations*, 1904).

8   William Domhoff, "Wealth, Income, and Power, http://whorulesamerica.net/power/wealth.html (accessed March 22, 2013) [emphasis added].

     E. N. Wolff, *The Asset Price Meltdown and the Wealth of the Middle Class* (New York: New York University, 2012).

9   Chris Hedges and Joe Sacco, *Days of Destruction, Days of Revolt* (New York: Nation Books, 2012); Tavis Smiley and Cornell West, *The Rich and the Rest of Us: A Poverty Manifesto* (New York: SmileyBooks, 2012).

10   Smiley and West, *The Rich*.

11   Ibid.

12   See table A-15, measure U-6, Bureau of Labor Statistics [BLS], "Employment Situation, April 2013," http://www.bls.gov/news.release/pdf/ empsit.pdf (accessed April 3, 2013).

13   National Employment Law Project [NELP], "The Low-Wage Recovery and Growing Inequality," http://www.nelp.org/page//Job_Creation/ LowWageRecovery2012.pdf?nocdn=1 (accessed April 1, 2013).

14   Kathryn Edwards and Alexander Hertel-Ferandez, "The Kids Aren't Alright: A Labor Market Analysis of Young Workers, *Economic Policy Institute,* http://www.epi.org/page/-/bp258/bp258.pdf (accessed April 1, 2013).

15   BLS, 2012.

16   Bruce Western, *Punishment and Inequality in America*, (New York: Russell Sage Foundation, 2006); United States Department of the Treasury and Department of Education, "New Report From Treasury,

Education Departments: The Economic Case for Higher Education [press release], http://www.treasury.gov/press-center/press-releases/Documents/The%20Economics%20of%20Higher%20Education_REPORT%20CLEAN.pdf (accessed April 1, 2013).

17   Richard Vedder, Christopher Denhart, and Jonathan Robe, "Why Are Recent College Graduates Unemployed? University Enrollments and Labor Market Realities," *Center for College Affordability and Productivity*, http://centerforcollegeaffordability.org/uploads/Underemployed%20Report%202.pdf (accessed April 1, 2013).

18   Ibid.

19   Charles Blow, "A dangerous 'new normal' in college debt," *The New York Times,* http://www.nytimes.com/2013/03/09/opinion/blow-a-dangerous-new-normal-in-college-debt.html?_r=0 (accessed April 1, 2013).

20   Blow, "Dangerous."; Jennifer Liberto, "Obama's College Tuition Plans Face Tough Fight, *CNNMoney,* http://money.cnn.com/2012/09/17/pf/college/college-costs-obama/index.html (accessed April 1, 2013).

21   Blow, "Dangerous."; Donghoon Lee, "Household Debt and Credit: Student Debt," *Federal Reserve Bank of New York*, http://www.newyorkfed.org/newsevents/mediaadvisory/2013/Lee022813.pdf (accessed April 1, 2013).

22   Lee, "Household Debt."

23   Elvina Nawaguna, "Student Loan Bill Tying Rates to Market Passes House," *Reuters,* http://www.huffingtonpost.com/2013/05/23/student-loan-bill_n_3327109.html (accessed May 23, 2013).

24   Katie Allen and Graeme Wearden, "Eurozone Unemployment Hits New High," *The Guardian*, http://www.guardian.co.uk/business/2013/apr/30/eurozone-unemployment-record-high (accessed April 30, 2013); Eurostat, "Euro Area Unemployment Rate at 12.1%," *Eurostat* (news release), http://epp.eurostat.ec.europa.eu/cache/ITY_PUBLIC/3-30042013-BP/EN/3-30042013-BP-EN.PDF (accessed April 30, 2013).

25   Claire Provost, "Egypt: Tackling Youth Unemployment," *The Guardian*, http://www.guardian.co.uk/global-development/2011/aug/03/egypt-education-skills-gap (accessed April 1, 2013).

26   Peter Coy, "The Youth Unemployment Bomb," *Bloomberg Business-Week*, http://www.businessweek.com/magazine/content/11_07/b4215058743638.htm (accessed April 1, 2013).

27   Abraham P. DeLeon, "Against the Grain of the Status Quo: Rethinking Pedagogy Through a Politics of Infiltration," in *Anarchist Pedagogies,* (ed.) Robert Haworth (Oakland: PM Press, 2012), 312–325.

28   John Dewey, *Democracy and Education* (Mineola, NY: Courier Dover Publications, 2004 [1916]).

      Noam Chomsky, *Chomsky on Democracy and Education* [Otero, C.P. Ed.] (New York: Routledge/Falmer, 2003).

29   Henry Giroux, "Democracy's Nemesis: The Rise of the Corporate University," *Cultural Studies/Critical Methodologies* 9, no.5 (2009): 669–695; Stanley Aronowitz, *The Knowledge Factory: Dismantling the Corporate University and Creating True Higher Learning* (Boston, MA: Beacon Press, 2000); M. Yates, "Us Versus Them: Laboring in the Academic Factory, *Monthly Review* 51, no. 8 (2000).

30   Neo-classical economics, see: Kalle Lasn, *Meme Wars: The Creative Destruction of Neoclassical Economics* (New York: Seven Stories Press, 2012); Ferguson, "Predator Nation," 2012.

31   See Henry Giroux, *The University in Chains: Confronting the Military-Industrial-Academic Complex* (Boulder, CO: Paradigm, 2007).

32   Giroux, "Democracy's Nemesis," 2009.

33   Richard Brenneman, "U.C. Berkeley: BP project impractical, dangerous, critics charge," *Daily Planet*, http://www.berkeleydailyplanet.com/issue/2007-05-01/article/26939?headline=BP-Project-Impractical-Dangerous-Critics-Charge&status=301 (accessed April 1, 2013).

34   There is some reason to problematize our argument here. Public schools and universities are partial extensions of the state. In this sense, presenting them as "public" spaces does not necessarily connote them as "free" spaces free of the problematic consequences of hierarchical state rule.

35   Stanley Aronowitz, *False promises: The Shaping of American Working Class Consciousness* (Durham, NC: Duke University Press, 1992); Stanley Aronowitz, "Against Schooling: Education and Social Class," *Social Text* 22, no.2 (2004): 13–25; Stanley Aronowitz, *Against Schooling: For*

an *Education that Matters* (New York: Paradigm, 2008).

36 Jean Anyon, "Social Class and the Hidden Curriculum of Work, *Journal of Education* 162, no. 1 (1980): 67–92; Jean Anyon, "Social Class and School Knowledge," *Curriculum Inquiry* 11, no. 1 (1981): 3–42.

37 Paulo Freire, *Pedagogy of the Oppressed, 30th Anniv. Edition* (New York: Continuum International Publishers, 2005 [1970]).

38 As Aronowitz (Aronowitz, "Against Schooling," 21) explains, "by reflection I mean the transformation of experience into a multitude of concepts that constitute the abstractions we call 'knowledge.'"

39 Aronowitz, *Against Schooling*, 20.

40 Chomsky, *Chomsky on Democracy*, 2003.

41 Allan Antliff, "Breaking Free: Anarchist Pedagogy," in *Utopian Pedagogy: Radical Experiments Against Neoliberal Globalization*, ed. Mark Coté, Richard Day & Greig de Peuter (Toronto: University of Toronto Press, 2007): 248–265; Abraham DeLeon, "Oh No, Not the 'A' word! Proposing an 'Anarchism' for Education," *Educational Studies* 44, no. 2 (2008): 122–41; W. T. Armaline, "Thoughts on Anarchist Pedagogy and Epistemology," in *Contemporary Anarchist Studies*, (ed.) L. Fernandez, A. Nocella, R. Amster, A. DeLeon, & D. Shannon (New York: Routledge, 2009): 136–146; Judith Suissa, *Anarchism and Education: A Philosophical Perspective* (Oakland: PM Press, 2010).

42 Anna Day, "Egyptian Youth Activists Extend Support for Youth Across the Arab World," *The Nation*, http://www.thenation.com/blog/160153/egyptian-youth-activists-extend-support-youth-across-arab-world, (accessed April 1, 2013); Patrick Cockburn, "After the Euphoria: On the Arab Spring Uprisings," *The Nation*, http://www.thenation.com/article/170611/after-euphoria-arab-uprisings, (accessed April 1, 2013).

43 Malia Yollan and Elizabeth Harris, "Occupy Wall Street Protesters Shifting to College Campuses," *The New York Times*, http://www.nytimes.com/2011/11/14/us/occupy-wall-street-protests-shifting-to-college-campuses.html?pagewanted=all, (accessed April 1, 2013).

44 Public Broadcasting Service [PBS], "Need to Know: Banned in Arizona" [video documentary], http://video.pbs.org/video/2335625906, (accessed April 1, 2013).

45 Antonio Gramsci, *Selections from the Prison Notebooks*, (ed.) Quintin Hoare and Geoffrey Nowell Smith (New York: International Publishing Co., 1971).

46 "The Communists have not invented the intervention of society in education; they do but seek to alter the character of that intervention, and to rescue education from the influence of the ruling class" (Karl Marx and Friedrich Engels, "Manifesto of the Communist Party: Chapter II, Proletarians and Communists," (1848), https://www.marxists.org/archive/marx/works/1848/communist-manifesto/ch02.htm#100, (accessed April 1, 2013).

47 Max Weber, *The Protestant Ethic and the Spirit of Capitalism* (Boston: Unwin Hyman, 1930 [1905]).

48 Armaline and Armaline, "Education's Diminishing Returns," 2012; Aronowitz, *False Promises*, 1992; Aronowitz, "Against Schooling," 2004.

49 Paul Willis, *Learning to Labour: How Working Class Kids get Working Class Jobs* (Westmead, UK: Saxon House, 1997).

    Lois Weis, *Working Class Without Work: High School Students in a De-industrializing Economy* (New York: Routledge, 1990).

    Jay MacLeod, *Ain't No Makin It: Aspirations and Attainment in a Low-Income Neighborhood* [3rd Ed.] (Boulder, CO: Westview Press, 2008 [1987]).

50 PBS, "Need to Know," 2013

51 Gramsci, *Prison Notebooks*, 1971.

52 Giroux, *The University in Chains*, 2007; Giroux, "Democracy's Nemesis," 2009.

53 DeLeon, "Against the Grain," 2012.

54 Robert W. Cox, "Gramsci, Hegemony and International Relations: An Essay in Method," *Millennium-Journal of International Studies* 12, no.2 (1983): 162–175.

INTERVIEW WITH
QUÉBÉCOIS STUDENT ORGANIZER JAMIE BURNETT

INTERVIEW BY ABBEY VOLCANO, MAY 2013

Abbey Volcano: *Can you start off by telling us a bit about the Québécois student movement and your role in it?*

Jamie Burnett: I moved from Ontario to study in Québec, at McGill University, a few years before the strike. It might be worth explaining a bit of the history behind McGill, which was founded in 1821 by a member of Québec's English-speaking merchant elite, who at the time was Canada's richest man and only major slave trader. In the 1960s, McGill was the only large secular university in a province where almost everyone spoke French, which meant that working class people in Québec couldn't really go to university. Its very existence as a symbol of elite privilege and a material barrier to accessible education became a catalyst for the development of a very powerful student movement, which to this day is virtually entirely French speaking.

I tried to get involved with student activism as soon as I came to Montréal, in 2009. Even a few months after I arrived, the movement had begun to strategize around the tuition hikes that were then being proposed. But not much was actually happening at McGill. Later, I was elected to a minor position in the campus-wide undergraduate student association, SSMU, beginning in September 2011, before the unlimited strike began in February.

We did what we could at McGill. We were lucky to be at McGill during a major labor strike, as the campus had already been politicized. The student strikes we organized were among the first-ever unlimited strikes in the Anglophone universities, even though similar, better-organized strikes had begun in the francophone schools in the 1960s. They were relatively small, but they helped to politicize or radicalize cultural and institutional spaces in a pretty new way.

Volcano: *Since the beginning of the economic crisis, students all over the world have been particularly targeted with austerity measures. How were Canadian students affected in particular? Can you talk a bit about the specific measures that were instituted there that led to the student uprising in Québec?*

Burnett: Firstly, the educational system in Canada varies significantly between provinces, especially between French-speaking Québec and the rest of Canada. The system in Québec is organized differently, with a large system of almost-free public colleges, and university tuition is about half what it is elsewhere in Canada, at around CAN $3000 a year for full time studies. Secondly, the tuition hikes in Québec, which precipitated the strike, have a bit of a complex relationship with the classical model of European austerity.

In fact, the original proposal from Québec's establishment right— former politicians, business leaders, and the association of university rectors—was to *increase* state expenditure in education, as an indirect subsidy to business through for-profit research and training technical workers, with a concurrent increase in tuition fees. Now, it was argued even at the time that the commitment to increase state funding was a sham, and in fact the new Parti Québécois government has brought in a small increase while decreasing funding. All the same, the differences with austerity as it is typically understood should not be elided.

Volcano: *And how did Québécois students respond? What tactics did they use to struggle against austerity?*

Burnett: As I noted above, the strategic conversation about how to respond to the tuition increases began in 2010, two years before the tuition hikes were set to take effect. The earliest parts of this campaign involved brief strikes with thousands of students, tiny by historical standards in Québec, but unprecedented in English-speaking North America.

The left of the student movement fairly easily reached the consensus to mobilize for an unlimited general student strike, bringing in as many students as possible across Québec in a campaign to shut down the entire educational system and issue an ultimatum to the government. This sort of tactic has been central to the student movement in Québec since its nascence in the late 1960s, and seven out of the nine times it has been attempted, it has won major concessions.

A build-up of small strikes and street demonstrations led up to an unlimited strike in February 2012, which lasted up to six months in some schools and put severe pressure on the state by nearly cancelling an academic year. There's a sort of pincer between the student movement on one hand, and educational sector collective agreements that prevent changes to the academic year on the other. By the summer, business people and college administrators were calling on the government to concede, and negotiate with the students.

Volcano: *The movement there seemed to take on a radical character from early on. It looked from the outside that students in Québec often understood that the roots of this recent calamity lie in capitalism rather than in this or that social policy. How did that radical character crystallize and what kinds of tensions were present with more liberal and conservative students? How did those tensions play out on the ground in movement work?*

Burnett: Unlike in the rest of Canada, where a bankrupt right-wing social democracy runs the labor and student movements, and in the United States, where you don't even have social democracy, things are a bit better in Québec. There are fewer illusions about political parties, and a collective memory of the very recent mass struggles that produced secular, social democratic Québec in the 1960s and 1970s. Both the labor movement and especially the student movement have therefore retained a lot of political autonomy, from the political parties and even from social democracy itself.

That's not to say there isn't a right wing, social democratic establishment in Québec. There certainly is, and it has substantial control over the student and labor movements. Liberal and conservative students were actually a tiny minority, mostly confined to McGill and a few small regional schools; they tended to support the tuition increase. Within the student population itself, the main arguments came from a social democratic position, represented by the Fédérations étudiantes universitaires/collégiales du Québec (FEUQ and FECQ), along with the Parti Québécois, which argued in favor of lobbying the government for a tuition freeze; and from a radical left, represented by the Association pour une solidarité syndicale étudiante, the ASSÉ, along with its strike coalition CLASSE, which advocated an unlimited general strike which would force the government to make postsecondary education completely free. It's a bit of a simplistic picture, but that's essentially what the debate was and remains, both on the level of national politics and on the ground with students.

Volcano: *How did students in the movement in Québec connect their organizing struggles with the wider working class? Were particular attempts made at bridging those demographics successful or not? In what ways?*

Burnett: The student movement in Québec has a very particular mode of organization, which is, to an extent, unique in the world, because it balances aspects of North American labor organization with aspects of European student politics. It is very focused on the specific situation of students within their own educational institutions, which makes it very easy to mobilize students. Additionally, students organized within their own schools can interrupt the reproduction of their own labor power, which creates a form of pressure usually only matched by things like general strikes, major blockades, and insurrection.

However, this focus on students-as-students creates limitations when it comes to reaching out to other workers, especially from that part of the working class which does not, or cannot, attend university. When university tuition is massively state-funded, but still inaccessible to many, it's easy enough to mount a populist campaign against privileged university students.

There's an interesting paradox here though, one that I think has implications for ideological debates happening outside of Québec. The ideological defense on the part of the student movement against accusations of privilege was to try to build working-class solidarity in asserting the position of students within the working class; but that equation of the situation of university students with less-privileged parts of the working class left the movement under-prepared to build solidarity off-campus.

That's not to say there weren't very serious attempts. Public sector unions, especially in the educational sector, did have a few serious conversations about joining the general strike of students, some even adopting strike mandates with varying degrees of commitment. However, the labor movement is a lot less democratic and a lot less militant than the student movement, and their support came rather late. The most serious commitment on the part of the labor movement was from educational workers, to respect student strikes that ended only a few days later. Outside of the organized labor movement, there were small efforts to form neighborhood assemblies of students and workers. Those efforts are on going, albeit on a small scale.

What remains to be seen is the long-term, democratizing and radicalizing effects of the student strike on labor organizing, particularly among youth and within the educational sector. These effects may be quite deep, without being immediately obvious on the surface.

Volcano: *I went to Montréal to watch things unfold and participate in some of the demos in the summer of 2012. I remember police randomly chasing groups of people around and, at times, the demonstrators seemed to have control over the streets instead of the police. Can you talk a bit about how these struggles over control of the streets fit into the wider political economic struggles?*

Burnett: That's a very broad question, one I don't feel completely qualified to answer. However, the issue has become very current. While the Parti Québécois cancelled parts of a special law that basically banned most protests, Montréal and other municipalities passed nearly identical bylaws. Just as protests were beginning again this past spring, municipal police began very aggressively enforcing the bylaws, performing mass arrests against anyone in the vicinity of any public demonstration not approved by the police. The repression has been severe, and Montréal's city council recently defeated a motion to overturn the bylaw, effectively endorsing the repression.

It's clear enough that the upper administration of the Montréal police has made a conscious decision to dedicate massive resources to political repression, and with the political support of three levels of government, resistance against it has become very difficult. Clearly, the policing of the strike in the summer was mediated by public consciousness of and support for the movement, and this consciousness and support will need to be expanded even though our conditions for organizing are more challenging. The state has an incredible repressive capacity, and while ultimately we have the real power, building the consciousness and solidarity to use it is not easy.

Volcano: *Relatedly, how did outside solidarity and sympathy figure into the movement?*

Burnett: Without making too much of the separation between the two, I'd make a distinction between support in the streets, and more abstract organizational support.

Political support of a broad spectrum of civil society, from labor unions to artists and musicians to college professors, and even to conservative social democratic politicians, was certainly significant. In some cases, this entailed substantial support for strikes on the ground by workers in universities and colleges, and in other cases, it took the form of financial and legal support in the hundreds of thousands of dollars, which was especially significant for those Québec student unions working on shoestring budgets with unpaid executives.

However, I'd like to also note the importance of physical support in the streets, where we were joined by nonstudent allies in bodily resisting repression. This came from politicized, radical communities that existed before the strike, but it also came from parents and teachers standing up for their students, radicalized by the vicious repression of students' collective organizing. This form of solidarity was as brave as it was crucial, especially because, as I noted above, a lot of the strength of state repression relies on the illusion of public indifference.

NECESSARY STEPS IN TOUGH ECONOMIC TIMES
NEW YORK STUDENTS TAKE TO THE STREETS IN THE WAKE OF OCCUPY

MARIANNE LENABAT

COLLEGE AND UNIVERSITY STUDENTS IN NEW YORK CITY, LIKE THEIR counterparts elsewhere in the United States and around the world, had been struggling for years under increasingly punitive conditions, including skyrocketing tuition and debt, dwindling educational resources, and undemocratic administrations. But in the wake of the Occupy Wall Street (OWS) movement that began in Zuccotti Park on September 17, 2011, they began to take action. Inspired by OWS's protest against economic and political injustice, students in New York mobilized against the tide of policies and practices eroding the quality of their education and sentencing them to a lifetime of debt. In a short time, a vibrant student movement spread across the city, driven by indignation and in solidarity with other students, and generating a level of activism not seen in decades. The successes and failures of that movement provide some interesting lessons about student struggle in the context of capitalism in crisis, especially the need for sustainable organizing strategies to complement more spontaneous moments of uprising.

THE ROOTS OF STUDENT UNREST: HOW CAPITALIST CRISIS IS UNDERMINING EDUCATION

IN MANY WAYS, students have been hit as hard by the catastrophic effects of capitalism as workers, the unemployed, and other sectors of
the population. Most recently, decades of "neoliberal" and "austerity"
policies have dramatically reduced funding for public education at
all levels.[1] At both public and private universities, programs and resources have been cut, while user costs, such as tuition, have risen dramatically.[2] All of this has dramatic effects. Students are being forced
to work more and more hours to pay for their schooling, and/or take
on significant amounts of debt.[3] Many end up saddled with tens or
hundreds of thousands of dollars in loans to repay, according to terms
so draconian that the amount repaid can end up being many times
greater than the original sum borrowed.[4] And this is not to mention
the countless individuals who do not manage to access, or complete,
higher education programs.

Politicians and university administrations justify the policies that
have brought education to this crisis point by saying that they are
"necessary steps" to control increasing costs in "tough economic
times." However, just as we see in almost all other areas of society,
these measures are really part of a radical restructuring to serve the
interests of those at the top, at the expense of everyone else.[5] Thus,
tuition increases have actually gone hand-in-hand with a reduction
in the amount spent on teaching, as administrations turn more towards low-paid, temporary instructors.[6] At the same time, administrative salaries, such as for presidents and provosts, have dramatically
increased.[7] In other words, a shift is taking place to make universities
resemble corporations, where those at the top make hundreds of times
more than those at the bottom.

Meanwhile, the federal student loan program is set to turn a bigger
profit from student loans than any American corporation.[8] In fact, student loans not only generate massive profit for private banks through
interest, fees, and penalties, but they can now be "securitized"—that
is, bundled and resold to investors. The federal government then
guarantees these investments, which means that even if students
default—and many do, since unemployment remains high, repay-
ment terms are punitive, and loans can never be discharged through

bankruptcy—investors reap their profits. This creates an incentive for more lending, regardless of whether students can reasonably afford to take on the loans or not.

In short, costs, risks, and penalties are being shifted downward, onto the vulnerable (students and their families), while profits, protections, and benefits are being siphoned up, all in the name of bowing to the pressures of the market.

In this process, education suffers significantly. It is increasingly treated as a commodity—as something created and sold just for the sake of generating a profit. University administrations come to view their academic programs as revenue streams, cutting those that aren't as profitable, and treat their students as consumers, drawing them in with a rosy picture of their college "experience," with less thought to actually providing them with quality schooling and career prospects afterwards.

This trend was obvious in the colleges and universities around New York City in 2011, and it was fueling student unrest. At the New School, President Bob Kerrey (the former senator from Nebraska who had also previously managed a chain of restaurants and fitness centers), undertook an expensive rebranding campaign, while aggressively expanding the school, including building a brand new $300 million "University Center" in Greenwich Village. The project, financed almost entirely by bonds (that is, debt), funneled a small fortune to members of the school's Board of Trustees.[9] Meanwhile, the majority of the school's library was placed in storage, students struggled with very little financial support, and tuition increased at a rate of 5 percent per year.[10] After a student occupation, the resignation of two provosts, and the passage of a vote of non confidence by the faculty, Kerrey was forced to resign. But he would go on to make headlines when he received a record three million dollars in compensation the year after he stepped down—a decision made by a small, ad hoc committee of his appointees to the Board.[11]

Public universities in New York, meanwhile, faced diminishing funding from state and local governments, and their administrations compensated with policies that many felt compounded the problem. The Board of Trustees at the City University of New York (CUNY) proposed a massive tuition increase—30 percent over the course of five years—that would undermine access to a historically important institution for the education of the working class in New York.[12] To compensate, the leadership of the university was proposed a new

"Pathways" program to help disadvantaged students, which on closer inspection actually amounted to little more than lowering curricular standards and a series of cost-cutting measures, such as reducing classroom time, which would hurt students even more.[13]

Similar problems existed at other universities around the city. In response, some organizing efforts had started taking shape. New York Students Rising (NYSR), for example, was formed in May of 2011, with the intention of uniting students at public universities across New York, decrying the fact that they "are under-funded, increasingly influenced by private corporate interests, and run by unaccountable administrators who receive a disproportionate amount of university resources."[14] However, their momentum—and their degree of coordination across different universities—was nothing compared to what would arise in the wake of Occupy.

THE RISE OF STUDENT ACTIVISM IN THE WAKE OF OCCUPY WALL STREET

OCCUPY HAD ITS precedents too. For one thing, it was inspired by mobilizations elsewhere that year, including the wave of popular uprisings throughout the Middle East that came to be known as the Arab Spring, and the massive protests against antiunion legislation in Madison, Wisconsin.

Closer to home, it was preceded by another encampment that June, parked across from City Hall to protest Mayor Michael Bloomberg's latest austerity budget, which included a massive round of teacher layoffs. Nicknamed "Bloombergville" after the "Hooverville" tent camps that arose during the Great Depression, many of its participants went on to help plan the launch of Occupy Wall Street on September 17, after the call was placed by the Canadian counterculture magazine, *Adbusters*, to peacefully occupy the symbolic seat of financial power.

When Occupy launched, its original intention was to point the finger of blame at the financial industry, which had caused a massive, worldwide economic collapse through its own reckless behavior, and at the government, which had bailed it out rather than hold it accountable. However OWS's concerns soon proliferated, quite naturally, as it attracted more participants, whose own experiences of injustice ranged from the racist policing policies of the NYPD to intolerable workplace conditions.

Soon after September 17, students began meeting at their respective universities to discuss how to "plug in" to OWS, meaning both how to provide support to it, and how to bring its energy to their own campuses. Students already had issues like debt around which to struggle, and with Occupy Wall Street, those issues finally began to look like political practices that could be challenged, rather than mere economic inevitabilities. At New York University, a group formed calling itself NYU4OWS. One of its main activities became organizing lectures and teach-ins in public spaces such as Washington Square Park, to "bring education out from the classrooms into public spaces," and to symbolically protest the treatment of education as a "consumer good."[15] It soon became a collaborative effort with students from CUNY, The New School, and Columbia, and the group renamed itself "The People's University."

Like many people in New York and across North America, students were being swept up in the excitement of this new political movement, especially as events unfolded. An OWS march across the Brooklyn Bridge on September 30 had resulted in one of the largest mass arrests in American history.[16] Galvanized by this, students at various universities decided to organize a walkout in protest. On October 5, they streamed out of classes and then marched down to Foley Square, where they joined a massive rally organized by labor unions. The turnout from across the city was enormous, in part because many professors had canceled classes in support of the action.

The momentum of Occupy was also generating an enthusiastic solidarity between students at different universities. The differences that existed between them—such as whether they attended a private or public institution—seemed politically insignificant. On October 15, the first "All-City Student Assembly" was held in Washington Square Park. It brought together postsecondary students from across New York City, who, borrowing from Occupy Wall Street formats (including the people's microphone and an agenda-less, open-ended meeting), reported on issues at their respective campuses, from concerns about Columbia University's expansion into Harlem, to New York University's attempt to bust unionizing efforts among graduate students. The Assembly continued to meet weekly throughout the fall, and on November 17, the two-month anniversary of OWS (and as it happened, two days after the eviction of the encampment in Zuccotti Park), it coordinated a "Day of Action" for education. A massive rally, including postsecondary as well as high school students, was held in Union Square, and then marched south to Zuccotti. Some students deviated from the march to launch a planned occupation at a study center at The New School. The occupation was meant to serve as an educational space open to all, and to draw attention to issues like student debt.

The occupation organized itself according to the same model used in Zuccotti Park, holding general assemblies to decide both logistical matters (food, personal security, holding the space, etc.), as well as its political program. A series of discussions and teach-ins were organized, some involving sympathetic professors or public figures (including the French socialist, Olivier Besancenot). It organized radical film screenings, cobbled together a food supply, painted the walls with radical slogans, and maintained the space around the clock.

But the occupation, which lasted one week, was also arguably a sort of turning point of the student movement that fall. Other New School students who were not part of the occupation dissolved it: they voted for its dissolution at a General Assembly meeting (these were, after all, open to everyone).[17] These students had been dissatisfied with being unable to use the space for study, suspicious of the occupiers and their intentions, and generally bemused by the political activity that had exploded in their midst, and so voted for a "return to normal." Moreover, serious divisions and tensions were arising for the first time amongst the student activists themselves. There were deep disagreements with regards to strategy, including whether to engage antagonistically or cooperatively with university administrations, and whether a commitment to nonviolence extended to all acts of law breaking, including the defacement of private property. Blocked in their attempts to achieve significant institutional or economic change, they began feeling and expressing frustration amongst themselves.

Student activism continued throughout the fall, however. On November 21, the Occupy Student Debt campaign was launched in Zuccotti Park. The idea was to get one million student debtors (as well as faculty and parent sympathizers) to sign an online "debtors pledge," after which they would default en masse, until reforms were put in place to the student loan system, such as bankruptcy protection and interest-free loans. Participants in the launch event then marched to Baruch College, where the CUNY trustee meeting was being held to discuss the proposed 30 percent tuition increase. When students were refused access to the meeting, they gathered in the lobby and outside the building, where police displayed shocking brutality against them (a common occurrence throughout Occupy-related protests), pushing students to the ground, injuring several, and taking many away in handcuffs. Police violence, and subsequent student and faculty outrage, were significant enough to force the university to pay a third-party agency to conduct an inquiry into their actions. (The Kroll Report later found no evidence of wrongdoing on the part of police or campus security, and even, incredibly, no evidence of injuries to protesters.)[18]

The following Monday, on November 28, CUNY trustees met again. This time, they canceled classes so that the entire campus could be closed early, and the meeting was held without interference, despite the fact that these forums are constitutionally mandated to be open to the public.[19] A massive protest gathered outside, again met by a huge police presence. As students shouted and demonstrated, the full tuition increase was approved. To add insult to students' injury at being forcibly excluded from proceedings, the new budget allocated millions of new dollars to campus security.

BUILDING SOLIDARITY WITH OTHER STRUGGLES

PART OF THE significance of Occupy Wall Street was how quickly solidarity was cultivated among various struggles. What started as a small gathering of activists exploded when "ordinary" workers, students, and community members joined in. One early example of this was a demonstration by seven hundred Continental and United Airlines pilots outside the New York Stock Exchange on September 27, just ten days after the occupation had settled into Zuccotti Park. The show of force lent significant credence to the then-nascent movement, which was being derided in the media as a "dwindling" "carnival" whose "cause...was virtually impossible to decipher."[20]

That solidarity proliferated in all directions. For its part, the student movement was equally enthusiastic about joining forces with both Occupiers and with labor. They organized marches to feed numbers to rallies organized by unions; they walked the picket line alongside locked-out Sotheby's workers; they met with and lent support to their school janitors when the latter's union entered negotiations for a new contract; and they folded academic labor concerns (especially regarding adjunct and part-time faculty) into their concerns about the future of postsecondary education.

There was also solidarity with parents, teachers, and students from the public K-12 school system, who were protesting massive school closures and layoffs under the administration of Mayor Michael Bloomberg. The mayor's office had created a "Panel on Education Policy" (PEP) to investigate "underperforming" schools and determine whether they should be closed in favor of opening private charter schools. Virtually every single school that came before the PEP was indeed voted closed. Frustrated by this, families and educators began showing up at PEP meetings in increasing numbers—the meetings were open to the public—eventually adopting the tactic of the "people's microphone" to disrupt the proceedings and voice their opposition. At one meeting, the cries of protest were so loud that the panel members were required to speak to one another through microphone feeds to noise-canceling headphones. These campaigns, which went by names like "Occupy the PEP" and "Occupy the DOE [Department of Education]," were actively supported by university students, who attended their meetings and showed up to actions.

University students in New York also reached out to student movements elsewhere. They issued a statement of solidarity with those pepper-sprayed on the UC Davis campus on November 18, 2011. They attempted to organize nation-wide "Days of Action" to raise awareness of education-related issues on March 1st and April 25th 2012—the latter being the date that student debt allegedly reached one trillion dollars in the United States. In May of 2012, they organized "casseroles" marches, fast-moving marches through the streets, banging pots and pans (in French: casseroles), to echo those taking place in Montreal, where students were opposing not only a significant tuition increase, but a draconian law curbing protest and outlawing the massive student strike that was taking place there (for more on this, see the interview with Jamie Burnett on the Quebecois student movement in this collection).

By late spring of 2012, the main organizing effort among New York students had become the "Free University." First held on May Day 2012, it put on a full program of lectures in Madison Square Park for one day. Some were regularly scheduled classes relocated from nearby campuses; others were one-time lectures or panel discussions on issues central to student struggles, or to Occupy. In September, another Free University was held, this time one week long, to coincide with the start of fall semester classes. It again included local faculty and students, but also brought in student organizers from Montreal and Puerto Rico, in order to exchange lessons learned in the struggle. Students in New York were looking for long-term organizing strategies to continue and strengthen the fight in New York.

PRACTICAL LESSONS FROM THE STUDENT STRUGGLE IN NEW YORK

A NUMBER OF practical lessons can be gleaned from the student organizing that took place in New York in the wake of Occupy Wall Street.

On the positive side, what OWS accomplished, in general, was taking the hardships that have been meted out to students (and workers and everyone else) in the name of economic necessity, and recasting them as the deliberate measures of those who own and control our society and economy—in other words, as class warfare. That is not to say that these measures are the capricious or willful acts of a small number of people. They are in fact imperatives of the capitalist economy, seeing as it depends on constant expansion, on constantly finding new areas in which to make profits, and on increasing those profits at an increasing rate. But as OWS has shown, this just proves that capitalism is unsustainable and insupportable—it fails to adequately deliver "goods" like education, it ruins lives through debt, and it deprioritizes and sacrifices every other value in favor of profit-making.

The good news is that, because capitalism is a human creation, it can be replaced. The struggle to do so starts with resisting capitalist policies and institutions, and challenging the narratives that support them. Students in New York were attempting to do just that, by questioning exploitative debt practices and austerity policies in education (at a time, it is worth noting, when profits were reaching record rates).[21]

The question is, what kinds of strategies are effective? Much of the explosion of student activity in the wake of OWS came from excitement about a new movement taking place, rather than from patient, long-term organizing. The first student walkout that occurred on October 5, 2011 happened with only the scarcest planning, considering that the idea for it was hatched only days earlier. By contrast, the nation-wide walkout and rally planned for March 1, 2012, which students had begun organizing in December, never materialized. Generating large, single-day events is much harder over the long term, as individuals develop activism fatigue.

For that matter, we can also see the limitations of single day, one-off events, or more broadly, what we may call an "activist" model of resistance, as compared to an organizing model. Students in New York, like their counterparts in Montreal, used large and visible street protests to communicate their demands and show their strength. However, only the Montreal students ground their universities to a halt with a strike, and only they were successful in fending off a proposed tuition hike (equal to that faced by students at CUNY).

Related to this, there are lessons to be learned with regards to democracy and organizing models. The massive strike in Montreal wasn't planned by a self-selected group of student activists. Assemblies were created in every department, holding weekly meetings to decide what steps to take next. When a vote was taken to walk out on strike, it was felt to be a decision made by all of the students, rather than a small fraction of them. In New York, however, the student occupation proved contentious in part because of the isolation of the students involved, and over time the momentum for student actions declined, in part because these efforts only ever involved a minority of students.

Student struggles will always wax and wane, including in places with a long history of militancy. What is perhaps most important is that, while they rage on, those struggles train a new generation of students, through both positive and negative experiences, imparting lessons about how to be effective in the future, which they can pass on to their younger comrades.

CONCLUSION

STUDENTS IN NEW York started their struggles in 2011 at many disadvantages. They had a fragmented history of student resistance from which to draw, were dispersed throughout a variety of institutions, and faced a multitude of targets—the New York state government, which makes budgetary decisions, their respective administrations, and the student lending agencies—each of which was difficult to strike at, and each of which could blame the other for growing student hardships. What students accomplished, in a very short time, was to politicize the policies that undermine them, and invoke the idea of struggling against them in unity. As they reflect upon their own experiences, and look to those of students elsewhere, they have the opportunity to sharpen their strategy going forward.

The chord of resistance cannot be unstruck. This became apparent in May of 2013, when, for the first time in its 154-year history, Cooper Union announced that it would begin charging tuition. Students immediately occupied the president's office, issued press releases, exposed the gross financial management of their institution, and demanded a repeal of the tuition proposal, as well as a seat on the Board of Trustees. The administration expressed its sympathy with the occupiers, but insisted that its hands were tied by financial necessity. Students refused to move.

ENDNOTES

1   Tamar Lewin, "Financing for Colleges Declines as Costs Rise," New York Times, March 6, 2013, A17.

2   Catherine Rampell, "Why Tuition Has Skyrocketed at State Schools," New York Times, March 2, 2012, http://economix.blogs.nytimes. com/2012/03/02/why-tuition-has-skyrocketed-at-state-schools/ (accessed May 26, 2013).

3   Rob Lieber, "Battling College Costs, a Paycheck at a Time," New York Times, February 10, 2013, BU1.

4   Student Debt Now Exceeds Both Credit Card and Car Loan Debt in the US. See Meta Brown et al, "Grading Student Loans," Federal Reserve Bank of New York website, March 5, 2012, http://liberty-streeteconomics.newyorkfed.org/2012/03/grading-student-loans.html (accessed May 26, 2013) and Maureen Tkacik, "Column: The student loan crisis that can't be gotten rid of," Reuters, August 15, 2012, http://www.reuters.com/article/2012/08/15/us-student-loan-crisis-idUSBRE87E13L20120815?fb_action_ids=623435977798&fb_action_types=og.recommends&fb_source=aggregation&fb_aggrega-tion_id=246965925417366 (accessed May 26, 2013).

5   A recent article in fact makes the case that, for the amount that the federal government currently spends on postsecondary education, the tuition of every student in the country could be covered. Instead, these federal expenditures are funneled into programs that help generate private profit through loans. Jordan Weissmann, "How Washington Could Make College Tuition Free (Without Spending a Penny More on Education), *The Atlantic*, March 8 2013, http://www.theatlantic.

com/business/archive/2013/03/how-washington-could-make-college-tuition-free-without-spending-a-penny-more-on-education/273801/ (accessed May 26, 2013).

6   "Adjunct" staff now make up 76% of classroom instructors. Tarek Barkawi, "The Neoliberal Assault on Academia," *Al Jazeera*, April 25th, 2013, http://www.aljazeera.com/indepth/opinion/2013/04/20134238284530760.html (accessed May 26, 2013).

7   Richard Vedder, "How to Tell if College Presidents Are Overpaid," *Bloomberg*, May 12, 2013, http://www.bloomberg.com/news/2013-05-12/how-to-tell-if-college-presidents-are-overpaid.html (accessed May 26, 2013).

8   Shahien Nasiripour, "Obama Student Loan Policy Reaping $51 Billion Profit," *Huffington Post*, May 14, 2013, http://www.huffingtonpost.com/2013/05/14/obama-student-loans-policy-profit_n_3276428.html (accessed May 26, 2013).

9   This includes John Tishman, whose Tishman Construction was awarded construction management, and Douglas Durst, whose Durst Organization acted as developer.

10 In 2011, Eugene Lang College, the undergraduate liberal arts portion of The New School, was granted the dubious honour of ranking as the fifth most expensive college to attend in the United States. "Most Expensive Colleges for 2011–2012," *Campus Grotto*, October 6, 2011, http://www.campusgrotto.com/most-expensive-colleges-for-2011-2012.html (accessed May 26, 2013).

11 Jack Stripling, "Lucrative Payments to Bob Kerrey by the New School Irk Critics in a Time of Austerity" *The Chronicle of Higher Education*, May 31, 2012, http://chronicle.com/article/Bob-Kerreys-Pay-From-the-New/132063/ (accessed May 26, 2013).

12 Until the mid-1970s, CUNY did not charge tuition at all, and admission was open to all those who wanted to attend—the fruits of a struggle by black and Puerto Rican students in the late 1960s.

13 Michael Busch, "What CUNY Pathways Means for Undergraduates," The Nation, January 16, 2013, http://www.thenation.com/blog/172243/what-cuny-pathways-means-undergraduates# (accessed May 26, 2013); James Dennis, "CUNY's Pathways Initiative and the Future of Higher Education Reform," CUNY Adjunct Project, http://

cunyadjunctproject.org/2013/02/18/cunys-pathways-initiative-and-the-future-of-higher-education-reform/ (accessed July 14, 2013).

14　New York Students Rising, "About," http://nystudentsrising.org/wp/about/ (accessed May 26, 2013).

15　People's University, "About," http://peoplesu.tumblr.com/about (accessed May 26, 2013).

16　Al Baker et al, "Police Arrest More Than 700 Protestors on Brooklyn Bridge," *New York Times*, October 1, 2011, http://cityroom.blogs.nytimes.com/2011/10/01/police-arresting-protesters-on-brooklyn-bridge/ (accessed May 26, 2013).

17　The occupation general assembly had agreed to make decisions on the basis of a two-thirds majority, rather than consensus. For insightful commentary on the occupation, see Arya Zahedi, "Reflections on the New School Occupation," *Insurgent Notes*, January 14, 2012, http://insurgentnotes.com/2012/01/reflections-on-the-new-school-occupation/ (accessed May 26, 2013).

18　The report, titled "Review of the Events Occurring at Baruch College on November 21, 2011," can be accessed here: http://www.cuny.edu/about/administration/chancellor/Kroll-Report2013.pdf. For commentary, see "12 Things to Know About the Kroll Report," Occupy CUNY News, January 25, 2013, http://occupycunynews.org/2013/01/25/12-things-to-know-about-the-kroll-report/ (accessed May 26, 2013).

19　"The meetings of the Board of Trustees of The City University of New York are open to the public, and the Board welcomes the interest of those who attend." City University of New York, "Meetings of the Board," http://www.cuny.edu/about/trustees/meetings.html (accessed May 26, 2013).

20　Gina Bellafante, "Gunning for Wall Street, With Faulty Aim," *New York Times*, September 23, 2011, http://www.nytimes.com/2011/09/25/nyregion/protesters-are-gunning-for-wall-street-with-faulty-aim.html (accessed May 26, 2013).

21　Yepoka Yeebo, "Corporate Profits at All-Time High as Recovery Stumbles," *Huffington Post*, March 25, 2011, http://www.huffingtonpost.com/2011/03/25/corporate-profits-2011-all-time-high_n_840538.html (accessed May 26, 2013).

INTERVIEW WITH RUDY AMANDA HURTADO GARCÉS

A MILITANT IN THE COLOMBIAN ANTI-NEOLIBERAL MOVEMENT

INTERVIEW AND TRANSLATION BY YESENIA BARRAGÁN AND MARK BRAY

Yesenia Barragán & Mark Bray: *Please tell us about yourself and your student organizing in Colombia.*

Rudy Amanda Hurtado Garcés: My name is Rudy Amanda Hurtado Garcés. I was born on March 29, 1989, on the banks of the River Timbiquí, in the department of Cauca, located on the southern Pacific coast of Colombia.

I started organizing for the autonomy, dignity, and self-determination of my Afro-Colombian community at a young age, first as a high school student at the Colegio Justiniano Ocoro in the municipality of Timbiquí, and then at my university. When I was sixteen years old, I was accepted to the Universidad del Cauca in Popayán, where I studied anthropology and began to be part of the student movement there, participating in assemblies, marches, and strikes at the university.

As a student and militant at the Universidad del Cauca, I began to investigate the socio-historical origins behind the structural poverty plaguing my black community and the indigenous, working-class, campesin@, and poor folks' communities in Colombia, which led me to realize that both colonialism and neoliberalism cause the violent, systematic extermination of the oppressed peoples of the world, privileging the national oligarchy and bourgeoisie. I then set this as my point of reference, in order to undertake the process of antisystemic rupture. Weaving the working-class struggle with the campesin@ movement, I began to think about the revitalization of the struggle of black youth in Colombia, given that the only option that capitalism offers most of us is going to war.

Barragán & Bray: *What do you mean by going to war?*

Garcés: In order to contextualize the situation in Colombia for those who are unfamiliar, there is currently a political, armed, and socio-cultural conflict in this country, which has lasted for a very long time. It is founded upon the system of slavery and colonialism in Colombia, which produced conditions of oppression, and generated direct and fundamental contradictions between the slave master (the Spanish, in the case of Colombia) and the enslaved (Africans, kidnapped and sold in the Americas). These contradictions were confronted by the insurgencies launched by the Africans and their enslaved descendants (and by insurgency, I specifically mean antisystemic rupture in front of a system of oppression). One path of resistance was through the creation of *palenques*, which were spaces created by runaway slaves beyond the reach of the slave masters and the state. These spaces created scenarios of collective, antisystemic construction, and negated the universes of domination of the slave societies at the time. A historic example that still exists today is the famous San Basilio de Palenque, located outside of Cartagena. For centuries onwards, there were confrontations between the *palenqueros* and the colonial army. This political-military process was essential during the Wars of Independence in the early nineteenth century, under the flags of Simón Bolívar, and other areas of South America, where there were Spanish colonies. Many of these societies fought for the liberation of their territory from the Spanish crown.

Jumping forward in time, in the 1950s in Colombia, other guerrillas were born, such as the FARC (Fuerzas Armadas Revolucionarios de

Colombia, the Revolutionary Armed Forces of Colombia), the ELN (Ejército de Liberación Nacional, the National Liberation Army), among others, that developed in the wake of the deterioration of the conflict in Colombia. The militarization and the recruitment worsened the situation faced by our communities, whether precipitated by the army, the guerrillas, or the paramilitaries. (Paramilitaries are private armies paid for and financed by the bourgeoisie, multinational corporations, national corporations, and even the politicians [to target leftists]).

With the rise of neoliberal reforms in the 1990s, a special kind of cultural politics was created for the recognition, protection, and preservation of "ancestral communities," like my Afro-Colombian pacific coastal communities. In the new Constitution of 1991, Article 7 created Article 55, which established Law 70 in 1993, recognizing that historically we occupied *tierras baldías* (common lands) in the Pacific. At the same time, while these socio-cultural politics were being established, an armed, political, and sociocultural conflict formed in the Colombian Pacific, occupied by black and indigenous communities that live in the most biodiverse zones of the world, known as the Chocó Biogeográfico, which converted this geopolitical region into "geographies of war."[1]

Barragán & Bray: *Besides fighting in the war, what other options are available to your community?*

Garcés: In this context of war, the only other option for young Afro-Colombians is to work as precarious laborers for national or multinational companies or corporations, or as domestic workers in the houses of the middle and upper classes. Because of this, very few of us are able to reach or finish high school, or even remain in our ancestral and collective territories.[2] Becoming aware of this, I came to the following realization: that the university is a giant slave *hacienda*, and the society is the mine where autonomy, self-determination, and dignity are extracted from our communities.[3] For this reason, I believe that we should create *libertades palen(k)es* (free *palenques* for our times, and so began the Palen(k)e Universitario del Cauca, which I helped create and organize, with the goal of confronting colonialism and neoliberalism as student militants.

Barragán & Bray: *Could you tell us a little more about Palen(k)e Universitario?*

Garcés: The Palen(k)e Universitario is a space for Afro-Colombian student-militants, which began in the Cauca region, one of the historic epicenters of the armed, political, socio-cultural, and economic conflict in Colombia. Working with other young, black student organizations based out of the other public universities across the country, we have articulated scenarios of construction and deconstruction of our ancestral and collective territories, seeing the university as a platform of struggle for confronting the racist, classist, and sexist system. We have also articulated this process to the general student movement in Colombia, as we push for a stronger emphasis on "ethnic" and "popular" recognition.

My work in the student movement has been mostly pedagogical. In a country that is unfamiliar with the history of black peoples, I work with the broader leftist movement, such as the Congreso de los Pueblos (The Peoples' Congress), to educate them.[4] Through various strategic alliances with several student groups with strong popular community bases, I help generate critical discussions concerning the visions of Afro-Colombian communities that cannot be homogenized in the construction of another world that is not just possible but, moreover, necessary. We have articulated our collective, ancestral, territorial politics to other students, which we learned from the example of the Soweto uprising in South Africa, which has significantly expanded the focus of the larger student movement.[5]

Barragán & Bray: *You work particularly within the Afro-Colombian student and the wider community movement. What unique struggles are embedded within both of them?*

Garcés: [As opposed to other groups,] the world vision of the Afro-Colombian student movement is rooted in the territory as our collective and ancestral reference point. We, the Africans, were the first globalized merchandise traded and sold through kidnapping, sold to the European invaders and exploiters and brought to a place they called America. This process required a dehumanization of Africa and its populations, in order to justify this holocaust. Because of the African Diaspora in the Americas, our education and teaching has been self-created and managed through communal processes within our communities.

In Colombia, the system of higher education has been in the hands of the elites who, for the most part, are white. They have isolated the black population from this setting. Our presence is nonexistent in the universities; whereas, on the other hand, you can see that the armed forces and police are full of black youth between the ages of eighteen and twenty-seven, or that our women are working in the houses "cleaning the underwear of the whites" and cooking food in their kitchens; others are exploited as members of the working class in the factories of the sugarcane and mining industries. Within the student movement in Colombia, we have analyzed that only 1 percent of black youth are able to gain admission to universities, and only 0.5 percent are able to graduate.

The situation I have just described has inspired us to take on a slogan from the philosophy of our rebellious black ancestors: "LIBERTAD O MUERTE!" (Freedom or Death!) In this sense, our challenge is to generate discussions concerning the truth of our past, and question why our black communities have the highest levels of poverty in the community. According to the PNUD (Programa de las Naciones Unidas para el Desarrollo en Colombia; Program of the United Nations for the Development of Colombia), in their report "Socio-economic Situation of the Afro-Colombian Population Under the Objectives of Millennial Development (2010)," 38.3 percent of Afro-Colombians live on US$2.50 a day, while 56 percent live on US$4.00.

Our demands are: equal access to education (bearing in mind the sociohistorical context of our communities); that our ancestral knowledge, which is thousands of years old, be respected and valued; and spaces within our universities for passing on non-Eurocentric knowledge. For this reason, our work has been based on the triad of Culture-Territory-Education; we simply cannot think without bearing all three in mind. For us, this is the path towards communal self-government, in order to guarantee the right to territory and exercise our cultural and ancestral practices.

Barragán & Bray: *What kinds of politics are at play among student radicals in Colombia, and how do they affect organizing and strategy on the ground?*

Garcés: In the political context of the 1990s, with the government of César Gaviria Trujillo and the new Constitution of 1991, as I mentioned before, the country opened up to neoliberalism (that is, they rented out the country to large national companies and foreign multinational corporations) and, at the same time, the government conceded some ethnic rights for collective lands of ancestral territories. These two developments generated a very complicated debate concerning the goals of "ethnic" and "popular" social movements in this country.

Nevertheless, the student movement in Colombia has been a generator of mobilizations and direct actions against the neoliberal policies that have been established in this country. "In the heat of the masses," we confront the exploitation of our natural resources and the criminal policies of the state. One of the slogans of the student movement is "la Educación como un bien común" (Education as a common good), where the sectors of the population who have not had access to it can enter these spaces, which were previously the privilege of the elites. As a student movement organized with class and ethnic consciousness, we are part of the working classes of our country, where the strategies of struggle combine with the workplace struggle that we carry out in our territories, communities, towns, and organizational processes inside our universities. Within this process of political-student militancy, we disseminate information in order to strengthen our movements for self-determination, self-government, and self-management of our territories, which the forces of capital are fighting to control. It's important to understand that in Colombia, after "the death of Jorge Eliécer Gaitán,[6] on the 9th of April of 1948, a violent outburst of social and political conflict was produced that did not respect any social strata; political terrorism affected all classes, each distinct class depending on their social, economic, and political circumstances, in order to resist the offensive of the sectarian barbarism of the political parties."[7]

During this period known as *la Violencia*, the war between the two main parties (the Conservative Party and the Liberal Party) facilitated the birth of the FARC and ELN. The rise of these guerrillas is central to the historical development of the student movement, since one of the founders of the ELN was Camilo Torres, a priest, guerrilla fighter, and one of the founders of the Department of Sociology at the Universidad Nacional de Colombia.[8] This created a direct link between the students and the insurgency. In this light, the student movement in Colombia has historically been a military target of the state, its political forces, and paramilitarism, under the argument that we, the organized students, are guerrillas.[9]

Barragán & Bray: *What has changed since the economic crisis of 2008? What form does austerity take in Colombia?*

Garcés: Because of the geopolitics of capital, Colombia is a country that has become the backyard of the economic powers. The austerity policies in the European Union and the United States affect us directly because these crises and measures imply the worsening and extension of the exploitation of our natural resources through concessions and free trade agreements (for example, in 2012, the United States signed the TLC, Tratado de Libre Comercio, or the free trade agreement). Neocolonization is the name for this boomerang process. While they increase your taxes in the European Union and the United States, they condemn us to exploitation.

But the ways in which austerity has been implemented in Colombia have been through the privatization of healthcare and public services, among them education. In 2011, for example, the Colombian government under the current president, Juan Manuel Santos Calderón, and the Minister of Education, María Fernanda Campo Saavedra, tried to privatize higher education under a reform to Law 30 of 1992, which organized the public service of higher education in Colombia. Through mobilizations, permanent assemblies, and a long, nation-wide student strike that lasted more than three months, we defeated this reform that tried to convert our education into a for-profit system, by fighting in the streets.

Barragán & Bray: *How have you connected student struggles to broader anticapitalist initiatives or workers' struggles?*

Garcés: Neoliberalism has arisen to privatize our education, in order to transform it into a privilege of the upper classes, around specific races, converting this process into an oppositional relation produced and deepened by capitalism. The labor struggle in Colombia is also essential for the student movement insofar as the coming together of these distinct struggles shows that the Colombian people should have self-determination. Therefore, we consolidate ourselves into one unified block of struggle against capitalism because we know that it is the system that privatizes, exploits, murders, and creates laws in favor of the elites, cutting the hard-earned rights of the working classes.

We can see an example of this with the recent strike of the coffee workers that took place between February 25 and March 8 of 2013, where the demands were focused on the international price of coffee, bank loans, the monopoly of the Colombian Federation of Coffee Workers, and the fact that the majority of land worked by the coffee workers in this country is being expropriated by the banks.[10] Hundreds of students took to the streets of Popayán, for example, to demonstrate solidarity with their struggle.

Barragán & Bray: *How has your movement dealt with internal political diversity?*

Garcés: Various ideological positions can be found within the student movement, which certainly complicates our tasks ahead. It's definitely a reflection of the political context of our country, where we find right wing, moderate, armed left wing, or left-democratic tendencies. The visions of the black and indigenous communities can converge, but can also collide when it comes to the anticapitalist question and struggle. But we believe that it is necessary that the student movement have these contradictions, in order to produce debate and consolidate our strength as we confront capitalism. The most important thing to bear in mind is that the broader student movement has been defending the interests of the working classes since its birth in Colombia.

Barragán & Bray: *How do you see the Colombian movement in the context of international struggles against austerity and neoliberalism?*

Garcés: When we, in the [global] South, return our gaze to the [global] North and see the demonstrations of the Indignados marching in New York, in London, in Spain, in Greece, and so forth, we understand that we need to globalize our hope of struggle against the capitalists. That is, just like here, over there people are fighting day after day against imperialism. It is capitalism that is producing "the two faces of the same coin." That is, austerity for you and neoliberalism for us. In both struggles and movements, we are attacking the global politics of the International Monetary Fund and the Inter-American Bank of Development. The conditions of oppression create these rebellious mobilizations and strikes against the privileges of the national elites.

In March of 2012, I had the opportunity to march in the streets of New York alongside comrades in Occupy Wall Street. It was really interesting to see that not everyone is a Yankee imperialist in a country like the United States, but that there are conscious peoples who question imperialism within the heart of empire. For me, Occupy Wall Street is an anti-imperialist movement because it questions the law of austerity that privileges the banks that are impoverishing the working classes of the United States, all just to maintain the monopoly of capital.

When Barack Obama won the elections in 2008 and entered the White House, I thought that because he was African American that he might transform the imperialist world politics exercised by the United States on its citizens and the rest of the world. But I discovered that he too was an imperialist—even more so, continuing to worsen the situation of the historically oppressed classes.

ENDNOTES

1   This concept, proposed by a comrade, Isnel, who is a member of the Movimiento Palen(k)ero del Cauca, asserts how our territory has been conditioned by elites in such a way that the conflict is resolved through violence and that our communities are massacred, militarized, and forcibly displaced.

2   In Colombia, through Law 70 of 1993, we, the black communities, have the recognition of collective titles for the use of our lands, consolidated in ethnic-territorial entities called Consejos Comunitarios (Community Councils). This doesn't imply that we are outside of the internal conflict of our country; on the contrary, our territories have been the center of the geopolitics of the war in Colombia.

3   Note from translators: *hacienda* is Spanish for estate. Historically, these were the first large land grants given to *conquistadors* after the conquest of the Americas. They were later owned by powerful Spanish and local white merchants, slave masters, and elites, continuing well into the nineteenth century, after the end of colonialism.

4   *Congreso de los Pueblos* is a broad-based, pan-left social movement that aims to build peace, community, alternative economies, and autonomy for Colombian society. For more, see http://www.congresodelospueblos.org/.

5   Note from translators: Beginning on June 16, 1976, the Soweto uprising was a series of uprisings led by high school students in South Africa against apartheid policies, with an estimated 20,000 student demonstrators. More than 100 young people died.

6   Note from translators: Gaitán was a famous populist politician in Colombia and leader of the Liberal Party who was killed on April 9, 1948, sparking a series of protests known as the *Bogotazo*, which spiraled beyond the city. Many historians argue that Gaitán's death sparked the development of the current-day civil war and guerrilla insurgencies.

7   Carlos Medina, *FARC-EP Y ELN Una historia política comparada*, doctoral thesis, Universidad Nacional de Colombia 2010, 123.

8   The Universidad Nacional de Colombia is the largest public university in Colombia, created on September 22, 1867.

9   Some writers say that paramilitarism has existed as a criminal strategy, financed by the bourgeoisie in order to maintain their power, since the beginning of *la Violencia* in the 1950s.

10   For more, see http://www.desdeabajo.info/component/k2/item/21710-las-razones-estructurales-y-coyunturales-del-paro-cafetero.html.

PATHS WRITTEN IN CONCRETE

THE CHILEAN STUDENT MOVEMENT OF 2012

MÓNICA KOSTAS, SCOTT NIKOLAS
NAPPALOS, AND FELIPE RAMÍREZ

IT HAS BEEN A DIFFICULT JOURNEY FOR CHILE'S LEFT TO ARTICULATE resistance since the carnage of Pinochet's mandate. Out of the ruins of a dictatorship's legacy, the Chilean student movement has managed to organize one of the most important mobilizations in recent years. Not only has the student movement garnered popularity due to its vast size, but it has also attracted international attention for the consistency and militancy of its student body. Looking back at its beginnings, Chile's student movement rattled the shackles that hold education hostage in an environment of profiteering. The magnitude of the protests not only exposed the problems of the Chilean education system, but also highlighted a rotten network of systemic problems that affect all sectors of Chilean society. Students are still fighting today to have their demands met—their struggles have not been resolved or even properly addressed—but through their organizing, they shook an entire administration, causing a reshuffling of the current conservative government of Sebastián Piñera, and a considerable drop in his approval rating.

This piece hopes to offer a brief and concise background of the Chilean student movement and an analysis of the strategies that pushed it along. We also provide an interview with Felipe Ramírez, member of the Federation of Libertarian Students (FeL) and 2012 secretary of the Federation of University of Chile Students (FECh).[1]

HISTORY OF A STRUGGLE

The struggle arises from a deep dissatisfaction with the Chilean educational system. Presently, only 25 percent of the education system is financed by the state, while the remaining 75 percent is paid out of the students' pockets, coming for the most part from loans. This model was set up during the 1980s under Pinochet's rule. His desired trajectory of privatizing education culminated in the LOCE law (Constitutional Organic Law of Education), which he passed just four days before relinquishing power. This law left it up to the private sector to manage and finance education, which allowed it to rapidly become a pervasive and lucrative business. Basically, "any group of people with the sufficient capital and space could employ a handful of professors and set up a university."[2] Today, even the universities that are officially public are financially supported by the private sector and therefore charge, per month, approximately the same amount as a minimum wage monthly salary.

In 2006, high school students led a series of mobilizations between April and June, culminating in a call for a national strike, to which more than 250 educational establishments responded, and between six hundred thousand and one million students adhered. Dubbed La Revolución Pingüina (the Penguin Revolution, in reference to the students' uniforms), these mobilizations struggled against the LOCE and demanded the abolition of testing and transport fees, among other claims. These struggles occurred not under Piñera's conservative government, but under the presidency of Michelle Bachelet of the center-left Concertación coalition, the same electoral coalition that negotiated the present electoral system and won against Pinochet. As they would again in 2011, the mobilizations of 2006 attempted to expose the need to restructure the impaired education system. These fights were met with heavy repression by Chile's *carabineros* (military police), but the violence against the resistance marches failed to hold back the movement. After a couple months of the government moving slowly with the few reforms it had initially offered, the marches re-activated, and successive strikes and mobilizations took place between

September and October. The LOCE was eventually replaced by the General Law of Education in 2009, which served to attenuate the fights but did not really bring substantial changes.

Certainly, indignation among students kept building and the mobilizations of 2011 and 2012 demonstrated a clear sign that students' patience had burst. The first protests of this heated period were called by the Confederation of Chilean Students (CONFECh), a grouping of student federations from the traditional universities (created before the 1980s). These traditional and older universities have a history of student organization that still thrives today. For example, all students participate on some level by electing annual federation representatives through a mandatory and secret vote.

The mobilizations were called over issues of tuition financing, scholarship delays, and problems with student ID cards. During the first marches, the movement gathered in large numbers throughout Chile's main cities. On June 14, 2011, the Ministry of Education announced that 184 schools were supporting the movement with some form of protest—122 schools were occupied, and the remaining 62 went on strike. They mainly demanded reforms to the educational system and increased involvement by the state, rather than relegating education to the private sector.[3] After a month of various strikes, the government of Piñera, a right-wing billionaire whose initial fortune comes from introducing credit cards to Chile in the 1970s, offered a deal to create a new educational fund and to facilitate access to student credit loans. The main organizations rejected the offer, claiming that more profound changes needed to take place. The government continued to issue successive proposals to reform the education system in slight and vague ways, such as promising to ensure quality of education, but the changes were too small, ambiguous, and questionable to satisfy the movement.

Though there's much continuity with previous cycles of student struggle, some important features stand out. The violence of the *carabineros* against the students, common at protests in Chile, resonated with the broad populace and spurred opposition to a state response perceived as being as too close to dictatorship-era practices. Rather than being able to castigate students as greedy or privileged, the government was put on the defensive and the student struggles gained support from many sectors. One important example was the copper miners (representing the lion's share of Chile's whole economy), who went on strike in solidarity with the student struggles. A back-and-forth existed between the students and other popular struggles, and created an explosive environment of combativity, uniting different sectors under a class banner. Likewise, the students showed themselves to be creative in exposing and protesting the regime using widespread occupations, murals throughout neighborhoods and universities, flash mobs, large-scale demonstrations of public mass kissing, nudity, and any means available to maintain pressure. Centered around concrete demands about education, the protests kept radical messages at the forefront of Chilean society, demanding both the immediate and the revolutionary, and constructing political forces and practices that mirrored their ideals.

ORGANIZED FORCES OF THE LEFT

THE MOST PROMINENT leaders of the mobilizations came out of the aforementioned traditional, organized universities. For example, Camila Vallejo, the 2011 president of the FECh, gained ample recognition in local and international media. As a daughter of Chilean Communist Party members under the dictatorship, Vallejo joined the Juventudes Comunistas (Communist Youth) while completing her geography studies at the University of Chile. She aimed to expose the lies about Chile being a progressive country, a place that had overcome a dictatorship, and a nation with a left-wing government up until Piñera. She wanted to show that the old repressive society was, in many ways, still intact and the state response toward the student mobilizations involved the same old repressive tactics from the past. Her compelling arguments and well-spoken statements helped leverage large numbers on the street (at its peak, the mobilizations were composed of around 200,000 students). Yet, regardless of her political prowess, the media insisted on concentrating on her looks and portrayed her as a sex symbol. The Juventudes Comunistas are one of a few major tendencies within the student movement. The right-wing trade unionists have their own organization, founded by a major ideologue of the dictatorship, Jaime Guzmán, and is found mainly at the Catholic University. One of the main center-left trade unions is part of the Concertación, a coalition of left and center-left parties, ranging from the Christian Democracy to the Socialist Party, who were in power from the end of the dictatorship until the victory of Piñera's conservative administration. The National Student Union is a leftist force mostly known for rejecting the reformist tendencies of the Juventudes Comunistas, the Autonomous Left, and the Concertación. However, they are known for "a chronic incapacity of overcoming atomization, and cannibalism…and lack internal cohesion."[4]

The Izquierda Autónoma (Autonomous Left), more commonly called the Autonomous, are a grouping who come from the autonomous section of the now defunct Movimiento SurDa (Left Movement), formed in the early 1990s, which had a revolutionary and pan-Latin Americanist perspective on left politics. It is a tendency that aims to be to the left of the Juventudes Comunistas, though in practice they are seen as falling more in the realm of the Concertación. They support "progressive" Latin American governments, and recently garnered a lot of attention when they snatched the presidency of the FECh from Vallejo, under the leadership of Gabriel Boric. As Boric is quoted as saying, "We don't have a problem in saying that the left of the twentieth century failed. Many of those who imagined a different world ended up building totalitarian ones."[5] Despite their strength being their denunciation of the reformism of the more traditional tendencies, they are paralyzed by internal disagreements, and their work is mostly limited to educational struggle.

The Federation of Libertarian Students (FeL) occupies another section of the revolutionary left. We will now provide a closer look into its history, emphasizing herein its struggles and lessons. The FeL grew out of a lack of national groups capable of weaving libertarian theory and practice in a coordinated effort. Essentially, the late 1990s saw ample resistance against laws that severely harmed students' education (such as the previously mentioned LOCE). Throughout these struggles, the organized student body became more radicalized in its ideals, but was unable to develop coherent and solid practices.

There was a frustrating dissonance between what the students wanted and the actions that took place. Out of this impotence came the birth of several groups who aimed to consolidate the radical talk with the radical walk. The Congreso de Unificación Anarco Comunista, (CUAC or Congress of Anarcho-Communist Unification) was formed in 1999, and developed activism in university spaces. In 2001, the Asamblea Coordinadora de Estudiantes Secundarios (ACES or Coordinating Assembly of High-School Students) was created with the goal of defending students' rights and fighting for a free education. In 2002, there was a visible growth in the number of radical and libertarian militants, with members of the CUAC getting elected to a few FECh positions. The lessons of CUAC and its key members would prove a strong influence on the direction and formation of the FeL.[6]

Eventually, a call went out for a national libertarian university student's conference, which became the Encuentro de Iniciativas Anarquistas (Conference of Anarchist Initiatives). The conference brought several groups and nonaffiliated radicals together. Two clearly divided fronts emerged, one of which went on to become the FeL, and the other eventually formed the Revolutionary Anarchist Current (CRA). The major differences between the two was that the CRA wanted to focus on consolidating different left student groups and use anarchist propaganda to build support for the anarchist cause, while the future founders of the FeL sought to focus on social insertion as libertarian militants within student struggles, but not limit their activity either to the left or the student movement, and instead advocated a politics based in society in general.[7] The FeL was formally created in 2003, and the CRA later went onto create the Coordinadora Anarquista (Anarchist Coordinating Committee), which focused mainly on propaganda within the student left.

Social insertion is a concept from the especifista tradition of organized anarchism in the Southern Cone of South America, though its influence has now spread globally. The Federação Anarquista do Rio de Janeiro (FARJ) uses the concepts of social work and social insertion to elaborate an anarchist practice of struggle in movements of the exploited. In their text Social Anarchism and Organization, they write, "The anarchist organisation does social work when it creates or develops work with social movements, and social insertion when it manages to influence movements with anarchist practices."[8] The focus on struggles of the exploited, and creating an anarchist praxis and militancy within those struggles, was key for the militants who initiated the FeL, which was not an especifista organization, but rather a broader, intermediate, libertarian coordination; likewise the objective to create libertarian practices not in ideas alone, but as a living material practice of the exploited, defined of their orientation and struggles. To these ends, the FeL would undertake a series of experiments and interventions in student struggles and in the broader communities of the exploited as well. FeL militants created groups of muralists in popular neighborhoods, practiced popular education to engage the exploited around issues of their own struggles rather than instructing or lecturing, and participated in the day-to-day struggles of students in protesting, occupying, and fighting for their interests.

The founding members of the FeL initiated and participated in a wide array of student organizing and struggles, spreading libertarian coordination through the universities in Chile. As the FeL grew and refined its directives, this work led to them winning positions in various university federations throughout Chile between 2003 and 2006, and they progressively came to the forefront of the student movement, based on their activity in student centers. In 2005, five student leaders were elected to the CONFECh from the FeL, and, in the same year, the high school FeL was created (Frente de Estudiantes Libertarios Secundarios). This latter front played an important role in the occupation of a high school which spurred the 2006 high school student mobilizations, the previously mentioned Revolución Pingüina. In the struggles of 2011–2012, the high school student groups pressed on when the university struggles simmered.

In 2011, FeL coordinated the student groups, calling this entity "Luchar: Construyamos universidad popular" (Struggle, let's build a popular university), united by direct action and democracy both within the fight and in the university.[9] Luchar participated in the elections of the FECh, and they won enough votes for their member, Felipe Ramírez, to take the general secretary position. In 2012, Fabian Araneda of Luchar won the vice presidency of the FECh and Luchar members also occupied positions in several student federations throughout the country, where it maintains its bases.

LEARNING FROM STUDENTS

THE TRAJECTORY OF the Chilean student movement and the reflections of Felipe Ramírez in the following interview offer lessons, not just for student movements, but also for liberatory struggles in general. In terms of Chile, it's unclear where these struggles will lead in the near future. Far from dead, in 2013, the students have shown that they have not yet demobilized. Whether the movement continues to maintain pressure or enters a more dormant period, the students of Chile show no indication that these issues are resolved or the fights are over. It is likely that the very same dynamics will continue to create new generations of militants in Chile, and new educational crises will send the population into the streets.

There are a few elements worth highlighting and evaluating. First, the objective context of Chilean society in the financial crisis played a central role in the rise of the student movement and specifically influenced the role of libertarians within those movements. Earlier battles with Michelle Bachelet set the stage for the explosions under Piñera, but it would be hard to understand the most recent cycle of struggles without looking at the global context of protests and disruptions that unfolded following the 2008 world financial crisis. As Felipe Ramírez suggests, different periods in the struggle created different roles, problems, and proposals for student militants. The politics of the FeL grew alongside the trajectory of the student movement and the ruptures in broader Chilean society with the decomposition of the fights and forces of prior eras. Society allows struggles to strike a series of accords and follow certain avenues. When these break down, new possibilities emerge and institutionalized forces of the left can either be left behind or be seriously threatened by more radical alternatives. Openings created by these breakdowns allowed the space for students to disrupt larger aspects of society than they otherwise would have. This created problems for the political forces integrated into that system and all it was based on. The Juventudes Comunistas, for example, both benefited from the legacy of their party and ultimately suffered as a result of it. The Communist Party benefited from its historic role in the Allende government, the repression, and the struggle against Pinochet. At the same time, the political and economic failures of the Concertación period and the inability of the official forces of the left to offer a radical alternative was undermining in the context of the upsurges of action around the student struggles. This was true of the historic left in general, but particularly the Communist Party within the student movement, which is seen to have faltered significantly in responding to Bachelet's center-left government and Piñera's attacks.

In times of pitched struggle and rupture, new potentials often emerge for revolutionary agents that were previously closed. Likewise, the existing political divisions can begin to break down, as the basis for their politics are shifted by the movements in the streets. Chileans sought answers to their problems, which were worsening day by day. The repression of the students, which resonated with the Pinochet era, stripped the regime of its moral credibility for many. While the left had its political programs and stances, the actions taken by students (and then by workers and communities) exposed both their impracticality and their inability to go beyond mere band-aid solutions. This pushed the FeL out of its cocoon. In a moment when popular forces were reshaping the left, the libertarians of the FeL were able to create, in practice, through struggle, a politics rooted in the perspectives and struggles of the students, and pose revolutionary alternatives to capital and the left. The libertarians were able to drive a wedge and put forward concrete political proposals, which pushed the movement forward, and exposed many dead ends.

Second, previous generations of student struggle in Chile provided a cultural memory that allowed new militants to advance beyond the mistakes of their forbearers. However, this point can be overstated. Too often, in the United States and Europe, there is a fetishism about Latin America that ignores the intense class and political contradictions at play, and the challenges to revolutionaries that exist in all countries. It is not that there are not gaps, lulls, or large popular forces antagonistic to the left in Chile (there are), but rather that the organized minority of militants within the student movement have been able to create the means to sustain their lifelong work and pass on their experiences. Chileans face many of the issues that we do in the United States. The culture of militants is distinct, however, as Chileans' commitment to creating a material living anarchism within these fights, and in other social sectors, gives them the strength to carry on in ways distinct from the North American activist world. That reality and orientation shapes the experience both of radicals and students in Chile, giving life to their theories and practices. There are seeds of these processes in the US as well, but they are more embryonic and preparatory.

Lastly, it's worth reflecting on the relationship between the politics and political struggle of the libertarians and the conjuncture of society as a whole. We are, in many ways, in the early days of the FeL, in which we think of our tasks in terms of the broad histories, ideas, and arguments as the motive of our path. In the United States, alienation from popular struggle is reflected in the thinking of the left in general, given the disassociation of the left and the state of popular communities. The student movement and the FeL illustrate a different relationship, one where the needs and potentials of the moment come to define where the lines of political struggle are drawn. The contradictions of austerity, debt, and the Chilean state create a prism of material conditions, and the libertarians intervene through that prism, reflecting their own images through the light of the popular breaks from normal politics. Any truly libertarian alternative is based exactly upon this: collective breaks from politics internalized within capital, and the construction of revolutionary praxis, in dialogue with those experiences. This alternative is not imposed upon a situation, but is constructed by organized minorities trying to trace emerging potentials, and intervene to catalyze ruptures. In the United States, there are now more opportunities for this work than at any time in recent history. It is a profound lesson worth mulling over.

It's worth remembering that the Chilean student struggle did not achieve most of its core goals. Indeed, many of the changes that occurred took place outside education issues altogether. The student struggle was, however, intensely embarrassing for the government (just as it was under Bachelet), and was perhaps the key factor in bringing about a reshuffling of the government. Those fights and the reopening of the wounds of the Chilean ruling class provided space for workers and communities, both to fight alongside the students and to carry their own struggles further. In times of rupture, we see this rippling effect, where destabilization in one sector can open up new potentials across broad sections of society. In this way, the contribution of the student movement, and the FeL within it, has been critical to our time. Across the globe, students, militants, and protesters looked to the inspiring struggles of 2012, and particularly the actions of the students, mine workers, and Chilean protesters taking on a bankrupt regime. These circuits of resistance create new struggles, shift the ground under the feet of the ruling class, and provide us with chances to build our politics by marching, as the FeL did, with our people.

INTERVIEW WITH FELIPE RAMÍREZ OF THE FEL
INTERVIEW CONDUCTED BY S. NAPPALOS,
TRANSLATED BY MÓNICA KOSTAS, AUGUST 2012

S. Nappalos: *How does the system of representation function for students in Chile?*

Felipe Ramírez: OK, we must make a distinction. The Chilean student movement is divided between high school and college. There are two organizations that tie the high school movement. One is the ACES (Coordinating Assembly of High-School Students) and the other is CONES (National Coordinator of High-School Students). These two organizations have their own models of representation and structure. At the university level, the movement is unified by CON-FECh (Confederation of Students of Chile), which is the larger federation of the student federations in different universities. Usually, it gathers the more traditional universities, basically the ones that existed before 1981, which is when the dictatorship generated a new law for universities, and during last year, a series of private universities (that emerged after 1981 and did not have an official organization) have been incorporated. These federations have to make annual choices on direction and objectives in a democratic manner, without the intervention of authorities from the university, so that that there is transparency and respect for the autonomy of the student body at the time of choosing their leaders. It basically functions like that.

Nappalos: *And with 2011, how were the students agitated? For example, was it a spontaneous fight or were there joint campaigns from different groups? Was it just some groups? How did it happen?*

Ramírez: I think that the mobilization of 2011 can be classified as many things, except spontaneous. Not because political groups had been doing specific work that was dedicated to make this happen, but because the objective circumstances of the country were the conditions that made students come out to protest. On the one hand, it was a combination of the end of a retreat produced both by the defeat of the high-school movement in 2006 and the university retreat after the mobilization of 2005. Both 2005 and 2006 were very intense years for mobilizations, and then both defeats (and movements) converged in 2008, when a new law for education was approved. The year 2009 marked the lowest point in mobilizations and then, in 2010, we started seeing important signals that the movement was waking up and that the circumstances were generating a more active student movement. Combine this with the fact that 2005 saw the defeat of the student movement and the creation of equity loans, and that the first generation of students entering with those credit loans was graduating in 2011. All the damage and all the debt that accumulated since 2006, with the new credit loans, exploded in 2011. There was the debt of the CAE (the equity loans from the state), as well as debt from other loans born of this new system of financing—like the CORFO credit, which had an interest rate of 8 percent and allowed family assets to be confiscated from students, expropriated as part of payment. All this produced an environment that, for anyone—it implied a social explosion. At the same time, the country was generating a mobilization; there were mass demonstrations in the Magallanes area in the far south. Just at the beginning of this year, there were massive demonstrations on the issue of power plants, environmental issues, and so on. There was an atmosphere that allowed you to predict that 2011 was going to host a powerful mobilization. No one imagined it would be so strong, but overall we could see it coming. Within that environment, the different organizations tried to fulfill their roles. The leftist organizations of every stripe and color tried to position themselves and come up with certain guidelines as the year developed.

Nappalos: *There was a period where FeL was small, and a period where FeL grew and became very large. What changed? Was it only the objective situation, or were there different strategies?*

Ramírez: I think the most crucial thing for the growth of FeL and for the strengthening of the national organization was its political maturity. At first, the FeL was an organization that had very few political plans. Proposals regarding the student movement emerged in a complicated context in 2003. There was a big mobilization against the financing laws that were being implemented. Overall, the financing issue that exploded in 2005 formed a powerful movement that ended up with the agreement between the heads of the student movement and the ministry of education to create the state-run credit, Crédito con Aval—the entry of banks to the finance system. Facing these situations, the FeL began to slowly start building the framework for its political line, its proposal for education and the funding issue—all of that somehow congealed in 2011. The mobilization caught us with an organization that was starting to grow along with the heightening of the student movement, and we saw high school students go on to college. These students were coming in with a history of struggle and mobilization already and they were interested in the left, which also allowed us to accumulate part of the growth process. The year 2011 forced the organization to understand that anarchism cannot remain a sum of values, a sum of nice words, or books that were written 140 years ago. It cannot solely be about moral principles, or ethical ones. Anarchism has to be made into concrete politics, and without it becoming that, it dies. Faced with this dilemma, the organization thankfully opted for political discussion, and for the creation of concrete proposals to give to the movement, understanding that we are not fighting for the revolution in the short term, but for the specific conditions that accumulate towards a project of the working class. That has allowed us to grow and consolidate as a national structure and also carve out a place among the leftist organizations.

Nappalos: *In the press, we hear only about the big issues in the student struggle, such as free education, privatization, and debt. Are there other smaller fights, where the FeL participates or other students are involved (for example, if classes are canceled or similar things)?*

Ramírez: Well, that's a big topic. On the one hand, there are structural issues, as in the structural models of Chilean education; on the other, there's the concrete interaction of the educational structure within the institutions themselves. It is impossible to separate the internal conflicts, the curriculum of our departments, the precarious conditions, the lack of economic resources within each college, the educational policy of the Ministry of Education, and finally the role of the state, and the unlimited power of the private corporations within the educational system. Every college and every department has small struggles, they have local claims, but what really matters and where you actually define the future of education, is not in these struggles, but rather in the struggles around structural issues. Nothing matters if you lose the large-scale national struggle, that is to say, you can postpone the effects of structural policy, but not forever. There's no simple solution to a problem that affects all universities equally.

Nappalos: *What happened with the struggles of 2011, and which battles are present now?*

Ramírez: Well, 2012 is characterized by the student movement having to confront the fact that the conflict of 2011 is not over. There is neither an agreement nor a complete defeat. What eventually will happen is that the student movement will return to school without acknowledging a defeat and letting the summer holidays be a kind of ceasefire. In 2011, during the first semester until July, what the movement tried to accomplish was to retake the demands of the previous year, considering that the government, the state, and the political parties had control over political initiative (through reforms like the tax reform, austerity measures like the ministry's educational proposals, and so on). Basically, what it ultimately sought was to disarm the regrowth of the student movement after the impasse of the summer. While that proved to be difficult during the first semester, right now, in this precise moment in August, we can see high school students trying to appropriate their struggle. There's already dozens of high schools taken all throughout the country, and we hope to see different universities generating mobilizations soon. We want the last half of August and the first half of September to allow us to see a much stronger movement than the one we've seen this year.

Nappalos: *How will the elections affect the student struggle? Because October's coming soon...*

Ramírez: Sure, there are local elections coming up, and the reading we get is that the parties of the reformist left, who play in the arena of municipal elections, and next year's presidential and parliamentary elections, want to steer the demands of the student movement toward institutionalization—the objective being to strengthen their own political alternative as a tool for conflict resolution. We think this is an illusion that is often created on any electoral path, especially with the big parties, like the democratic one and so on, who are largely responsible for the current situation. Neither the state nor the political party system delivers basic conditions to the social movement, or to the student movement in particular, to be able to see them as a solution. Of course, it all presents a problem because the idea that the elections are part of the solution will be presented with great force and from many sectors. Keeping that in mind, we have to see how we are able to maneuver and prevent the social movement from being co-opted.

Nappalos: *What relations and exchanges are there between the student movement and other struggles in Chile, such as workers, households, etc.?*

Ramírez: I think, starting from 2011 with the series of fights that I already described, the regional conflicts that developed in Magallanes, as in Aysén, in the northern mining areas, the environmental struggles, the student struggles, and the different trade union struggles and mobilizations taking place, allowed us to understand one thing: Chile is a country deeply dependent on the capitalist periphery of the world. A place where resources are highly concentrated in a few hands—in a few families. The ones responsible for the environmental conflicts with thermal or hydro plants, the poor working conditions, the low wages, the extreme privatization that we already have in the education system, the debt problem, and having to pay quadruple the cost of rent, are all the same culprits. They are the same entrepreneurs; they are the same faces, and the same holdings—national or international, repeated again and again.

So, the enemy is clear. It's not a matter of values, not a matter of uniting the different causes due to some metaphysical reason, it is a concrete thing. We face an economic, political, and social system that is concrete, that has concrete and real expressions in our daily lives, and which deeply intersects with the different spheres of our lives. In that sense, the student movement as well as other struggles have been slowly trying to understand this reality and trying to articulate in some way or another a political alternative to deal with these facts. It is a long and very difficult process in a country that is just recovering from the defeats suffered by the popular movement. Chile is slowly rebuilding its organizations after the defeats of the years '88 and '73, when fear reigned massively. That fear was pervasive even up to 2011, so the social organizations are still really disarmed. We have seen some pretty encouraging signs, however. Some union sectors, such as the miners or longshoremen, where libertarians have a pretty important position, have organized sympathy strikes paralyzing labor, which is something not seen since the days of popular unity. So there are some encouraging signs that are positive, though they're isolated at the moment. These still allow us to believe that it is possible to move towards a reconstruction of the popular movement and they also allow us to slowly build a political alternative.

ENDNOTES

1   The University of Chile is perhaps the most politically significant university in Chile, given the centrality of Santiago, and the age and position of the university itself.

2   Manu García, "Radiografía del Movimiento Estudiantil Chileno," Anarkismo, http://www.anarkismo.net/article/22805 (accessed April 1, 2013).

3   Educar Chile, "El movimiento estudiantil chileno de 2006 a 2011," http://www.educarchile.cl/Portal.Base/Web/VerContenido. aspx?ID=209692 (accessed April 1, 2013).

4   García, "Radiografía del Movimiento Estudiantil Chileno."

5   Juan Pablo Garnham and Nicolas Alonso, "El país de Boric," *Qué Pasa,* http://www.quepasa.cl/articulo/politica/2012/08/19-9280-9-el-pais-de-boric.shtml (accessed April 1, 2013).

6   Frente de Estudiantes Libertarias, "Historia del FeL," http://fel-chile. org/?page_id=271 (accessed April 1, 2013).

7   Felipe Ramírez, "Felipe Ramírez, candidato a la Fech por 'Luchar': 'Una construcción social de un proyecto educativo,'" *El Ciudadano,* http://www.elciudadano.cl/2011/11/28/44636/felipe-ramirez-candi-ato-de-luchar-por-la-fech-"una-construccion-social-de-un-proyecto-educativo"/ (accessed April 1, 2013).

8   Federação Anarquista do Rio de Janeiro, translated by Jonathan Payn, "Social Anarchism and Organization," http://libcom.org/library/social-anarchism-organisation (accessed April 1, 2013).

9   Coordinadora Luchar, "Qué es Luchar?," http://luchar.cl/que-es-luchar-2/ (accessed April 1, 2013).

THE END OF THE WORLD AS WE KNOW IT?

TOWARD A CRITICAL UNDERSTANDING OF THE FUTURE

DERIC SHANNON

"As you watch the world crumble, try taking your Armageddon with this sprinkling of irony: Over the last three decades, business has got virtually everything it wanted, and its doomsday scenario from the 1970s has come true because of it."
—Thomas Frank

ONE REASON I BEGAN THE TITLE OF THIS COLLECTION "THE END OF the World..." is because I'm not filled with optimism about the prospects for the kinds of deep changes I desire in the ways we live and organize our lives. And even beyond my desires, there are also simple questions of survival at stake. The risk of nuclear annihilation is still real and the world's owners don't seem particularly moved to rid ourselves of it. One former Secretary of Defense (William Perry) and a former Assistant Secretary of Defense (Graham Allison) have both estimated the chance of a "nuclear attack...at more than 50% over the next ten years."[1] In 1995, Russia "mistook a meteorological rocket launched from Norway for an American submarine launched ballistic missile, and the Russian 'nuclear football,' used to authorize a nuclear attack, was opened in front of President Boris Yeltsin."[2] Luckily he didn't use it—this time.

As well, we're living in what looks like the beginning (or perhaps the middle) of an environmental collapse. In a capitalist system based on constant growth and rooted in the fossil fuel economy, we may find ourselves dealing with this collapse instead of finding some way to avoid it—particularly if capitalism is allowed to continue to run rampant, commodifying everything in its path, and reducing the entire nonhuman world to instruments for human use and profit.[3] This year, we have already seen a summer arctic ice cap almost completely decimated. Scientists suggest that, in just twenty years, the ice cap will be gone.[4]

The science behind global warming is so overwhelmingly accepted that even business press magazines like *The Economist* readily admit, "there is no serious doubt about the basic cause of the warming. It is, in the Arctic as everywhere, the result of an increase in heat-trapping atmospheric gases, mainly carbon dioxide released when fossil fuels are burned."[5] In the same article, the authors go on to warn us that "it is hard to exaggerate how dramatic this is. Perhaps not since the felling of America's vast forests in the 19th century, or possibly since the razing of China's and western Europe's great forests a thousand years before that, has the world seen such a spectacular environmental change. The consequences for Arctic ecosystems will be swingeing."[6] But never fear—this calamity could also bring about profits:

> In the long run the unfrozen north could cause devas-
> tation. But, paradoxically, in the meantime no Arctic
> species will profit from it as much as the one causing
> it: humans. Disappearing sea ice may spell the end of
> the last Eskimo cultures, but hardly anyone lives in an
> igloo these days anyway. And the great melt is going to
> make a lot of people rich.... The Arctic is already a big
> source of minerals, including zinc in Alaska, gold in
> Canada, iron in Sweden and nickel in Russia, and there
> is plenty more to mine... The Arctic also has oil and
> gas, probably lots.[7]

Spoken like a true economist! Given the challenges we face, given the sociopathic obsession of capitalists with profit, given their virtual ownership of our governing institutions, and given our continued failure to constitute any real and substantial threat to their suicidal culture, it's easy to find hope a rare commodity indeed.

Nonetheless, there is a distinct difference between discussions about *probability* and discussions of *possibility*. It seems much more *probable* that capitalists will either bring us to ruin through some nuclear disaster or through environmental devastation, than that humanity will wage a successful war on capitalism's institutions of profit-making-at-all-costs and end the separation of humanity into competing nations based on glorified lines drawn on maps. I'm not attempting to motivate anyone here to act out of "catastrophism."[8] But I *am* attempting an honest assessment of the very real risks we're dealing with at present.

However, there are also *possibilities*—a myriad of possibilities in a historical moment such as ours. And, despite a feeling of pessimism, there are still plenty of reasons to support anticapitalist efforts and engage in those efforts ourselves. Life is, after all, a process of meaning-making. It is an attempt to make our own sense of the senseless, to find and make meaning in the face of absurdity. And no matter how hopeless we might feel, the forms of life that are available and coherent under capitalism are fundamentally alienating, violent, boring, monstrous, and unethical. I don't want to live in a world where some work to live, while others live just by virtue of owning things. And I don't want to live in a world where people are reduced to work, commodities, and other objects. Further, I don't want to live in a world where we take this boring and alienated state of affairs and attempt to manage it ourselves or run it democratically. This means that there is a lot to be done and it also means recognizing the possibilities we're given and acting on them—because to do so is to *make meaning*.

So, there are issues of basic survival that are arguments in themselves for dismantling our prevailing systems of domination. There are ethical reasons and, perhaps more fundamentally, reasons of making life *meaningful* in an absurd and meaningless world. But Marx was right all those years ago, in saying that there are also issues of material interest (which are also wrapped up in issues of ethics, survival, and meaning-making). Do you want to live in a world designed in such a way that you can be turned into a commodity, rented, exploited, surveilled, ruled over, expropriated, and then beaten and tossed in a cage for resisting these designations? I don't.

If we can agree on that, then that leaves which lessons we might take from the latest round of crisis, ruling class attacks on workers, and movements against. I can't distill all of them and have absolutely no interest in providing a political "line" or "program" (which I'm not sure are ever all that useful). I think the chapters in this collection speak for themselves, so I won't summarize them—readers are encouraged to take what's useful from those contributions, and reject and critique what isn't so useful. But I do want to close with a few modest lessons that I think have been made obvious by contemporary anticapitalist practice and its limits, all of which, too, should be scrutinized, critiqued, and perhaps, in places, rejected.

THE POSSIBILITIES AND LIMITS OF "PUBLIC" SPACE

A central aspect of many of the movements against has been the occupation and use of "public" space—where we can meet, where groups can make decisions, where we can plot together, and where we can experiment in some limited fashion in social relations of our own choosing. This has obviously been a powerful tactic that was easily generalized, evidenced by the fact that square occupations were central tactics in the movements against all over the world and involved millions of people.

The strengths of this particular tactic are pretty obvious. For one, it provides a physical space for people to meet up and for unaffiliated folks to "plug in." Secondly, it provides a space for confrontation with the state (when they attempt eviction) and these confrontations can provide valuable lessons in and of themselves. As Matthew Adams explains in his chapter, it's "notable how many liberals became radicalized after experiencing a police beating"—never mind the experience of actually temporarily *winning* in these confrontations. This also calls attention to just how un-public these spaces are. Rather, "public" spaces are owned, operated, and controlled by the state (in the case of Zuccotti Park, it was a "privately owned public space") and when that control is made obvious, it allows us to imagine what a real "commons" might entail—something we simply do not have in existing society.

The main weakness of public square occupation is, perhaps ironically, also that it is *public*. That is, our daily lives typically put us in apartments/homes, workplaces, schools, all sorts of bureaucratic offices—for hours and hours at a time. Although many of us spend a bit of time in public squares, the bulk of our daily lives are spent elsewhere. And what is the purpose of struggle if not to change daily life? What might occupation look like as a tactic applied to the spaces where we spend most of our daily lives? What kinds of possibilities might that provide? This isn't a new insight either—note, for example, the many offshoots of the various movements to occupy public squares. Shane Burley's analysis of Take Back the Land and Occupy Our Homes and Jorell A. Meléndez Badillo's examination of *los rescatadores de terrenos* in Puerto Rico both provide examples of people taking *living* space. Or consider Marianne LeNabat's cataloguing of student organizing in New York City, catalyzed by Occupy. These examples point to ways to extend the "movement of squares" into daily life.

GIVING UP ACTIVISM

DEVELOPING ANTAGONISMS AROUND so-called public spaces, while leaving daily life untouched, share some of the problems that Andrew X detailed in his piece, "Give Up Activism," for the eco-radical magazine, *Do or Die*.[9] Written shortly after the Battle of Seattle, this piece was a reflection on the successes of various activist mobilizations and a critical assessment of their failure to launch any substantive threat to capitalism. At that point in time, it seemed we had some traction—after all, we'd successfully stopped the World Trade Organization Ministerial Conference from taking place, effectively shutting down one of the most powerful capitalist organizations in the world with street theater, some minor property destruction, and a whole lot of bodies in the streets. This seemed like a good time to step back and start taking critical stock of ourselves.

What lies at the center of Andrew X's critique of activism is an examination of what he calls "the activist mentality":

> By "an activist mentality" what I mean is that people think of themselves primarily as activists and as belonging to some wider community of activists. The activist identifies with what they do and thinks of it as their role in life, like a job or career. In the same way some people will identify with their job as a

doctor or a teacher, and instead of it being something they just happen to be doing, it becomes an essential part of their self-image.... The activist is a specialist or an expert in social change. To think of yourself as being an activist means to think of yourself as being somehow privileged or more advanced than others in your appreciation of the need for social change, in the knowledge of how to achieve it and as leading or being in the forefront of the practical struggle to create this change.[10]

Activists, then, are people who see themselves as specialists in "social change" or "social justice" or some other, more or less, meaningless abstraction. There really isn't a theory behind activism—it exists for its own sake—but the locus for "social change" (or whatever) comes *from activists*. It is a politics of specialists, by specialists, for specialists, and typically relies on strategies of recruitment. Activist politics typically take place in public spaces, where the specialists meet to "do actions" or protest in order to "speak truth to power" and so on, tendencies Abbey Volcano critiques in her chapter on gender and sexuality in the movements against.

The alternative is locating antagonisms in our daily lives. Instead of going "out there" to "do actions" with fellow specialists, we might intervene in our schools, our workplaces, our neighborhoods—places where we actually spend most of our daily lives. We might find co-conspirators among people outside of tiny fringe ideological groups, and the movers of history might be ordinary people who don't need to be led by activists, political organizations, or other self-appointed representatives. We might give up activism.[11]

WHAT IS IT WE WANT?

PART OF THE problem with vague terms like "positive social change," "social justice," or their many variants, are that they're more or less devoid of any real meaning. The same might be true at present of socialism—take a look around the world, particularly in Europe, at what the various socialist parties are doing. If they are, indeed, socialist, then a capitalist is certainly not required in order to put into place lethal austerity measures, and then set the police to beating anyone who complains too loudly. But it might make sense to have some larger conversations about what we want, how we articulate that, and the dangers in a) being indecipherable; and b) becoming pandering populists.

Mark Bray analyzes this problem in his treatment of the way Occupy Wall Street articulated the decline of American Empire and the kinds of alternatives they put forward. Antonis Vradis describes how meaning itself seems lost in Greece, while Yesenia Barragán shows how the ruling class has successfully recuperated the discourse of sustainability and the "green" movement.

But what concerns me most is when we seem to mistake a certain kind of *form* for a certain kind of *content*. This is common when antagonists call for things like a "consensus society," "radical democracy," or "self-management." Calls for consensus or democracy—without considerable elaboration—elevate the form of decision-making over the content of the decisions made. The same is true of self-management or calls for democratizing production or work. The rhetoric, although easy on the populist ear, can often lead listeners to believe that all we are asking for is to take what exists and run it ourselves. But I have absolutely no interest in "self-managing" my job. I would imagine most workers feel that way—it's not as if liberation just entails making democratic decisions about the miserable and boring workplaces we're assigned to, in order to make a life under capitalism. These sorts of calls require, at the least, elaboration. Better, perhaps, would be different terminology altogether.

Indeed, much of the liberatory rhetoric we inherited from the past is centered on the means of production. A decent society would certainly produce things, but in the industrial juggernaut in which we currently live, much of what we produce is useless shit we're conditioned to want by an advertising industry that manipulates our desires. Surely a liberatory project wouldn't just mean seizing society as it exists and self-managing it. It would also mean destroying much of the means of production we have produced—those which serve little purpose except to perpetuate a society organized around commodity and spectacle. This means rethinking productivism (a mentality obsessed with production and output) and capitalist technology and technique. Seizing the proverbial "factory" may provide less radical potential than ridding ourselves of it.

MAKING THE END OF THE WORLD THE END WE WANT

I MADE THE case earlier that we live in a time of a myriad of possibilities, but not all of those possibilities are all that pleasant. We have seen widespread resistance to global capitalism and the state in the age of austerity. People all over the world have started taking to the streets to register their discontent—in some cases, this has involved overthrowing governments (though replacing them with new ones); in others, it has involved confrontations with power and privilege; and in some rare cases, it has involved some minor concessions from the ruling class. But most of the stories about contemporary uprisings, if we're going to be honest, are stories of loss. Luckily for all of us, these stories last decades, if not centuries, and the current wave of revolt can be situated in a long history of struggle and self-activity.

But we live in a time where our rulers have developed a spying apparatus so great that they can record our interests, our networks, and our desires to degrees that were previously unimaginable. Their methods for manipulating those interests, networks, and desires have also become more sophisticated and complete. And in many cases, this has created a situation where the dispossessed come to support and participate in their own exploitation, oppression, and confinement.

This makes the act of revolutionizing society all the more complicated. In order to do so, we need more *snapshots*, more collections of stories and analyses from social antagonists. We need criticism and self-criticism in our process of altering our institutions and our *selves*. So, an honest engagement with possibilities for the future is one wrapped up in our present condition. Under austerity and under the eyes of economists and politicians, social life is something that happens *to* us. Under those eyes, history is seen as a progression of political and economic processes affecting anyone without power, rather than processes of struggle that produce the present and have the capability of creating a different future. And although things might look bleak—the *probabilities* can be overwhelming, weighed against the many *possibilities*—an understanding of the future that does not give in to debilitating catastrophism and contains some degree of confidence that ordinary people can do extraordinary things presents us with a contemporary situation ripe with prospects. The trick, perhaps, might be learning to articulate our desires, without accepting anything less than the conscious creation of our daily lives, and the destruction of those things that create social misery.

ENDNOTES

1   Testimony of Matthew Bunn for the Committee on Homeland Security and Governmental Affairs United States Senate, "The Risk of Nuclear Terrorism and next Steps to Reduce the Danger," http://belfercenter.ksg.harvard.edu/files/bunn-nuclear-terror-risk-test-08.pdf (accessed July 21, 2013).

2   Martin E. Hellman, "Defusing the Nuclear Threat," http://nuclearrisk.org/ (accessed July 21, 2013).

3   Wayne Price, "The Ecological Crisis is an Economic Crisis; the Economic Crisis is an Ecological Crisis," *Anarkismo,* http://www.anarkismo.net/article/17024 (accessed July 20, 2013).

4   Juan Cole, "Arctic Summer Ice Cap Will Be Gone in 20 Years: NOAA (Time-Lapse Video)," http://www.juancole.com/2013/04/arctic-summer-years.html (accessed July 21, 2013).

5   Special Report, "The Melting North," *The Economist,* http://www.economist.com/node/21556798 (accessed July 21, 2013).

6   Ibid.

7   Ibid.

8   For a look at the limits of catastrophism, see Sasha Lilley et. al, *Catastrophism: The Apocalyptic Politics of Collapse and Rebirth* (Oakland: PM Press, 2012).

9   Andrew X, "Give Up Activism," *Do or Die,* http://www.eco-action.org/dod/no9/activism.htm (accessed July 20, 2013).

10   Ibid.

11   For a thoughtful response to Andrew X's piece, see J. Kellstadt, "The Necessity and Impossibility of Anti-Activism," *Libcom.org,* http://libcom.org/library/anti-activism (accessed July 21, 2013). Interested readers might also see the critical exchange between Chris Dixon and Sasha K, beginning with Chris Dixon, "Finding Hope After Seattle: Rethinking Radical Activism and Building a Movement," *The Anarchist Library,* http://theanarchistlibrary.org/library/

chris-dixon-finding-hope-after-seattle-rethinking-radical-activism-and-building-a-movement (accessed July 21, 2013) rejoined at Sasha K, "'Activism' and 'Anarcho-Purism'," *The Anarchist Library*, http://theanarchistlibrary.org/library/sasha-k-activism-and-anarcho-purism (accessed July 21, 2013).

CONTRIBUTOR BIOS

Matthew Adams is a temporary worker for a large tech company in Seattle by day, and an organizer for the Seattle Solidarity Network by night. He is a member of the Industrial Workers of the World and the Workers Solidarity Alliance.

Ernesto Aguilar is a media professional for Pacifica Radio and technology coordinator for various activist projects, including People Of Color Organize and Feminist Current. In addition, he is a speaker on media access, criminal justice, race, and public policy, with extensive training and research experience in these and other fields.

William Armaline is the Director of Human Rights and an assistant professor in the Department of Justice Studies at San Jose State University. His areas of interest include political economy, critical race theory and antiracism, critical pedagogy and transformative education, critical ethnography, inequality and youth, prison abolition, and drug policy reform. His recent publications include: (1) *Human Rights in Our Own Backyard: Injustice and Resistance in the United States* (UPenn. Press, 2011); (2) "What Will States Really Do for Us? The Human Rights Enterprise and Pressure from Below" (*Societies Without Borders*, 4[3]: 430–451); (3) Works on political economy, critical pedagogy, and transformative education in *Accumulation of Freedom: Writings on Anarchist Economics* (AK Press, 2012), *Contemporary Anarchist Studies* (Routledge, 2009), and *Academic Repression* (AK Press, 2009).

Yesenia Barragán is a doctoral candidate in Latin American History at Columbia University, where she studies the abolition of slavery and emancipation in Colombia and the Americas, in addition to neo-liberalism and social movements in Latin America. Currently the Solidarity Coordinator for AfroColombia NY, Yesenia was most recently active in Occupy Wall Street, and the student, immigrant rights', and environmental justice movements in the 2000s. Her book, *Selling Our Death Masks: Cash-for-Gold in the Age of Austerity*, is forthcoming from Zero Books.

Angie Beeman is an assistant professor at the City University of New York-Borough of Manhattan Community College. Her research interests include racism theory, media, social movements, and gender. She has published research on racism and film in *Ethnic and Racial Studies*, predatory lending in *Critical Sociology*, and domestic violence in *Violence Against Women*. Her dissertation, which received an award from the Society for the Study of Social Problems, examined the strategic use, limitations, and challenges of color-blind ideology in grassroots, interracial social movement organizations.

Paul Bowman is an IT worker, a trade unionist, and a time-served anarchist militant. Currently living in Dublin, he is an organizer for the Independent Workers Union and the Workers Solidarity Movement. He is also one of the editors of the *Irish Anarchist Review* and a regular contributor to this and other WSM publications, on the topics of the global financial system, the Eurozone crises, communism and organizing.

Mark Bray was a core organizer with the Occupy Wall Street Press Working Group and is a member of the Industrial Workers of the World (IWW). He has been a political organizer involved in various groups and campaigns over the years and is the author of *Translating Anarchy: The Anarchism of Occupy Wall Street* (Zero Books, 2013). Mark is also a PhD candidate in European History at Rutgers University, where his research focuses on anarchism, human rights, terrorism, and state repression in Spain at the turn of the twentieth century.

Shane Burley is an organizer, author, and filmmaker now based in Portland, Oregon. He is a co-founder of Rochester Red and Black and the Metro Justice Housing Committee, and a long time organizer with Earth First! and Take Back the Land. He is currently working on housing and labor projects with the Portland Solidarity Network and the coalition project, Housing Is for Everyone. He contributes to a number of publications, including *Waging Nonviolence, Red Skies at Night, Anarkismo, Labor Notes*, and Occupy.com, as well as writes a regular blog on housing justice for LibCom called Eviction Free Zone. He has recently completed a documentary about the intersection of the housing justice and Occupy movements called *Expect Resistance*.

Jamie Burnett is a student activist who was involved with organizing for the 2012 Québec student strike at McGill University. He is presently a student at the Université du Québec à Montréal (UQAM) and a member of the Association pour une solidarité syndicale étudiante (ASSÉ).

Colleen Casey is an assistant professor at the University of Texas at Arlington in the School of Urban and Public Affairs. Her current research focuses on access to credit; specifically, the effects and implementation of policies and programs designed to stimulate reinvestment in low-income, urban communities. Her work has been published in journals such as the *Journal of Planning Education and Research* and *Critical Sociology* and she has co-authored reports for the Brookings Institution. Most recently, she served as a visiting scholar for the Federal Reserve Bank Atlanta in the Community and Economic Division, focused on research related to disparities in access to credit for low-wealth, minority entrepreneurs.

Noam Chomsky is Professor Emeritus in the Department of Linguistics and Philosophy at the Massachusetts Institute of Technology. He is the author of over one hundred books spanning subjects such as war, terrorism, politics, and mass media.

Abraham P. DeLeon is an assistant professor at the University of Texas at San Antonio in the Department of Educational Leadership and Policy Studies. His critiques are grounded in radical social theories and have been influenced by cultural studies, anarchist theory, critical discourse studies, the postmodern tradition, critical pedagogy, and postcolonial studies. His articles have appeared in *Educational Studies, The Urban Review, Critical Education*, and *Equity & Excellence in Education*. He has also authored numerous book chapters in various edited collections and was a member of the editorial collective that produced *Contemporary Anarchist Studies: An Introductory Anthology of Anarchy in the Academy* (Routledge, 2009) and *Critical Theories, Radical Pedagogies, and Social Education: Towards New Perspectives for the Social Studies* (Sense Publishers, 2010), co-edited with E. Wayne Ross.

Nick Driedger is a regional organizing coordinator for the Canadian Union of Postal Workers, a member of the Industrial Workers of the World, and a truck driver. He is a regular contributor to Recomposition Blog and is also in the editorial collective.

Luis A. Fernandez is an associate professor at Northern Arizona University, where he teaches in the criminology department. He is the author and editor of several books, including *Policing Dissent*, published in 2008, and *Shutting Down the Streets: Political Violence and Social Control in the Global Era*. His research and teaching interests revolve around protest policing, social movements, immigration, and issues of social control of late modernity.

Miguel Ángel Fernández has been a member of the CNT since 1991. During these years, he has held different posts related to social communication, propaganda, and culture, such as: press, propaganda, and culture secretary of the Local Federation of Madrid and regional secretary of the Center on different occasions; director of the CNT newspaper from September 2003 to December 2007; press, communication, and propaganda secretary of the Permanent Confederate Secretariat; responsible for web page content on the Confederate webpage (cnt.es) from 2009 to 2011. Currently, he holds the post of organization secretary in the syndicate of Graphic Arts, Communication, and Spectacles of Madrid. He has been a member of this organization since re-founding it with other comrades in 1998. Before that, he was affiliated, first and as a student, with the Organization of Teaching and later in the Organization of Various Trades, both also of the Local Federation of Madrid.

Benjamin Fogel is a journalist and activist from Cape Town, South Africa, who writes on the intersection of popular culture and politics, social movements and class struggle in South Africa. Occasionally, he tries his hand with theory. He has contributed to numerous publications, both in radical and bourgeois presses. In his spare time, he listens to hip hop and rants.

Christian Garland is a writer and theorist, and Fellow of the Institut fur Kritische Theorie, (InKriT) based at the Free University, Berlin. He has research interests that include critical theory (Adorno, Benjamin, and the original Frankfurt School), and the intersections between "autonomist" Marxism and class-struggle anarchism. Recent publications include the chapters "Illuminated in its Lurid Light: Criminalization, Political Repression" and "Dissent in the UK" (2012) in *The Criminalization of Resistance in the Era of Neoliberal Globalization*, ed. J. Shantz, (Durham NC: Carolina Academic Press) and "A Secret Heliotropism of May '68: Historical Postponement, Mimesis, and Nostalgia" (2012) in *Movements in Time: Revolution, Social Justice and Times of Change*, eds. CA Lawrence and N. Churn (Newcastle: Cambridge Scholars Publishing).

Davita Silfen Glasberg is College of Liberal Arts and Sciences Associate Dean of Social Sciences at the University of Connecticut, and a professor of sociology. She has taught both undergraduate and graduate courses, and authored or coauthored six books and dozens of scholarly journal articles on issues of power and oppression, human rights, finance capital and the state, predatory lending, and inequality and diversity. Her most recent article (coauthored with William T. Armaline), "What Will States Really Do for Us? The Human Rights Enterprise and Pressure from Below," is published in *Societies Without Borders*. Her latest books are *Political Sociology: Oppression, Resistance, and the State*, coauthored with Deric Shannon (Sage/Pine Forge Press); and *Human Rights in Our Own Back Yard: Injustice and Resistance in the United States*, coedited with William T. Armaline and Bandana Purkayastha (University of Pennsylvania Press).

Uri Gordon is an Israeli activist, teacher, and writer. He has been active with the Negev Coexistence Forum for Civil Equality, and in global networks including Indymedia and Peoples' Global Action. He teaches politics at Loughborough University, and is the author of *Anarchy Alive! Antiauthoritarian Politics from Practice to Theory* (Pluto Press, 2008), as well as numerous articles on the theory and practice of contemporary anarchism. His work has been translated into ten languages.

Nate Hawthorne is a member of the Industrial Workers of the World and thinks you probably should be as well, unless you're somebody's boss. He co-edits http://recomposition.info, writes an occasionally political blog at http://libcom.org/blog/1578, and has reservations about author bios.

Rudy Amanda Hurtado Garcés is an Afro-Colombian activist, born and raised near the River Timbiqui, Cauca, Colombia, located on the southern Pacific coast of Colombia. She began organizing at a young age, both in her Afro-Colombian community and as a high school student at the Colegio Justiano Ocoro in her hometown of Timbiqui. At the age of sixteen, she began to study Anthropology at the Universidad del Cauca, located in Popayán, Colombia, where she started to organize in the student movement. At her university, she co-founded Palen(k)e Univeristario del Cauca, an Afro-Colombian student activist organization dedicated to confronting the rise of multicultural neoliberalism, racism, classism, and sexism.

Monica Kostas is an Argentinian graphic artist living in Miami, where she works closely with Miami Autonomy and Solidarity (MAS) and the Miami IWW branch. She focuses on workplace organizing, and is also interested in student struggles, mass culture, and radical feminism. Monica often contributes translations, artwork, and writings to MAS and has also recently contributed to a forthcoming book of worker stories by the Recomposition editorial collective.

Marianne LeNabat teaches and studies philosophy in New York. Her work focuses on solidarity, spontaneity, and collective action, with particular attention to recent political movements. Outside of academia, she has been involved in student, workplace, and tenant organizing.

Gayge Maggio is an Italian@ butch, autonomist Marxist, and nurse living Deep Lezzin' it up in New England. She is an RN, street medic, herbalist, NREMT-B, and nurse practitioner student. She has spent over a decade and a half as an organizer, notably being a former Trans-Fix NorCal and Camp Trans organizer. Much of her organizing has revolved around linking up trans and gender non-conforming communities into networks of mutual aid, and linking their struggles to workplace struggles. She is currently involved in Rebellious Nursing!

(http:// www.rebelnursing.org), networking and organizing with other radical nurses. She is particularly concerned with the racial and gendered divisions of labor built into health care work, queer and trans health, and with helping to create bottom up, community controlled healthcare and wellness.

Jorell A. Meléndez Badillo is a history teacher by trade, a singer in a punk rock band for kicks, and a full time anarchist by conviction. He is a member of the Colectivo Autónomo C.C.C., and has an M.A. in History from the Interamerican University of Puerto Rico. He has presented and published papers in various international forums and publications, and was an organizer for the Third Annual North American Anarchist Studies Network conference in Puerto Rico. At the moment, he is currently undertaking several research projects related to Puerto Rican radical politics and migration patterns.

Ayn Morgan is an assemblage and sound artist focusing on surveillance, freedom of information, and media activism. She maintains the Eigengrau Press, which publishes interviews, sound collage, and essays on activism through music and art. She also curates The Chestnut Tree, a weekly experimental and Creative Commons music program on KPFT Houston and ∃ radio.

Jasmin Mujanovic is a PhD candidate in political science at York University in Toronto. From Sarajevo, Bosnia-Herzegovina, he has resided in Croatia, Slovenia, Germany, and now Canada. His dissertation is on the topic of the socially stunting history of the state and participatory democratic alternatives thereto in Bosnia-Herzegovina. His commentary is regularly posted at *Politics, Re-Spun* but has also appeared on *New Left Project, ZNet, Balkan Insight, TransConflict* and in several academic journals and texts.

Scott ("Nikolas") Nappalos is a nurse living in Miami, FL. Nappalos has contributed articles to *The Accumulation of Freedom: Writings on Anarchist Economics* and *What Would it Mean to Win* by the Turbulence Collective. His writings have appeared in *Industrial Worker, Anarcho-Syndicalist Review*, and he is a regular contributor to the Anarkismo network. Scott is a co-founder and a member of the editorial collective *Recomposition: Notes for a New Workerism*, an online publication of autonomous workers struggle and organization. Presently, he is preparing a manuscript for a book of philosophy and metapolitics addressing emergence, power, method, cognition, and intentionality. Scott is a longtime organizer in the workers movement, member of the Industrial Workers of the World, and one of the founding members of Miami Autonomy and Solidarity, a revolutionary political organization.

Sean Parson is an assistant professor in both politics and international affairs and sustainable communities at Northern Arizona University. He has conducted and published research on a range of topics, including homelessness activism, climate justice, critical animal studies, revolutionary environmentalism, and political ecology. His current research interests revolve around decoloniality, anarchism, and environmental resistance movements in the United States.

Harpreet Kaur Paul read Law at King's College London and International Economic Law, Justice and Development at Birkbeck, focusing on the globalization of human rights. She briefly practiced law at a commercial law firm in London, before working with NGOs seeking to make critical interventions at the United Nations, including Global Policy Forum and Amnesty International. She currently volunteers with a London-based collective (Platform) that combines art, activism, education, and research in campaigns that focus on the social, economic, and environmental impacts of the global oil industry.

Adam Quinn lives in Vermont and is an undergraduate student at Hampshire College, studying history, social theory, and anthropology. He is currently researching, writing about, and (hopefully) participating in the history of the anarchist movement in North America.

Felipe Ramírez is a militant of the Libertarian Student Front (FEL) at the University of Chile since 2007, and a member of the Libertarian Communist Federation of Chile (FCL). In 2010, he was a member of the plenary of delegates of the Student Federation of the University of Chile (FECh); in 2011, during the student mobilizations, he was the president of the Center of Communication Students; and, in 2012, he was the secretary general of the FECh. At present, he's assisting Fabian Araneda who is vice president of the FeCh for 2013, and representing their tendency.

Deric Shannon is a former Indiana boy, most recently relocated to the deep South. He has written books, book chapters, and journal articles on social movements, political economy, food justice, human rights, sexuality, culture, and political sociology. When he's not organizing or working, he's playing music or walking around aimlessly.

Dustin Shannon works as a freelance teacher, translator, and editor. He lived for fifteen years in Spain but currently resides in the USA.

Chris Spannos is a writer, editor and publisher. He edited the book *Real Utopia: Participatory Society for the 21st Century* (AK Press, 2008). He participates in many social movements. Currently, he is editor of *NYT eXaminer* (www.nytexaminer.com).

Marie Trigona is a writer and media maker whose work has focused on social movements in Latin America. She has reported for Free Speech Radio News, Radio France International, Z Magazine, the Buenos Aires Herald, NACLA-Report on the Americas, Dollar & Sense, among many others. She currently resides in Seattle, where she works with a union and dances tango.

Abbey Volcano is currently living in Eastern Connecticut. She has worked as a clerk at a health food store, a barista, a secretary for a non-profit, and more recently, as a graduate assistant. She has organized in movements around reproductive freedom, food justice, and sexuality. Currently, she is writing on the state in its many forms, political economy, and the ways that both effect and are affected by sexuality. When she's not watching Buffy, she is dreaming of a world without the limits set upon us by capital, where she can take up her rightful role as Fox Mulder's animal companion.

Antonis Vradis is a member of the anarchist collective Occupied London, based deceivingly enough in Athens. The collective has published a book on the situation in Greece (*Revolt and Crisis in Greece*, AK Press, 2011) and continues to offer its "irregular updates" via its blog at http://blog.occupiedlondon.org/. Antonis is also Alternatives Editor of the journal *CITY*.

INDEX

"Passim" (literally "scattered") indicates intermittent discussion of a topic over a cluster of pages.

A

B

O

P

Support **AK Press!**

AK Press is one of the world's largest and most productive anarchist publishing houses. We're entirely worker-run & democratically managed. We operate without a corporate structure—no boss, no managers, no bullshit. We publish close to twenty books every year, and distribute thousands of other titles published by other like-minded independent presses and projects from around the globe.

The Friends of AK program is a way that you can directly contribute to the continued existence of AK Press, and ensure that we're able to keep publishing great books just like this one! Friends pay $25 a month directly into our publishing account ($30 for Canada, $35 for international), and receive a copy of every book AK Press publishes for the duration of their membership! Friends also receive a discount on anything they order from our website or buy at a table: 50% on AK titles, and 20% on everything else. We've also added a new Friends of AK ebook program: $15 a month gets you an electronic copy of every book we publish for the duration of your membership. Combine it with a print subscription, too!

There's great stuff in the works—so sign up now to become a Friend of AK Press, and let the presses roll!

Won't you be our friend? Email friendsofak@akpress.org for more info, or visit the Friends of AK Press website: www.akpress.org/programs/friendsofak